P9-CZV-633

JERRY WEST

JERRY WEST

THE LIFE AND LEGEND
OF A BASKETBALL ICON

ROLAND LAZENBY

ESPN BOOKS

BALLANTINE BOOKS   NEW YORK

Published in the United States by ESPN Books, an imprint of ESPN, Inc.,
New York, and Ballantine Books, an imprint of the Random House Publishing
Group, a division of Random House, Inc., New York.

BALLANTINE and colophon are registered trademarks of Random House, Inc.
The ESPN Books name and logo are registered trademarks of ESPN, Inc.

Library of Congress Cataloging-in-Publication Data

Lazenby, Roland.
Jerry West : the life and legend of a basketball icon / Roland Lazenby.
    p.   cm.
Includes bibliographical references.
ISBN 978-0-345-51083-9 (hardcover : alk. paper)
1. West, Jerry, 1938–   2. Basketball players—United States—Biography.
3. Los Angeles Lakers (Basketball team)   I. Title.
GV884.W4L39 2010
796.323092—dc22
[B]   2009043777

Printed in the United States of America on acid-free paper.

www.ballantinebooks.com
www.espnbooks.com

9 8 7 6 5 4 3 2 1

First Edition

Book design by Karin Batten

Title-page illustration: Jerry West (Getty)

For my father, William Lowry "Hopper" Lazenby,
a West Virginia boy with a pure,
two-handed set shot

For Tex Winter and all truth-tellers

For my wife, Karen, the best proof I can
find that there's a god in heaven

TIGER, tiger, burning bright
In the forests of the night,
What immortal hand or eye
Could frame thy fearful symmetry?

In what distant deeps or skies
Burnt the fire of thine eyes?
On what wings dare he aspire?
What the hand dare seize the fire?

— WILLIAM BLAKE

Contents

INTRODUCTION

IT'S MAY 1999. JERRY WEST SITS COURTSIDE IN THE EMPTY GREAT Western Forum in Los Angeles. It is the end of an era. His era. It is the last NBA season for this building, which has been the stage for much of his basketball life, a wrenching forty-year struggle for meaning. For those four decades, as a player, as a coach, as an executive, Jerry West has led the Los Angeles Lakers. He *is* the Los Angeles Lakers. And now his hour has come round at last. The only others present are young superstar Kobe Bryant, who is shooting free throws after practice; a freelance writer who is trying to engage West in a conversation; and a stunningly pretty television reporter who keeps exchanging furtive glances with the legend. Only the presence of the woman seems to pull him from his dark thoughts and push him toward a hint of a smile. He is troubled because the San Antonio Spurs are about to sweep his Lakers from the play-offs. Down three games to none in the series, his team has just finished a practice before the fourth and final game. The season, indeed his historic tenure with the team, is hanging by a thread. And so the people around him are an immense distraction.

Jerry West, who seemingly sees everything, is peering into the immediate future and recognizing a developing scenario that absolutely nauseates him. (Those around him might scoff and say that everything seems to nauseate West.) He is pondering these things, half listening, when the writer suddenly mentions the very name that is the source of his trouble.

Phil Jackson.

The name brings West instantly and completely into the moment. His troubled face tightens.

"Fuck Phil Jackson," he says.

Taken aback by West's sudden fury, the writer attempts to clarify his comment.

"No," West interrupts. "Fuck Phil Jackson."

He says each of the words with emphasis to burnish his intent.

Sportswriters covering the Lakers have long been used to West exploding in anger during interviews. They laugh about the uptight persona that often leaves him launching F-bombs in response to one of their questions, but they hardly ever report his responses.

This time is a bit different, however. The sixty-one-year-old West is addressing the central issue of his career, perhaps even of his life. On the surface, it is about coaching versus talent. But in reality, it's far deeper than that, perhaps even Oedipal.

West is certain that talent supersedes coaching in the business of basketball. It is a business about which West knows as much as a person can know. It is the obsession to which he has dedicated his life. There is the perception among the sport's media, fans, players, coaches, agents—even the entrepreneurs and owners—that no one has ever cared more, given more, sacrificed more, done more for basketball than Jerry West.

That is why he is the "Logo," the player upon whose photograph the National Basketball Association's red, white, and blue logo is said to have been modeled. He is the very image of the sport, the brand of a multibillion-dollar enterprise that has captured the fascination of millions of humans around the globe.

And yet, on the core question of his life, the core question of the game he adores and knows so well, Jerry West is probably wrong. In fact, I know he is.

I was the reporter sitting in the Forum with West on that day in May 1999. Over my years of covering the NBA, I have had about twenty substantive, in-depth interviews with him. His focus on coaching versus talent is a running theme of those conversations. One time he told me, "You can tell your friends Tex Winter and Pat Riley that coaching is important, but it's mostly about talent."

The coaching-versus-talent thing was an issue that would hit West like a tsunami in the coming months, and he would cling to his beliefs like a person clinging to a tree, trying not to be swept away by a great tide.

Of course talent matters. West had spent his adult life assembling talent for the great Lakers championship teams. His 1999 roster brimmed with talent, including the mammoth center Shaquille O'Neal and the resplendent young wing player Kobe Bryant. To play alongside them, West had acquired an array of polished, intelligent players. And yet here these marvelous Lakers were, once again facing dismissal in the play-offs, an underachieving collection of overpaid—dare I say it?—talent.

That tsunami headed West's way was none other than Phil Jackson, the man who coached Michael Jordan and the Chicago Bulls to six National Basketball Association championships in nine years. I had just watched Jackson engage in a titanic struggle with the vice president of those Bulls, Mr. Jerry Krause. Mr. Krause was a friend and confidant of Jerry West's. They had long shared beliefs and phone conversations and gossip, the kind of talk that only NBA executives share. Mr. Krause was determined to prove that it is the "organization"—a team's scouting staff and administration that collects talent—that wins championships. Organizations were the most important thing in basketball, according to Mr. Krause.

Jerry West believed much the same thing, though he would express it in other words.

Phil Jackson, in essence, rolled right over Jerry Krause in this debate. Within weeks of cursing Jackson in our conversation, West would stand before the television cameras in Los Angeles and announce that he was hiring Jackson to coach the Lakers. And soon Jackson would turn the great force of his personality and his skill to the task of rolling right over West himself. It would not be pretty. I will explain this in detail, but right now I am getting ahead of the story.

My task here is to explain the mystery that is Jerry West, the most influential figure in the history of American basketball. My best clue was provided almost twenty years ago in an interview with that most perceptive of basketball men, Pete Newell. Newell had coached West on the 1960 U.S. Olympic team and was amazed and puzzled by the talented but tortured young player, so beset by inferiority complexes and insecurities.

After an early Olympic practice, West had come to Newell and confided that he didn't think he belonged on the team because he just wasn't as good as the other players selected, particularly Oscar Robertson. West expressed his thoughts about leaving the team and heading back home to West Virginia.

Newell recalled with a chuckle, "I told him, 'Jerry, if you're not going to Rome, then I'm not going either.'"

But the conversation would play on Newell's mind long after the Olympic Games were over. How could such a high-level player harbor such doubts about his own abilities?

After much thought, Newell concluded that West's personality had much to do with his background in his home state. Newell told me, "If you want to understand Jerry West, then you have to understand West Virginia."

That clue struck a true note with me. I was born in Bluefield, West Virginia, to a father who was one of the best two-handed set shooters to come out of the hills of southern West Virginia. My father, William "Hopper" Lazenby, worshipped Jerry West. I often tell people that there were two pictures on the wall of our home when I was a boy. One was of Jesus. The other was of Jerry West.

The picture of Jesus, I tell people, was hung higher than the picture of Jerry, but only by about an inch or two.

That punch line was at least figuratively true.

So when I heard Newell's advice, I knew he had laid out before me the challenge of a professional lifetime. Understanding West Virginia would prove to be a long, torturous trip into the baseness of mankind. Still, Newell was right. Many, including West's own family members, have observed that there was something about Jerry that very quickly attracted the allegiance of people all over the state, particularly people such as my own father. Like the place itself, with so much natural wealth and beauty, there is a complex character to the people, because so many of them have come from downtrodden circumstances. So many of them have fought so valiantly, yet lost again and again and again, and still they've kept fighting. That, as much as anything, perhaps explains the statue they've erected to West outside the state university's field house at Morgantown.

He has had an up-and-down relationship with his home state over the years, one that the seventy-one-year-old West still can't quite understand. In the summer of 2008, he was asked to appear at a basketball fantasy camp in West Virginia. Eddie Barrett, the retired sports publicist, recalled pulling up at the hotel for the camp one morning and seeing West standing out front. "He was dressed in all white, this bright white running suit, and he had sunglasses on and was tan," Barrett, an old friend, recalled with a chuckle. "He looked like Elvis."

Fans in California and other places have always been struck by the mythical nature of West's aura, but it reaches a different level in his home state. "He doesn't understand the feeling that the people of West Virginia have for him," explained Willie Akers, his college teammate and longtime friend. "When he goes to Morgantown and goes to a basketball game, there's always a crowd of people eager to interact with him. He has to have someone, an escort, take him around and back and forth because of that crowd. He'll sign autographs, but he has to have a guard so he can watch the basketball game, because they'll ask him questions. He doesn't understand when they introduce him at public appearances why there's always a standing ovation, and he doesn't understand why they still think that much of him."

As a young man, West held some awareness of this connection, but his years in Los Angeles led to an alienation from his home state. Then, more recently, as he aged and read more and learned more, his life and his relationship with West Virginia again came into sharper focus. "The culture there is different," he explained. "The opportunities there are limited for people. Life has always been spelled out for the people there because of that limited opportunity."

As he spoke, I could sense the emotion rising in his voice.

"But that place laid the foundation for who I am," he continued. "A lot of outsiders make fun of it and say negative things about West Virginia. A lot of the negative things are just people's opinions. Fuck them."

It has always seemed as if this anger could boil to the surface at any given moment with West. Why is this polite, accomplished gentleman given to fits of such vitriol? That question sits at the core of this mystery.

There are other clues. One leapt out at me from a fifty-year-old photograph, both comical and telling in its intensity. The photo is from signing day, 1956. Local high school star Jerry West is signing to play college basketball at West Virginia University. There have been literally thousands of photographs taken of West over the decades, yet this is the one, found in the long-ago pages of a small Mountain State newspaper, that says so much about who he is and the family chemistry that wrapped him so tightly and made him, to use his own words, "so crazy."

He's standing there with his parents, Howard and Cecile West, and WVU's handsome young coach, Fred Schaus. Of the four, there are two sets of eyes that emit the same quiet fury. Their energy and indignation are absolutely radioactive. Mother and son, eyes burning like Blake's tiger, obviously share something unspeakable, something far away and deeply troubling. The occasion should have been joyous. Just weeks earlier, West had experienced what he has often described as one of the true moments of delight in his entire life: leading his East Bank High School team to the state basketball championship. But here he is, still buzzing over his success, and yet as the shutter snaps, his eyes radiate this stern message: This is no time to smile, not even a goofy eighteen-year-old, I-rule-the-world-in-this-moment sort of grin. For mother and son, the visages are fixed fiercely, because there are things to be done. Houses to be cleaned. Clothes to be washed. Porches to be swept. Shots to be hoisted. Games to be won. Discontent to be nurtured. Unhappiness to be endured.

His face reflecting immense parental pride, Howard West poses there with his wife and son, enjoying this moment seemingly in ignorance of just how alienated he is from both of them. The elder West, a nondescript guy in the slightly worn suit of a 1950s working man, was said to be a nice person, one who had survived a harsh upbringing to become a community figure known for his warm deeds toward friends and neighbors. Yet there is something deep within him that is profoundly unfulfilled; something almost sinister that neither he nor his family can ever quite contend with.

On his father's side, Jerry West's English ancestors landed at Jamestown, Virginia, and later helped settle the wild, bloody frontier that would become West Virginia. Yet this photograph suggests just how much of his persona Jerry West drew from his mother. Cecile Sue was a Creasey, a forthright clan that settled in West Virginia's magnificent Kanawha Valley in the nineteenth century, hearty people who made their living on the keelboats that hauled salt and other goods along the Kanawha River down to the Ohio.

With his long frame and thirty-eight-inch arms, West would seem to have been right at home among the keel-haulers, pushing and pulling those boats in the hearty, hardscrabble milieu along the river a century earlier. Like the keel-haulers before him, the brooding and sullen young man in the picture appears preoccupied with the constant and distressing need to find a place to employ his seemingly boundless energy.

"I've always been a nervous person," West would admit many times. In fact, his restlessness before games is almost as legendary as his jump shot.

He and his mother would share a psyche often driven to distraction by this nervous energy. Later in life, this no-nonsense woman would greet warmly the occasional strangers who traveled to the family home in the little village of Chelyan (Shill-yun) to worship her son. She would serve homemade lemonade and even pull out scrapbooks to revisit his glory days. But, beyond such moments, there was little charm about Jerry West's mother.

Patience was not her virtue, nor was it her son's. An unadulterated demand for perfection was their shared burden. The mother saw it in her son at an early age because she recognized it in herself.

"He's always wanted perfection," she would confide to sportswriter Bill Libby in 1969. "I think he's come closer to it than most. But I doubt he's satisfied. He's still the boy he always was, who wants to be perfect and just can't understand why he can't be."

The expectation of perfection is a gnarly and contentious quality, impossible to endure yet essential to greatness. It is the central quality in basketball's select few, the truly great players according to Tex Winter, who coached basketball brilliantly for six decades and intensely followed every detail of the game in the process. "That's the one thing about those rare players like Kobe Bryant and Michael Jordan and Jerry West and Oscar Robertson—they want to be the best, and they are never satisfied with anything less. That's what makes them what they are. They're all very complex."

Such complexity would remain the core of West's anxious persona his entire life. At age seventy, reflecting on his career and trying to explain it, he said, "I'd like to see a perfect world in basketball. It's not perfect, and that drives me crazy."

His approach also drove those around him somewhat crazy. Standing there with the Wests on that signing day in 1956, was Schaus, the man who would share so much of West's life yet never quite gain his full confidence. The coach was smiling and relaxed in this moment of victory. He had just signed the state's best player, this scarecrow of a forward he had watched perform magnificently in West Virginia's high school tournament. Months earlier, Schaus had scouted those tournament games with Hot Rod Hundley, his varsity star at the university, and he had pointed out to Hundley two high school players that he liked, one a big man, the other this energetic but thin forward.

"The other one's a nice player," Hundley told his coach. "But if you have to pick one of them, get the skinny one."

Schaus did just that, and in so doing set in motion the karma that would define both his life and West's.

Schaus would coach West for nine straight seasons, three at West Virginia University and six with the Lakers, a phenomenal stretch of almost one thousand games. Then he would serve as general manager for five more Lakers teams that West led. More than anything, they would share an unrivaled frustration.

They would lose the 1959 National Collegiate Athletic Association championship by a point to the University of California team coached by Newell. In Los Angeles, Schaus, West, Elgin Baylor, and their Lakers faced the confounding Bill Russell and the Boston Celtics six times for the league championship in the 1960s. Six times West and the Lakers lost. Each time they watched as Celtics boss Red Auerbach lit up his victory cigar and hooted.

"There were an awful lot of times I wanted to shove that cigar down his throat," Schaus once told me.

As the losses to the green-clad Celtics piled up, West got to the point where he could not stand the sight of green, would not wear anything green, did not want anything green around him. "It got to the point that it controlled my life," said West.

For the first five times that his Lakers lost, the Celtics were favored. But in 1969, the Lakers had home court advantage, they had the giant Wilt Chamberlain, they had every reason to believe it was finally their time.

But they lost game seven in Los Angeles to Russell and Company. West had competed maniacally and was named the Most Valuable Player of the series, the only time in league history that the MVP came from the losing team.

In those days, *Sport* magazine awarded a fancy car to the finals MVP. Already inconsolable over the loss, West recoiled at the sight of the auto.

It was green.

The moment branded Jerry West indelibly, existentially, as the great Sisyphus of basketball. Only a West Virginian could understand the profundity of such frustration. And so, perhaps an advisory label is in order. In searching for clues to the mystery of Jerry West, I have followed the advice of Pete Newell, may God rest his soul. I have included lots and lots about West Virginia.

My old man would have liked that.

Roland Lazenby
October 2009

Jerry West

1

Our grandfather wasn't much of a man.

—Charles West

SAGA

THE SMALL BOY PLACED EVERYTHING THAT WAS HIS, MOSTLY A FEW tattered clothes, in a paper bag and set out over the hill for the long walk in the cold to a neighbor's farm. It was Christmas 1910, and his mother had just died. There had been a pine coffin and a hurried funeral, and now he was all alone. Fear and confusion welled up in his ten-year-old heart as he trudged along, holding tightly to that bag.

For the rest of his life, Howard West would think back to that frightful day and his trek over that hill. His mother, Salena Kile West, had slipped away at age forty-one, worn down by a succession of troubled maternities amidst a world of toil. She had birthed nine children in fourteen years, a succession of labors that defined the wretchedness of subsistence farm life in rural West Virginia in the late nineteenth and early twentieth centuries. It was a life wrought with unrelenting difficulty for women in that age before rural electrification. Pregnant year after year, all the while faced with the staggering work load of a farm woman: the cooking, washing, cleaning, cutting wood, and tending stove fires seven days a week. Salena had some-how raised the brood of children needed to scratch out a life from the thin soil of the West Virginia hills in rural Roane County, northeast of Charleston. Like so many women of the period, her life had been an act played out in drudgery and isolation. Her first six pregnancies had brought the supposed blessing of six boys to help with her husband's work, but that also meant that for much of her life, she had been the only female to support a family of seven farming males.

The troubled life of Salena Kile West sprang from circumstances all too familiar for generations of rural women. "Living was just drudgery then," a farm wife from that era recalled. "Living—just living—was a problem. No lights. No plumbing. Nothing. Just living on the edge of starvation. That was the farm life for us."

Without electricity, all of a family's water had to be drawn by hand from either a deep well or a nearby creek. A joke of the times was that farm families had "runnin' water"—you had to run back and forth to get it. An extensive federal study of farm family life of that era said each person used an average of 40 gallons per day. That would have been 440 gallons daily for Salena Kile West's family as she neared her end. Water for cooking. Water for scrubbing the unrelenting farm dirt from clothing. Water for working those washboards that left her hands raw. Water for cleaning the small domicile that housed Salena, her husband, Maxwell "Maxie" West, and their nine children. Water for cooking to feed them all.

Yet hauling water and cutting wood, however difficult, weren't the worst of her plight. That would have been the woodstove itself, which had to be kept roaring hot all day long, seven days a week, summer, fall, winter, and spring. Farm life—and a farm woman's exhaustion—centered on that woodstove. When it went out, the cook fire was in-fernally difficult to restart, thus it required constant fuel and attention, a welcome enough distraction in winter but a pitiless ne-cessity in summer. And with no electricity and no refrigeration, the preparing and canning of vegetables and produce had to be done as they came ripe and were harvested in the heat of summer and early fall. Farm women had to get things preserved and into jars before they spoiled, just another exhaustion in farming's relentless agenda.

In a speech before Congress, Representative John Rankin of Mis-sissippi recalled the era and his mother "burning up in a hot kitchen and bowing down over the washtub or boiling the clothes over a flaming fire in the summer heat." Everything had to be ironed by heavy irons heated on those woodstoves, and Rankin told of seeing his mother "leaning over that hot iron hour after hour until it seemed she was tired enough to drop."

The history of the American frontier—and make no mistake, West Virginia remained a fixture of that frontier in 1910—has been written as a man's story, yet the history itself was borne and endured by women like Salena Kile West. Likewise, the story of her grandson, Jerry West, would seem to be a man's story, yet in so many ways, his success was a product of the strong and enduring women among his forbearers.

Stories passed down through the West family say that the birthing process over the years had been particularly hard on Salena, a typical problem of that era. One federal study said many farm women of the early twentieth century had almost no access to medical care, particularly during childbirth. As a result, a large percentage of them suffered from tears of the perineum, the area between the anus and vagina. These tears, many of which were third degree and left unrepaired, according to the report, were so bad, so painful long after birth, that it was difficult to see how farm women "managed to stay on their feet." And, of course, many didn't.

It was this cumulative effect of the nine births and the harsh life that brought Salena to an early grave, according to family legend. She apparently continued to bleed long after the last birth. In her final exhaustion, she lay in bed as Christmas neared, worrying about her nine children: the little girls, Lula, almost two, and Thelma, three, and Sylvia, six; and her handsome collection of sons, Herman, eight, Howard, ten, Frederick, twelve, Holly, thirteen, Lee, fifteen, and Earl, sixteen. What would happen to them? Who would care for them all?

Her husband, Maxie West, hardly inspired trust. If fact, Charles Dickens couldn't have drawn up a finer scoundrel. Maxwell West himself was a product of West Virginia's harsh farm life: Born into a family of tenant farmers in 1869, he was a working adult, a farm laborer, by age eleven, illiterate and doomed to remain that way his entire life. The harsh challenge of subsistence farm life ennobled some men; others it simply ground under and reduced to pathetic desperation, leaving them dreaming of escape from the long hours, the harsh conditions, and the many mouths to feed. According to legend, Maxie West was a coarse man cut from the wretchedness of the land.

Decades after he was gone, family members would harbor passed-down memories of his teeth, badly stained brown by years of chewing and smoking tobacco, and his revolting table manners. He would eat peas with his knife, scooping them up on the blade and letting them roll into his open mouth.

What little control Salena West had over her husband lay in the deed to their small farm. It was in her name, handed down from her family. Small West Virginia farms weren't worth a lot in those days. Although they were needed to feed the many mouths in a family, many of those tracts were valued at less than $200, according to federal records. Then again, $200 was a lot of money in rural West Virginia in 1910. The land was Salena's. And she drew some satisfaction from the idea that she would leave that farm to help sustain her brood.

There, on her deathbed, Salena made Maxie promise that if she signed the farm over to him, he would keep the children together. Eying the deed, he promised dutifully to keep them all in his care and custody.

Within hours of her funeral—"She wasn't even cold before he packed off those children," said granddaughter Hannah West—he made it clear that he never planned to fulfill Salena's wishes. Instead, Maxie West moved quickly to the task of parceling the children out to neighboring farms.

"The phrase his children used later when they were adults was that he 'turned them out,'" recalled Charles West, Maxie's grandson. Apparently Maxie sold the farm quickly. He left it and his nine children behind and found work as a barber in the nearby town of Spencer.

Records show that just six months after burying Salena, Maxie married a local woman who already had an eight-year-old boy and a ten-year-old girl of her own. This second wife, who worked as a domestic servant, soon bore Maxwell two more children.

Records from the era don't say how or why, but Maxie's second wife died in 1915 at age thirty-eight, just a few months after giving birth to a daughter and four short years after taking up with Maxie. Just as he had done the first time he lost a spouse, he quickly abandoned his second family of motherless children by sending all four children to live on her father's farm in Roane County. Unburdened of his offspring, Maxie West would remarry twice more over the ensuing years.

In all, Maxwell West fathered eleven children, and, according to family legend, he boasted of another. In one of his marriages, an underage stepdaughter in her early teen years became pregnant, and Maxie confided to relatives that her child was his. His wife soon learned Maxie's secret. Understandably outraged, she contacted authorities, and Maxie West was arrested and charged with statutory rape. Arrest and prison records in West Virginia are notoriously incomplete for that era, and no record of Maxie's incarceration has turned up, but his grandchildren heard all the family stories about him from their mothers. For decades, women in the West family would say that Maxie West was the kind of relative to be avoided. And no matter what, never leave him alone with the children.

IT WAS TO A NEIGHBOR'S FARM that little Howard West trudged that week of Christmas 1910. Rolla Starcher, a sheep farmer, had agreed to take him in. Starcher, a distant cousin of Salena Kile, had been married for years to wife Bertha. Typical of the families of rural Appalachia in 1910, the Starchers' three adult children still lived with their parents on the farm. They welcomed Howard warmly into their home, and in time it would become clear that, as harsh as the circumstances were, the Starchers had saved little Howard West. His mother's death meant that he would not have to grow up in the close company of his dreadful father.

He had to work hard on that farm, Howard West would later tell his children, but it was a good home. He would have fond memories of farm life, of chasing lambs around and playing in the fields as a boy. And every year as an adult, he would get on a bus and ride back to Roane County to visit the old Starcher homeplace. Howard's own children viewed the Starchers as the closest thing they had to grandparents on their father's side of the family. On occasion, Howard and his children would visit the grave of Selena West in a small cemetery on a remote hilltop in Roane County. The marker was primitive, and obviously her pine coffin had rotted, because the ground around the grave was sunken. But the story of her labors and privation had survived in family legend. And those who visited her felt a gratitude toward her and a sorrow about her life and the scattering of her children.

That scattering would profoundly shape Howard West. It seems that his entire life he would retain some element of that ten-year-old making the lonely walk over that hill. Long after he was gone, his own grown children would recall his obvious longing and need for family. He would hold his small children on his lap, singing them to sleep at night with verses from "Streets of Laredo" or "Barbry Allen." He would tell them he loved them and always seemed quick to display his pride in them. At the same time, Howard West was also known for his harsh temper. He was well aware of the dark recesses of his anger and always warned his children not to test him. If you heeded that warning, you could avoid the consequences of his fire. On the other hand, if you persisted in pushing him? Well, his children said they quickly learned that challenging him could prove quite painful.

A NOBLE BEGINNING

His grandmother's grim tenure and death on a West Virginia farm in 1910 would seem to suggest that Jerry West descended from a pack of dirt-scratching hillbillies. Yet that was hardly the case. When the West family line arrived in America just after the seventeenth century turned, it bore the crest of English nobility: a design featuring three leopards, portending perhaps West's own catlike playing style. In fact, it's hard to imagine a more colorful lineage than that of Jerry West. His direct family tree shows an astounding array of heroes and villains, wealthy landowners and occasional paupers, soldiers and profiteers, Indian fighters and dandified gentlemen, dating from the first moments of the English settlement at Jamestown and running through some of the bloodiest days in American history.

West's ancestors include Thomas West, the second Baron De La Warr of Wherwell Abbey in the English county of Hampshire. Thomas West claimed noble lineage but worked as a poor justice of the peace in Elizabethan England until he married into money. With financial backing, he was able to lay claim to privilege and establish himself as a baron. His son, the younger Thomas West, assumed title. This younger West, the third Baron De La Warr, was one of the financiers behind the Jamestown colony in Virginia. De La Warr, of course, would be corrupted over time into "Delaware," and Thomas West would become known as Lord Delaware. The state of Delaware, even the Delaware Indians, were named after him, based upon his claim to be the first Englishman to visit that territory.

One of Jerry West's ancestors served as the Crown Governor of Virginia, and the line of his ancestral grandfathers became some of the wealthiest landowners on Virginia's Eastern Shore for hundreds of years. Yet another ancestral grandfather of West's was Edmund Scarborough, a notoriously rapacious colonel in Colonial Virginia and the largest landholder on the Eastern Shore. Scarborough served as speaker of the House of Burgesses. He owned a fleet of ships, which allowed him to conduct trade up and down the coast of America, including the selling of arms to Indians, who called him "Conjurer." According to the book *Squires and Dames of Old Virginia* by Evelyn Kinder Donaldson, Scarborough was known for his harsh temper and ruthless business practices. Supposedly, in 1671 he invited local Indians to a feast where he promised the Great Spirit would speak to them. Once the Indians had gathered, he reportedly ordered his artillery to open fire on them. That same year, Scarborough died of small pox and left his vast holdings to his children, including daughter Matilda and her husband, Lieutenant Colonel John West. Evelyn Donaldson wrote: "Edmund was tempestuous and would fight at the drop of a hat . . . Scarborough however built a dynasty in America which was heard from in every generation. He left his widow Mary Scarborough and five children very well-to-do."

SCARBOROUGH'S GRANDSON WAS SCARBURGH WEST—the English spelling had been abbreviated—and he was the West who headed the family history down the path to West Virginia. His will, probated on April 29, 1760, in Accomack County, split his land between his two younger sons but left his eldest, Edmund West, and two daughters a mere two shillings each and "no more." Just what caused Edmund West to fall into such disfavor is unclear, but it perhaps explains why Edmund would eventually pack up his family and depart from a life of relative comfort and safety in Accomack to head out into the wilds of the Virginia frontier at a time when it was aboil with conflict. It also perhaps helps explain how the status of this particular line of the family slipped over the decades from landed gentry to hard-luck hillbillies. Edmund West was to join the settlers who braved the frontier that would become West Virginia. They all were in search of unclaimed land and the opportunity that it seemed to offer. What many of them found instead was another sort of opportunity: the opportunity to get scalped.

WEST'S FORT

By the dawn of the eighteenth century, Virginians had crossed the sloping Blue Ridge Mountains and begun to settle the broad Valley of Virginia, later to be known as the Shenandoah, that reached up into Maryland. The Blue Ridge comprised the southern boundary of the great valley, and its northern edge was formed by the Allegheny range—the beginning of the great Allegheny Plateau, that large mass of mountains and crags that faces north and covers today as much as four-fifths of the state of West Virginia. Back then it represented an imposing fortress to early explorers, red or white, who managed to climb the crest of one Allegheny ridge only to find an unbroken vista of similarly steep ranges stretching out in the distance. The harshness of the landscape seemed to be relieved only by equally narrow valleys and often turbulent rivers.

The emptiness enhanced the mystery of the place. For a thousand years, mound-building Indian tribes had inhabited various sections of the region, but when white explorers crossed into the Virginia frontier in the early 1700s, they found almost no one living there. Some historians suggest that the harsh Iroquois had chased other tribes from the place to claim the fat hunting lands there, but no one really knows why most peoples had quit the country that would become West Virginia.

The only indisputable fact is that it was an empty, difficult land. If white men visited, they often chose to go around rather than over those ranges, just as did George Washington, who first visited West Virginia as a young military officer during the French and Indian War. A land surveyor by training, Washington returned to the region in 1770, making his way up by Pittsburgh and then down the Ohio River, before heading back up into the lower elevations of the Allegheny Plateau to explore the choice lands in West Virginia's Kanawha Valley.

The fierce tribes, the Shawnee, Mingo, Chippewa, Ottawa, and Delaware, among others who lived along the Ohio River, eyed the hunting grounds in the territory jealously. While few of them, if any, attempted to live there, they made frequent trips down into the Kanawha and Greenbrier valleys to terrorize and torture any white folks foolhardy enough to linger. They particularly enjoyed the slow roasting of captives in their council fires and, over the course of the very turbulent seventeenth century, collected what had to be thousands of scalps. The French and English and even the Dutch, who had eyed opportunity for land and timber and political influence, all jockeyed to curry favor with those tribes as they parried for control of the territory. Taken as a whole, the Virginia frontier was a very dangerous place, as British general Edward Braddock discovered in 1755 when he marched a force of 1,400 crack European infantry and about 300 irregular colonial militia into the West Virginia wilderness on their way to attack the French near Pittsburgh. Hacking their own road across the rugged terrain, Braddock and his men were surprised by a force of maybe 300 Indians and French and were badly routed. The blunder cost Braddock and about 500 of his men their lives in a slaughter that startled the colonies just as the demise of General George Custer's Seventh Cavalry would shock the country a little more than a century later.

Any number of settlers and colonial militia would meet Braddock's same fate during the French and Indian War, and for decades thereafter. But the British defeat of the French in 1763 and subsequent treaties with various tribes created a new hope for the place. To encourage development, the Colonial governor of Virginia began offering land incentives for those brave enough to settle that trans-Allegheny region. As might have been expected, it was only a matter of time before the incoming crowd violated whatever treaties had been arranged and the Indians took to their warpaths again, trying to kill off settlers.

THAT WAS CLEARLY THE CASE by the late spring of 1773 when Edmund West and his young family boarded a boat in Accomack and headed up the Chesapeake Bay and into the mouth of the Potomac River. They traveled as far as Alexandria, where they likely purchased a Conestoga wagon. From the port at Alexandria, they headed over

the Blue Ridge to the broad green richness of the upper Shenandoah, with its serenity and lush fields, and from there they moved up into the Allegheny Range and then across the lower reaches of the plateau. The flow of settlers stopped in Moorefield, at the upper waters of the Potomac, then down to Petersburg for a final stopover before pushing through the mountains into harsh and dangerous territory. The Wests were part of a great migration of colonials into the Greenbrier, Tygart, Monongahela, Kanawha, and upper Ohio valleys, but beyond the pristine Tygart Valley, Edmund West and his family pushed into Lewis County and settled at Hackers Creek, not far from what would become the community of Jane Lew, West Virginia.

John Hacker, an Irishman who had come to America in 1748, had settled the area along the creek three years earlier and made a home there. By 1773, Edmund West's family and a number of other whites had joined Hacker. Fear of Indian attack guided their every move. Edmund West's eldest son, Edmund Jr., would marry Mary Ann, Hacker's daughter. Beyond those ties, the two families would brave and suffer the wild country together. That fall and winter brought an immediate test for Edmund West and his family. The large influx of settlers and the lack of a growing season for most of them meant there simply wasn't enough grain to feed them all. Historians say the conditions brought a "starving time." West was almost forty-four years old at the time, and while it would seem he hardly had any experience at pioneering, he would survive and soon gain some reputation as an Indian fighter. To that end, Edmund West Sr., his sons, and neighbors built West's Fort for protection. Typical of many frontier forts of the era, it was a basic large log building with a surrounding stockade; a place where families could retreat when hostiles threatened their homeplaces. They also used it as a meeting place when times weren't so bad.

While conditions were already bad across the trans-Allegheny region, they would turn dramatically worse with the colonies pushing for independence in 1775. The English Crown's representatives began striking alliances with the tribes along the Ohio River as events turned toward war. The British withdrew their garrisons from their larger forts across the frontier, leaving settlers defenseless. Indian tribes in America had long been used to playing the various political games between the European powers vying for control of the headwaters of the Ohio River and thus the frontier. For the first two years

of the Revolutionary War, the tribes remained mostly neutral, but they shifted in 1777 and began siding with the British. The Allegheny Plateau turned violent again, and 1777 would long be remembered as the year of the bloody triple sevens, with Indian raids on settlements. Attacks mounted that fall—one ambush killed a Colonial officer and twenty men, a scenario that occurred several times—and many families abandoned their settlements and fled east. Not Edmund West, however. His son Alexander turned seventeen that year. Of Jerry West's many ancestors, young Alexander West was the first noted in historical accounts for his athletic feats. Frontier life required hardiness, and from various reports, Alexander West had that. He was swift enough to chase down the mountain trails in pursuit of ambushing Indians. He was a crack rifleman. Most important, he was a willing participant.

As the British grip tightened on the Ohio Territory in 1777, a charismatic young officer in the Virginia militia named George Rogers Clark wanted to drive deep into the Midwest to defeat the English and stop the Indian attacks they were foisting on the Virginia and Kentucky frontier. Rogers raised a troop of rangers to take the Midwest back from English control in 1778, and young Alexander West joined the mission as a private in a company of Virginians under Captain George Jackson.

Unfortunately, West's Fort was attacked by Indians in both 1779 and 1780, and twice the Wests and other inhabitants were forced to abandon it. In one incident, Indians surrounded the fort and settled in for something of a siege, with the frightened settlers inside unsure what to do. Finally, Jesse Hughes, one of the Wests' neighbors, snuck out of the fort at night and ran to a nearby fort in Buckhannon, where he got help and brought back a party of men to fight the Indians and chase them away. Indians burned West's Fort at one point, and he and his neighbors apparently rebuilt it out of beech trees and renamed it Fort Beech.

Alexander West returned to his family after his enlistment was up. As colonials grew increasingly weary of the heavy burden of fighting, it became harder for the Continental army to recruit enlistees. Not only did Alexander West serve with Clark for more than a year, he rejoined the army for a second stint in 1781 and served another seven months until the British were defeated. His service would be an item of West family pride for generations.

BLOODY DECEMBER

For decades, the tribes along the Ohio River had formed unlikely alliances, first with the French and later with the English, to fend off the advances of what was clearly an alien invasion. With the defeat of the mighty British in 1781, the tribes were left to fight on alone. They did so with increasing nastiness and desperation. It wasn't until more than a decade after the Revolutionary War ended that the young American government finally sent an army deep into the Midwest to deliver the crushing blows that subjugated the native people and opened the territory to a new host of predators: land speculators, then salt miners, and, finally, the grand array of coal and chemical and oil companies that turned the pristine Kanawha Valley into a grim patchwork of polluted waters, played-out coal mines, dilapidated trailer parks, and seedy little strip malls, a debasement accomplished with amazing swiftness over the course of two hundred years. Of course, that's a deeply negative take on events. Many parts of the valley remain vibrant today, but there's little question that industrialization left its blight on the region.

Over its decades in the New World, the West family would march in step with this settlement and eventual industrialization of the land. Certainly a dark moment in that procession came on December 5, 1787.

It must have been unseasonably warm that winter morning near Hackers Creek. Although he was getting along in years, almost sixty, in fact, Edmund West was busy hauling fodder to his stable. In a scene played out hundreds of times on the West Virginia frontier, the Shawnee war party stole along Hacker's Creek, where they first met twelve-year-old Martha Hughes, who was coming down the creek from a visit to John Hacker's place. She was carrying the new puppy he had given her. The raiders took young Martha and her puppy captive first but didn't kill her right away. Next they came upon Edmund West. The old man supposedly begged for his life, but they quickly tomahawked and scalped him right there in front of Martha. His sons Edmund Jr., Alexander, and Charles were off hunting, probably not a coincidence for the raiders. They went immediately to the cabin of Mary Ann Hacker West, where she was cooking a meal with Margaret Hacker, her eleven-year-old sister, and Billy West, the youngest son of Edmund West Sr. The Indians forced their way inside, killed and scalped Mary Ann and struck a blow to the head of Margaret, who tried to take cover behind the door. Billy was hiding under a bed, but they pulled him out and quickly tomahawked him, once above each brow, according to legend. Although the cabin was a bloody mess, the war party took the time to consume the meal Mary Ann West had been preparing. They also scalped the still-living Margaret, sensed she wasn't dead, and struck her with more blows before dragging her body outside and throwing it over a fence.

The wife of Edmund West Sr. was home with two daughters and feared the worst when he failed to return from work. She and her daughters went to the home of neighbor Jesse Hughes and sought his help in looking for the elder West. Hughes was likewise worried because his daughter Martha hadn't come home. Hughes and the three women went to warn Mary Ann West and happened upon the carnage in her cabin. The women were sickened by what they found, and Hughes rushed them back to safety without realizing that Billy West was still alive or that Margaret Hacker had been thrown over the fence. Hughes returned the women to his cabin, where he kept watch over his family until the next day when neighbors gathered to investigate the incident.

Billy West was found nearly a mile from the cabin, standing in Hacker's Creek in a daze, his brains oozing from his wounds. He died three days later and was buried next to his father.

Margaret Hacker, scalped and badly injured, had risen and walked to the empty cabin of Edmund West, where she lay down on a warm hearth before growing sick and crawling into a bed. She would wear a scarf over her scalped head for the rest of her life and go on to bear ten children before migrating to Ohio and dying at age forty, like so many put-upon frontier women.

Martha Hughes was taken captive by the raiders and carried deep into Ohio, where she lived with the Shawnee for three years until one of the many treaties of that era brought her release and return to her family.

Alexander West would recover from the murders of his father and brother and live to the ripe old age of seventy-four. His son Thomas would come to be known as Thomas Sr., and, like his father before him and so many other West Virginians, was a military man. When hostilities reignited with the British in the War of 1812, Thomas joined one of dozens of companies that formed on the Virginia frontier to rush to combat. Thomas lost a leg in the war and returned home in 1815 to begin a long life as a military pensioner, perhaps a factor in the further financial decline of the family. He lived to be ninety and watched as his own son, Thomas Jr., went off to war in 1861. Records indicate that a half dozen Thomas Wests from West Virginia served in the Civil War. Of the group, only Thomas West Jr. fought for the South, which was typical of the area that would become West Virginia.

For years, residents of the western part of Virginia complained that the state was dominated by the economy and mind-set of its Southern plantations. The war only deepened those divisions and led to the establishment of the new state of West Virginia, a dominion already beset by land speculators and opportunists. It was the settlers and pioneers who had paid for their land holdings with their blood and sometimes their scalps. But title to the lands too often eluded their grasp and wound up in the hands of the large business interests and the coal companies, which would lead to yet more bloodshed. In due time, the state would find itself facing another violent agenda: the mine wars, the nasty struggle over labor rights for West Virginia's downtrodden miners.

All of that had yet to unfold when Thomas West Jr. arrived home in Roane County from the Civil War. Just a few years later, he would add a new son, Maxwell West, to his large farm family. The genetic strain that would become Jerry West had traveled a long, hard, narrow road through the centuries to this appointed hour. Maxie West would do his part, then slink away into ignominy, leaving his ten-year-old son Howard to trudge over that hill in December 1910, heading toward a world of still more dark, harsh turns and yet somehow just enough wondrous beginnings.

If the men were dead, that was the end of them; but the women must face the future, with its bitter memories, its lonely and desolate struggle for existence. The women must see the children suffering, dying by slow stages of deprivation.

—Upton Sinclair, *King Coal*

WEST, BY GOD, VIRGINIA

Cabin Creek, 1912 to 1938

AFTER HE BECAME A FAMOUS MAN IN LOS ANGELES, STORIES ABOUT Jerry West would sometimes erroneously describe his father Howard as a coal miner. That certainly made for nice copy. There was even a story, quoted in some publications, about Howard West coming out of a mine with his face blackened by coal to shake the hand of John F. Kennedy during the 1960 presidential campaign. Howard West did shake Kennedy's hand that year (he told the young senator that he was supporting Hubert Humphrey in the Democratic primary), but he didn't shake it as a miner. Jerry West's father worked for several years repairing and greasing the wheels of the cars that hauled coal out of the mines, but he never dug a single lump of the stuff himself. Still, the coal industry defined many of the major elements of his life, just as it did for just about all West Virginians in the early decades of the twentieth century. Across much of the state, coal was king, it was true, but it was hardly a benevolent dictator. In fact, it seemed to inspire the worst in all sorts of people.

Having come through its days first as a frontier, then as a battle-ground for the American Revolution, the state next found itself caught in the middle of the Civil War. The smoke hadn't even cleared from that great conflict before the next bloody, ugly chapter unfolded. It was a class warfare that seized the entire state by the throat, pitching those with big money against those fighting the tyranny of that money.

"I used to work for a coal company," said Jerry West's sister Hannah. "It was a very prominent coal company, and the guy who was their treasurer, he once told me they deserved every bad thing that ever happened to them. They were just lousy human beings."

Why was the struggle so nasty in West Virginia? Perhaps because it was the kind of place where backwardness could frustrate greed. The renowned British geologist Richard Cowling Taylor had visited the state in 1848 and described its vast untapped store of wealth as "that magnificent, central, elevated region within whose borders slumbers in undisturbed darkness untold millions of acres of coal."

Such talk had speculators dreaming of getting at those deposits. But the coal boom that seemed so certain to explode was delayed by the Civil War and by West Virginia's lack of banks. It was a costly, difficult task to build the railroads necessary to haul out the coal through the state's steep, craggy terrain. With no entity to finance either mining or railroad building, the exploitation of the state's resources was slow in getting started and yet so brutally efficient when it finally did. For the most part, West Virginia remained a place of natural grandeur until well past 1880. "Forests of oak, ash, cucumber wood, and poplar covered the hills," wrote journalist Winthrop Lane in describing the place before the coal boom. "Bears lumbered through the wilderness and wildcats howled at night. No railroad had yet penetrated the region . . . The earth reposed peacefully."

Yet once the war ended, companies in Europe and Pennsylvania and New York saw the benefit of financing the prospecting. The ensuing push to get at the coal would bring its own peculiar madness. Within a few short years, operators began digging, blasting, and scraping tens of millions of tons of coal from the hills. The great Allegheny Plateau, and especially the once lovely Kanawha Valley, were soon enough pocked by hundreds of mines. Cabin Creek and its twin, Paint Creek, begin about twenty-five miles east of Charleston and cut their winding way through and across the plateau, forming its southeastern edge, till they feed into the Kanawha River south of Charleston. Locals liked to point out that there was a coal tipple or mine at every bend in the road along the twenty-five miles of Cabin Creek, right to the point that it reached the river, where the coal was loaded onto barges and hauled off to stoke the great fires of American industry. The mining operations soon stretched across the breadth of much of the plateau, with their coal and coke all spawning and feeding the stupefying array of chemical plants that came to dominate the once pristine valley.

And it all happened at such a deadly price. Building the railroads over and through the mountains to get at West Virginia's prize jewels cost hundreds of lives, many of them itinerant African-American laborers brought up from the cotton fields of the Deep South who died in anonymous droves. The losses in the coal industry would run even heavier. Between 1880 and 1920, more than 4,300 coal miners died in a steady stream of incidents, some that killed hundreds at a time. Thousands more were injured or suffered the dreaded cough of the black lung.

The mining companies soon faced a rising din of bitter complaints and then a series of strikes by miners hoping to organize into a union. The industry, fearing that it would lose control over the resources and thus lose huge amounts of money, responded swiftly with a brutality that matched the very conditions in the mines. The suppression of mine workers evolved with sheer ugliness.

From the mining industry's earliest days, coal operators brought in miners from across the European Old World—Welsh, English, Belgians, Italians, Slavs, Austrians—not to mention a steady stream of Scots Irish from the eastern seaboard and African-Americans in hopes of diluting and defusing any demands from the labor pool. Where the state's settlers had once struggled against the frontier and the Indians for their very survival, the descendants of those same people now battled corporations and even governments. Their new neighbors suffered alongside them while mourning, in an array of foreign tongues, those who had died in the disasters.

Whatever their ethnicity, the miners worked in brutal servitude, described by American Federation of Labor founder Samuel Gompers as "a most desolate life." A miner, working on his hands and knees in cramped, damp spaces deep underground, would dig with a pick and shovel as much as ten tons of coal per day. He lived in constant fear that the company would "short weight," or systematically underweigh, his tonnage to keep him in that servitude. It also meant no food on the table for mining families living on the edge.

"Many times in miners' homes, I have looked into family cupboards that contained only a little food, perhaps for a single meager meal," wrote West Virginia senator Robert Byrd, himself the son of a miner. "I have seen the haunted look in the eyes of men who did not know how they were going to provide for the immediate wants of their half-starved and ill-clothed children and wives."

Instead of money, miners were often paid in company scrip. The miners and their families lived in company shanties in company towns, attended company churches and company schools, and spent company scrip at company stores, saw company doctors, and even patronized company whores.

"You didn't even own your own soul in those damnable places," an elderly miner would recall years later. "The company owned everything."

The suppression only bred more contempt, and it soon boiled over into a violent conflict between activists who wanted to organize the miners into unions and the operators who fought unionization at every turn. The site of that first major outbreak hit south of Charleston in the mines along Cabin Creek and Paint Creek, where miners went on strike in 1912.

The violence at Cabin Creek marked a dark turning point in the great labor struggle of what came to be known as the West Virginia mine wars, a bloody shooting conflict between striking miners and the army of company detectives hired as thugs to enforce the labor conditions. The companies brought in the security force to evict the families of striking miners from company houses. The miners took up residence in nearby tent cities as the strike dragged into 1913 before the state declared martial law and began charging and trying striking miners for treason.

"The West Virginia mine wars involved nearly every form of violence," wrote historian David Alan Corbin, a student of the era. The conflict ran for a decade, regularly boiling over into shootouts, street fighting, gangland-style hits, and, finally, martial law, a bizarre drama stirred by labor leaders such as Gompers and the great Mary Hams "Mother" Jones, the small, feisty old woman who so passionately took up the miners' cause. She came on the scene as part of the strike at

Cabin Creek and Paint Creek in 1912–13 and attacked the coal companies with salty language that stirred the humor and hearts of the striking miners. The Cabin Creek conflict saw authorities and coal company detectives load a Gatling machine gun on a train and ride up the mountain shooting randomly into the tent camps of the striking miners, a crime that prompted Congressional hearings. Federal testimony revealed that even some company thugs recoiled at the lowness of the deed. (For many years one of Jerry West's relatives had a bullet hole in the wall of her house left by the gunfire.)

Before the mine wars were over, 20,000 armed miners would gather near Cabin Creek and set out on a ninety-mile march with the goal of lynching the union-busting sheriff of Logan County. A running gun battle ensued. To restore order during a particularly heated uprising in September 1921, President Warren G. Harding sent in 2,100 troops, a chemical warfare unit, and the Eighty-eighth Light Bombing Squadron led by General Billy Mitchell of World War I fame, all of which suggested that while the state may have been remote, it certainly retained a capacity for the fantastic.

HOWARD'S QUEST

The ongoing coal battle seemed to be everywhere at once, a drama covered by newspapers the world over. If young Howard West knew about it up in the isolated farming country of Roane County, he likely read it in a newspaper. Like his father before him and like many in his own generation, he had been required to work on the farm as soon as he was old enough. Schooling was not the priority. He had been able to go through only the sixth grade, which must have been disappointing for him as a boy, because he loved to read; absolutely loved it. Whenever he could get his hands on a discarded newspaper, he'd read every word. Old magazines were special prizes. In time he would become a man of letters in the only way that his narrow life would allow: He used the newspapers to educate himself. They offered Howard West what little intellectual salvation he would find.

"My dad was very intelligent and very frustrated that he was very intelligent and not educated," said Barbara West, his youngest daughter. "I think that's why he read a lot his entire life."

It also suggests that, like his father before him, Howard West desperately wanted to escape the confining life on the farm. And like his father, as soon as he got the opportunity, he took it. At seventeen, he told Rolla and Bertha Starcher good-bye, packed up his few belongings, and set out in search of his own place in the world.

His first stop was the U.S. Navy. That seemed like a good enough place to try to find a home. The year was 1917, and he gained enlistment as part of America's armament for World War I. Howard served about nine months in uniform and was hoping to do a lot more when his travel plans abruptly ended in Norfolk, Virginia, where he was stationed. The federal government was looking to trim the costs associated with an expensive war. He and many others like him were cut loose early from their commitments, given an honorable discharge, and sent on their way.

For the second time in his young life, he was homeless. First his father and now Uncle Sam had turned him out. Although he served only a short time, the navy had also exposed Howard to the growing port city of Norfolk, which revealed in a few short months the world beyond West Virginia. Just as important, it brought him a broader array of reading material to feed his huge hunger for learning. In many ways, his time in the service was as close as Howard West would get to formal education.

With just this taste of the outside world, he abruptly faced a decision. Should he go back to West Virginia? Every day the papers were filled with stories that made you wonder if society itself was coming unbolted. All across the Allegheny Plateau, anarchy was in the air. It stood to reason that Howard West had second thoughts about going back. He looked around and apparently realized that the best landing place was with his favorite older brother, Holly, who had found work in an Akron, Ohio, rubber plant. Mr. Henry Ford's automobiles had taken off in a big way, and the world needed tires. Holly and his wife were bunking with another couple who worked in the rubber plants, and he said they had room for his little brother.

"Every teenager went to Akron to find work in those days," Charles West said of his father's next move.

It was a destination for a generation of Midwesterners migrating away from small farms. What they found once they got there was the hard news faced by farm boys and girls all over the planet: The new, industrialized world meant long hours in miserable circumstances for low wages. Akron was the ideal place for the rubber convergence. There was plenty of water, cheap coal from nearby West Virginia, and a flush labor pool to keep wages low. Howard West would spend several years toiling in Ohio's rubber factories until he abruptly moved again.

West Virginia hardly seemed an inviting alternative, yet something pulled him back. The bloodshed and scenes of armed, angry miners engaged in a standoff with federal troops played to headlines in newspapers and magazines around the world, which only deepened West Virginians' profound sense of humiliation and isolation. For decades afterward, the state's textbooks and history books made scant mention of the conflict, an indication of that shame. The region's character had suffered yet another major blow, one more in a long chain of events that seemed to cast it as a backward place. In the aftermath, generations of West Virginians would harbor a sense of indignation over the treatment of miners. As Jerry West himself noted, by the 1950s, just about anyone who espoused Democratic or Populist ideals had a good chance of getting elected in just about every community. "The Republicans were all associated with Herbert Hoover and the Depression," Charles West recalled.

Populism appealed to Howard West. The mine wars eventually opened the door for the unions in the state. He would become a union man and a Democrat, and an outspoken one at that. "Dad thought it was his duty to write a letter to the editor of the Charleston paper every two weeks," explained Barbara.

It wasn't that Howard agreed with every element of the party platform or blindly followed union direction, Charles West said of his father's fundamental beliefs. He didn't. Despite his lack of formal education, Howard West was an independent thinker willing to speak his mind to challenge the state's problems. Unfortunately, there was plenty to challenge. If nothing else, the mine wars had laid bare very basic and very deep divisions in American society. They presaged the coming hurt and hard times that would roll across the land, staggering even those who had thought their world stable.

Howard West had many shortcomings as a young man, but overconfidence in the stability of everyday living wasn't one of them. Life had taught him different lessons. He decided to leave Ohio and return to West Virginia in the early 1920s, probably to find a good job. In looking back years later, his own children understood that he was

really searching for something much deeper—much more basic—
than that.

CECILE

Restlessness defined that generation that came off the farm, just as it
defined Howard West. About the time that the conflict in the coalfields reached a crescendo, he made his way down to Charleston,
where he took a job at the Kelly Axe Company. He hadn't been there
long before he apparently began looking yet again for better
prospects.

"To use an expression, he was as poor as Joe's turkey," said Patricia West Noel, his eldest daughter.

How or why he went to Charleston, family members aren't exactly
sure. His older brother Earl was working as a barber there, and it is
suspected that Howard made that the next stop in his search for family.

Just two years after he had been sent to live with the Starchers, he
learned that one of his older brothers, Lee, who had gone to live and
work on a nearby farm, had been killed when a horse kicked him in
the head, and the incident apparently only deepened his longings for
family. He confided once to his children that as a boy he had sat in the
room with Lee's body after the incident and saw an angel there.
Clearly, whatever divine connection Howard West saw in life, it came
to him through that sense of family.

Probably he was drawn back to West Virginia by a sense of opportunity. Another wave of migration was bringing thousands of people
into the area as jobs opened in the new oil and gas and chemicals operations of the Kanawha Valley. Metropolitan Charleston alone had
better than 100,000 inhabitants in its heyday, and the southern end of
Kanawha County ballooned to at least that. Historians say that in the
decades leading up to World War II, as many as 120,000 people lived
in the scores of little communities that dotted the valley south of the
city. Malden, Pratt, Rand, Dupont City, Ward, Cedar Grove, Handley,
Belle, East Bank, Glasgow, Chelyan, Cabin Creek, Chesapeake, and
many others, all of them connected by the creeks and hollows that fed
into the river and by the dirt roads that fed into West Virginia Highway 61. In the 1930s, bus and streetcar services would extend from the

city along Route 61 into these communities. Years later, when Jerry West went to Los Angeles to play for the Lakers, his mailing address in Cabin Creek evoked backwoods images for his teammates and fans, but the circumstances were more complex than that. Cabin Creek had an identity as part of a bustling industrial corridor.

The early decades of the twentieth century had brought an expansion of the chemical industry in and around Charleston, as DuPont and other corporations sought to take advantage of the great stores of resources available. Soon some shortsighted soul thought to boast that the Kanawha Valley was the chemical center of the world. In just a few decades, West Virginia's industrialization had become one large gaseous, water-fouling, soul-stealing endeavor. All you had to do to realize that was to take a whiff of the air.

The area's first big coal-fired, cinder-belching power plant was built beside Cabin Creek and Chelyan. For decades it coated the surrounding communities with cinders and ash with seemingly little attempt to monitor the emissions.

"My mother was a large-eyed woman, you might say," said James Creasey, one of Jerry West's cousins who grew up just down the street from him. "She was always trying to get one of those cinders out of her eyes. She'd use a handkerchief rolled up on one corner and stick it in to try to get it out of her eye."

The only relief from the cinders would be the foul winds that blew up the Kanawha River from Charleston. "If the wind blew up the river, we got the smell from DuPont's chemical plant," Creasey recalled. "If it blew down the river, you got the ash from the power plant. You got it coming and going."

In one form or another, cinders dominated the landscape. They were also used to pack the dirt roads throughout Chelyan and Cabin Creek, and if that wasn't enough, the constant traffic of the coal-hauling trains brought more emissions to the air as they chugged seemingly nonstop on the five tracks that ran right through the heart of the small riverside villages. The residue collected on everything, the houses, the people, the stores, especially the porches. People in Cabin Creek and Chelyan were always sweeping the film of cinders and ashes from their porches.

Outsiders have often been confused by the very nature of Cabin Creek itself. First, there's Cabin Creek, the body of water, which stretches for miles down from the hills south and east of Charleston into the Kanawha River. The creek accompanies a vast, rich vein of coal, which means that Cabin Creek is also perceived as an area. Then there's the community of Cabin Creek, which sits at the mouth where the creek enters the Kanawha River. It's particularly defined as a community because a federal post office is located there.

Cabin Creek, the village, is also joined by its twin, the adjoining community of Chelyan. In their heyday, both communities offered an array of churches, a collection of stores, several auto dealerships, and, of course, a full menu of nearby coal and industrial operations.

Oil had been discovered near Cabin Creek just after World War I, thus adding to the mad rush for whatever. This great transformation was well under way by the time Howard West found his way to the area in 1922. Just exactly how he got down there is unclear, but he soon found work at the Pure Oil refinery nearby. The company had built a brand-new facility shortly after the discovery of oil in Cabin Creek. Supposedly one of the geologists who discovered the oil sent a telegram to Henry M. Dawes, who had financed the drilling. The telegram said that the "oil is as pure as gold."

"That's how they came up with the name Pure Oil company," Charles West said. Somebody had an angle on a job there for Howard West, family members say, and that was all he needed.

Soon Howard took up residence at a boarding house in the area. Fortunately, the proprietor was a great cook who turned out fruit pies to die for, the only problem being that she served them in very small slices. "She expected the boarders to quote scripture around the dinner table," Charles West said, repeating a tale his father told him. One night when it came Howard's turn to offer up some holy words, he bowed his head and said, "She who cutteth the pie in more than eight pieces shall not enter the kingdom of heaven."

It's also not clear how or where Howard West met Cecile Sue Creasey, but it's fairly certain that Howard's wit drove the process. The chemistry was relatively simple. He was twenty-two and an extrovert with a round face and an easy smile. And he was living in a strange place. She was seventeen, redheaded, and almost five foot ten, maybe taller.

"Mother's family was always big boned," recalled her eldest child, Patricia. "The boys were big. My mother was bigger than the other girls. My mother was like a horse."

And she was filled with contradiction. To begin with, her name was

Cecile, and her family pronounced it "Cecil," like she was somebody's uncle or brother.

"My mother lived at the Cabin Creek junction," said daughter Hannah Lou. "She worked at a little department store up there." Their father must have walked in that store and struck up a conversation, the children figure. From family accounts of his personality, it's fair to assume that Howard playfully teased her about her name. Whatever he said, it clicked. Cabin Creek was crawling with Creaseys. Cecile had lots of family living right there. Howard must have liked that, because he had none of his own.

She had to have been an awkward teen, large, painfully shy, and profoundly unhappy, just as she was most of her adult life. Supposedly, her eyes were the giveaway. Photographs taken of her often caught her unhappiness, no matter what the occasion. Patricia was struck by this while looking at an old family picture. "Mother had the most stern look on her face. I don't think she ever enjoyed much of anything," she said. "She never stopped to smell the roses. She just felt like she had to go at a terrible pace her whole life."

Perhaps such an assessment is unfair. Perhaps she was happy at seventeen, but her children don't know for sure, just as they don't know how Cecile Sue Creasey met Howard West. Unhappy people in an unhappy marriage aren't inclined to talk about their days of romance, if there ever were any.

What is known is that at the time they met, Howard was outwardly possessed of a gentle way. Most of all, he was aching to be loved, and therein lay the tragedy in everything, because she had been superbly conditioned not to give it.

That doesn't mean they didn't have reason to hit it off. Cecile's older sister Kate was attractive, self-assured, and among the first graduates of East Bank High School after it opened. But Cecile, like Howard, never finished high school. Her home was at least a mile walk from the school (sometimes, perhaps in moments of youthful daring, she would hitch a ride to school on the trains passing through the village, she later told her daughters), but that walk itself factored into her failure to finish, she would later explain. She and Howard came from the same West Virginia working and farming class—their ancestors had even traveled similar journeys to the frontier and likely walked some of the same hard roads. As with so many of those who migrated into West Virginia, the battle for life in the isolated region had managed to downgrade their financial condition and social status. Both their families had hit rock bottom, or near it, which meant that the primary bond between Howard and Cecile was their hope that they could climb back up together.

THE LONG WALK

Much like Howard West's forbearers, the Creaseys and other families that made up Cecile's line of ancestors had come from England. One family, the Huddlestons, entered at the port of Pennsylvania, probably as indentured servants, where they lived for a few generations until one of three brothers supposedly lost all of his possessions in a court case. The three then apparently retreated south down through the great valley of Virginia and across the Blue Ridge into Bedford County, a strikingly scenic area marked by the sloping hills of the Virginia Piedmont, so beautiful that Thomas Jefferson kept a second home there, his beloved Poplar Forest.

Meanwhile, the Creaseys had come into Virginia's port of Richmond in the late 1600s, also perhaps as indentured servants. A succession of generations of Creaseys lived and worked on farms around Richmond and later nearby Goochland County, Virginia, until the early nineteenth century when they too made their way west to Bedford County.

Apparently Bedford County, attractive as it was, offered little in the way of cheap, available land, because a steady stream of Bedford inhabitants migrated to the Kanawha Valley in the 1800s, the lure there supposedly being opportunity, land, and work in the salt industry. In 1834, young Henry Lewis Creasey left his family behind and walked over the difficult, rocky Allegheny range to Paddy Huddleston's inn in southern West Virginia, a place once frequented by the legendary Daniel Boone and other frontier figures of the day.

Young Creasey fell ill with the measles while at the inn and had to stay two weeks to recover. Once he was better, he walked down to the salt operations on the Kanawha River and found a job working on the flatboats hauling salt down the Kanawha to the Ohio River and on to the frontier river town of Cincinnati. He worked for a week, collected his wages, and walked back to Huddleston's inn to pay the bill he had run up during his illness. Creasey family members have long cited their ancestor's walk as a testament to the clan's forthright approach to living. His bill paid, Henry Lewis Creasey returned to the Kanawha River and pursued a rigorous career in the water freight business. In time, he came to be known as Captain Creasey and owned two boats, the *Modoc* and the *Winona,* that he ran up and down the Kanawha, hauling salt and freight to Ohio. His success attracted other members of the Creasey clan to the area, especially after the Civil War.

Henry Lewis, meanwhile, became a man of property. His forthright actions with Paddy Huddleston also paid off in that he married into the Huddleston clan and eventually moved to Cabin Creek, purchased a large piece of land, and split it among his children, including Joseph Creasey, Cecile's father. Unfortunately, Joe Creasey wasn't nearly as successful as Henry. He spent his life working for the Chesapeake and Ohio Railroad as a car knocker, keeping wheels greased, which, like just about everything else in West Virginia, seemed to involve backbreaking toil. During the Depression, the railroad required him to work for weeks at a time away from home, way up Cabin Creek, in Cane Fork, where he and another worker were forced to live in an old boxcar.

"He was a great big man and had a white handle brush mustache," Patricia West Noel recalled of her grandfather. "He was a handsome man, a good-looking man."

"PawPaw" Creasey, as he was known to his grandchildren, was years older than his wife, Cass. Afterward, the word passed down among the women in the family was that you should never marry an older man because if you do, you have to live an older life, without the pleasures of a younger woman. Cass had long, beautiful hair, but, typical of the time and her nature, she kept it wrapped in a tight bun.

According to family legend, Cass Creasey was prone to bitterness and thus quite hard on her daughters. Although she could be kind to her grandchildren, Hannah Lou West would sum her up as "kind of cold." Family members suspected that this coldness begat Cecile's many insecurities and thus her coldness to her own children.

"Her insecurities came from the way she was raised," explained daughter Barbara West. "I don't think the Creaseys were warm as a family."

"My mother was not a loving woman," sister Hannah agreed. "She never said I love you, she never put her arms around you. Dad rocked you and told you he loved you. But her mother was kind of cold like that."

Her children would struggle with the fact that she rarely, if ever, told them she loved them. Not any hugs or kisses, not a lot of coddling or cuddling from Cecile. And when they got kids of their own, she would warn her daughters sternly not to spoil them with kisses and sweetness. To modern sensitivities, this might seem grounds for psychiatric intervention, but there were mitigating factors. Cecile was a child of a harsh and unforgiving world. She was a machine of a female, a product of generations of conditioning, built and bred to withstand the brutality of the frontier. Her own mother and grandmother had lost three children each. Her mother would live into her eighties but would spend her later years lost in a world of dementia, where she often fretted and wanted to keep track of her babies.

So in a very real sense, Cecile learned her lessons well. She coddled no one. And for her children she required a standard every bit as rigid as her own mother's. That was the pioneer way: Protect your children; protect your heart.

"Hannah didn't think Mom paid much attention to the children," said Patricia. "Now, she took care of us. When we were growing up, we didn't have much. I tell you one thing. We always were clean. We had a clean bed to sleep in. But she never really went anywhere with us or never really did anything with us. She was set in her ways. She liked to cook and keep house."

"She and I we weren't as close," Hannah admitted. "She was a fault finder. And this is where I'm like my Dad: I need someone to approve of me, and he did, too. Mother was a perfectionist. You were never supposed to do anything out of line. You were supposed to be perfect."

"I wouldn't say that I was very close to my mother at all," said Barbara. "She worked very hard her whole life. I think she was crippled by her insecurities. While my mother and I had a cold relationship, I appreciated her for her accomplishments and abilities."

Those modest achievements would be reflected in the accomplishments of her children. And that would perhaps be a fair and final measure of Cecile Sue Creasey West. Through a haze of disappointment and profound heartache, she raised up a brood that would be known for intelligence and kindness—the fine fruit of a mysterious tree—a brood that also happened to include the one great player to become the symbol of a game that would find fans and devotees all around the globe.

THE PATH

The union that first seeded Jerry West's life, then shaped it so dramatically, has come to rest obscurely in family memory. It seems entirely likely that Howard and Cecile had to work and save to get married. There is some belief among the children that someone in her family helped him get the higher-paying job at the new Pure Oil refinery in Cabin Creek. It also stands to reason that she continued her job clerking in the small store until enough money was saved.

The place of the marriage or even details about their wedding day also remain obscured, for the most part. It is assumed that they got married at the Baptist church in Chelyan. As a railroad man, Joseph Creasey had no choice but to work Sundays while his family attended the local Baptist church. At some point in the Creaseys' lives, the church elders advised Cecile's father that he and his family were no longer welcome in the church because of that work schedule. Sunday was for the Sabbath, they said, and Joe Creasey wasn't keeping the Sabbath. In the Bible Belt of that era, such a move was a severe ostracizing. The hypocrisy of that unrealistic expectation so angered the Creaseys that they apparently rarely, if ever, attended any church again.

Hannah said that she and her siblings later attended the Methodist church in Chelyan with their cousins, the Trails, her grandmother's family. "If it hadn't been for them, I would have never gone," she said, adding that neither her mother nor her father made regular church attendance a part of their lives.

Hannah said her mother attended the Baptist church in Chelyan for at least part of her early life and probably was married there, but no one in the family seemed to know for certain.

What is known is that they married on August 27, 1923. Cecile's parents probably weren't able to offer much assistance. The Creaseys still owned the house on the land that Henry Lewis Creasey had given them, but they lived no life of comfort. "All of Momma Creasey's sons went to work in the coal mines when they were right young," explained Patricia West Noel. While the Creasey boys eventually found other lines of work, the message was clear: They had to make their own way in the world, and they had to do it quickly.

Their father, Joe Creasey, would have to work hard his entire life as a car knocker on the railroad right up until the day they found him standing in Cabin Creek, dazed and confused, an apparent stroke victim.

The Creaseys certainly had no means to help the young family get started, and Howard West had no family support of his own. But he did have the fine-paying job at the Pure Oil refinery, and that was enough to allow the couple to pay rent on their first home.

Some family members recall that the first house was the typical four-room coal company house, although Charles West says it was not actually owned by a coal company. Regardless, one thing is indisputable. The house had three bedrooms and "a path," Patricia said with a chuckle, *path* being a euphemism for an outhouse. The Wests were part of the great American transition from a rural to an urban culture. While the communities south of Charleston were quickly becoming industrialized, that didn't mean they all had plumbing, just as many of them had no electricity.

The house sat facing the Chelyan Methodist Church across a dusty side road. The Wests moved in, and Cecile quickly set about the business of scrubbing the place spotless. The first child, Patricia, was born two years later, on August 20, 1925. Charles came on October 20, 1927, then David on November 21, 1929. All three were born right there at home.

"David as a baby had a form of croup," recalled Patricia. "Mom said he was scrawny. She was crying about him. The doctor said he would be all right. He had to take shots."

Cecile West formed quite a bond with this scrawny second son. As the years unfolded, it became clear to everyone in the family that David was her favorite.

Eventually, Cecile would give birth to six children, but unlike Salena Kile West, having one after another, Cecile's children would be spread over parts of three decades. Which meant that the first segment of the family came of age in the 1940s; the second, Hannah Lou and Jerry, did so in the 1950s; while the last child, Barbara, graduated high school in the early 1960s.

It was the first segment of the family that spent their early years in that frame house in Chelyan. "I remember going barefoot a lot," recalled Patricia. "We played a lot. There were just three of us for a long time. Myself and Charles and David. There wasn't much for us to do; we'd go out and go all in the hills there."

In the early 1930s, Howard West moved his family from Chelyan into a frame house in the Kanawha River community of Coalburg, just a couple of miles down Highway 61 from Cabin Creek. The house sat beside the river, and it had a huge yard, which Howard West filled with a fine garden and a henhouse, two important elements in helping the family through the cash-strapped decade. And, of course, this second house also had a "path."

"When we lived in Coalburg, we walked a whole lot," Patricia said, adding that as a child when she walked to school, bus drivers rolling down Highway 61 would stop and pick her up and drop her off at Mission School, the elementary school she attended.

"I didn't have much of anything when I was growing up," Patricia said. "What I had was clean. We just didn't have a whole lot. We had a Christmas tree. Had lights on it. There weren't a whole lot of presents. One year I got a watch, and that was all I got."

If Cecile was ill or needed a break from the constant cycle of cooking, Howard would make a little sawmill gravy on Saturday mornings, a little grease and flour and a can of milk—normally the fine makings for sausage gravy, except that the Wests couldn't afford the sausage.

"Our lives weren't fancy," Charles West said. "My mom wore a cheap cotton dress. She didn't have much more."

The great wave of economic downturn following the bank failures of the early 1930s soon rolled across the country, sending millions into unemployment, then soup lines. The era might well have been called the Great Humiliation. Times grew tight in the West household, but they were far from destitute. "I remember the Depression," Charles West said. "One of the early things I can remember about my dad is he worked shift work at the refinery. It was about three miles away. He never owned a car and walked to work or hitched a ride with a coworker. He always had a big garden. He would take corn and pole beans to the store and exchange it for sugar and coffee. We lived approximately a mile from the railroad yard in Cabin Creek. When I was a little boy, these guys would come to the door, and they were hobos. And they smelled and they had cinders all over them, because they were riding the freight trains. My dad would make my mother fix them some leftovers or fry them an egg or make them some toast or something. He would question them. 'Where ya from?' 'Nebraska.' 'Where ya going?' 'Washington, DC.' 'What ya going to do when you get there?' Then if my dad was working, my mother wouldn't open the door if a hobo came to the door. I remember my dad was making one hundred twenty-five dollars a month, and he lost eighty-eight dollars in a bank failure. Around 1932 a small bank in Cabin Creek went under."

Despite the disappearance of his meager savings, his job at the Pure Oil refinery allowed Howard West to gain even a measure of prosperity. Cecile had long wanted a Chambers stove, and they were able to save a few dollars each week and eventually purchase it. There were flaws in the West marriage, but the couple always showed the willingness to huddle together to go over their finances each week to figure out a way to save a few dollars. "I remember my mother and dad talking on payday. 'Howard, we could save eight dollars this way,' she'd say." Cecile was vigilant with her money, a trait her youngest son would inherit.

"Mom got that Chambers stove; it was her pride and joy," recalled Patricia. "That's what she wanted, and she got it. At that time, it was really one of the better stoves. We had a kitchen cabinet that was white enamel. The furniture, the table and chairs, were white enamel. I hated it. That was my job. Every Saturday I had to clean that stuff and do the kitchen floor. I had to wash dishes all the time, and I can tell you I cried many a tear in that dishwater. And you had to iron everything. I can remember even having to press out diapers."

The Wests weren't alone in their limited prosperity. In fact, the entire Cabin Creek area fared well with its array of employment, as opposed to other regions where the work stopped altogether. "My father's brothers in Akron were standing in soup lines," Charles West said. "His brother Holly would be humiliated for years by the memory of standing in those soup lines. We always had a home. I can remember it wasn't too much of a home. It didn't have insulation or anything like that, but we always had food, a clean bed, and clothes."

Mindful of his brothers' plight and focused on his love of politics, Howard West hung on the many words of President Franklin Delano Roosevelt's fireside chats as he listened to the radio in the evenings. As the public works programs of the federal government kicked in to provide Americans relief, they brought upgrades in the West family condition. First, there was the Works Progress Administration, the good old WPA. "My dad had a certain amount of pride about him,"

Charles recalled. "From the WPA, the Works Progress Administration, you could get a concrete form for an outhouse. They made them, and you could get them free. My dad dug his own holes, and instead of a two holer, we had a three holer."

The federal relief money and Howard and Cecile's furtive efforts to save each week eventually made it possible for them to get a government-backed loan to buy a house, which they did in late 1937, early 1938. The family had continued to expand. Hannah Lou was born in November 1935, and again the birth had come in bed at home right there in Coalburg. The new house would take the family back up the river a little ways to Chelyan. It was a nice place, newer, roomier. Even better, it had indoor plumbing.

Cecile was pregnant yet again as they signed the papers and moved into the new home. Even though they now had indoor plumbing, the Wests decided they would be able to go to the clinic in Chelyan for the birth of this latest child.

Jerry Alan West arrived on May 28, 1938, at the clinic in Chelyan.

The doctor who delivered him noted that he had exceedingly long arms. He came home to a crib in his parents' bedroom and nursed with his mother, as was customary.

All in all, the Logo's arrival in this world rated hardly any notice. If anything stuck in the memory that year, it came at Halloween, when eleven-year-old Charles and the family listened in horror to the radio news updates that Martians had landed and had launched attacks in key places around the country. The radio show, based on H. G. Wells's *The War of the Worlds* and staged by dramatist Orson Welles, left young Charles trembling with fear as he went to bed that night fully believing that the end was near. His mother was never warm, always stern and standoffish, but that night she turned surprisingly tender, even going so far as to tuck him in bed and quietly assure him that there was no need for his fear; that somehow he and every member of the family would be all right.

If only that had been true; if only Howard and Cecile West had been able to keep the family safe, to keep it moving forward without interference from the large, dark forces of life. But ahead lay staggering heartbreak, losses for which there were no answers, and then an amazing turn of events that no matter how long or often they thought about it, still kept them blinking in wonder over the course of their entire lives.

We lived in Chelyan. It was a town of about five hundred people. We lived right in town. I was the next-to-youngest of six kids. My father worked for a coal mine. He didn't follow sports much. He enjoyed the political arena. He enjoyed that side of it. Politics is serious in the coal industry.

—Jerry West

HEARTBREAK

Chelyan, West Virginia, 1938 to 1951

OVER THE YEARS, MAXWELL WEST HAD FOUND OCCASION TO VISIT HIS son Howard, a development greeted with dread by Cecile West. One time, Maxwell showed up unannounced at her door, and Cecile was forced to spend a fearful afternoon alone with her father-in-law until the children got home from school and Howard arrived home from work. She was furious with the circumstances.

"He was a womanizer, and my mother had high moral standards," Charles West said. "She didn't want to be around him."

The West children saw quite a contrast in the families of their parents. The Creaseys lived nearby and were always around. The Wests never were. And if they did come around, Cecile wasn't quick to welcome them.

Every few years, the brothers and sisters of Howard West would try to get together. Sometimes Howard would board the bus and ride to Akron for these reunions. Other times the West siblings would gather at Howard and Cecile's house in Chelyan. Howard's children remembered their uncles Darcy and Holly teasing them.

"They would come here. We didn't have enough room to put 'em up," Patricia recalled. "We'd just pile them up all over the place. Mother would just cook like mad for them. Darcy would come in, and they'd start playing setback [a card game of the era] till two or three o'clock in the morning."

Sometimes Maxwell West would join the clan.

"They'd go over to Coal River and pick him up and bring him in," Patricia said of her grandfather.

"There was a lot of fun, a lot of love, shown when my father and his brothers and sisters would get together," Charles recalled. "Dad made fun of one of his sisters, who would feed her dog a pound of hamburger and a quart of milk every day."

Despite their occasional eccentricities, the surviving West children seemed remarkably well adjusted, considering what they had been through. And they remained relatively accepting of their father, despite his actions when their mother died. Later in life, Maxwell took a fourth wife and moved to Highcoal, West Virginia, way up Cabin Creek from Chelyan, high in the mountains. If the Wests hitched a ride with relatives all the way to Highcoal for a visit, it would take more than an hour to go by the roads. Instead they'd take a shortcut, riding into the hills and stopping at a railroad tunnel that cut through the mountain. It was a good hike through the tunnel, and probably dangerous, but they could save time and gas, Charles remembered.

In February 1941, Maxwell West died, and Howard, Cecile, and several of the children made the drive up to Highcoal for the funeral, walking through the dank tunnel to get there. "We didn't know much about him, except that we had heard about the things he did," Charles said of their grandfather. "My mother always had such a negative opinion of him, she didn't talk about him much to us." With his father's passing, Howard West laid a bitter family chapter to rest.

Jerry West was three when Maxwell died and never knew the man whose actions had shaped his father's life. Indeed, in a number of ways, Jerry's experiences growing up would be quite different from Howard's. Whereas his father's childhood milieu was the farm, Jerry West's life unfolded in a river town. As a boy, he would spend countless hours exploring the Kanawha River that ran near his house and its nearby woods and creeks. Family members say that on one of his many outings, he found a bloated, putrid body, one of the river's victims, in the water. While the mystery of that event resonates Huck Finn, Jerry West's early years came with an edge more suited to Dickens.

As he moved from diapers to short pants, the thoughts of his parents turned from the Depression to the growing dark cloud of World War II. By 1941, the conflict was upon them. Just as they had with previous wars, West Virginians responded in droves. Howard, in his early forties, went to the draft office in hopes of enlisting. He was itching to get out of town, but recruiters told him that his work at the refinery was considered essential to the wartime effort. He wasn't going anywhere. He had five children, three of them in high school, one in grade school, the last a mere toddler.

Oldest daughter Patricia turned seventeen that year, and like her father, she too wanted an escape from her mother's disapproving eye. Patricia fell in love with a local boy in uniform named Jack Noel, and they got married just a few weeks before he shipped off with the Marines to fight the war in the South Pacific. It happened quickly, then Patricia found herself back at home, working and paying rent to her parents while helping with the chores around the house and pensively watching the news from the war.

Her situation hadn't gotten better, just more expensive. She would harbor hard feelings the rest of her life over her situation as the eldest in a family where her mother was always raising children. "I kind of resent the fact that I didn't have much of a childhood, because my mother had a lot on her and I just had to help her out," she said. "I look back on it, I didn't get to go anyplace because we never had any money. I'd say that after I got big enough and figured out a lot of things, I just think there should have been some forethought."

If nothing else, the 1940s would confirm that for the Wests there was no such thing as family planning. Their frame house, which sat behind a doctor's office, looked like most of the others in the community. "A number of houses in town were all built with the same plan," cousin Jim Creasey said of Chelyan. "There were no sidewalks. All the streets were dirt. The main road was paved, but as soon as you got off the main road, everything was dirt."

As the war years moved by, Jerry made his way toward grade school. It soon became clear that he had inherited his mother's shyness and all the complexity that came with it. "I've always been kind of a solitary person," he once explained. "I don't need a lot of people around me to function." Cecile West kept order in her limited world by focusing on cooking and cleaning her house. She kept her most developed relationships with her sisters, her cousins, and her closest neighbors. Sometimes they all got along famously, sometimes they didn't.

"On my mother's side, the Creaseys all lived together in Cabin Creek," Charles West recalled. "Sometimes among one or another of the sisters, there'd be some animosity. It had to do with my grandmother, who in her late age was having some difficulty. Her youngest daughter and her oldest daughter were fighting over who was taking the best care of her. But for the most part, they all got along."

James Creasey recalled that his own mother would join the tight-knit group of Creasey girls and their sisters-in-law for regular gossip sessions on the Wests' back porch. "You'd have trouble getting a word in between the group of them," Creasey remembered with a laugh.

Sitting in the shadows on that porch, taking it all in, was little Jerry. He would come to harbor a lifelong love of gossip. When West first arrived in Los Angeles to play for the Lakers, teammate Elgin Baylor quickly picked up on that gossipy nature and nicknamed West "Miss Louella" in reference to the Hollywood gossip columnist Louella Parsons. Later, as a team executive, he would be known as a notorious gossiper in NBA circles, with reporters, fellow NBA team figures— anyone who knew the good inside stuff. Of course, no one in the NBA has the inside scoop like the general managers. By virtue of their jobs, the team executives spend their lives on the telephone, incessantly chatting about players and coaches, sifting through a zillion tidbits of information to decide which players to trade for, which ones to avoid, which coaches to hire, which ones to fire.

In many ways, Jerry West was born and raised to fill such a post. Actually, the Miss Louella tag doesn't quite explain his skill. Gossip is very different in a small town than in a city. As Jim Creasey said of the Wests, "We could look out our front window and see in their back window, so everybody was pretty close in town."

In a small town, all of your neighbors know your business as well as your name and your daddy's name. That knowledge becomes the grist of gossip, and talk in a small town can be prying. True, city newspapers have long featured gossip columnists to reveal details about celebrities. But the individual city dweller is protected by the anonymity that comes with population, while people living in small towns are at the mercy of their neighbors. Respectful and friendly neighbors such as James Creasey's family are often abundant. Small towns can be wonderfully relaxed. Yet they can also be invasive and cruel, because the gossip is based on the ups and downs of people's lives. Thus, everything is magnified in small communities. In fact, one could argue that only in a small town is shame truly shame.

Plus, gossip is often the premier entertainment in a place where life can unfold slowly and with more than a bit of boredom. That ennui can produce gossip plump with intriguing and often exaggerated details, the everyday comedy, heartbreak, drama, exposure—all of the elements necessary for a good mortification when serious things really do happen. Unfortunately for the family of Howard West, the 1940s would bring them far too many moments of deep humiliation. Cecile West may have been a shy mountain girl at heart, but like her son Jerry, she was possessed of tremendous personal pride. Humiliation was not something she did well.

Like her mother before her, she was "ramrod straight," an erect woman, with her red hair now graying with resplendent distinction as she entered her forties. Howard often teasingly called her "Red" when the mood between them was agreeable.

"She was kind of a tall woman," Jim Creasey said. "Her husband wasn't that tall. Jerry got his height and everything from her. Back then everybody had to walk to the store. The store was at the end of our street. That's where you'd see her. You'd see her walkin' to the store."

If it wasn't the store, it was a stroll to the post office in Cabin Creek, about a mile away. The family lived on the north side of Chelyan and might have used the post office there, except for the railroad tracks.

"We were in north Chelyan," Jim Creasey explained. "We were right on the river. The east side of town had their own post office, and another small store over there. We all actually got our mail at the Cabin Creek address. If you used the Cabin Creek address, you didn't have to walk across the railroad tracks. It was about five tracks wide. They did a lot of switching up trains there. People didn't like to walk across the railroad tracks."

Because Cecile rarely went to church, those walks to the store or the post office were her primary public appearances, which raises perhaps the only mystery in the scenario. How could shy, closeted Cecile West possibly know any details about her neighbors? The answer to that again goes back to the Creasey girls. Cecile's oldest sister, Kate, the sister she looked up to and remained close to, served as the local postmistress. It was no coincidence that the first successful newspaper in America in the early eighteenth century, the *Boston News-Letter,* was published by the Boston postmaster. Postmasters know everything about their communities. Sister Kate knew everything about the lives of the people of Chelyan and Cabin Creek, their comings and goings, their bills, and their troubles. The post office not only dispensed and delivered mail, it served as a primary social center in those small West Virginia communities, and the postmistress was a hard-working hostess of sorts. When Cecile wasn't pregnant, she would sometimes work part-time in the post office with her sister.

Kate also helped Cecile's oldest daughter, Patricia, get a job in the post office. Patricia would ultimately rise to the role of postmistress herself. In that role, she came to know much about Cabin Creek and Chelyan in the 1940s and 1950s.

"The community was friendly," Patricia observed. "People were close. Maybe one set of families would marry another set of families. There were a lot of just good, hard-working, poor people. We didn't have much crime. We had about three colored families. They were nice families. They worked on the railroad. And then we had about three gay men in the community. Nobody bothered them. They just went on their way."

Up in the many hollows around Cabin Creek were the coal-mining families, many of them of immigrants, Patricia recalled, which implies that long before it became a social norm of modern life, the talk in Chelyan was quite multicultural. For example, that was how Kate learned about the new family of Welsh miners in town, who had emigrated to Australia only to find the Depression once they got there, so they had soon moved again, to West Virginia, where work was available even in the hardest of times.

Aunt Kate knew about everyone, white, black, straight, gay, poor, rich—just one of several reasons that Cecile West idolized her oldest sister. It meant that the gossip that turned up on the West back porch was rich and meaty.

After all, like every community, the villages of Chelyan and Cabin Creek had their attractions, Jim Creasey recalled. "There was a beer joint where all the men went. Then there was Wade's, another joint down the road. And there was gambling around town, on Friday night, and Saturday night through Sunday morning—not in Chelyan proper, but in the area."

Wade's Pool Hall in Cabin Creek was a hot spot that Jerry learned about as soon as he was old enough to run to the post office for his mother. "Cabin Creek was about a mile away," he recalled, reflecting a good gossiper's eye for detail. "That's where we got our mail. I'd run there and back. Maybe that's why I was in such good shape to play basketball. I remember running past Wade's Pool Hall on a Saturday morning. You could tell how wild a time the coal miners had had the night before by how many of the windows were broken out."

So the Creasey girls likely had plenty to discuss on Cecile's porch. If Cecile truly enjoyed those moments on the porch with her sisters, they appeared to be the few in her life.

In addition to gossip sessions, the house's big back porch was where the West girls spent many hours ironing the constant flow of laundry that came through the household and made its way to and from the clothesline. One of the big chores was ironing their father's work clothes, which were steeped in the strong odors of the refinery. They had to be ironed just right to meet Cecile's standards. This may seem like a minor detail, but in an Appalachia cut from the frontier, clean households could be scarce.

"Mother was a workaholic," Patricia said. "Well, her whole family, they were Creaseys. And all those girls, I always told them they were nuts about dirt. They always had spic and span houses. Whatever they had was clean. You didn't tear anything up, and you didn't get things dirty. You might get dirty yourself, but you were always cleaned up. I always remember if you were lying on the floor and went to sleep, Mom always woke you up and made you go in the bedroom."

"Mother was a perfectionist," Hannah agreed. "You were never supposed to do anything out of line. You were supposed to be perfect."

Of all the family traits, this perfectionist strain would loom in Jerry's profile. As a woman who had grown up in the rural narrowness of early twentieth century West Virginia, Cecile West's idea of perfection was less grand in scope than that of her son's, yet it embodied perfection's every effort and element.

Her masterpieces were Sunday dinners. And the heyday of those dinners came in the thirties and forties before her family was crushed and broken by a series of events. Charles recalled attending Sunday services on his own as a boy, and as soon as he returned home, Cecile would order her eldest son into action. "She'd say, 'Get off those good clothes. We need three fryers.' I'd cut the heads off with a hatchet, and she'd do the rest," he remembered.

She would dress the birds immaculately, fry them to tenderest perfection, and plate them with an array of fresh vegetables—pole beans, carrots, peas, potatoes—all plucked from the massive garden that Howard West tended and the chicken house that kept her family supplied with fresh birds and eggs. The main courses of the meal were all scrumptious, her children would recall decades later, but her fresh rolls and desserts, all made from scratch, were what qualified Cecile West. "My mother was the van Gogh of rolls," said Barbara West. "She was an incredible cook, but more important than that, she was an incredible baker. She was a perfectionist. You've heard about her hot rolls. Her hot rolls were like a masterpiece—the structure, the uniformity. They were delicious."

On the spot, she could turn out from scratch a white cake with apricot filling, a three-layer cake with white meringue icing, Charles recalled longingly. "Her idea of recognition and praise was cooking a great Sunday dinner. That was an event at our place."

As much as her children appreciated her great skill in the kitchen, they couldn't help but be left with the feeling that something was missing.

"I don't want this to be a criticism, but she wasn't into parenting," Charles observed. "Years ago when I was young, we called it 'raising kids'; now the term is 'parenting.' She wanted to see that we were clean and presentable to go to school and things like that. Don't get me wrong, she was a good mother, but she didn't dote on us or anything like that. Hannah and Barbara were straight-A students. She was proud of them and Dad was proud of them. I want to be careful here and not say that she took us for granted, but on a scale of ten as a parent, mother might be a six and dad would be an eight or a nine."

Hannah West remembered that no matter what she did, it never seemed enough for her mother. Hannah might earn excellent grades, but when she made a B in typing, it seemed that was all her mother could focus on. "I always thought I was one of the ugliest girls in school," Hannah said. Then she met her boyfriend, who explained to her that she was one of the most attractive. "That was the hard part of her being a perfectionist," Hannah recalled. "There just wasn't that much that pleased her."

At night, at the end of her long days, Cecile West avoided the temptation to rest and turned instead to her needlework, sewing and stitching designs.

"If she had rested at night, I think she might have felt she was lazy," Hannah said. "I guess she just felt she had to be working all the time. She really had a hard time later when her health began to deteriorate, and she couldn't relax. All of us in the family have read a whole lot. She just never read anything. I think she thought anything like that was a waste of time. The nearest thing she had to recreation was doing that needlework. She didn't miss recreation very much. She didn't believe in it."

Nor did she believe in Howard. As the years had worn on, the marriage had suffered, first from their basic differences, then from much deeper divisions. "My mother and dad were very different personalities," Charles West observed. "My mother was a hard worker. I used to kid her that her idea of a good time was to clean her house up one day and go back and clean it up again the next."

Howard West, on the other hand, was born to occupy the center stage in a small town. He craved attention in the best and worst ways. At one time or another, he seemed to have served as president of everything, from the PTA, to the union local, to the American Legion post, to the local Democrats club. His round face broke easily into a smile, and he sought out the many haunts, wherever people were wasting a little time—playing poker at the American Legion hall or hanging out at the local gas station.

"He liked people, and people liked him," Charles recalled. "He had a winning way about him, a way of provoking people conveniently. He would see a guy he knew, and he would say something about the Republicans or Herbert Hoover or someone like that. And this would get the guy excited. One time he got into a political discussion with a guy who had false teeth, and the other guy said, 'Howard, how do your feel about that?' And my dad would say, 'No truer words were spoken through falser teeth.'"

The wit always seemed on display, especially whenever he talked politics. He loved the Democratic party, but he never seemed to lack a sense of humor about it. Over his long tenure in politics, Howard

West entertained the likes of West Virginia senator Harley Martin Kilgore and the infamous Wally Barron, a key figure of Democratic machine politics in West Virginia, who would later serve time in prison for corruption as governor. (He was one of three West Virginia governors to achieve that distinction.) Howard West himself served as a cog in that machine, and it seemed like every politician, local and state, felt the need to pay a visit to the West house.

"All of these people came to see my dad," Charles West recalled. "He was either president of the Cabin Creek Democratic Club, or if they couldn't get anyone to be president, he was acting president. They would look my dad up especially around election time. I came home one afternoon, and my dad said, 'I wish you'd been here. This guy running for office, Wally Barron, before he sat down, he'd told me three lies!' Here was the problem with my dad: It seemed like he always supported the wrong faction. But he always went to the Democratic meetings in Charleston. We didn't have a car, but we had fabulous bus service to Charleston. It was thirty-five cents both ways. It wasn't a real handicap, not having a car. Two things prevented it: We didn't have the money, and it wasn't necessary anyway, because the bus stop was about a block away from our house. We could hear the bus at the end of the line."

When it came to union work, Howard West didn't have to take the bus. That would involve longer trips on the train, all the way to the big city of Chicago, which must have thrilled him with the freedom and power it offered. The West Virginia mine wars earlier in the century had presaged the great labor struggles of the 1930s, headed by John L. Lewis. The Depression had impressed upon the Roosevelt administration the folly of not allowing the working class to prosper. Big labor suddenly came into vogue. The National Labor Relations Act, or Wagner Act, passed by Congress and signed by FDR in 1935, had opened the door for all sorts of unionization in West Virginia. Howard joined the Oil Workers International Union, a CIO affiliate, and soon found himself holding office in the local.

"He would go to Chicago to the group meeting, and they would plan their strategy on how they were going to try and improve working conditions and maybe more monetary benefits and that kind of thing," Charles West said.

Already brimming with the desire to read—he soaked up encyclopedias he bought from door-to-door salesmen, used copies of *Time* magazine, the local paper, anything available, really—Howard plunged into the literature of labor law. He subscribed to and pored through the mountains of labor literature, publications, and pamphlets—anything to prepare him for dealing with Pure Oil management.

"They would have negotiations," Charles recalled. "My dad would be the bait to argue these points, particularly about seniority. The company didn't want to recognize seniority, and that's one point the labor union wanted, was to recognize seniority."

In time, the union experience had an effect on his standing in town. Over time this extremely gregarious refinery worker came to be viewed as a quasi-lawyer figure in Chelyan and Cabin Creek. He became a notary public, began doing his neighbors' short form income taxes, and assumed an array of duties around the area.

"Jerry's father was kind of a man-about-town," Jim Creasey remembered. "He'd go around and help everybody fill out their income tax for a dollar or two. His dad was very intelligent. He knew a lot of law. He'd advise people on what they could do when it came to dealing with the state or county or things like that."

When Creasey's own father was killed in a railroad accident in the mid-1940s, it was Howard West who helped his mother cope with the ordeal. Creasey remembered that advice and help as crucial to the family finding its way in the aftermath.

For another woman in the community he became a "committee," an official overseer of her affairs. The woman, a domestic servant, fell into financial trouble and had to go on public assistance after her husband was sent to prison. Howard West managed her money and wrote her checks to pay her bills. He was advised that he could take 15 percent for managing her affairs. "When she died, he closed out her checkbook," Charles said. "He told me he never took a cent."

The largest of his community efforts came on behalf of the American Legion, where he served first as a service officer and recruiter, then as post commander. "Dad always had a soft place in his heart for veterans," Patricia recalled. "He always thought the World War I veterans got a raw deal."

Those feelings intensified dramatically after the U.S. Army attacked its own veterans on the Anacostia flats in Washington in 1932. Tagged the "Bonus Army," tens of thousands of World War I veterans and their families converged on Washington that year as the Depression wore on. They had been promised a bonus for their war service, payable at a later date, but with the hard times, the veterans had come to the nation's capital to ask Congress for payment right away. President Hoover grew weary of the act and ordered troops under General Douglas MacArthur to attack the Bonus Army with tear gas and fixed bayonets, which quickly came to be viewed by the public as one of the most shameful episodes in American history. Several Bonus Army protesters were killed and hundreds injured, an outcome that inflamed veterans like Howard West. It also perhaps explains his kindness toward the hobos who knocked on his door during the Depression; many of the nation's thousands of hobos were homeless veterans.

One way to counteract such treatment of vets was to build the Legion's membership. Howard West and the local post commander began working the area aggressively to find members.

"The commander had a car, and they would go up and down Cabin Creek getting people to join for three dollars a year," Charles West recalled. This work became more important as World War II dragged on, taking its grim toll as families lived in fear of bad news about their loved ones. Patricia's husband, Jack, was wounded on the Pacific Ocean island of Saipan, but he would return home to resume a full life and play a role in Jerry's upbringing. Cecile's nephew Glen, the son of her brother Fred, wasn't so fortunate. A tail gunner on a B-24, he was killed the day after D-day in 1944. He would be buried on a hillside in London Memorial Park, not far from Cabin Creek.

The event only spurred Howard's efforts for the Legion. He wanted the Legion to be more than a membership drive, so he also worked in other ways. "We had a sick neighbor, and he was a veteran," Patricia recalled. "So Dad wrote a letter to get the man admitted to the VA hospital in Beckley. His family was really grateful that my father did that."

"My dad was what they called a service officer," Charles said. "In those days, if a veteran had died, you could get a foot marker for their grave. My dad was a notary, so he would go around getting information about the deceased, about their service time, to prove that they deserved a marker."

Sometimes it involved quite a bit of detective work. When Cecile's uncle died, Howard set to work tracing his Civil War service record.

"Dad got Uncle Dave Creasey a Civil War marker for his grave,"

Patricia said. "He had died and was buried a little bit up Cabin Creek. Dad got him a marker. He got quite a few people a marker who had discharges."

Somewhere Howard had dug up his papers. One of the Creasey boys had gone off to war, then failed to come home at the appointed hour, which prompted Henry Lewis Creasey to go to Virginia to find him. "He didn't come home," Patricia said of her great-uncle. "His dad went over to Virginia and got him. I saw his discharge. It was on a lined sheet of paper. It was handwritten."

For other veterans, Howard used his power as notary to support evidence of their birth, which was important for those born on the farm, Charles explained. "This involved quite a bit of work. If you were born at home and the doctor failed to record your birth at the courthouse, there would be no record of your birth. The census taker would come around, and they would record people's birth. To get a birth certificate, you had to get a delayed birth certificate, and my dad would fill out these forms. A lot of the old-timers had a family Bible, and he would attest the birth record in the family Bible."

In his constant mulling about the community in pursuit of these unofficial duties, Howard often learned a lot about his neighbors, information that certainly also made grist for gossip back on the Wests' porch. Much to Cecile's mortification, time would show that Howard himself could also be the subject of such talk as well.

"My dad and mother had their differences," Charles said. "My mother resented my dad going to the American Legion. He didn't drink. But he loved to gamble. I don't know if he had gambling debt. He liked to go to the American Legion and play poker. If he won, he'd talk about it, but he never mentioned it if he lost."

From working at the refinery to pursuing his community work and card playing, Howard's dizzying array of activities often left him short of time for his family, an issue that factored into the fraying of his relationship with Cecile. Although his children have fond memories of him singing them to sleep at night, that didn't mean he was around much during the day.

"I remember him just kind of working," Patricia said. "He wasn't involved with us too much. He went to work in the morning and came home at night, and that was it."

If there was daytime interaction with the family, it came each Sunday at Cecile's glorious dinners. Then Howard would hold court with his children, asking them about school, joking and teasing with them. "He always had an odd little grin," Patricia said. "You could tell he was amused when we might be talking to him and everything. And we could sit there and talk quite a bit."

Yet, for the West family, the imprint of Chelyan in the 1940s was far more than Howard's conversations around the table during Sunday dinner or Cecile's gossip sessions on the back porch. The West siblings were soon caught up in the web of their parents' union and the lack of trust that came to define it. It was either that, or the absence of forgiveness that followed the disappearance of that trust. Either way, the relationship between Howard and Cecile West deeply affected their children, but none more so than their fifth child, Jerry. In some ways, he would spend the bulk of his young life a prisoner of their dysfunction. And yet that disconnect between his parents was also the thing that pushed him along so furiously on what he has described as an amazingly improbable course to basketball greatness.

DAVID

West has often maintained that his early life was dominated by an intense shyness. That shaped his earliest choices, as soon as he was old enough to venture out on his own. "I was very active," he said. "When I couldn't fish or go hunting, basketball was my other drug. My shyness was the reason. They were things you could do by yourself."

Over the full course of his life, fishing would remain one of his few escapes from the pressures he heaped on himself.

"He was usually on the river bank," said sister Hannah.

"I particularly liked to fish," West admitted, "and developed an appetite for doing that. It was a solitary thing I could do, or go in the woods all the time."

The outdoors wasn't a love that he shared with his father. "He didn't follow sports much. He enjoyed the political arena," West has often said, disdain obvious in his voice.

"My father was a bookish man," Hannah said. "That was why he and Jerry really didn't have anything in common. Jerry was a hunter and fisher from a very young age, and Dad liked books and history and he liked to talk to people. I always said he should have been a politician or he should have been a preacher, because he definitely had the gift of gab."

Nor was the outdoors something Jerry did with his oldest brother. Charles was an industrious sort who favored his father's side of the family and went to work at age nine in a local store resacking heavy one-hundred-pound bags of potatoes into smaller bags for the customers. Charles, eleven years older than Jerry, was driven to independence and work, consumed from earliest adolescence by a drive that allowed him to work a series of jobs while pushing his way to a college education.

Charles would admit many years later that he was so busy working all the time—thirteen hours a day in Charleston, including bus travel back and forth—that he hardly had the opportunity to notice much about young Jerry. Hannah, on the other hand, was not quite three years older than Jerry and tomboy enough to enjoy her little brother, as she recalled. "We used to be big playmates. There gets to be a time when a girl has different interests. But for a long time we really were big playmates, because I used to be pretty good at throwing and catching a ball."

There were more sociable options than fishing and basketball in sports-rich Chelyan. "Sports was mostly it," Jim Creasey said. "That was the only thing that was free. We had a ball field down in the lower end of Chelyan, and all the companies—coal companies and Appalachian Power and so forth—had teams. They'd come out and play on Sunday, and everybody would go down there and watch."

Although he was too small and scrawny and shy to play in those games, little Jerry West witnessed them hungrily. Overlooked in his vast portfolio is that West is among the greatest spectators in the history of sport. As a sports executive, he would spend vast amounts of his adult life studying keenly the movements of athletes on the field of play. Scouting was about what you could "see" of an athlete's abilities, and Jerry would become known for seeing just about everything.

He grew up loving baseball, especially Ted Williams and Stan Musial, and listening to games on the radio, or reading about them in one of the papers his father brought home. In Los Angeles, before he became too famous to attend games (autograph seekers would invade his peace), he liked to follow the Dodgers.

As a boy, like everyone else in the community, he'd watch the local games in Chelyan. A lot of times the competition, softball or baseball, pitted north Chelyan against south Chelyan. This was the premier entertainment on weekend afternoons in the summertime. In the fall, the kids got together and played pickup football, some tackle, mostly touch. There were no streetlights or traffic lights, so summer evenings made a perfect setting for games of tag.

In those early years, it was mostly the outdoors, the river, the woods, that offered West a pathway to himself.

When it did come time for Jerry to venture out, the "big brother" role would fall to David, nine years older than Jerry. David was possessed of a sweet nature, one that inclined him to enjoy time spent with the earnest little fellow.

Joe Chrest, one of Jerry's high school teammates, recalled that his own father worked long hours. Chrest also had a brother about ten years older who did everything with him. "My brother was my father figure, because my father worked all the time," Chrest explained, adding that many West Virginia families had the same dynamic, like Jerry and David West.

It was David who explored the river and woods with Jerry. It was David who shared his love of sports, who introduced him to basketball. Some have interpreted this to mean that David taught Jerry the game. Jerry has said many times that was not the case. David introduced him, but Jerry learned the game alone, beginning at age six. Longtime Boston Celtics coach Red Auerbach once described the allure of basketball in its simple geometry. "Smooth floor, round ball," Auerbach liked to say. In the rural world of Jerry West, that would be "Dirt floor, round ball," the simple beginnings of his lifelong infatuation with the game. It's a familiar story. The ball was big, the hoop was high, and Jerry was challenged.

"I started shooting the basketball earlier, when I was shooting from between my legs because I couldn't get it up to the basket," he recalled. "Then I remember I got to where I could shoot it two-handed. Those were the days when it was just something to do, something to pass the time. When I look back at it, everything you learned, you learned by yourself."

The same was true for fishing and exploring the mysteries of abandoned mines and other intriguing sites in and around Chelyan. Much he would do on his own. But when he was too young to go alone, it was David that Jerry pestered to take him fishing, family members said, adding that it was David's good nature that often left him inclined to agree.

"He was the older brother I tagged after a lot," West acknowledged.

When David couldn't go, there was sometimes an older, married neighbor, or Patricia's husband, Jack Noel, who took Jerry along to the riverbank. In time, Jerry became pretty good at angling, even though fishing on the Kanawha was quite an endeavor. The big prizes were the huge catfish lurking in the depths. Occasionally local fishermen would haul in a cat as big as a man, said cousin Jim Creasey. "I can remember one time seeing a big catfish hanging from the clothesline pole, and its tail was touching the ground. There's still some big old cats in the river. People just don't catch them very often."

In the 1940s, some people in the area still lived off the water. "There was a gentleman who lived out on the riverbank, and he had a lot of children; seventeen to eighteen kids," Creasey said. "He worked at the power plant, and he'd come in off the midnight shift sometimes, and he'd have to go out and catch breakfast for the family. If you were good at it, there was plenty of fish there."

Even though he couldn't swim, young Jerry would borrow an old boat from a neighbor and head out on the river looking for catfish, bass, and anything else he could hook. Catching them was relatively simple. He just had to dig a few worms from his father's garden, roll up some dough balls in his mother's kitchen, and make sure to clean up after himself. Then he'd head out on the bank, where he could get lost for hours.

"Mostly I recall he was a loner," Charles West said. "He would always be off fishing by himself."

Still, these early experiences fishing and playing basketball connected Jerry to his older brother, as much as he had any connection with his siblings. Over the years, he would speak often of that growing feeling for David. Jerry turned seven the spring that David was sixteen. Although he was slender, David played both football and basketball, which was part of the reason that Jerry revered him so.

"During the time he was going to school, obviously I was younger," West said. "I looked up to him a lot."

Cousin Jim Creasey recalled similar admiration. "David was several years older than us," he said. "When he played football, he wasn't big. I remember one time a big boy from another team, maybe it was

St. Albans, was running down the field, a big boy. And David got him down, but he had to work to get him down."

"He played football at one hundred thirty-five pounds," sister Hannah recalled. "You know, you could play at that size in those days. Among my friends who used to go to East Bank High are a couple of guys who used to play with him. He was a substitute center, and their first-string center got hurt; I think he broke a leg or something. And David had to play for him against Logan High School. The guy who was the center for Logan was a Golden Gloves champion in boxing. And that guy hit David every time coming through the line. David couldn't even eat afterward, his face was so swollen. Those guys still talk about his guts. David's high school coach was my geometry teacher when I was at East Bank. He told that story in class one time about the courage David had. A lot of people would have said, 'I'm not playing against that guy.' He was very brave."

Family members say that David possessed a variety of qualities that made him their mother's obvious favorite. First, the West daughters said, their mother clearly looked more favorably upon her male children. Of her boys, it was obvious that David and Jerry drew much of their likeness, their genetic identity, from their mother, while Charles acknowledged that he favored their father. This perhaps explains the sibling rivalry between the elder West boys, although those things are fairly typical, especially in a family where the mother is not generous with her affection.

"He was almost a perfect person. Everything he did, he did for a purpose," Jerry said of David. "Kind, gentle, thoughtful, he was the apple of my mother's eye."

"He was my mother's pride and joy," Charles agreed.

David was the perfect son for the perfectionist mother. He was neat and clean and quiet and mannerly. But her affection was not something that he particularly sought. He was just a loving, pleasant boy, with a sense of other people. Although the family was not religious, David was decidedly spiritual. In high school, he attended prayer meetings regularly. He thought deep thoughts and was considerate. He just had an accepting way about him, his siblings said. He wasn't much of a complainer, and he was the one in the family who seemed to love everyone else without condition.

"He always saw the best in people," Charles explained.

"I don't know what it was about David," Hannah said. "There was just something special about him. He was a very decent young man."

He had a way with people, although he was not overtly political like his father. He wasn't a backslapper or a hand shaker, just a nice guy who could put people at ease with his smile.

Especially Cecile. There seemed to be little question that she drew some strength from David, and took both comfort and pride in his presence and appearance. In a world where few things or people met her standards, David did. As he neared his final year of high school, it was a comfort she would need. In 1947, just shy of age forty-two, she learned she was pregnant again.

"I'm pretty sure my mother was humiliated at being pregnant at her age," Charles said.

Her sixth child, Barbara Ann West, was born on August 11, 1947. "Cookie, when she was born, she was so little," Patricia said. "Now mother nursed her, but her milk wasn't rich enough for her. She had to take her off of it. She kind of whined a little bit."

Cecile nicknamed her "Cookie," ostensibly because of the round face she inherited from Howard. Older brother Jerry had his own nickname for his new little sister. He called her "Donut."

"Cookie had a big round face and a sweetness about her," Charles West recalled. "My dad adored her. Cookie was spoiled rotten."

It could have been wonderful, if only a new baby had been the family's one big challenge. In a short time, there would be much more to endure.

MINERAL WELLS

Labor had always been a hard game in West Virginia. Howard West must have known that. Yet he had always been eager to assume the presidency of virtually every organization he had come in contact with. The union was no different than any of his other activities, except that his growing interest in labor law drew him into a nasty situation in 1947, and before he realized what was happening, his comfortable life in Chelyan had evaporated. In its place was a nightmare.

The first sense of trouble probably came in early 1948 when he traveled again to Chicago to attend the Oil Workers International Union meetings. Its leadership and members were steeling themselves for a major strike against the six refineries that the Pure Oil company operated in the eastern United States. "Dad recalled that at that meeting, people said, 'We're gonna bring the company to its knees,'" recalled Charles.

For the company at large, that may have worked, but for the refinery at Cabin Creek, the situation couldn't have come up at a worse time. The oil field there was showing signs of playing out, and when the union went on strike at the six plants that year, workers in Cabin Creek were at a substantial disadvantage.

As president of the local, Howard West was not allowed to vote for the strike, but the tally was unanimous. Yet instead of the quick settlement that workers expected, the strike dragged on at Cabin Creek. At other refineries in the Pure Oil system, the company made enough concessions to settle the work stoppages. In Cabin Creek, there were no concessions. So the strike ran on, first to thirty days, then to sixty, and the workers soon turned their anger on Howard West. By the third month of the strike, his evenings became a run of angry phone calls from furious wives struggling to feed their children with their husbands out of work. The tone of these calls was especially difficult for Howard, who had always sought the love and approval of his neighbors and community.

"Until the strike, he was held in high esteem in the community," Charles said. "Then when things went bad, these women would call up my dad and say, 'You SOB, you caused the strike!'"

His workers weren't totally without pay. If they walked picket lines at Pure Oil gas stations and other company locations, they were paid $10 a day. But as the company began settling with each of its other plants, the pressure increased on Howard and the workers at Cabin Creek. It became clear to some that Howard was too eager to please everyone.

"It came to a time they voted a strike, and Dad was right in on it," daughter Patricia recalled. "It was very hard for him. He made a lot of enemies among the employees because every time they were ready to negotiate, well, Dad wavered."

"At that time he had some age on him," Charles West observed. "He was about forty-eight. My dad wasn't a rebel rouser. He didn't have to cuss to express himself. He could speak judiciously." Yet his

eloquence somehow deserted him under the circumstances. It became clear that soon Pure Oil would shut its Cabin Creek plant. Its
younger workers there were offered jobs at its remaining five refineries, Charles recalled. "Older workers like my dad were left holding
the bag. He was humiliated. He really suffered from this, the humiliation."

"When the refinery shut down, they blackballed him," Hannah
said.

Stung by that humiliation and the pending loss of his job, Howard
perhaps panicked, began looking around, and decided to go into business for himself. He learned about a rural gas station for sale in Mineral Wells up near Parkersburg, more than an hour from Chelyan. He
had a sister living there, and after studying briefly the financial numbers for the station, he entered into an agreement to buy it. That, of
course, required selling the home in Chelyan and moving the family
to the country, near Parkersburg.

David had just finished high school, Hannah was nearing her thirteenth birthday, Jerry had just turned ten. And, of course, there was
the new addition, Barbara, in diapers. To Cecile's relatives, the move
seemed absolutely harebrained.

Added to the scenario was speculation that the move had little to
do with Howard's union troubles. Some family members would later
point to his gambling at the American Legion. Howard had gotten
into trouble there, they said. Some family members say that he violated the trust of his marriage just once and spent the rest of his life in
an unsuccessful attempt to gain Cecile's forgiveness. Other family
members say his transgressions were more extensive. Whether it was
gambling or marital issues or the nightmarish union affair, the situation still added up to a lot of anger, especially later, after the whole
thing had turned bad.

Selling the house and packing up meant that for the first time in
her life, Cecile would be away from her mother and sisters. She was
forty-two, with an infant. And Hannah and Jerry faced fears similar to
their mother's. They both inhabited a comfortable world of school
and play in Chelyan. They entertained no desire whatsoever to sever
ties with their friends and move to a strange place.

"My grandmother Creasey tried to get her to not sign that deed,"
Patricia said of the sale of the family home.

"They sold the house and moved away," Charles remembered. All of their hard-earned equity went into the gas station. There were many tears shed at their leaving that summer of 1948. And, as some in the family guessed, the situation was doomed to end badly.

"A man who had never owned an automobile decided to buy a service station?" Hannah wondered. "This was in Parkersburg and he moved us up there out in the country."

"My dad had no experience with cars," Barbara said. "My dad was a very outgoing man, was very encouraging with his children to try to get education. In fact, he said once he thought about going back and getting his GED."

Perhaps if he'd had more education, Howard might have seen another option, rather than taking this huge risk. "He wanted a second chance in life," Charles offered as an explanation. "He didn't see the emotional impact it would have on my younger sister Hannah Lou and Jerry. It was very hard on Jerry and Hannah because they had friends in school. Jerry was in grade school and Hannah was in junior high."

Howard West was uprooting Jerry at the same age he had been when he was uprooted by his mother's death. Because the Wests moved out in the country and had no car, nor could they drive, the children faced extremely long bus rides to school and back each day. "I had to get up at the crack of dawn and go to school in Parkersburg," Hannah recalled. "And I didn't get home until dark in the evening. I was gone from dawn to dark. We were miserable."

Just as bad was the isolation of being the strange new boy at school.

Rather than face these things, Jerry rebelled, Hannah said. "Jerry was hiding from the school bus so he wouldn't have to go to school."

It was a misery that planted the first seeds of what would grow into an intense dislike of his father.

"He was very unhappy," recalled Patricia, who remained behind in Cabin Creek with her own family. Sensing that things had gone terribly wrong, she and her husband, Jack, rode up to Mineral Wells to check on the family. Charles went along for the ride.

"We went up there," Patricia said. "I can remember Mother just crying and crying about it because they had nothing."

Howard and his family were isolated in an unfriendly place. Charles recalled his father telling him during that trip that not long after he took over the station, he encountered a strange situation with the local Masons. "He told me about people stopping there at the station, trying to give him a secret handshake," Charles said, adding that his father at first failed to recognize what was going on.

Considering Howard's personality, he might well have tried to join the Masons, but they were a secret organization not readily open to new membership.

"His sister lived in Parkersburg, and they would come out and take my mother to the store," Hannah said. "It was ridiculous."

The emotional toll was one thing, but the downward spiral gained quick momentum with no appreciable income to support the family. Perhaps there has never been a more ill-suited service station owner.

"He was not mechanically inclined," Patricia said. "He wasn't making much money selling gasoline. Dad sold tires to those people up there on credit. They never paid him a penny for all of that. They were farmers up in there."

"He bought this service station and was shown the volume of what he could expect it would do," Charles said in his father's defense. "The guy [previous owner] misrepresented what he was doing in business. Dad had looked at the sales records of the station and felt like he could make a go of it. It was just a bad decision."

Unable to make his loan payments on the business, Howard watched what little cash he had drain away, then apparently panicked again and simply packed up and walked away, taking his family back to Chelyan just months after having left.

"When Dad let it go, he was not making any money," Patricia said of the foreclosure.

"The bank took that back," Hannah said. "We didn't try to sell it or anything."

Howard, homeless as a boy, now found himself turned out once again, this time bankrupt with his family in tow. The Wests retreated to the house of Cecile's seventy-eight-year-old mother, who had begged her daughter not to agree to his plans in the first place. They would live with Mrs. Creasey until Howard could find a job and a rental house for his family.

"We came back to Chelyan. Penniless," Hannah remembered. "Moved in with my grandmother until we could find a house. It was awful."

"My dad was a proud man," Charles observed. "He tried to do the best he could for his family. I'm sure he suffered mentally from all of that."

Suffering, like anger, was not in short supply in the West household. The animosity that settled upon the relationship between Howard and Cecile was like a frost, family members said. A frost that stayed and stayed and stayed despite Howard's repeated efforts to thaw it, to find forgiveness. The ordeal and her humiliation, not just over the financial disaster but over Howard's violation of her trust, had hardened Cecile's heart. In another age, another culture, in other financial circumstances, divorce might have been possible. But Cecile had no such option in the late winter of 1949. For her, it seems, the only option lay in a seething tolerance. Their mother's anger, in fact, would settle in her youngest son Jerry, probably because he drew so much of his nature from his mother's side of the family. That anger would fester and grow as conditions worsened over the coming years. Before it was all said and done, Jerry's heart hardened too.

More than a decade later, the incident still weighed on Howard's mind. In a 1959 interview for a Charleston Sunday newspaper feature on Jerry, his father brought up the issue. "I didn't realize until then how much a boy could be hurt by taking him away from friends and familiar surroundings," Howard told writer Skip Johnson.

But even then, Howard couldn't address the full truth of the incident, his failure in business, telling Johnson instead, "I quit my job and moved back to Cabin Creek, and I intend to stay here."

He had not quit a job; he had lost all the equity he possessed. The Wests would live in a series of three rental houses, trying to recover, Hannah recalled. "The houses they moved into were substandard," Charles said.

Fortunately, Cecile's large family offered plenty of connections for recovery. That's how Howard found the job at the large mining concern, the Oglebay Norton Company, servicing mine equipment.

"Mom's second cousin was married to the sheriff of Kanawha County, and he got Dad this job," Patricia explained.

Howard worked in Kayford, some fifteen miles south of Cabin Creek, which left him hitching rides to work with neighbors. There were frequent work stoppages, which made it seem that he seldom worked a full week. As tenuous as this appeared, it was a job Howard would keep for the next fifteen years. The new job focused on repairing and servicing the wheels on the large machines that hauled the coal out of the mines, and it required that Howard join the

United Mine Workers of America. He did so, but he had learned his lesson.

"He didn't even attend meetings," Charles recalled.

Perhaps the biggest casualty of the family upheaval was David. Just seventeen and finishing high school when the turmoil began, he found his own life unsettled at a vulnerable age. Patricia recalled his difficulties at finding a job and the accompanying despair. "He would come up to the post office and come to the back door and want some money," she remembered.

She would give him what she could. She felt sorry for him and would help him buy clothes or things that he needed whenever she could.

For a time he found work at the new Kroger grocery store. The chain had opened in the region, and it needed baggers and grocery boys. But David didn't see much of a future there, so he joined the army and entered the service in January 1949.

"He couldn't find decent work or anything like that," Charles said. "He joined the service out of futility, I suppose."

Increasingly, the Cold War mentality had gripped global politics as the midcentury neared. There was much fear in the air. The United States rearmed, and as in previous times of conflict, thousands of young West Virginians saw the service as an opportunity.

"The young guys like David used the army as a haven because they couldn't find any work at home," Charles observed. "It's always been a poor man's world to me."

THE MUD WALLOW

Even though his family's circumstances were less than ideal, Jerry was ever so glad to be back in Chelyan. David was gone to the military, and Jerry missed his brother terribly. But as he turned eleven, he came to the age where he was getting out and playing with other children more. He weighed less than one hundred pounds, but he was coming into a sense of his own body and realized that although he wasn't big, he had amazing quickness. He could dart around and make it pretty difficult on anybody who wanted to catch him. He loved football, but when he tried to play on the junior high team in seventh grade, there wasn't a uniform small enough to fit him. So he became the team's manager. In retrospect, West came to view this rejection as a blessing in his life. He could have easily gotten caught up in football and maybe even ended up like David, playing as an undersized substitute. Instead he answered by returning to his backyard, to a goal he had put up all by himself.

"I did it. I put it up myself," he once remembered. "I was young. Back then, you learned how to do things for yourself. You could always find a hoop. You could find an old one that someone discarded and use that. I used to live near a bridge, and underneath the bridge was an old hoop that was torn down. No one used it, so I took the hoop. The backboard was plywood. It wasn't painted. Occasionally there'd be a net. They'd take one down over at the junior high school, and you'd have the chance to use it. Or somebody'd give you one. This was right before junior high. I was in the fifth, sixth grade.

"I was little and skinny," he explained another time. "The other guys wouldn't let me play pickup football so I was all alone. I found out you could play basketball by yourself, so that started it."

Having the goal had its advantages. He could shoot anytime he wanted, mostly after school till well after dark, and all day on Saturdays if he wanted. He would sometimes get whippings from his mother for getting dirty and playing right through dinner till past dark. But having the goal meant he would find some company, although that wasn't necessarily always his top priority.

"He got out in the backyard," Hannah remembered, "and he played with a kid named Petey Simms and another one named Kenny Kirk."

It was mostly H-O-R-S-E and other shooting games, and soon he was good enough to command a little respect from the older kids in the neighborhood.

"They put up a hoop in the backyard there at the house down in Chelyan," Patricia recalled. "It rained, and I called it a mud wallow. It didn't take too long before they wore grass down in the backyard. Mother got on him. So they planted grass and started playing on a hoop down the street that a neighbor set up. There was a road out there—it wasn't paved. A walkway into that house called the Wagon Road. This neighbor put up an old hoop for them to play on that street, and they just played and played and played."

Jim Creasey was about five or six years older than Jerry and had played on the team in junior high at that time when the balls still had laces. He remembered distinctly when Jerry began playing with the older kids.

"When Jerry first started playin' out in the neighborhood, we were several years older than him," Creasey recalled. "He was really big on H-O-R-S-E. He was really big on that. He would get out there for hours and just shoot one shot. Then he'd move to another spot and shoot another shot. He could wear all of us out on that, just standing in one spot. He did a lot of that on that dirt court. In H-O-R-S-E, if he was shooting in front of you, you were done."

When they played regular pickup games, the situation was a little different, Creasey said. "The older kids could shove him around a little bit. We were bigger. You could push him a little bit. We were all about six years older than him, but he could hold his own. He had that jumpin' ability way back then and those long arms. He was very quick. There was a place called Keffer's court. There was a girl there named Janice, Janice Keffer. Back then girls just didn't do anything like that, but Janice was a good athlete. She was our age. Her daddy put up this real nice backboard and everything for us. It was a rather large yard. That was where Jerry done a lot of his early playin'. The girl Janice was left-handed, and she could hold her own against a lot of the boys—softball, basketball, what have you. Really a good athlete. That was where we did most of our playin', in that yard. The court was just beat-down dirt. Half court. But it was nice and firm unless it rained or something. We played year-round. I can remember going out there when my hands were so cold I thought my fingers would fall off. But we always played."

When there was no one to play with, Jerry didn't mind all that much. He could play for hours by himself. Family members recall that in the wake of the family disaster, the atmosphere in the West household held that coldness, the unpleasant air of contempt. The hard feelings between Cecile and Howard were palpable. Basketball became Jerry's retreat from this unpleasantness.

"For some strange reason, it was something that I could find solace in," West recalled. "It was a peaceful place for me. I could be anything I wanted to be, in regards to what people would say about me being too small, being too little. It really didn't make any difference in my own mind. I could play all these mental games, these mental exercises. All kids do that. And for some strange reason, basketball became a love for me. But no one knew about it, because I wouldn't tell anyone."

KOREA

Patricia West Noel served as a postmaster for seventeen years. Before that, she was a mail clerk in the post office at Cabin Creek, where she worked long hours pushing the correspondence along during World War II, in the days when letters meant everything to people. Those who handled the mail were often mindful of that, as was Patricia as she carried out her duties during the Korean War. Hostilities had broken out in late June 1950 when North Korean troops launched a surprise invasion across the 38th parallel and into South Korea. Folks at home weren't sure just what the conflict was all about, but it didn't take long to get the message that things were going to get nasty in a hurry.

"A lot of the boys went overseas," Patricia recalled. Which meant that people were often in the post office early each day, waiting pensively for the mail to be put up, anxious about their loved ones, eager for news from overseas. Patricia knew exactly how they felt, knew all too well the peculiar sensations of dread and longing.

As the war stretched over three long years, the number of Americans killed in the conflict mounted to 33,741, including 801 West Virginians. Thousands more suffered serious injuries.

David had been stationed in Japan with the twenty-fifth infantry division, thirty-fifth infantry regiment, which put him in the funnel for immediate action. In Japan, David grew close to his unit's chaplain and sent back home photos of himself posing with the chaplain's family. His fellow soldiers took to calling David "Preacher." At the time hostilities broke out in Korea, the thirty-fifth was in south-central Honshu as an occupational force. It was deployed to South Korea in a matter of days and soon found itself in the thick of the action near Pusan, trying to stop the onslaught of advancing North Korean units. Inexperienced and ill equipped to match the battle-ready North Koreans, the thirty-fifth took heavy casualties. Later, critics would blame General Douglas MacArthur, in charge of troops in the Pacific theater, for failing to take the threat in Korea seriously.

"That fall and that winter, they were almost driven out of Korea,"

Charles West said of the American forces. "It took them time to rearm and reinforce, and David saw the most bitter part of the fighting. The troops were green. The Koreans, they would play havoc at night with our inexperienced troops. It was very difficult, but they began to get seasoned, and their battle tactics were better, and they began to get tanks and things like that. They drove the Korean army north, and George Marshall had the command in Washington."

Finally, Korea had gotten MacArthur's attention. "It was MacArthur that cut them off," Charles remembered. "And he retook Seoul, but he let the bulk of the Korean army escape back to the north."

On August 17, 1950, David's unit was fighting in a rice paddy when Corporal Don Woody, a comrade as well as a fellow West Virginian, was wounded. David went to his aid under fire and would later be cited for bravery and awarded the Bronze Star. That December, the story made its way to the Charleston paper, and Woody, from the community of Institute, not far from Cabin Creek, cited David's action in saving his life.

The fighting through the fall and winter had been harsh for soldiers on both sides to endure, in terrible conditions, and especially difficult for the poorly equipped Americans. David's two-year commitment came due in January 1951, but he was frozen in service because his country needed him right where he was. Not long after that, the Wests learned that David, a sergeant working the dangerous job of a forward observer for a heavy mortar company, had contracted hepatitis.

"They took him off the front," Patricia said. "They kept him in Japan for about sixty days. David wrote to everybody. He even wrote to my aunts."

"He was so interested in everybody else but himself," Hannah explained.

He seemed particularly interested in the poor people of Korea and the suffering he witnessed, Hannah recalled. "He would say he was going to be a missionary to those people because they have nothing. And now that I'm a little bit older, I think that that is ironic because we didn't have very much either. We had all the necessities. We never went hungry or anything like that. We never went on vacations. Those things were just not available. Yet his focus was on them, on their needs and suffering."

When Cecile first heard that he had hepatitis, she thought it might be good news. He was sick, he was past his commitment date, she figured. "When Momma and I found out that he had hepatitis, we thought he would come back home," Hannah said. "He went to the hospital in Japan. And we had read in the paper where this general's son had hepatitis and they sent him home. So we were thinking David was going to get to come home."

David, though, was no fortunate son, and while he was long past the time for his enlistment to end, he was needed. As soon as he was well, he was shipped back to the front.

"When they took him back to Korea, I thought, 'That's it. I don't think you're going to make it,'" Patricia recalled. "In fact, I had a terrible dream that he didn't make it. At that time, we had a railroad there. In the dream, I could see where they put him on the big platform where they unloaded the mail. I could see that just as plain. I can remember being very disturbed by that dream."

The family got terrible news late that April. Their first cousin, Cecile's nephew Jimmy Creasey (not the same James Creasey who was a distant cousin and neighbor), was killed when his National Guard plane crashed at the Charleston airport. "The plane was bringing soldiers from Fort Knox, making their approach to the airport," Hannah said. "They crash-landed. One guy lived two or three days; the rest died right away."

They brought Jimmy's body home and buried him near Glen Creasey, who had been killed after D-day. The entire family was shaken deeply by the accident. Someone noted that both Jimmy and Glen had been the third child in their families. That left the Wests with more dread. David was the third child in theirs.

As a postal worker, Patricia also knew she might be the first to get the news if something happened to David. But that wasn't exactly how it came down.

"When the telegram came about David's death, there was a man who worked for the railroad," Patricia recalled. "He knew me because of the post office. He knew it would upset Mother, so he got a neighbor from across the street to break the news. It was just terrible, and we went down the road as soon as we found out. Mom was at home. Dad wasn't. He'd go up there to the filling station to loaf and tell lies and all that stuff," she recalled with a laugh.

"David was twenty-one in the preceding November," Hannah said. "He was wounded on the sixth of June in 1951, and he died on the eighth."

Yet it would be six months, not until December, before his body arrived in Cabin Creek.

"Mom nearly died during that," Patricia said. "She fretted over how they prepared the body. She said, 'David was always so clean with hisself. He'd get a bathtub of water, wash himself, and let that out. Then he'd get a tub full of water and rinse himself.' That played on her mind."

War seems to be the world's way of dealing out her harshest blows. The perfectionist mother had lost her perfect son.

"Back then you had a little red and white flag with a number of stars on it for the number of people you had in your family in the service," Jimmy Creasey said. "I can remember that flag at the Wests' house. Mom went to their house several times. Mom and Mrs. West were pretty close. They done a lot of talking about it."

The months rolled by. Summer came and went. Then the fall. After an interminable wait, word came in December that David would soon be home.

"Dad and I went up to the station when they unloaded David's body," Patricia said. "It was December, and it was so cold. I think he was buried the sixteenth of December. He was on the train in car number three. They unloaded him at Cabin Creek there."

The ordeal, including the long wait, had traumatized the entire family. The army sent two soldiers to accompany the body, to stand guard at attention by the casket, taking turns in relief. Charles thought the months of waiting had inured him to the pain of David's death. He didn't understand—none of them did—just how staggering those moments at the funeral would be. "When I saw that casket, I nearly fainted," Charles said. "It was so traumatic."

They buried Sergeant David West near his cousins Glen and Jimmy Creasey on a hillside in the London Memorial Park. As a service officer for the American Legion, one of Howard's duties had involved working the funerals of servicemen. He had presented a folded flag to bereaved family members about a dozen times over the years. Now it was his turn to receive a folded flag. David's death was the first time Hannah had ever seen her father cry.

"I was already married when David died," Patricia said. "I can remember ironing—we did a lot of ironing back then—I can remember ironing and crying about him. I thought he got cheated out of life."

"They put him back over there, and he had that devastating wound," Hannah said. "We felt that he was not sufficiently recovered from hepatitis when they sent him back."

Their tears for David would never stop, really. They would cry during media interviews decades later in telling the family story, during a trip years later to the Korean War Veterans Memorial, in their private moments, and especially when the men who served with David contacted them to explain what had happened.

His fellow soldiers explained that they wanted to be near "the Preacher" in combat, that they were sure that if they stayed close enough, they would be protected by his goodness. "They said they thought God wouldn't allow something to happen to somebody as good, as devout, as David," Charles recalled.

War, of course, cares nothing at all about goodness. And David's goodness certainly didn't protect the men standing near him beside a stream in Korea that June day as David's unit engaged in action near Korea's "Iron Triangle." The mortar shell landed amid the group of them, killing a half dozen outright. David's leg was badly injured. Still, his fellow soldiers were surprised to learn two days later of his death. They had seen him leave the field. He was reading his Bible as he was being Medevaced to a MASH unit. The next day, doctors amputated his badly injured leg. One of his fellow soldiers visited David in the field hospital and came away thinking he was going to make it, but David died the next day in the MASH unit.

"There was a wasted life and a life that I know would have done a lot of good," Hannah said. "David and I were very close. We went to church together, and he was the ideal big brother. I hate war to this day."

REBELLION

For the loss of David, the federal government paid a $10,000 death benefit, which the Wests split. They took $5,000 and purchased a house with large, spacious rooms, to which they would add a big front porch. In his later years, Howard West loved sitting on that porch and waving to his neighbors as they walked past.

"When David died Mother could finally buy a house, because he left her money," Hannah said. "He's responsible for them having a house."

With the other $5,000, they purchased an annuity, which paid Cecile $75 a month beginning at age sixty-five.

But there was no joy to be found in any of it, not for a long time. The entire family suffered in the months and years afterward, especially Cecile and Jerry. Mother and son plunged into their own depressions in the wake of the event.

"We suspected afterward that my mother had had a nervous breakdown after David's death," Charles said. "The children, especially Jerry, were neglected."

The mental pain—first from her husband's betrayal and business failures, then the terrible blow of David's death—was soon followed by physical agony. Shortly after David was laid to rest, Cecile developed horrific kidney stones that required surgery. "She had stitches from her navel to her spine," Charles recalled. "It took her eight to ten days to recover."

Jerry was just thirteen, and his siblings said he showed all the classic signs of depression. He stopped eating, he became withdrawn, and he insisted on spending even more time alone. Seeing the entire family staggered by David's loss and his mother's breakdown had left him riddled with a mix of guilt, anger, confusion, and intense sadness.

"He was loved by everyone," West would recall years later. "You would say to yourself, 'My goodness, why didn't it happen to me?' Because this person was so good, and it was a devastating thing. It really changed me a lot."

His boyish aggressiveness turned to a strange passiveness. He did little of anything, but the worst part came with his stubbornness, Charles remembered. "After David's death, he wouldn't eat. He developed scurvy. His skin took on a leatherlike appearance. My mother grew very concerned and sent him to the doctor. The doctor said he's not eating and began giving him vitamin shots."

Years later, sportswriters would be told that the vitamin deficiency developed from his intense interest in basketball, that he was playing and shooting so much outdoors that he had failed to take time to eat. This interpretation became a comical element in the West stories written in newspapers. In reality, there wasn't much comical about it.

Certainly West was using his time shooting the ball to get away from difficult conditions inside his home, as sister Barbara explained. Basketball became a haven for his troubled mind. But the scurvy stemmed from his depression, not his love of hoops.

His refusal to eat triggered another major family issue: a series of "brutal" physical confrontations with his father, Hannah said. West himself would describe them as "physical abuse," though these incidents have been at issue for years in the family. The older siblings, Patricia and Charles, weren't living in the household at the time, didn't witness the incidents, and were reluctant to characterize them as abuse. The younger siblings tended to be more matter-of-fact about them. But both sides seem to agree that they first arose over Jerry's refusal to eat after David's death.

"Jerry was stubborn. Mom and Dad tried to force him to eat," Charles offered. "Jerry refused. That's when Dad gave him a whipping. Hannah witnessed it."

Yet it wasn't just the eating. Charles said it was fair to assume that Jerry's anger probably mirrored his mother's. The series of events, beginning with Howard's troubles in Cabin Creek and the family's move to Mineral Wells, all capped by the loss of David, had left Jerry quite resentful of his father. The level of anger in the household was high.

"Jerry was rebellious," Charles said. "Remember the dysfunction that's going on with the relationship between my mother and dad. I never experienced it, but Hannah Lou said it was caustic."

"During that time, things were really cold between my parents," Barbara West said. "Jerry and Hannah went through that, and it had a lasting effect on both of them. My mother was a very shy person. She didn't have a lot of confidence. I'm not sure Dad did a lot to build that confidence."

There were other pressures as well. In addition to the anguish and family conflict, the Wests continued to struggle financially, despite Howard's job with Oglebay Norton.

"When I graduated, my dad was only working two or three days a week," Hannah explained. "They had a lot of wildcat strikes, you know. He had always been a big union man. Toward the end of his working career, he said he thought the union was making a mistake and sheltering people who really didn't want to work. They'd make up an excuse to have a wildcat strike and walk out. He needed the money. He still had Jerry and Cookie at home, and I was still living at home. I guess I was reasonably self-sufficient. I was talking to Patricia one time about the miserable amount of money I was making at that time. And she said, 'I don't know what Mom and Dad would have done without that money because that's what they used to buy groceries.'"

The tight money could only have stoked the charged atmosphere in the household.

"I remember only three incursions," Hannah said. "I know Jerry has said he had an abusive father. Dad warned you when you were getting in trouble. He would say you've gone just about too far. And Jerry just plunged on in. I don't know what he was trying to prove. It cost him."

"My father had an extremely explosive temper, and when you would cross ways with him, his temper would come up," Barbara explained. "He would tell you to stop or else you could get a beating."

Charles and Patricia formed their opinions of the situation based on their experiences with their father's temper and from Jerry's and Hannah's accounts.

"He did have a temper," Patricia said of her father. "I think it would have took a lot to provoke him."

Howard's anger was not something she witnessed often in her years at home, she added. "He liked his family. Now, Cookie and Jerry had different personalities than the rest of us. Different. I said I didn't know which branch of the family tree they fell off of," she added with a laugh.

"I don't know about friction between Jerry and my father," Charles said. "All I know is he thought Jerry was rebellious. One time Jerry called my father a liar. I don't know what that was all about. It really upset my dad. I don't know if he whipped Jerry or not, but it was quite a confrontation. When we got into a discussion around the dinner table, he would kind of say, 'It's okay for you to disagree with me but don't insult me.'"

"Let me tell you this: Jerry didn't respect Dad, like the rest of us did," Patricia allowed. "We would never have said things to Dad like he did. So that's what it was, from what I can tell. I guess he was growing up and thought he could get away with it. But he did not."

Regardless of the family perspective on the confrontations, the incidents clearly registered in Jerry's mind as unwarranted and abusive. They would be the basis for a lifetime of resentment. At the time, such a physical response from a parent was fairly routine in Appalachian culture, where even teachers whipped and paddled wayward students. In more recent times, it would likely be the grounds for criminal charges against Howard West. In Jerry's mind, the incidents were a further violation of any trusting relationship he had with his father. There's little question these incidents played a major role in seeding and shaping his furiously determined approach to his life, especially to basketball.

"That was tragic in my life, in my family's life," West said of the loss of David. "That was the thing that formed the nontrusting, angry way that I played. That was very devastating for me and my family."

"My dad was a fair disciplinarian," Charles said. "He whipped me a couple of times, and both times I deserved it. Sometimes mother would make cookies, and sometimes I would get in and eat more than my share. And my mother would slap at me. My dad would whip me. He wouldn't make me pull down my pants. He would say, 'Now, Charles, you're going to get into trouble.' He would invite me to behave, then spank me if I didn't. Hannah indicated he had a temper. Remember, there's some dysfunction between him and my mother about that time. My mother was not an affectionate, lovey-dovey-type mother. My dad would brag on us. Every time the relatives would come to visit, they would say, 'Howard always brags on his children.' "

Indeed, over the next decade, as Jerry rose to the highest station of basketball, Howard West would puff up with pride over his son's accomplishments and quiet humility.

"When one assists in rearing a son whose humility and depth penetrates even the most generous public acclaim . . . that is a parent's richest reward," Howard would tell the Charleston newspaper years later.

"He was very proud of Jerry, he really was," Hannah said. "It gave him something to talk about. He read all the sports. My dad was on top of things. He was very proud of Jerry. I don't think he knew the malice Jerry bears him."

Charles West said he's pretty sure his father had no idea of the tremendous antipathy Jerry held for him. It was all part of West's quiet fury, a fury he shared with his mother, a fury from which the mere vapors would carry him far and wide in the greater world. Yet at the same time, it robbed him of any great joy in his accomplishments. In joy's place, Jerry West would settle for self-disapproval, for his own harsh criticism, or the perceived slights of others—anything, really, that would push his quiet fury and competitive indignation. If nothing else, he knew he had to keep that alive. To the people who grew to know and admire and even love Jerry West over his playing career, this was easily the most unsettling thing about his deep complexity: He never seemed to find any joy in it. They often suspected, but they never really knew, that all the fervor of his great heart he drew from some deep and hidden injury, something he held onto, something dark and mysterious, something from far away and long ago.

I was little and skinny. The other guys wouldn't let me play pickup football, so I was all alone. I found out you could play basketball by yourself, so that started it.

—Jerry West

THE LOCOMOTIVE

BY ANY STANDARD, THE SCOPE OF THE OBSESSION IS IMPRESSIVE.

"People would look at you and say that you border on being so obsessed that it's not healthy," West said while looking back on the seven decades of his relationship with basketball.

As the years rolled by and he added experience in the game—first as a college and pro player with an exceptional knowledge of his peers; then as a coach, and finally as an executive and scout—Jerry West came to possess a hyperencyclopedic knowledge of basketball. Over time he acquired a view of the entire fabric of the sport. In his quest to keep the Lakers stocked with the best talent, he came to know all of the players, the great, the good, and the mediocre in era after era. He studied their moves and their backgrounds, learned their tendencies and their skills, and evaluated everything that he could "see" about them.

Pretty much, Jerry West learned it all, perhaps more than any other human being. As he acquired this knowledge, he often thought back to his own experience playing the game. And he soon came to an inescapable conclusion: His rise to the top of the sport was absolutely and completely improbable.

Jerry West was entirely without pedigree when he began his basketball journey. He was not from a family that had any sort of substantial athletic experience, or from a family that even prized such experience in any way. "No one at home encouraged me," West remembered. "I was on my own." He did not receive top-notch, or even good, early instruction. In fact, he received hardly any instruction at all. "When I look back at it, I wish I had been in an area that was bigger, because I liked it," he said. "But everything you learned, you learned by yourself. And you don't learn things good that way."

Perhaps, but the world has long been fueled by the genius of the self-taught, from Ben Franklin to Abe Lincoln. What did they used to say of Anna Pavlova, the great Russian ballerina? "She learns only from God." The same could be said of West.

He made his way into the top levels of the game even though he was unable to handle the ball well and despite the fact that his shot was strangely flat, the product of shooting outdoors in the wind. He also lacked the ability to go to his left, but that didn't hold him back either. Perhaps the most puzzling item of all was that he rose through the ranks of the game despite a physique that appeared absurdly frail.

At the height of his high school experience, when he was getting attention from college coaches, Jerry West was six foot three and weighed little more than 150 pounds. Even when he was drafted into the NBA, he was no specimen.

"People forget that he weighed one hundred and seventy-two pounds when he came to this league," said Marty Blake, the longtime NBA talent scout. "One hundred and seventy-two pounds. He weighed nothing."

As a Lakers executive, West came to understand that there are certain players, the very elite among the elite, who, in his words, "have a little extra dust sprinkled on 'em at birth." West realized that he, too, had the "dust" and was simply born for the game. "If I wasn't raised the way I was raised, saw the hardships," he once explained, "I'm not sure I would have risen above being someone who ended up in the same situation, except for one thing: I had a round ball that somehow loved me, and I loved that."

THE BLADE

Andrew Clark Shaver, better known as "Duke" to the folks in town, coached West at Chelyan Junior High. Shaver, who drove an old Ford and smoked cheap cigars called "penny stinkers," knew as much basketball as most junior high coaches in those days. His main focus was conditioning, so basketball became a lung-burning experience for his players.

Seventh grade was the first time West actually got to play the game indoors, but he spent much of that time running wind sprints and doing duckwalks and other torturous exercises. Having discovered the delights of a gym and the magic of a ball bouncing on a wooden floor, West would make much use of the junior high facility over the years. "He'd go over there at night," recalled Joe Chrest, his East Bank teammate. "If he couldn't find anybody to go with him, he'd go over there and play by himself."

Because West was so slight, he didn't get to play in either of the two games for which he actually got to wear a uniform as a seventh grader. By the eighth grade in 1951–52, he dressed out for all the games but looked absolutely emaciated in his uniform and got to play only a little. For ninth grade, he had grown a bit, got to play a lot, and was team captain. Duke Shaver took a longer look at him in practice that year and decided he had "jelly legs," his way of saying they were lively.

"Jerry had nice legs," his brother Charles observed. "They weren't real muscular, but they were perfectly formed."

And amazingly strong. Willie Akers, Jerry's high school opponent and then his teammate at West Virginia University, said the first thing he noticed about West was how thin he was, but Akers quickly learned that the sinewy West possessed great strength in his legs, in his arms, even in his hands and fingers—all the appendages and limbs necessary for basketball. Later in pro basketball, defensive-minded guard K. C. Jones would quickly learn the same thing about the slender West: "He was very strong."

That strength superbly complemented his quickness and leaping ability. He didn't have to play long that ninth-grade season before word circulated among his schoolmates that Shaver thought Jerry was exceptionally good—good enough, in fact, that he might someday be a great player. West remembered being typically immature as a ninth grader, but the chance to play created hope that he might earn a spot on the East Bank High varsity someday.

Charles West recalled walking into the family home in 1953, Jerry's ninth-grade season, and seeing his younger brother in the family room lying on the floor with paper and pencil. "I asked him what he was doing," Charles said. "He said, 'I'm figuring my average.' I said, 'Figuring your average? How many points are you averaging?' I think he said thirteen or fourteen points. I knew that was pretty good for junior high school."

"The scoring made Jerry well known around the valley, even in ninth grade," recalled Joe Chrest, who played against West in junior high. "And he was fierce on rebounding even back then. He's always been that way."

That spring Jerry played on his junior high softball team, and it went all the way to the championship game in the school league. But that would be about the last of his days in other sports. That summer between the ninth and tenth grades, he grew six inches, transforming almost overnight into a rather freakish figure. His clothes didn't fit his strange new frame. He felt extremely self-conscious, at well over six feet and little more than 110 pounds, with his sticklike limbs and long arms.

"He reminded me of a jockey because of his build," Chrest remembered. "We called Jerry 'the Blade' because he was so thin."

At least part of his appearance could be attributed to his malnutrition after his brother's death. West remembers brutally painful clumsiness that year that left him falling down steps and tripping over air as he walked through the house.

"Every kid who goes through a growing spurt experiences something completely different in life," West later recalled. "And that was different. I could fall up steps, and I could fall down steps. It was awkward. Clothes—nothing would fit. My arms were so long that shirts would be up to here, and you would try in your own way to go to school and look presentable. But it was an awkward period for me. Very awkward."

The awkwardness alone sent him back to the usual retreats: the river and the lonely outdoor goal. "I would go fishing from morning till night," he said. "And I could play basketball from after school till way past dark." He constantly experimented with the one-handed shot, and that's where the perfectionism he shared with his mother really started to become a factor. It's what made him a good shooter. But these hours alone would bring much more than a shot. They would form the early basis of what would become his kinesthetic genius, the self-taught comprehensive understanding that he would gain of every single element of the game. In time, he would command the complete knowledge of even the most nuanced detail of every skill required to play. He would come to own all the fine points and little secrets to defending, passing, rebounding, shooting, stealing, moving without the ball—virtually anything that happened on a basketball court. This understanding was not mere basics but literally the physical language of every basketball movement, available only to the rarest talent. It wasn't just a function of obsession, either. It was the core of his gift, the ability to see in complete detail the minutiae of every fundamental. Most players spend years around the game and never acquire such knowledge. Over time West would see and hungrily absorb every little piece of it. And if no fundamental applied, he'd easily make up his own. That was the joy of teaching himself.

He went to East Bank High as a tenth grader and wanted to go out for football that fall. Chrest remembers Roy Williams, the head football coach who also coached basketball, taking a look at the sticklike West, laughing, and replying, "No, I'm saving you for basketball."

"Jerry could really punt the football, and he would have probably made a really good end," Chrest remembered. "But he was frail."

So frail that, despite his surprising skill level, West was initially placed on the junior varsity, or what was known as the B team, when basketball season began. "Jerry was really good as a sophomore," Chrest recalled. "But Coach Williams was the kind of guy who didn't play underclassmen. He stuck with the seniors even when the game was out of reach." Yet West played so well early that season that even Williams relented, Chrest said. "That was the first year he ever really started playing underclassmen."

Williams brought the skinny sophomore up to the varsity for a few games. Although records are nonexistent and memories conflicting, West apparently played his first varsity game on January 1, 1954, against Charleston High, and went scoreless. A few games later, he flashed a glimpse of the future by scoring a dozen points against rival DuPont High on a night when three East Bank starters were out with colds. At the end of January, the East Bank Pioneers played Beckley, coached by the legendary J. P. Van Meter, who guided his teams to great success. The power for East Bank was a six-foot-four post player named John Plybon, who scored 28 points that night and would go on to lead East Bank to two wins in the state play-offs that year. West scored 5 points. It seemed pretty clear that he could contribute on the varsity level. But trouble struck in a game not long after that.

"I had just got a chance to play for the varsity team in a game, and I had a big last quarter in the game," he recalled. "The coach maybe started looking at me a little different, but I wanted to play one more junior varsity game against our local rival."

On one play, he went up to block a shot and came down awkwardly. Coach Williams, figuring that West's foot was sprained, tried to play him later, but it hurt too much for West to go back in.

The next day he walked a mile on the aching foot to the doctor's office, where he learned it was broken. He was devastated. "I could only make the B team at first but finally made the varsity about midseason," he recalled. "Even though I broke a bone in my foot, I knew it was my sport."

He would miss the rest of the season while working his way through a series of casts. "I clowned around and kept breaking it," West explained.

"Back then with a break of that type, the doctors used a cast that ended up coming up to your crotch, basically," Barbara West remembered. "Mama helped Jerry put on his clothes every morning so he could go to school. And every evening he would go out in the backyard with this makeshift hoop, and he would shoot from the same position."

Stationary in his cast, West would spend what seemed an interminable amount of time in one spot, shooting the same shot over and over, for hours. He had always hoisted one-handed shots and worked to perfect them. Now he stepped up the pace and made the one-hander his primary shot from each spot that he worked.

"Then he would move to another position the next night," Barbara said. "And I'm just convinced that he became a master shooter because of that. Seeing him shoot, one would see the right arm out and the left with his hand under his elbow, lining up everything. He's so consistent in his shot."

West would retain that mode of focus throughout his career. Youths attending his summer basketball camps years later would remember the thrill of watching him drain dozens of jumpers in a row or shooting free throws blindfolded.

In 1992 a reporter walked into the Lakers' preseason training camp at Klum Gym at the University of Hawaii early in the morning, hours before the first session. There was West, well into his fifties, alone on the court shooting shot after shot, delivering one perfect sixteen-footer after another. The ball would settle through the net and hit the floor with just enough spin that it headed back to West. He hardly had to move to retrieve it. Then he began pausing and studying the goal for an unsettling amount of time between shots. Later the reporter asked him why he was studying the basket so intently, and West said, "Because each goal is different. You have to look at it and figure out what's different about it." The reporter later figured that West had sighted the goal probably no fewer than two million times since those grade school days, when he first began lofting a ball at a hoop suspended above the dirt outside his home. And here he was, five decades later, pausing and studying again, as if he were seeing something for the first time, discovering something that others simply couldn't see. Those moments with the goal were the process of West's lifetime, the essence of his study of every little detail of the game, his mother's perfectionism at work.

ELEVATION

It wasn't just the injury that sent Jerry West back out in the yard to practice as he sat out the rest of his sophomore year. The relationship between his parents continued to play a role as well, sister Barbara said. "Again, I think in the extremely frosty environment in which we lived, shooting was a great escape."

The beatings from his father brought him mental toughness at a young age, West said later. Some people in the community apparently saw Howard West as a gambler and a womanizer, though it's not clear if that was mere perception or reality. There was even talk that he drank excessively too. But Charles West insisted that his father rarely ever drank alcohol, not even a beer, and almost never at home.

With mixed feelings about his father, Jerry found a new role model and father figure of sorts in his coach, Roy Williams. It seemed that West very much wanted to earn his coach's approval. That spring of

1954, as the red bud bloomed in the Kanawha Valley, he finally shed his cast and turned the full force of his energy to the game. The little bit of playing time and success as a sophomore had opened the window of hope. All of the starters at East Bank had been seniors. West knew that if he improved, there would be a lot of opportunity to play. To do that, he had to please Roy Williams.

"He was an exceptional coach, in some ways the best I ever had," West has said many times.

Taken at face value, Williams might not have seemed ideal. A former football player at West Virginia University, his primary focus at East Bank was on the gridiron. There, on the field during practice, he'd often have a cigarette hanging from his lips. "He'd be smoking in the huddles in football," Chrest recalled with a chuckle. "He'd be blowing smoke in everybody's face. He'd say, 'I don't want you boys smoking like me. I smoke enough for all of us.'"

The smoking alone could easily have turned West against him. Years later Jerry would complain to family members that he intensely disliked his father's smoking. (This became another item for later family debate—Charles said his father smoked a pack a day, while Jerry believed it was more like three.) And years later West would tell family members that while he thought a lot of Lakers owner Jerry Buss, he found the "body odor" of Buss's tobacco use extremely distasteful. Despite a lifelong aversion to smokers, there were legitimate reasons that West could overlook the constant puffing of his high school coach. Most importantly, Williams was an extreme perfectionist, and in him West had found a kindred spirit.

Their shared perfectionism reached sort of an ideal state in practices. West Virginia was sports crazy in the 1950s. East Bank, like other public high schools, required its athletes to take the early bus to school each day to begin their classes early to make room for an accelerated sports practice schedule. Athletes took only four classes each day, Chrest recalled, and were turned loose from class shortly after noon each day to begin strikingly long hours in sports.

"With Coach Williams, we practiced four or five hours a day," Chrest said. "And he was typically old school. You weren't allowed to have any water in practice."

Chrest explained that there never seemed to be any school counselors in those days to make sure that athletes took a certain number of courses to fulfill degree requirements. "Back then, the sports were everything to those communities," Chrest recalled. "I only had four classes a day. It was mostly sports, not academics. All the players did well in school, for the most part. Coach always wanted to see our report cards, but there wasn't too much emphasis on academics. We got out of school at twelve-twenty each day. Practice started at one-thirty, and we wouldn't get finished till almost six."

Williams made the most of those four-hour marathon sessions each day, Chrest explained. "Everybody liked Coach Williams even though as a coach he was really hard nosed. He drove you to the limit all the time."

Williams's practices featured long periods of scrimmaging matched by interminable hours of drilling, topped off with one long wind sprint after another to end the day. Also typical of the era, Williams watched the proceedings with an eagle eye, ready to correct his players with salty language whenever they made mistakes. Even so, he had a way of fussing that seemed to leave no permanent scars, Chrest said. "He would chew you out and then just kind of laugh about it."

Williams seemed to respect his players, and he wasn't much for humiliating and belittling them. Because he had their respect, he had the ability to inspire them as well. Much would be made of West's ability to lead the team back with furious rallies, but those rallies usually followed a halftime talk in which Williams managed to inspire while upbraiding and correcting.

Williams was keenly aware of the talent in both football and basketball at all the junior high schools that fed East Bank, and it was obvious that he knew all about West's potential long before he got to the varsity—which only made sense, since Duke Shaver was his brother-in-law. "Coach Williams and Jerry got along real well," Chrest said, adding that their close relationship caused no problems with the other players. "I always thought it was because Jerry was a good player and Coach was just being a coach. I don't remember him getting on Jerry that much, because Jerry was such a good player. But he did call him down a few times, mostly if Jerry got out of position on the floor or something."

"He was a wonderful person and someone who I absolutely admired a lot," West recalled of Williams. "He was more than a coach. He was a kind of father figure to me. I think at that stage in anyone's career, you need someone who's supportive and encouraging. He watched me go from this ugly duckling to a prince as a basketball player almost over a three-year period. A lot of those things that happened to me in my life were because of him."

Williams drilled and drilled and then drilled some more to instill team play and fundamentals. "He was really strict in the repetition of plays in practice," Chrest said. "We'd run them over and over and over. That was the perfectionist in him. We did drills till they were just right."

The entire mind-set of the state in the 1950s focused on "West Virginia basketball," a running, up-tempo style that fans adored. In fact, Hall of Fame college coach Cam Henderson, at Davis & Elkins College, then at Marshall University, is credited with pioneering the concept of fast-breaking basketball. Henderson coached many men who went on to be head coaches at high schools and colleges around the state, including Red Brown at WVU, so that up-tempo style ran in the blood of West Virginians. Fans across the state had seen it and played it in their high schools for decades. In 1954–55, West Virginia Tech coach Neal Baisi perfected the style. His team averaged better than 100 points a game, unheard of in college basketball. That caught the attention of Fred Schaus, Brown's successor at West Virginia University, who employed Baisi's style. His teams, featuring star player Hot Rod Hundley, soon thrilled fans with the attacking and running game. Roy Williams flat-out loved it. All West Virginians did. He pushed his teams again and again through the running process until they knew just what to do.

Over time, the scarecrow called Jerry West would become the perfect fast-break weapon. He had those long arms "and could jump like somebody six-eight or six-nine," Chrest recalled. The East Bank running game relied on West to get the defensive rebound, fire the outlet pass to the guard in the middle of the floor, then beat it up the floor to finish the break at the other end.

And the football coach in Williams came with a high appreciation for contact. "He'd have a drill with everybody rebounding, going for the loose ball," Chrest recalled. "There were no fouls called. We went at it, and it was always rough. I got a tooth knocked out doing those drills."

While West had taught himself much of the game alone in the backyard, his time with Roy Williams burnished his competitive toughness. His fearlessness as a college rebounder had its roots in

Roy Williams's rebounding drills. "I was never afraid," West would allow.

It's striking that at a time when West was rebelling against authority at home, he would find comfort and guidance in an authority figure at school, especially one who pushed his players through an intense experience with the game. Most of all, Williams was deeply involved in West's life for hours each day. Jerry's bitter complaints to his siblings years later would focus on the fact that Howard West was so busy politicking and backslapping around the community that he had almost no time for his own family.

Williams surely had some sort of ego, but he managed to coach the basketball team without conveying much of it. He made the game pretty much about the team, not about the players so much and certainly not about the coach. West flourished in this setting. "Jerry was good, but he just got better and better," Chrest said. "We always ran the fast break. Jerry was always the guy who'd go get the rebound and pass it out to the guards in the middle. We'd practice that fast break for long hours each day. A lot of teams we played against didn't like that fast break. Jerry could always get that rebound, and we could always run."

As if this practice schedule wasn't enough, West continued to put in the time at the neighborhood goal. He had come to master the one-handed jump shot with his long hours of work. By the first games that junior season, it was obvious that West's confidence was swelling.

Richard Gregg, who played at nearby rival Dupont High, remembers an early game from December 1954, West's junior season. Dupont was already wary of that "skinny kid at East Bank who could shoot the ball," he said. West had scored 12 points against them in that early game the previous season.

"We came out in a 2-2-1 zone," Gregg recalled, "and I was the one out front on the zone. I was just inside the key when we set up. On the first possession, he came down and stopped about ten feet from where I was standing and canned a shot. He was at least five feet from the top of the key, and that's the way it was all night."

What stuck in Gregg's mind about West's shot was how much he elevated when he took it. "I can still see his knees in front of me when he went up for that shot," Gregg said. West revealed his trademark: banging one last hard dribble before rising up for the shot.

"They beat us that night something like 77–37, and he almost outscored us by himself," Gregg recalled.

What is remarkable, in retrospect, is that at such an early stage in his emergence West had the confidence of his coach and teammates to take such a shot. A player taking that same shot in the modern game could easily find himself sitting on the bench, whether he made it or not.

"He was good at the jumper, even then," Chrest recalled. "He was so good, he did a lot of our scoring from the outside. From way outside sometimes. Coach Williams liked us to get a good shot. About the only one he gave the green light to for the long shots was Jerry. He'd take 'em out there and hit 'em from out there. It's too bad there weren't three-pointers in the rules back then. Jerry probably could have scored thirty-five to forty points a game. He scored almost 25 a game that junior year as it was. But he wasn't selfish. If somebody was open, he'd pass off and get 'em the ball."

West had high games of 37 and 38 that season, and his average would have been even higher if he had shot free throws better and his instincts had been more developed.

"I was green, and I didn't know anything about getting loose for shots or getting around a defensive man on drives, but I was learning," he told sportswriter Bill Libby.

In retrospect, West said he was almost a better shooter in high school than he was later in his career. At that age, he didn't dwell on negative things as much as he eventually would.

In time every team in the conference, every basketball fan in central West Virginia, got the news about Jerry West. There were some newspaper reports that junior season, but mostly it was word of mouth. Dupont, in the nearby community of Belle, joined East Bank in the hugely competitive Kanawha Valley Conference that included the two Charleston high schools, Stonewall Jackson and Charleston High. "We were big rivals, and we were only five miles apart. The Chelyan Bridge separated East Bank from Dupont," Gregg explained. The teams played again that season and twice more the next, and West and his teammates usually had their way with Dupont. "They were a great high school team," Gregg said. "They worked well together. It wasn't just West."

Chrest, however, emphasized that West provided most of the real talent at East Bank, with guard Jack Landers adding some much-needed athleticism. "The rest of us on the team were just kind of average," Chrest recalled with a laugh. "If we hadn't had Jerry, we wouldn't have gone very far at all. We just happened to have the horse to ride in Jerry."

People remembered his shooting, but it was his defense that destroyed other teams, especially if they had the lead and West was determined to bring his team back. Gregg and his teammates came to know that helpless feeling of watching as West ate up their lead by stealing the ball and laying it in. That would become a common experience for opponents. "It was like we couldn't get a ball past him with the pass," Gregg recalled. "And if you put it on the floor, he could steal it from you right off the dribble. He was fast with his hands, and he had that wide wingspan. I'm still amazed at how well he played in high school. There was all of this pent-up energy in him. He was always in motion. You never saw Jerry West standing around."

That energy made him a great rebounder, despite his size, Gregg said. "He was about six-three and had to be less than a hundred fifty pounds back then. He was very slender—a stick, really—but he controlled the ball games with that energy. He was everywhere, in constant motion, always after the ball, wherever the ball was. If he missed a shot, you never saw Jerry turn and go back down the floor after he shot. He was always going after the ball."

East Bank finished the 1954–55 regular season, West's junior year, at 11–12. He would later point out that it was one of only three times in his career that his team posted a losing record. The team actually won two games in the sectional play-offs before losing to end the season at only 13–13. Perhaps that explains why he wasn't even mentioned when the all-state team was announced after the season, even though he had been a unanimous first-team selection in the powerful Kanawha Valley Conference.

"My junior year, I guess, was when people started to hear of me," West recalled. "My high school team was nondescript in the sense that we had a 13–13 record. That was the only thing people knew me by my junior year. It was very disappointing because I hadn't been considered for any postseason honors or anything. I couldn't understand it, because people I had played against had made the all-state team, and they couldn't even make the all-conference team, which I got every vote for. I couldn't figure out why."

The snub angered him. "There was no way that they were gonna be as good as I was," he later recalled.

The 1955 postseason ended in the gym at Morris Harvey College (later to become the University of Charleston) in a regional loss that left West humiliated. The Pioneers had won two games in the sectional play-offs, then met Nitro, a team they had beaten by 20 points earlier in the year. At halftime, West and his teammates were up by 15 and seemed headed for greater things. That's when Williams decided to go to the stall game. West and his teammates lost their mojo and couldn't regain it. They lost 50–47, a stinging and bitter result for Jerry West, although he would grudgingly admit later that he had learned an important lesson about disrupting a team's rhythm.

Mostly he was bitter. He hated losing. As West and his teammates found their way that junior year, they had suffered several blowout losses. He learned that some people didn't hate losing the way he did. It was a trait he came to despise in teammates, especially as he made his way through the ranks of the game and came to recognize the condition. Some people just don't care as much, or even care at all sometimes, he realized. He could not abide that.

West decided then that he absolutely hated people who didn't understand what it meant to compete, who didn't hate to lose, who put the focus on themselves and not on the team. Yet more than all of that, he felt a self-loathing because of his own performance in that 1955 tournament. At its deepest level, his humiliation was personal. He never wanted to be in that situation again. "I started practicing after the 1955 season ended," he recalled, "and I didn't stop."

THE GOOD GUY

If there was any salve for West's disappointment, it came with his first contact from college recruiters. Fred Schaus, West Virginia University's bright young coach, made a point of talking to West after that season. It was the first contact in a relationship that would shape the entirety of West's basketball life. And it thrilled him. West Virginia basketball loomed large across the state. The sport had captured the imagination of schoolboys in the coal camps and mining towns since the 1920s. In Bluefield and Beckley and Huntington and Charleston and Morgantown and Wheeling and all the hundreds of little communities in between, they took pride in hoisting those two-handed set shots. The fervor reached a pitch in 1942 when the state university won the National Invitational Tournament in New York. The NIT was far bigger than the NCAA tournament in those days, and suddenly every boy's dream ran to Broadway.

After playing in the navy in World War II, Schaus himself had starred for the Mountaineers in the late 1940s. He then went on to play five years of pro basketball—four with the old Fort Wayne Pistons, one with the New York Knicks—before becoming the WVU head coach at just twenty-nine years of age in 1954. The star on those early Schaus teams was the ball-spinning Hot Rod Hundley, a first-team all-American whose antics stoked dreams and goosed fans across the state, including Jerry West.

"I used to listen to West Virginia when I was a little boy," remembered West. "It was very interesting because listening to these games, they would fade in and fade out. I remember a lot of times listening on the radio not knowing the outcome of the game until the next day because you couldn't get it. They liked basketball in West Virginia at the university. There was a statewide enthusiasm for the university team, and Marshall had terrific teams then too. And Morris Harvey had George King. He led the nation in scoring. I read the sports pages every day."

His brother-in-law, Jack Noel, had gotten tickets to a game at the field house in Morgantown when West was an adolescent, and the long trip to the game registered as a big event in his young life. They sat high above the floor and watched the players running around below. That moment stirred his thoughts about one day playing for the Mountaineers, but of course it was only a dream.

In that age of limited media, there wasn't a bigger star than Fred Schaus. And now here he was, telling West that the university was interested in him. He had coached two years at WVU when the East Bank star first caught his eye.

"I saw him play a game in high school," Schaus recalled years later, "and he got twenty-eight rebounds. I don't know how many points he scored, but when I saw the timing and jumping ability of that skinny little kid, I knew I had seen something special."

Even though West was just a teen, he sensed from the very start that Schaus wasn't entirely sold on his abilities because of his size. Yet Jerry liked the coach. More important, Schaus had quickly snared Cecile West with his charm. She would remain all for him and all for West Virginia throughout Jerry's recruiting, as coaches tried to persuade him to consider other schools.

"It almost got to the point where I didn't want these other coaches to come around," he recalled, "because she was so vocal about where she wanted me to go to school."

The scope of that recruiting would grow over the 1955–56 season. First came a few letters. Then new faces started showing up at the West house and at East Bank games. West would soon snag the attention of a growing number of college coaches, first from the Southern, Atlantic Coast, Southeastern, and Missouri Valley conferences, and then from teams all across the country. With each letter, West's confidence grew. He realized he would be able to play in college.

"I became pretty confident at a young age," he said, "and I think my senior year reflected that."

Perhaps the hottest on his trail was Virginia Tech coach Chuck Noe. Peppy and full of life, with a gift for gab and salesmanship, Noe had begun to drive the mountain roads in nearby West Virginia looking for talent in and around the coalfields. In time, he would pluck a number of fine players from the hills of the Mountain State. And unlike Schaus, Noe entertained no early doubts about West. The Virginia Tech coach was one of the first to look past the frail physique and the skinny legs to see the real competitive force that was Jerry West. He saw what Richard Gregg had seen. Time after time, West took over games. Sometimes, against weaker teams, he did it in the beginning of a game. But in the highly competitive Kanawha Valley basketball of the day, West did it against better teams at the end, with the outcome on the line. And newspaper reporters began describing West as very good "in the clutch."

"When the game is close or when his team is behind, you know he is going to come roaring out of there like a freight train," Noe said after watching West play.

Indeed, in a matter of months, Jerry West had rolled onto the high school basketball scene in West Virginia just like a locomotive. At the time, he had no real idea why he played as hard as he did, except that he was very, very hungry. Looking back on his life much later, he would realize that he was desperate to please his mother, to brighten her life, to make up in some way for the great loss she had suffered.

"The pressure I felt," West confided, "was to compensate, to account for my brother David's death."

It's hard to overstate the impact of his brother's death on West, especially at the formative age of thirteen, observed former Lakers team psychologist George Mumford. Mumford explained that over-coming the fear of death is an extremely vital and motivating concept in the warrior mentality. It fosters and drives the pursuit of glory as a victory over death. Obviously, the adolescent West couldn't articulate or understand what he was feeling, but in obvious ways he responded as warriors in every culture respond, Mumford pointed out.

And West had other motivating factors in his young life. Years later he would recall overhearing his neighbors once remarking as he passed by, "There goes that West boy. He'll never amount to any-thing." The comment, real or imagined, made West furious, and he would hold to that memory as a driving force in his competitive fe-rocity.

Yet his talk of the "angry way I played the game" would easily mystify opponents. They saw nothing of that, except for his intensity. Any anger was hidden behind his mask of stoicism.

West Virginia high school basketball featured a number of fine players in that era, all of them competing for status and the attention of college recruiters. One of them was Howard Hurt of Beckley's Woodrow Wilson High, who had already led his team to a state cham-pionship and would enjoy an excellent career playing for Duke Uni-versity. Reporters asked Hurt his opinion on just who was the best player in the state. Hurt demurred, mentioning West and other candi-dates. However, when reporters next asked him who was the nicest guy among the top players, Hurt had an immediate answer: "Jerry West gets that title. He's a real swell boy. He never complained and was always a gentleman on and off the court."

Added to the mystery of his rise in the game was that of his mag-netism. He was shy and reserved. Yet people liked West, really liked him. They sensed his humility was genuine. That extended to the stu-dent body at East Bank, where he was elected class president heading into the 1955–56 school year. His understated demeanor had won over a broad range of followers, and of course some of that was re-lated to the excitement he had created in the East Bank gym and the other small high school venues across the area.

"Anywhere he played, there was a crowd," Richard Gregg re-membered. "Our gym at Dupont High School only seated about five hundred people. It was packed when he played there."

Jerry West, who had hardly traveled in his life, tolerated those trips to games—rolling along the twisting and snowy West Virginia roads—

mainly because he loved the competition and the atmosphere, all despite the fact that he was a nervous wreck on game days. He was brimming with toxic amounts of energy, so much energy that the opening tip-off always resulted in the kind of high-octane explosion that left Gregg and other opponents awestruck.

Hazel Dawson Hawkins would catch the same early bus to school as West. Often they would find themselves in the same seat. She was dating a boy from a rival Charleston high school, and she wore his ring on a necklace. West saw it and made a playful comment.

"He'd just kid about it," she recalled. "I always rode right behind the driver because I had some motion sickness. If that seat was still available, Jerry would sit down, and we would talk. He wasn't a real talkative person. He was such a gentleman. He was very lean, very clean-cut. He wore his hair short. Back then he was so small, almost frail looking. He was so slender and long."

It was obvious that a lot of the girls took notice of Jerry and even had an interest in him, recalled Aileen Holbrook Kelley, one of his classmates. But Jerry was shy, and the 1950s was a more innocent age. Yes, Elvis Presley had begun to teach the nation's youth all about the pelvis, but such antics inspired more blushes than anything else. "I remember all of that stuff with Elvis and the music," West recalled. "I was kind of a typical kid. We all were attracted by Elvis's popularity and all that. But we didn't have a car in my family. I had no real ability to go out with girls then, or even the money to buy records."

When the East Bank kids did go out, they'd go to a small burger joint across from the high school, Kelley remembered. The place would get busy after school in the afternoons, or at night after basketball games. It was typical of the age, a place filled with booths where you could order a milk shake or a Coke. There was a jukebox. Kids would play songs and get up and dance. She doesn't recall West ever doing any of that. He was always reserved and polite, hanging off to the side, watching others dance. But he was always on the radar of most of the girls in school, she recalled.

West felt limited by his family circumstances. Howard had his job at the Oglebay Norton mine, but there were frequent work stoppages. Money was extremely tight.

"Things were up and down with the coal mines," Jerry recalled. "Everyone went through tough times, and we did. We found a way to get through it. Everyone back there had those times. It wasn't easy.

That was what made us strong. Those coal companies were multinational corporations. They didn't give a damn about the state or the people. They were there to make money for their shareholders. People in that state suffered a lot."

West worked odd jobs to earn the money to buy clothes and things he wanted. Mostly he mowed lawns. "I worked and bought everything that I had," he said. "I remember I got my first soft shoes. I got white ones and got them dirty pretty quickly. I was taught to respect people, taught to be fair, taught that it's what's inside that matters."

If West did go out, it was with a buddy like Ken Gregory, who played football at East Bank. Gregory at least had access to a family car, a '52 Ford. Gregory remembers that he and West were both quiet guys. They'd ride over to South Charleston to hang out at the Big Boy and other burger joints. "We never got in any trouble," Gregory said. "We were just riding over there looking for something to do. There wasn't a whole lot to do back then. Jerry was just a real good guy, kind of shy. The gym would be packed, and everybody would get excited when he played. But he never acted like a big shot or anything. Everybody liked him."

This admiration of West extended to the faculty of East Bank as well. He was selected to the elite group of students to attend Boys State, a summer honors program for West Virginia's top male students. It was there that he would meet Willie Akers, who at the time was recognized as the top player in the state. Akers had just led Mullens High in Wyoming County to the state championship. He was almost six foot five and a first-team selection for all-state. Akers recalled that there were several basketball players honored as allstaters among those selected to attend Boys State that summer of 1955. It was the first time that West had ever been away from home for any length of time, and he was miserable with home sickness.

"I had a classmate from Mullens High School that was in his cabin," Akers recalled, "and he informed us that there was a good basketball player rooming with him over there. Of course, there wasn't a lot of media at that time. I had never heard of Jerry."

The good players at Boys State got together to play some hoops, Akers recalled. It was an all-star group of players, and West was clearly an unknown.

Of that day, Beckley star Howard Hurt recalled that he and Akers were in a gym shooting during some free time at Boys State. They were talking about their selection to the All-State team when they were approached by two guys who wanted to play. One of them was skinny with really long arms.

"They must not know who we are," Hurt told Akers.

Once they started playing, Hurt and Akers were amazed at the skinny guy's leaping ability. "He stuffed everything." Hurt said. "That's the day I met Jerry West."

"We found out right fast that Jerry was the best player there," Akers recalled with a chuckle. "We recognized right off the bat how good he was."

THE TENSION

Any coach or recruiter could understand that Fred Schaus would have reservations about West in high school. It's often the case that a player with an overpowering presence or defensive ability will look great against inferior competition only to appear quite ordinary when facing top-level talent. And West was so thin! How could he possibly survive against competition that was both big and fast?

Years later, when West himself was a scout at the top levels of the game, he often harbored similar doubts about players, and quite often such doubts proved correct. As West often said, you can see pretty easily what a player can do athletically; the really hard part of the business is that you can't read a player's heart. That only reveals itself over time.

As basketball people everywhere would learn, Jerry West's game was about many things, but it was also very much about heart. And the greatest expression of heart in basketball comes from that rare player who, when things look bleak for his team, can summon the unexplained power to accomplish the heroic, to reverse the tide, to change the course and the outcome of a game.

Time and again over his career, Jerry West would bring tremendous displays of such heart, so much so that sportswriters and people everywhere would talk again and again about his play in the clutch, his ability to turn lost causes into winners, with magically explosive play—what Chuck Noe described as West "roaring like a freight train." This power was a part of West's game from the very beginning, but it would become a marvel once he reached the Los Angeles Lakers and began playing before a national audience.

Chick Hearn, the legendary broadcaster of the Lakers, spent many nights describing it to his radio audiences and began calling West "Mr. Clutch." One of the biggest mysteries surrounding West in Los Angeles—and there were many—would arrive after he finished playing and became the Lakers' general manager. By and large, West got far more agony than satisfaction from his job as an executive. During games, he would become a bundle of nervous energy and sometimes wind up out in the Forum parking lot while the outcome was being settled. Or he could be seen standing near section 27, peeking past the ushers at the action, his body twisted with tension. He would retreat from there to his office, where he often watched the game on television. There he could express his disgust in solitude. Other times he would leave the building entirely and drive around listening to the game on his car radio.

Such behavior soon became the brunt of jokes among the Los Angeles media. Reporters couldn't understand it. They saw it as another sign of West's well-documented zaniness.

"The amazing thing is that he is so insecure and so uncertain of things," offered longtime Los Angeles sports commentator J. A. Adande. "Here was this great team that he had put together, and he could barely even watch it. He'd disappear down the tunnel during games and head out on the road. This team he put together, his lasting tribute to LA, his last couple of years he wasn't even watching it. He was driving up to Santa Barbara. That stuns me more than a bit. Obviously the guy was Mr. Clutch as a player. Here he was with the game on the line, and he was the calmest guy on the court, wanted the ball in his hands. He could control everything and always come through in the end and make the shot. Here was this guy who was so cool under pressure, and yet sitting in the stands he would crumble. He was a mess."

High school teammate Joe Chrest, who lived for a time in Los Angeles and had the opportunity to observe West at work as a general manager, said West's difficulty in watching the Lakers play stemmed from his perfectionism. "Jerry has always had a hard time watching people make mistakes," Chrest observed.

Yet the full answer to this mystery perhaps goes back to Chelyan.

Cecile West couldn't travel to many of her son's games. She listened to them on the radio when they were broadcast. Cecile would grow animated and frantic as she listened to Jerry's games on the radio or watched them in person.

"We would sit around the radio and listen to basketball," Barbara recalled, "and my mother would get so worked up. She was very proud of Jerry."

"It made her nervous to go to the games," Hannah said, and she explained that West didn't do her any favors with the style of game he played in high school and later in college. "One time I thought she was going to knock a hole in the wall—they had so many come-from-behind games. It was a nip-and-tuck game, and she hit that wall with her hand, and I thought she was going to knock a hole in it. But she did get very nervous, and she wanted him to do well. A lot of those games were just crazy, pretty exciting."

West was so close to his mother in demeanor. Mother and son felt a connection, which meant there was something of her there in each game, in the fury of the competition.

"His build, his drive, I think comes from the maternal side of the family, and his competitive side also," Barbara said.

"She was a determined woman, absolutely," Hannah agreed. "I think that's where Jerry got his will, from her."

Was it also, in some ways, a repudiation of his father and his father's interests? Perhaps. At the very least, it was an affirmation of the unspoken bonds, of all that Jerry shared with his mother.

"Jerry always said to me, about dad, 'I prefer mom to dad,'" Barbara recalled.

Whenever possible, Cecile West would load into a car and ride with her daughters to take in the sights and see the big games her youngest son played. Each time, she would try to stay calm. But it never worked. "Mom would get excited," Patricia recalled with a chuckle. "And we would too."

EAST BANK

Rock 'n' roll was just starting to peek its head over the covers in 1955. "Rock Around the Clock" by Bill Haley & His Comets topped the U.S. pop charts throughout the summer, for eight consecutive weeks. Elvis was twenty years old and just getting ready to sign his first recording contract with a big label. The cost of a first-class stamp ran 4 cents, and the average family of four needed about $60 a week to pay the bills. Zenith had introduced its first twenty-one-inch TV screen, and soon followed with a fantastic gadget—the remote control—but viewers still saw the world in black and white. The airwaves offered *The Ed Sullivan Show* and *I Love Lucy,* but you were just about always out of luck if you wanted to watch basketball or most other sports. TV executives just hadn't discovered them. In many places, you even had a hard time finding NBA stories in your local paper. Not in West Virginia, though. Never mind that there were no franchises around, newspapers in the basketball-crazy state ran pro hoops stories on the front of its sports pages, mainly because George King, the dribble wizard from Morris Harvey College, was playing for the NBA champion Syracuse Nationals. The league had just installed the twenty-four-second shot clock, and speed was the new name of the game.

Bob Cousy and the Boston Celtics had yet to win a championship, but he was all the rage, with his fancy-dan, behind-the-back, no-look passes. As the high school season neared, the East Bank Pioneers would shoot around before practice and fantasize that they were the Celtics. Joe Chrest played Cousy, and Jack Landers pretended he was guard Bill Sharman.

And Jerry West?

"We called him Easy Ed Macauley," Chrest remembered with a chuckle. "We always imitated the Celtics because they were so well known."

Macauley was Boston's fan favorite, a six-foot-eight beanpole center and forward with a deadeye shot. Celtics boss Red Auerbach would trade McCauley the next year as part of a package that brought the draft pick that would become Bill Russell, the hydra who would rule the NBA for the next thirteen seasons. He would become the man who singularly doomed Jerry West to a future of misery, all perpetrated by the Celtics. So there was more than a bit of irony in this fantasy. In 1955 Russell was still largely unknown to sports fans in the East, although he had just led the University of San Francisco Dons to the 1955 NCAA championship and was about to lead them to a repeat in '56.

At East Bank, Jerry West was determined to have a great senior season, but neither he nor his teammates even dreamed of winning a state championship. After all, there was a host of strongly favored teams around the state, beginning with the Mullens High team that was led by Willie Akers and coached by Lewis D'Antoni, the father of future NBA coach Mike D'Antoni.

"I don't think any of us had any idea that we could go far enough to win a championship," Chrest said. "There were a lot of teams that were pretty good around the state back then. We weren't one of them."

That didn't stop East Bank fans from getting rowdy on game nights. The school's gym was just like all the other sweatboxes that dotted the valleys and ridges of the plateau. "That's how people passed the time back then, going to high school games," Chrest recalled. "Sports meant everything to all those little communities around the state. We had a small gym at East Bank, and they always packed it. And it was always noisy. People would be stompin' on those old wooden bleachers to beat the band. And it would be real hot inside. Even in the winter."

As the season wore on, it became clear that West was going to give them something to stomp about. He scored 39 points on opening night, and things just rolled away from there.

Word obviously had spread among college coaches about Jerry West, as the cards and letters poured in, and coaches squeezed into the gym at East Bank to watch him play. But Virginia Tech's Chuck Noe remained determined to stay ahead of the pack, just as the staff at WVU was determined to block him out.

"We had somebody at every game Jerry played his senior year, and we made sure nobody else talked to him," recalled Rene Henry, who served as the university's sports information director at the time. "One night we had to be in Charleston, and East Bank was playing a game at home. So I get there late and immediately come in and check with a couple of his family members."

Henry recalled that he was introduced to one of West's relatives "that was a deputy sheriff or with the police chief with Cabin Creek, or whatever. All of a sudden it was halftime, and I look around and there's Chuck Noe, the coach at Virginia Tech. I said, 'What are you doing here, Chuck?' And he said, 'I want to talk to Jerry West.' I said, 'You're wasting your time. Go ahead if there's somewhere else you need to be and leave.' He got pissed and huffy. At that time, this deputy sheriff came over and said, 'Is this guy giving you a hard time,

Rene? What do we need to do to help?' Noe's mouth dropped wide open. I said, 'He's from Virginia Tech, and there's no way Jerry wants to talk to anyone except West Virginia. I suggest he should leave now.' And the deputy said, 'I'd be happy to escort him to the county line.' Noe looked at me and just stormed out. Where else can you get that kind of support?"

Henry recalled that he and Schaus burned up the winding two-lane blacktop in and out of Morgantown as they pursued Schaus's busy recruiting schedule. If the WVU coach didn't think all that much of West, you couldn't tell that from his effort.

"Big-footed Fred Schaus spent a lot of time in that gym at East Bank," West teammate Gifford Basham told a Charleston newspaper in 1986. "The thing I remember about him is that his shoes were always shined. That impressed me."

True to his intentions, West established his trademark for furious performances that season. He scored 45 points each against Charleston Catholic and Stonewall Jackson. He scored 40 in an overtime home loss to Beckley but fouled out three minutes before regulation ended. That game featured a fun battle with Beckley's Howard Hurt, who scored 8 in overtime to seal the outcome. He finished with 38, while West watched from the bench, steaming.

Such performances drew reporters as well as coaches. *Charleston Gazette* sportswriter Bob Baker made the trip to East Bank to interview West and came away struck by the shyness that made it difficult for the skinny young star to produce much more than awkward one-word answers. Baker had wanted to ask West about comparisons people were making between him and Hot Rod Hundley, the showboating WVU guard who was thrilling and entertaining crowds while making a name for himself.

Although he mostly lowered his head and shuffled around that day, West would later admit that he loved all the attention. He had first noticed it in his breakout junior season. No longer was he just the bony kid skulking in and out of the shadows around Chelyan. Now he was the big man around town. What seventeen-year-old wouldn't love that transformation? But as the senior season wore on, and the Pioneers climbed higher and higher, West first became aware of the invasive nature of star worship. People just came up and talked all the time, said what was on their minds, and didn't seem too aware of your own feelings. Perhaps worst was the fact that his friends and neighbors loved him when the team won, yet if it lost, he could immediately sense their resentment. "If your team wins a game, you're great," he said. "And if it doesn't, you're not a very good person."

That proved a jarring adjustment for a reserved guy who didn't know what to say a lot of the time. He didn't quite fathom it then, but the last few days of his public privacy were draining away. In a short time, West himself would become the subject of a generation of schoolboy fantasies, first in West Virginia, then nationwide.

As February 1956 rolled by, he was just the leader of a high school team that had gotten the local folks very excited. All West knew was that there were things he liked about that, and things he didn't. Mostly he just loved being on the court. That's where all his troubles drifted away and he could lose himself on the tide of each moment. It seemed like the play-offs were upon them in a blink, and like that, the tide became a flood.

In the running game, it's hard to tell if your team is an offensive machine or a defensive force. That's the way it was with East Bank in 1956. Nine times the team scored upward of 80. And like that, the sectionals were upon them. The Pioneers dispatched Seth High School in the opener, then came up against local rival Dupont in the sectional finals. For two seasons, East Bank had owned Dupont, but that changed in the play-offs. The Dupont club had gotten better, especially defensively, and forced the Pioneers into a bad night. Even so, Jerry found a way to get them through. "We were ahead of them by about eight points with four or five minutes to go," Dupont High's Richard Gregg recalled. "Jerry stole the ball and scored four or five times in the last few minutes. We couldn't get the ball past him to get into our offense. It seemed like he stole everything. He was unbelievable."

From there it was back to the regionals at the Morris Harvey College gym, where the Pioneers had met their demise the year before. "The thing I remember most is that nobody gave us a chance in the tournament," Chrest said.

Up first was St. Albans, a team that had tied them for the Kanawha Valley Conference regular-season title, although the two had not played. East Bank made it an early night and looked forward to meeting Charleston High, a team that had whipped them during the season. Instead Nitro upset Charleston, and suddenly West and his teammates were facing a team they had beaten by 20 earlier in the year. Nitro quickly reversed those numbers, scored 17 straight points early, and led East Bank by 17 at halftime.

Roy Williams watched his players stew in misery in the locker room and reminded them of how important their pride was in overcoming a deficit. West and his teammates rolled out to the third quarter with a burst of energy and shut down Nitro for the first five minutes. They made shots and moved their feet on defense, and any signs of overconfidence vanished. By the start of the fourth, they'd cut the lead to 9. That's when Nitro made an ill-advised decision to slow the game down and try to freeze the ball. The crowd of two thousand screamed and banged the bleachers as the Pioneers erased Nitro's edge, with injured Bob Buckley scoring a layup on a bum ankle and Gary Stover doing the same, to push East Bank into the lead and then up by 5. At the end, West was dribbling to run out the clock.

Then hundreds of his screaming and crying East Bank schoolmates and neighbors rushed onto the floor for a wild celebration— and this was in the days before wild celebrations were copycatted from television. The enthusiasm was overwhelming.

"I'll never forget it as long as I live," West told Bill Libby.

Next up came another of the state's true powerhouses, Huntington East, in a game that would decide a berth in the state championship final four. Huntington East overwhelmed East Bank in the first quarter, taking a 9-point lead. West and his teammates steadied themselves in the second period but still trailed by 10 at halftime. And this was no Cinderella like Nitro. It seemed its whole lineup was six foot three or taller. Yet West and his teammates had the memory of that comeback, and they had Roy Williams again telling them in the locker room that they could do it, they could pull this one out too. Huntington East expanded the lead to 11 by the start of the fourth quarter. West, though, sensed that the opponent was beginning to tire, and he wanted the ball. The lead slipped to 5 with minutes left, then he stole the ball and laid it in to make it 3. West got it right back, hit a jumper, then tied up his man. The ref whistled a jump ball. Huntington East was up, 63–62.

"Jerry called a quick timeout," Joe Chrest recalled. "There were just seconds left."

The fans were going berserk, and Williams had to yell over the noise. Jerry had to have the jump ball, and he had to smack it down the left side as far as he could as Jack Landers broke toward the basket, the coach said.

"I knew I could get the jump," West said. He told his coach he could tap it forward to Landers and surprise the other team, because no one believed he would be able to get it.

The two teams lined up, the official tossed it up, and West's skinny legs took him to the ball.

"I slapped it down court," West remembered.

With the crowd going delirious, Landers scooped it up on the left side and drove hard to the hoop. "The defender was all over him," Joe Chrest remembered. "He was much taller than Jack. He went up on the left side and kind of turned his back to the defender and put it up with his right hand. Jack told us, 'I didn't even think it went in until I heard everybody yelling.' It was a miracle that it went in."

Once again, the East Bank crowd exploded onto the floor in delight. Their boys were going to the state final four at Mountaineer Fieldhouse in Morgantown the next weekend.

"Madness," West called it.

But suddenly he was facing his new friend from Logan, Willie Akers, as well as Willie's Mullens High teammates in the state semifinals. They were the defending state champions, and they had the great Lewis D'Antoni coaching them.

"Everybody thought Mullens was going to win it again," Chrest recalled. "They were a great team, and Willie Akers was really good. He had the reputation and the championship from the year before."

But Chrest said that he and his teammates had come to believe that West was the best. "Of course, Jerry outplayed Willie that game, and the rest is history."

Regardless, it would be far from easy. For that middle weekend in March 1956, Morgantown was crawling with fans, many of them giddy high school students. After all, East Bank hadn't been to the state final four since 1939, and Morgantown, one of the two teams in the other bracket, had never been there. Lots of college coaches came to town too. West Virginia assigned Hot Rod Hundley to host West during the weekend.

"We had assigned players to be with Jerry and all the other players we were recruiting at the time, so they were never out of anybody's sight," WVU's Rene Henry remembered.

The only thing that hadn't been covered were the frat houses. Henry happened to be a Sigma Nu member from his college days, so he dropped by that house because he had heard West might visit there.

"I walk into the Sigma Nu house, and damn if Chuck Noe's not there," Henry recalled. "I said, 'Chuck, I didn't know you were a brother. If you're looking for Jerry, we already have someone looking after him and bringing him up here to the house and showing him around.' Noe was waiting for him. I told him, 'Do I need to call some friends to take care of you, or are you going to mind your business and stay out of trouble in Morgantown?' "

Keeping West away from other colleges involved a lot more than scaring away Chuck Noe, who hardly dropped his efforts in Morgantown. The University of Maryland and Texas A&M led the growing array of colleges after West's commitment. His mind, however, was almost wholly on Mullens. Akers entered the game averaging 28 points. Mullens also had six-foot-seven Wilbur Blankenship. West, averaging 33 points a game, would have to contend with both in the frontcourt.

Rod Thorn, a talented freshman from Princeton, had seen his season end in a loss to Akers and Mullens in the sectionals. He talked his father into taking him to Morgantown to watch the championships. "Most people called Mullens the best team in the state with Willie Akers," recalled Thorn, who would follow in West's footsteps to the NBA. "Jerry was unbelievable. His team was very small. He played all over the place. But he was more forward than guard. He just kept scoring. Mullens had a hell of a team, but Jerry scored anytime he got ready."

With West on his game, East Bank jumped out to a 20-point lead at the half. The contest turned increasingly physical as Mullens tried to control West with its larger, bulkier lineup. At the end, West and his teammates stood up to the physical challenge and survived, 77–73. Akers, who had been hampered by foul trouble, finished with 27 points. West scored 43, with a tournament record 23 rebounds. Mullens had found no answer for his quickness and leaping ability.

"I think that was the roughest game I've ever played in," West told a reporter after the game.

"That game just drained Jerry," teammate Gifford Basham told the *Charleston Gazette* in 1986. "After the game, he didn't even eat supper. He just walked around campus. The man had tons of heart. They beat him to death, and he kept coming back."

West fouled out of the championship game against Morgantown High the next day with 39 points and his team well in the lead. The crowd of 6,500 in the fieldhouse gave him a standing ovation.

"I remember when I walked off the court, I felt sort of bad about having fouled out, and I had my head down," West told Bill Libby. "But I heard noise from that crowd like I'd never heard before. I looked up and the fans were giving me a standing ovation. I couldn't believe it. I was just overwhelmed by it, and I cried."

He had finished the season with 926 points in twenty-seven games, for a 34.3 average—the single-season scoring record in state high school basketball.

"Just one word, terrific," Morgantown coach Jack Roberts said of West afterward. "He is, without a question, one of the best shots I've ever seen."

West had set a three-game tournament rebounding record, with 56. He also set the record for field goals, with 44. Jack Landers, who along with six-foot-two Bob Buckley had helped West with the scoring all season long, was also named to the all-tournament team. But West was the center of attention.

"He's the best I've seen in West Virginia high school circles this season," Schaus told reporters afterward. "We would like to have him here. He'll replace Rod Hundley if he comes."

WEST BANK

Duke Shaver and his buddy Ellis McDaniels got up early that Sunday morning in East Bank and reworded the sign at the town limits in anticipation of the coming celebration.

It now read, *West* Bank.

The team's championship was the first Class A state title by a Kanawha County school in thirty-two years. West had finished his career at East Bank with 1,501 points, then the state's all-time record.

"They had this big parade up at East Bank and renamed East Bank West Bank for a day," Patricia recalled. "It wasn't much of a parade. It was a gathering, really. But that was a day that the Kanawha County Board of Education found their way up to East Bank. We were always sort of the outcasts. We never got much funding from the Kanawha County Board of Education. But some of the board members were there and put their two cents' worth in. We had a band and different people spoke. Jerry was kind of bashful.

He was captain of the basketball team. He didn't say much. He just acknowledged people. He said he liked the guys that he played with."

"No, the 1,068 citizens of East Bank haven't officially changed the name of their town," wrote Bob Baker in the *Charleston Gazette*. "They were just showing their excitement about Jerry West leading East Bank High School to its first state Class A basketball championship at Morgantown Saturday."

The big reception for Roy Williams and his players had been set for three o'clock that breezy March afternoon, but it was almost four before the coach and players pulled up in East Bank to cheers from the crowd.

"The oil line in my car burst," explained Williams, still hoarse from the jubilation. "Had to stop and get it fixed."

Fans had initiated a fund drive earlier in the play-offs to replace the coach's clunker with a new station wagon.

As the players got out of the cars in the team caravan, West emerged hugging the shiny trophy. Dignitaries from the schools all spoke, then the crowd filled with students began yelling for West and his teammates to make statements. "I think our team deserved to win. We are glad to win this for you," West told them.

"It was cold in Morgantown, but this team was hot," Williams said when it was his turn. "This reception overwhelms me. The team and I surely do appreciate it. We are tickled to death. These boys are tops; there is no greater bunch of guys anywhere. They are always well behaved—except when they get on a basketball court."

Beaming in the audience were Howard and Cecile West. "To me he's still the same old Jerry," Cecile told Bob Baker. "Praise doesn't bother him at all. He's been playing basketball since he was six years old."

THE FRONT PORCH SWING

Howard West loved his front porch. Fred Schaus grew to like it too. As the weather warmed, he visited the Wests, and Cecile received him there. She made no bones that she loved his elegant manners and nice suits. Jerry himself was hesitant, however. He thought that the coach seemed to be fulfilling obligations by visiting him while having more interest in Willie Akers and other more orthodox recruits.

The mail and telegrams that had piled up over the course of the season now became Jerry's chore to deal with, but he wasn't sure exactly how to do that. He came home from school one day and found three coaches from three different schools waiting on the porch. He didn't know what to say to them. Eventually Cecile took to shooing such visitors away, especially poor Chuck Noe, who had come to the house three different times.

About sixty major schools, most of them in the South and the East, had made a push for West, and that didn't include junior colleges. He visited a variety of them, and the ones he didn't visit still came in hot pursuit as he played in a series of high school all-star games that spring of 1956. He was offered all sorts of inducements, cash stipends, jobs that paid him more than Howard made—all of which opened his eyes wide to the world. One desperate coach invited West up to his hotel room, then broke down crying and pleading.

He listened with interest when the University of Kansas coaches tried to talk him into coming to Lawrence to play alongside Wilt Chamberlain. He visited Texas A&M and Marshall and Maryland and several other schools. For some reason, Maryland was the one he liked. It didn't have much of a basketball tradition or program, but he liked the people, liked their honesty. Then there was the matter of his visit to the school.

"He went to Texas A&M for a visit and then we flew to Maryland," Willie Akers recalled. "It was the first time I had been on a plane. I went to Virginia Tech a couple or three times. But the one I remember most was Maryland. We flew to Maryland, and we stayed in the old fieldhouse. They had dorm rooms in there. At two o'clock in the morning they had some players there who wanted to play. We turned the lights on in the place, but we didn't have any tennis shoes. So we played barefooted. I'll never forget that. We had a good time there. They took us out to eat. At that time, that was a big deal. There were seven or eight of us in the room."

West remembered that the first day at Maryland, the school's coaches had focused on a number of bigger athletes in the group. But apparently the coaches had secretly watched the players in their late-night game in the coliseum, and the next day the coaches fawned over West, virtually ignoring the taller players.

The story of the West Virginians coming to play barefooted at Maryland would soon leak out and draw laughs about barefooted hillbillies coming down from the hills. The other recruits, however, didn't laugh about the outcome of that pickup game. West had schooled them and hadn't even needed shoes to do it.

"It doesn't embarrass me to be called a hillbilly," West said later. "I'm proud of where I came from. I'm sure they didn't think West Virginia would produce any basketball players of any quality. It was pretty eye opening."

But as much as he liked the Maryland coaching staff, Cecile West remained determined. "There was never a question of where he was going or me," Akers contends. "His mother was very active in his life too, and she kind of got rid of a bunch of the other coaches. There were three of them at the door at one time. Chuck Noe was one from Virginia Tech, and she ran all of them off. She wanted him to go to Morgantown."

"He really liked Maryland," sister Barbara recalled, "and it got down to the choice between Maryland and West Virginia. He asked Dad what to do, and I believe it was Dad that said to him, 'Jerry, you haven't been out of state and away from home, and you're shy. The place where you can make a name for yourself is the state of West Virginia.'"

Ever the politician, Howard had other motives, Patricia recalled with a laugh. "Dad always wanted Jerry to come back to Cabin Creek and run for sheriff of Kanawha County."

All along, the obvious answer was West Virginia, where Hot Rod Hundley reigned as the silver-tongued star. West had made a pact with Akers and Butch Goode of Pineville High School that they would all attend the same place and announce their intentions together. But Jerry grew weary of the pressure and annoyance and just announced one day in early June out of sheer frustration. He later phoned Akers to apologize for jumping the gun. Akers didn't mind. He was happy to get it settled too.

"We kind of made a pact that we would go to the same school, and he called me and said he was going to sign with West Virginia," Akers recalled. "That was no big deal for me because that's where I always wanted to go. Then there was another fellow with us, Butch Goode, and he said that's where he was going too. So that's how it ended up. Jerry was very heavily recruited, but he got to go where he wanted to go, and that was West Virginia."

The real truth was that Jerry West really didn't want to go any-where. "He had always been a homebody," recalled sister Hannah with a laugh.

In many ways, Jerry West would have been completely happy stay-ing right there in Chelyan, fishing on the river when he wanted and hanging out at the local Esso when he didn't. But he already knew that life didn't work that way, that you had to keep moving forward. And once he got going and discovered all that was out there for him, Jerry West never did a whole lot of looking back.

Play as a team and eliminate all thoughts of personal glory.

—Clair Bee, West Virginia native and one of basketball's winningest
coaches and great innovators

THE DISCOVERY

Morgantown, 1956 to 1958

OVER THE LATE SUMMER OF 1956, HOWARD WEST SAT DOWN AT HIS typewriter and tapped out a letter to the sports publicity department at West Virginia University. Many years later, former WVU sports information director Eddie Barrett would discover the letter among old effects. It politely asked that Barrett list Jerry's address in the Mountaineers game programs as Cabin Creek, even though the family hailed from the nearby community of Chelyan. The family got its mail at the post office in Cabin Creek, Howard West explained.

Thus was born the nickname that would irk West for his entire playing career, Zeke from Cabin Creek, which was just another fun way of saying West was a yokel. The nickname wouldn't become a factor until he went to Los Angeles to play for the Lakers. There were elements of truth in the name, even at West Virginia University. Having led a sheltered life in a small town, West was uninitiated when he arrived in Morgantown in 1956. As a freshman, he was six foot three and maybe weighed 165 pounds, with those freakishly long arms. While his teammates no longer called him "the Blade," his gaunt features and length made him look, to use the Appalachian vernacular, like a "picked chicken." What clothes he had were neat and clean, but his wardrobe hardly came close to matching those of the other students on the campus. His father had been right in advising him to go to school in his home state. His twang was particularly high pitched, almost comical to those who met him, yet it wouldn't stand out quite as prominently in Morgantown. Besides, he was the quiet type. To the people he met, he hardly said anything at all.

Certainly he wasn't the first college freshman to be overwhelmed by the transition to a bigger place, and he had gone to Morgantown during the late summer to begin his adjustment. But when the rest of the student body of six thousand moved in late that summer, West was met with a horrific sense of isolation. He was from a town of five hundred people, and he simply wasn't used to anything remotely like the busy world around him. "I was terribly disillusioned by being away from home," he recalled. "I was so quiet and shy that I couldn't assimilate in almost any social condition."

Dorm life presented all sorts of obstacles. West had no earthly idea what to say to all of these new faces he was meeting. Quickly his college experience became clogged with new details, all of them made difficult by his discomfort communicating. He began to wonder seriously if college was something he wanted to do. "Every day was a struggle to get through," he would admit later.

Willie Akers roomed with West in a dorm that freshman year. "He was very backward," Akers said frankly. "We were both from small communities, and we were backward when we went off to college."

Eddie Barrett recalled an early visit that Akers and West made to his office. As freshmen, they wanted a copy of the publicity photographs the athletic department had taken of them in their uniforms. Barrett noted that West never spoke during the entire visit.

Before long, his silence and isolation led West to take desperate measures. He reached the breaking point and maybe figured that if he hopped a southbound train in Morgantown, he could get back home. So he headed down to the railroad tracks that ran near campus.

"Jerry got really homesick, terribly homesick," recalled his sister Patricia. "He went out and started walking down the railroad tracks down there. I don't know whether he was crying, but he was really homesick."

Akers saw the departure of his friend and figured he'd better get some help. "I think Willie got ahold of Coach Schaus," Patricia recalled. "He went there and got him and told him to come back. Coach Schaus called Mother after that and told her what happened."

West reluctantly returned to campus. While the dramatic moment brought the issue to a head, it didn't immediately resolve West's difficulties. That would take some time. What comfort he did find was mostly on the basketball court. After all, travel was limited on those winding two-lane West Virginia roads in the days before interstate highways. It wasn't as if Howard and Cecile could jump in the family car and drive to Morgantown. They still lived without a car, hours away in Chelyan.

Morgantown sat on a sharp bend on the eastern bank of the Monongahela River as it wound its way out of Pennsylvania through the steep hills of northeastern West Virginia. The small college city anchored a corner where the state lines of West Virginia, Pennsylvania, and Maryland intersected, seventy-five miles south of Pittsburgh.

"We got there and you couldn't get home," Willie Akers said of Morgantown. "It was about eight to ten hours home, and basketball took up all your time. And that's all we did, was play."

Today, with interstate highways, the drive is maybe half that time. Akers's hometown of Logan is deep in the coalfields southwest of Charleston, a long pull in 1956. You had to take Route 19 out of Morgantown, down through Fairmont and Clarksburg and Weston. From there you had your pick of winding, miserable roads finding their way west to Charleston. Chelyan was an hour or so closer than Logan, but no less complicated to reach. It's no wonder that West's best thought was to hit the railroad tracks.

Such crises were relatively common among freshmen at any college, but West's siblings said his upbringing obviously made his homesickness worse. "You see, we never ever went anyplace out of town," Patricia pointed out. "We hardly went anyplace around Cabin Creek. We didn't have a car. We didn't have the money. So he got terribly homesick."

West's salvation that first year, besides basketball, was the fact that Willie Akers had come to school with a black Mercury sedan. His father was in management with the railroad, which meant that Akers had a railroad job and could afford an auto. Before long, Akers would trade the Mercury for a red and black 1956 Ford convertible. As

Akers said, he and West may have been backward, but things weren't all bad. Before long, they were rolling in style around the steep streets of Morgantown. And when the weather turned warm, they dropped the top. In time West was no longer dwelling on hanging his head and listening to the lonesome whistle of a passing train. He settled in a bit, found a little comfort, and turned up the radio in Akers's convertible. Before he graduated, West would eventually save enough to get his own vehicle, a used Pontiac. But for the longest time, his days passed with Akers as his chauffer.

"We liked the same things, movies and stuff," Akers remembered. "We didn't have a whole lot to do with the women. We were afraid of them. We were bashful and backward, so we kind of hit it off pretty good."

The second year, things were a bit better, but only a bit, as West moved off campus with Akers and teammate Joe Posch.

The summer after his freshman year, West moved in with two older spinster sisters, Ann and Erlinda DiNardi, who had opened their home to the university's basketball players. It was just a matter of blocks from the field house. Hot Rod Hundley had lived there his senior year and kept the sisters in stitches with his antics. For that sophomore season, West, Akers, and Posch joined the sisters. "We were mostly a lazy, sloppy bunch, and we needed them," West remembered. Ann DiNardi was especially good at rousting the young West from bed in the morning so that he would get to classes and appointments, Charles West recalled.

Eddie Barrett, West Virginia's sports publicity director during the West era, recalled that the university provided athletes a $15 monthly housing stipend, although Barrett was pretty sure that the Dinardi sisters never asked the boys for money. The extra money in West's pocket didn't matter nearly as much as the fact that he finally felt like he was being mothered again.

"Her greeting was, 'God bless ya, honey,' and she'd give you a great big juicy kiss on the face," recalled Patricia West Noel with a chuckle. "She liked Mom, and Mom liked her. And Jerry just really liked her. She was just such a nice person."

"They became my surrogate mothers, they really did," West said of the sisters. "They paid a lot of attention to me, and I was a pretty fragile guy at that time in my life . . . Just living there was something that was unbelievably important to me."

"Ann Dinardi was the pharmacist at a local drugstore," Barrett remembered. "She owned this house two doors down from the field house. All those guys stayed with her. You know, it's one of those unspoken things. She loved the players."

The Dinardi home was torn down many years later. Barrett called it "an institution" in WVU athletics. "I know that a great deal of what I feel about the university today could be attributed to Ann Dinardi," West said.

Even if they weren't living there, other players from the team stopped by just for a taste of mothering offered by the Dinardis. Best as Barrett could remember, the house had only a couple of bedrooms and a single bath. It's comical to think of the tight fit: three large basketball players in the tiny house with the sisters. But it certainly served its purpose. If only everything else in love and basketball had worked so well for Jerry West.

Dinardi died in 2003 at age ninety-seven. That same year, West donated $100,000 to the university in her memory. "Without her direction I am not sure where we would have ended up," West said. "She was a gracious and loving mother to many, most particularly to me. I will forever hold her dear to my heart."

SHOWTIME

Whoever said the 1950s were boring didn't know Hot Rod Hundley. When West came to Morgantown in 1956, he arrived knowing full well that the university was essentially Hot Rod U. Hundley, too, knew he ruled. You could tell from the way he strolled down Morgantown's bustling High Street in nothing but a Speedo. "That was pretty spectacular stuff for 1956," Barrett recalled with a laugh.

From the frat houses to the nightspots, he owned hearts and minds. To Hundley, basketball was an opportunity to put on a show, and that seemed to tickle fans across the state. If the circumstances weren't a hoot, it wasn't Hundley's fault. He was plenty busy trying to make them that way. His life was so big that he needed two autobiographies just to tell all the tales. The first, written in the seventies with Bill Libby, was appropriately titled *Clown.*

He was the Huck Finn of basketball, abandoned as a child by a father he hardly knew and a mother who struggled emotionally and financially. As the story goes, Hundley was raised in the pool halls of Charleston. He also spent considerable time on the city's streets and basketball courts. At an early age, he learned that his big personality and athletic gifts would draw the attention that his parents had been unable or unwilling to give him.

Hundley already had the eye of a lot of college coaches when he scored 45 points in a high school all-star game in 1953, and suddenly everybody wanted the guard with the Harlem Globetrotters moves. The great coach Everett Case at North Carolina State invited him down to Raleigh, and Hot Rod had his mind set on the Wolfpack until the National Collegiate Athletic Association declared him and other players ineligible to attend State because Case had been holding illegal tryouts for recruits.

Red Brown, the Mountaineers' coach and athletic director, had desperately wanted Hundley for West Virginia and thought he had lost out until the NCAA ruling changed everything. Once he was no longer eligible at North Carolina State, Hundley quickly contacted Brown and told him he was on his way to Morgantown. Like just about everyone who made the trip in those days, the winding roads left Hundley carsick. Once he got there, it was Red Brown who got the motion sickness.

Freshmen weren't eligible to play varsity athletics in 1953–54, but Hundley quickly got the university's attention by scoring 50 points in his first game for the freshman team. From then on, the field house was packed early each night for the preliminary game, the varsity be damned. Hot Rod was the top ticket and he never failed to thrill. In another freshman game he rolled up 63 points.

"He was a showman," Eddie Barrett remembered with a laugh.

Hundley recalled a gaggle of alums pushing $20 bills his way, sometimes hundreds of dollars a week. The campus girls also became quite friendly, and the big shots seemed ready to slap his back too, he recalled. A local auto dealership made sure his lifestyle included wheels. Once hungry for attention, Hundley was soon overwhelmed. One week he abandoned school to move to Ohio, where a girlfriend was in school; another week the destination was back home to Charleston to enroll at a small college there. Each time, he later phoned Red Brown, wanting to return, and the coach always readily agreed and made the drive to pick him up.

"Rod never had anybody to teach him right from wrong," Eddie Barrett said. "He is a self-made person. He has personality flaws, and nobody ever told him. Red Brown was probably as much of a father to him as anybody. Red took Rod into his own home."

Brown, though, dealt with the dizzying Hundley that freshman year and must have realized there was no way he could coach this wild man. When WVU athletic director Roy M. "Legs" Hawley died suddenly of a heart attack in March 1954, Brown decided it was time to take the AD's job and let someone else coach basketball.

His ideal candidate was former WVU star Fred Schaus, a big, strong, smart guy who was playing pro basketball. Schaus had never coached, but Brown saw that as a positive. "The fact that [Fred] was young and was a hero of Rod's was in his favor," Brown explained in Hundley's book. "I was impressed with Fred's manner—calm, confident, fatherly, despite his youth, and I figured he'd make a good mentor for Rod."

Schaus was all of twenty-nine years old, but he was no tenderfoot. He had played at Newark High School near Columbus, Ohio, where he led his team to the state championship and was an all-state center in 1943. But like so many young grads in that era, Schaus headed off to the service, not college. Just seventeen, he started for the powerful Great Lakes Naval Air Station team in Illinois.

"Fred was a pretty good leader," Eddie Barrett recalled. "He was captain of every team he ever played on, except for that navy team, and that was only because he was seventeen at the time."

After the service, he chose West Virginia over Ohio State and went on to score 1,009 points in sixty-one career games for an average of 16.5 points per game. He was named a third-team All-American by the Helms Athletic Foundation and was elected class president in 1949. From there it was on to play for the Fort Wayne Pistons, where he would become a teammate of the disgraced Jack Molinas, who played a major role in gambling scandals in both pro and college basketball. Schaus's biggest pro season came in 1951, when he averaged 15.1 points and played for the West in the first NBA All-Star Game, held in Boston Garden on March 2, 1951.

Pro basketball wasn't much of a life in those days. Schaus had been embittered by his trade from Fort Wayne to New York in 1953, so he was very willing to listen when Brown talked about his coaching West

Virginia. They agreed on terms, and Schaus soon arrived in Morgantown. That September of 1955 the young coach got an instant idea of the difficulties ahead. He hadn't even settled into town when he learned that Hot Rod was off again, this time to the training camp of Eddie Gottlieb's Philadelphia Warriors of the NBA. Forty years before the move became popular— and legal—Hundley had the idea of going straight to the pros before he had played a minute of varsity college basketball. Like a lot of athletes, he didn't really like school all that much, and the pool hall ethos from which he had emerged led Hundley to ask the simple question: Why not get paid to play? By most accounts, Hundley acquitted himself with distinction in that pro camp, but the NBA had a loosely enforced rule that said players couldn't join the league until their college classes had graduated.

Gottlieb owned another prosperous pro club, the Philadelphia Sphas, a barnstorming team not in the NBA, and he apparently had Hundley talked into playing there until Hundley injured his knee and his future immediately turned cloudy. Hot Rod suddenly considered the fact that his career might be over and he had no education. Once again he phoned Red Brown, and yet again Brown rode to the rescue. "Red went to Philadelphia and brought him back to his home to keep him in school," Barrett remembered. "Rod didn't like school. And, again, he had nobody to counsel him."

Barrett was in a position to know virtually everything about West Virginia basketball. At age sixteen, he had become sports editor of the newspaper in Fairmont, West Virginia, and by his early twenties had been hired as the university's director of sports publicity. He later did a stint in the service, then returned to Morgantown in 1956 to resume his sports publicity job. He knew all of the people in and around the program. Barrett tirelessly promoted the teams that first Hundley and then West played on, and watched every minute of the West era unfold in Morgantown.

According to Barrett, Red Brown was a dapper, suave veteran of West Virginia's high schools and small colleges. The state had proven to be a veritable breeding ground for brilliant basketball coaches, some of the game's best minds. Clair Bee, the prolific author and fabled coach at Long Island University, came from West Virginia, as did Cam Henderson, the brilliantly innovative tactician at Marshall University and the father of fast-break offense and zone defense. To go with those giants of the game, both in the Hall of Fame, were men like Brown and literally dozens of top-flight coaches, such as Press Maravich, the longtime college coach and father of Pistol Pete Maravich. (For a brief time, Brown had hired Press Maravich as his freshman coach at WVU, but before Maravich reported for work, he was offered the head coaching job at Davis & Elkins. It's not far-fetched, said Barrett, that Brown could have then hired Maravich instead of Schaus as WVU head coach, which means little Pete Maravich could have followed Hundley, West, and Rod Thorn in the line of legendary Mountaineers stars.)

Brown was neither a great basketball coach nor a fine administrator (he hated making decisions), Barrett said. "Red Brown was a raconteur. He was a gentleman—big smile, big personality. He hobnobbed with the greats effortlessly because he was nonthreatening; a guy they liked to have around. He wasn't going to ask them a lot of tough questions."

In time, it would become clear that Red Brown had used more than a bit of salesmanship to advance West Virginia several levels in the hierarchy of college basketball. In the early fifties, he gained appreciation merely for his ability to hold things together amid turbulence. He had come to Morgantown to replace coach Lee Patton, who had died of a heart attack following a car wreck in 1950 after a game with Penn State.

When it came to Hundley, Brown had invested heavily. Like many at WVU, he truly cared about the irrepressible star. As Hundley progressed as a player and the team came to dominate the Southern Conference, Brown could be seen standing in the shadows at the key moments and responding quite emotionally at the result of his persistence in helping Hot Rod find his way.

With the immensely talented but undisciplined Hundley back in the fold, the rookie coach would build an impressive team. Yet there, in that moment, also was born the strange chemistry and playing style that would define Jerry West's lonely, frustrating struggles with the basketball powers that be. Those immediately involved in WVU basketball recall the young Schaus as a no-nonsense type of guy, yet one also swayed by Hundley's irrepressible nature.

"He had stern discipline, and Rod was set up to drive him crazy," Rene Henry said of the young Schaus.

"Schaus wasn't a showtime man," Hundley agreed. "He played serious basketball his whole life."

Yet that's not what the fans and opposing coaches saw. From other perspectives, the discipline seemed anything but stern. West Virginia basketball in those days featured elements of the Globetrotters and even the fast-breaking "Showtime" basketball for which the Lakers would become known. With the pep bands blaring, Hundley and the Mountaineers would dash onto the floor before each game and whip through a crisply entertaining warm-up with a blue and gold ball. Schaus brought the ball, but it was Hundley who supplied the show.

"I did it when we got the gold and blue ball," Hundley recalled. "Schaus brought it in. We'd always run layup lines, and I'd be the guy at the free throw line. They'd throw me the ball, and I'd roll it around my back. And then Schaus got it changed to a striped ball just for warm-ups. We'd look down the floor and the other team would be watching us warm up."

Hot Rod expanded it from there to include fancy scissor drills and any other gag he could come up with. "We were the only team that I've seen in college that did drills running with the ball in scissors and crossing patterns, kind of like the Globetrotters," Hundley said. "We're the only team I've seen that did it. People loved it. We always sold out no matter where we played."

The Mountaineers were quite spiffy, Eddie Barrett agreed. "Schaus put them in the high kneesocks like North Carolina wore with Frank McGuire."

"It was a two-toned ball," recalled Rod Thorn, who would follow both Hundley and West as a Mountaineers star and first saw the warm-up as a high school freshman. "It wasn't an ABA-style ball but it was flashy," Thorn said. "And Rod came out doing his twirls, running the ball up and down his back. Almost like the Globetrotters. I don't think Fred liked that, but Rod was so good, he kind of tolerated it."

After seeing the display, Thorn, like so many West Virginia fans, was even more motivated to follow the team on the radio. Lee Patrone, another WVU player from that era, recalled being in high school and traveling to see Hundley and the Mountaineers. Patrone was especially eager to see the warm-up routine, but when the Mountaineers took the floor, there was no Hundley. "Where is he?" Patrone wondered. Then he looked up to see a commotion in the upper reaches of the field house. There was Hundley, leading cheers.

Things might have been fine if Hundley had kept the antics only to warm-ups, or if Schaus hadn't used the old pro-style offense when his team slowed to the half-court or if Hundley hadn't taken so many shots. But all of those things contributed to a perception of the Mountaineers that would later become a similar perception of Schaus's Lakers teams with Baylor and West, a perception that they were somewhat undisciplined and focused only on their stars. In many ways, Schaus was just doing what he knew, Barrett observed. "He was a rookie coach learning on the fly."

The early NBA, formed in 1946–47, struggled mightily at the gate and took to scheduling doubleheaders with the Harlem Globetrotters so that NBA teams could draw enough fans to pay the bills. Then there was the issue of star power. From its earliest days, Eddie Gottlieb, of the Warriors, knew that he had to have a high-scoring star to get the attention of the media and the fans. In the early days of the game, that star for Gottlieb and the Warriors was a Kentucky hillbilly named "Jumpin' Joe" Fulks, who thrilled crowds with his newfangled one-handed shots. Gottlieb kept Fulks in the game to run up the star's point totals to impress fans and media. The coach set up the offense so that Fulks got the ball and got the shots, as he would later do for Wilt Chamberlain, and it worked well. Fulks became the first NBA player to average more than 20 points a game. He got plenty of media attention, and Gottlieb's Warriors survived in the hard-sell days of the game, when a lot of other cash-starved pro teams died off. That set in motion what would become a pro basketball practice of giving the ball to your star and clearing his teammates out of the way so he could score. That was the game that young Fred Schaus knew, and that was the game his Mountaineers, and later his Lakers, teams would play.

Hot Rod was his star, and Hot Rod got the ball. His first varsity season, Hundley took an incredible 756 shots, more than a third of the shots taken by the entire team. For 1956, his second season, Hundley upped that number to 814 shots attempted. Pete Maravich would later take more, but Maravich was playing for his own daddy. Hundley would average a hair under 25 shots per game over the 89 games of his three-year varsity career. Rarely did Hot Rod, who made about

35 percent of his college field goal attempts, get a look he didn't like over the course of a forty-minute college game. With an ethic long established by the two-handed set shooters in those West Virginia high school gyms, Hundley would lace up shots from way downtown, never mind that the three-point goal was years away from even being imagined.

By themselves, those shot totals are heavy and suggest that Hundley, as his detractors often alleged, was a ball hog. However, taken in the context of the Mountaineers' pressing style, they were not unheard of, especially in shot-happy Southern basketball. In 1954, Furman University's Frank Selvy, who would later play for the Lakers with Hundley and West, scored 100 points in a single game by making 41 of 66 field goal attempts.

Beyond Hundley's shot selection, the real perception that Schaus's West Virginia teams were undisciplined came from Hundley's on-court behavior. His antics were a lot of fun for the Mountaineers and their fans and infuriating for opponents. Richard Gregg will never forget the game he saw early in Hundley's career played between WVU and Washington and Lee University at Fayetteville, West Virginia. The W and L guards chased Hundley furiously all night with double-teams, and Hundley dribbled in and around and through them. The madcap pace continued the whole night until late in the game, when it was clear that West Virginia had won. Hundley stopped, grinned, and suddenly held the ball out for his opponents to take. First startled, one of them seized it and raced down the floor for a meaningless layup as Hundley laughed.

Rod Thorn saw another game, played in the old armory in Bluefield against Virginia Military Institute. "That was the night that Rod shot the ball from behind his back late in the ball game," Thorn recalled. "The game was essentially over, and from about fifteen feet, Rod shot it from behind his back, missed it, and it came back to him. He shot it from behind his back again and made it."

"His clowning didn't really take place until after the game was decided," Barrett said, adding that Schaus was willing to tolerate the antics because Hundley had so much heart and was so competitive when the outcome was at issue. Such playfulness might have been marginally acceptable if it had indeed come only after or before games, or if it hadn't inspired more antics by his teammates, or if it didn't leave the impression that Hundley was humiliating opponents.

In Hundley's second varsity season, WVU played in Miami's holiday tournament, the Orange Bowl Classic. "Gary Mullins, who played for West Virginia, had no teeth, and he was at the foul line," Rene Henry recalled. "Two guys from the other team kept changing places along the foul lane. Mullins is ready to shoot and three times the official takes the ball away from him, instead of telling the other guys to stay put so the free throw could be taken. Finally Gary fell straight on his back and acts like he's passed out. Rod goes running over, opens Gary's mouth and looks in, and Gary winks at him. Rod yells out, 'Is there a doctor in the house? He's swallowed his teeth! He's swallowed his teeth!' The two officials are going crazy. And Fred is over there on the bench just cringing, just dying."

Another time, Henry recalled, "They were playing William & Mary, and Rod had just made a shot. He's at William & Mary's end of the floor. He sits down on the end of the bench, takes a towel, rolls it up like a microphone, and starts calling play by play. And Boydston Baird, who is the coach at William & Mary, looks down and sees him and goes berserk."

"The opposing teams, their coaches, didn't cotton to it at all," Barrett remembered.

Schaus himself would establish a foot-stomping, glaring style on the WVU sidelines which he used to discipline his teams. "We called him the Stomper," said Lee Patrone. Yet Hundley was just so good, and so irrepressible, that even the stomping and fussing only helped so much in the cause. Many WVU fans loved the crazy stuff, but more than a few complained. "He was flamboyant, fun to watch," West said of Hundley. "People had an incredible love for him. And to some degree, I used to say to myself, 'I wish I could have his personality.' But that wasn't the case. I watched him go through some wonderful times there, but also some times when people would be critical because of the way he played the game."

Regardless, everybody seemed impressed with Hundley's array of skills. Old-timers from those days look at how the modern game is officiated with its liberal rules for traveling and palming the ball and wonder how a young Hundley would fare today. "Could you imagine if they had allowed him and Cousy to handle the ball the way they do today?" asked Rene Henry. "No one would have known where it was. The palming and traveling they don't call today? Rod's rookie year, he had some real klutzes on the Lakers. He would come down, and a teammate would be wide open under the basket, and he'd hit them from behind his back while he was looking somewhere else. It'd bounce off their chest or off the top of their head. They weren't ready for the ball."

Time would show that those teammates weren't the only ones not ready for Rod Hundley. Schaus's WVU team won nineteen games his first season in 1955, defeated Virginia Military Institute, Washington and Lee, and George Washington University to win the Southern Conference tournament, and advanced to the NCAA tournament for the first time in school history. In fact, his teams would win three straight Southern Conference titles with Hundley in the lead. The antics and pro style posed little problem in the conference, but each of those first three years, Schaus's teams lost in the first round of the NCAA tournament. The translation? The Mountaineers weren't ready for well-organized units that played as a team.

By his senior year, Hundley was set to break the Southern Conference scoring record during the tournament. He needed 2 points to claim the record and was fouled at the end of his last game. He went to the line and took them as contorted hook shots.

"He threw the hook shot around the back with the two free throws," Rene Henry recalled. "All he needed was one to break the conference scoring record. Fred just cringed. He couldn't look at it."

NEXT?

West would get his own heavy share of shots as a varsity star for Schaus, although nothing like Hundley. The situation irked Barrett for years. The coach had essentially given Hundley a free rein, the university sports publicist said. "Then he turned around and sat on Jerry West."

Where Hundley attempted an eye-popping 2,218 over eighty-nine varsity games, West shot the ball 1,660 times over ninety-three games, about 17.6 shots a game. Yet even that lower number would eventually lead to rumored team dissension in West's senior year, despite the fact that West shot better than 50 percent from the floor—at a time when NBA players were making fewer than 40 percent of their shots, on average. Hundley and West were the featured stars of Schaus's offense over the six seasons he coached at West Virginia, but West wasn't eager to share the showboating image.

"He played so differently than I did," West said. "I had kind of a boring, unexciting style . . . But the legacy he left at the university was wonderful. I mean, here was this great guy who had played a game that no one had ever seen before."

Hundley had ushered West around campus as part of WVU's recruiting effort during the 1956 high school championship series. They would become true friends and remain that way through decades of basketball association. They would share a common experience — going from the Mountain State to the Lakers — that no others would share, and in that they achieved a remarkable understanding of each other. West would be amused and at times deeply annoyed by Hundley's showmanship, would come to the same conclusion as many others: that Hundley ultimately wasted his bountiful talent, although many of those judging Hundley didn't do so harshly. Considering his background, they said, his youthful indiscretion was understandable, not to mention the fact that for just about all involved it was quite a bit of fun. Plus, there was always the fact that over the years as a basketball broadcaster — first with the Lakers and then for decades with the Utah Jazz — Hundley provided the game a voice of great wit and insight.

By early 1957, the freshman and the star senior were going at each other during WVU scrimmages, and although West very much remained a work in progress on offense, his defense was both stifling and deceptive, even for an accomplished ball handler like Hundley.

"West would guard Hundley in practice," Eddie Barrett remembered. "And Fred said sometimes West took the ball right off Rod's hands. Apparently Rod would go to pass, and West would just take the ball right off his hands. Schaus said that was the first time he had ever seen anything like that."

"The toughest guy who guarded me in college was Jerry West as a freshman," Hundley offered years later.

At that time, when he was a freshman battling the senior Hundley, the WVU varsity was ranked fourth in the country, West pointed out with a laugh. "And the scrimmages, you would have thought we were one or two steps behind them as freshmen. It was fun."

West may have had little use for Hundley's antics, but there was one thing he liked about the varsity's flashy approach. "Jerry said we'd like to have those high warm-up socks like varsity had," Barrett said, "and Fred said, 'When you make varsity, you can have them.'"

At six-three and 160 pounds, West led the undefeated freshman team with 19 points and 17 rebounds a game, and Akers wasn't far behind, averaging his own double-double over those games. Still, West's scrimmages against the varsity had given him a view of the adjustment he would make on the college level. "It was a learning process," West said later, "for me to be exposed to bigger, stronger players, to understand that there was a different skill level involved."

THE GOOD OL' SUMMERTIME

Once the year ended, West and Akers both retreated to Chelyan, where Akers bunked with the West family while he and Jerry drove back and forth to Charleston each day. During the day, they held down something of a make-work job doing public relations for a local dairy. In the evenings, they played in the highly competitive Charleston summer league for the area's top talent. The league was set up and run by Nemo Nearman, a former player for North Carolina. It was part of a network of summer leagues set up around West Virginia. These summer leagues were huge fan favorites, and they would remain a staple of summer entertainment until the college basketball gambling scandals of the early 1960s prompted the NCAA to outlaw them. Some believed those scandals were rooted in summer play, where it was suspected that gamblers gained exposure to athletes.

Nearman recalled that West actually missed part of the schedule that summer after his freshman year because he was in summer school finishing up his academic work. West was a physical education major and a decent enough student, but West has acknowledged many times that he wasn't exactly fully engaged in the classroom.

"Jerry and I were alike in this regard," Charles West observed. "If we really liked a subject, we tended to do well in it. If we didn't, we didn't do so well."

West would finish his time at West Virginia lacking a course or two for his degree requirements, which he would make up later. The summer courses apparently helped him keep pace, just as they have done for college athletes for decades. Once his summer work was finished, West hustled home to join the summer league with Schaus's blessing.

"They told me they had this player Jerry West who had played at East Bank High School, and they asked if we could work him into the league," Nearman recalled. "I remember sitting out there and watching him warm up before his first game. You could see the fluidity of his moves and see he was a natural. He was skinny, but he was a natural."

"We played June and July and maybe a little August, and then we would go back to school," Akers said of the summer league experience. "We played outdoors. We played on three courts, nice courts with bleachers around them, and they'd have three games a night. Mostly people came to watch you. You didn't have a lot of TV back then, and our team was pretty popular. It was really big-time basketball, and it would draw a couple thousand people, sometimes fifteen hundred. Hot Rod Hundley would come in to play. All the West Virginia guys would play. Every college was involved. Morris Harvey would bring players. Marshall would come in. Virginia Tech had three kids from Charleston, and one of them was Chris Smith, who was an all-time player from down there. It was real competition. You'd get a job in the summer and play basketball."

Over the next two summers, West and Akers would also spend time in Morgantown and ride over the mountains to Wheeling for a summer league there. Just across the river from southern Ohio, Wheeling also drew players from the Buckeye State. It was in the Wheeling summer league that West would play against a young Ohio State recruit named John Havlicek, who would later be his opponent for many years as a member of the Boston Celtics.

The summer league in Charleston would be particularly big in 1958 after Akers and West enjoyed a breakout sophomore season at WVU.

"Jerry and I were sophomores on the number one team in the nation," Akers recalled. "At the end of the season, we were ranked number one, and we came into Charleston with all these guys, and they wanted to see us play. It was quite a spectacle."

And quite a learning experience for West. Nemo Nearman recalled that Fred Schaus wanted West to use the summer leagues to work on specific aspects of his game. "Fred Schaus wanted to use Jerry in the pivot more his senior year," Nearman said, "so Jerry would play pivot pretty regularly in our league. But every time his team would get in trouble and need a basket or two, Jerry would move out and do his guard thing. Jerry played wherever he wanted to. He would take his man in the pivot and maneuver off of him. He did quite a bit of it that last summer because that's what Fred Schaus wanted."

There's no doubt that the summer league work played a major role in West's growth as a player and set the tone that fall of 1957 for his first varsity season. It also further established his close friendship with Willie Akers, perhaps the most important friendship of West's life, a friendship that would endure the kind of competition that could easily have distanced the two from each other.

1957 TO 1958

West saw Schaus as a good coach. Yet where others saw Schaus as a disciplinarian, West saw him as a coach who basically relied on friendliness rather than toughness, although the two would long have their differences, beginning that first varsity season. There were four returning starters for a team that had won a lot of games and yet another conference title. The team had size in six-foot-ten Lloyd Sharrar, and a scoring forward in Bobby Joe Smith, and plenty of quickness in guards Don Vincent and Joedy Gardner. The reserves included Bob Clousson, Bucky Bolyard (who had one eye), Jay Jacobs, and three rising sophomores: Akers, West, and Goode.

"People think it was the best team we ever had," Barrett said. "That '58 team was excellent. It was smart too. Joedy Gardner later coached at WVU and Northern Arizona. He was a good player too. The roster had some outstanding players. Sharrar was an athlete. He wasn't a natural athlete, but he was well trained."

West seemed the obvious choice as the fifth starter at small forward to everyone involved, except Schaus, who hesitated and took a long look at Akers, who at nearly six foot five was bigger than West, Barrett remembered. "Jerry was all basketball player, and there was a big controversy over who was the best player. People would ask Fred Schaus about that. The first thing Freddy did—and I'm sure Jerry resented it—was to say that the fifth starter would be either West or Akers. West and everybody else knew who the better player was, but

Fred kept insisting it's either West or Akers. They eventually started West, of course."

This competition did little to hurt the close friendship between the two players, even though the matter dragged on.

"It began with the very first game of Jerry's sophomore year," Barrett said. "In the third game of the season West Virginia beat [the University of] Richmond by a couple of points, and West scored the winning goal and had twenty-seven points on the night. I remember Freddie discussing it afterward with the media. I told him, 'They're not going to be asking you this much longer,' Freddie said. 'You know the answer, and I know the answer. But I'm not going to say it.'"

During the early stretch of games that sophomore year, the coach called West into his office and told him he wasn't sure he was ready to be a starter. Schaus told West that the team needed more production out of him if he wanted to stay in the lineup. Years later, West would recall the meeting and point out that because he was always so hard on himself, he was particularly thin skinned about criticism from others. Barrett said the situation seemed unnecessary and obviously factored in the dislike West came to harbor for Schaus over the years. "Jerry just resented that," Barrett said.

West was regarded as a raw, athletic property at the time, with a yet-to-be developed offensive game. He saw himself much as others did. "I was kind of a late bloomer as a basketball player," West would allow. "There are so many things as a player that I didn't do. I wasn't a very accomplished dribbler, at all. I probably was a better defensive player than I was an offensive player at that time. I was probably a better rebounder than an offensive player."

Yet even at that level, without a polished offensive game, he could change outcomes with his energy, determination, and athletic play. "They played Jerry by the basket, deep by the basket," Eddie Barrett said, "and he had a knack for being where the rebound would come off. And he had those long arms and that instinct and those quick reflexes. So he scored on put-backs, on follow-throughs. And on the fast break. If he wasn't on the wing then he was the follow-up man. He would follow the fast break man down the floor and follow up if the shot was missed."

A big factor in West's development that year came with the hiring of George King as an assistant coach. King had an easy grin that belied his toughness. He had been an undersized, do-everything post player at Morris Harvey, then somehow made the transition to playing the backcourt in pro basketball, where he would often entertain crowds with his dribbling exhibitions. Just before coming to West Virginia as an assistant, he had played a key role in the Syracuse Nationals' winning the NBA championship in 1955, the first year of the NBA's twenty-four-second shot clock. King had scored the winning points in the deciding game in the series and had gotten a late steal to seal the win. That provided more than enough clout to impress the young West. Many longtime observers, such as Barrett, would maintain that King was the second greatest player to come out of West Virginia.

King had traveled much of the same road that West himself was about to travel. Plus, he was young and still very competitive. He liked challenging West at one-on-one and other little contests. It was gym rat versus gym rat. "One of the things I said to myself when I played against him was, 'You know, he's not as quick as I am. I don't think he can guard me,'" West said.

West, though, soon realized that King knew lots of crafty tricks for guarding quicker people. Those sessions with King would teach him many lessons that would be valuable to him not just in college basketball, but later as well, when he played pro ball, West said. In a short time, he came to develop a closer relationship with King than with the head coach. Schaus was a big man, and he understood the ways of big men. Even then, West knew his future in the game would be on the wing, as a guard.

"It seems like you bond with an assistant maybe more than you do a head coach," West would explain later. "George was someone who taught me a lot about the game."

Before long, Fred Schaus had joined King as a teammate in playing two-on-two against West and Akers. It was during these battles that the coaches started to see Jerry West differently. They began to understand that they had a player who could achieve greatness.

THE RISE

The Mountaineers had reeled off six straight wins to open the 1957–58 season, and just before Christmas they traveled to Lexington, Kentucky, to play in the Kentucky Invitational Tournament against the

Universty of Kentucky teams of the famed Baron of the Bluegrass, Adolph Rupp. He had coached the Wildcats for almost forty years and in that time had built them into a cultural force in the state. Kentucky's Memorial Coliseum held better than eleven thousand rabid fans in those days. It was one of the biggest gyms in the country at the time and easily the most intimidating. The Baron's teams had won 129 straight home games from 1943 to 1955, by an average margin of 31 points. The fifth-ranked Wildcats just didn't seem to lose at their Kentucky home, but they lost that first night of their holiday tournament as West and the Mountaineers silenced the noisy crowd, 77–70. It was a huge win. There was little time to celebrate, though. The next night, the West Virginians faced the number one team in the country, the University of North Carolina Tar Heels, who had won the 1957 NCAA championship over Wilt Chamberlain and the University of Kansas to cap off an undefeated season. The Tar Heels owned a 37-game winning streak dating back to the previous season, but the Mountaineers ended that one too, 75–64, in the championship of the Kentucky Invitational, played before thousands of numb Wildcats fans—none of them more numb than Rupp himself, who watched another team play in their preseason tournament championship.

"We were somewhat aware of Jerry West before that game," said Dick Kepley, who played in the Carolina frontcourt. "We didn't play well that game, and West Virginia had a lot to do with that. But I remember there were a lot of comments about Jerry West in our locker room after the game."

The comments would grow after each performance that sophomore season. Kentucky went on to claim a fifth national championship for Rupp that spring of 1958, but the immediate glory after that December weekend went to the Mountaineers.

"We went right to number one in the rankings," Barrett recalled. Witnessing those upset victories would rank tops among the many highlights of Barrett's career as a sports publicist and administrator.

The Mountaineers returned home to the raucous delight of their fans and ran through two more wins before heading to play Villanova University at the historic Palestra at the University of Pennsylvania, where the crowds easily matched the noise in Kentucky. This time the noise worked for the home team. Villanova owned a 14-point lead with eight minutes left in the game—just the circumstances that time and again over his career would ignite a West "moment." On cue, he came alive in the closing minutes, scoring 17 of his team's final 23 points. In the last thirty seconds, he scored two goals, then hit Sharrar with the winning assist with just two seconds on the clock.

"There were several big games that year, but one of the biggest ones was that game with Villanova on January eighth," Eddie Barrett recalled. "It came during an NCAA convention for football coaches, so they all saw it happen. We got three baskets in the last 30 seconds and we beat them 76 to 75 and the crowd went wild. West got two of those baskets and passed off for the other one. That crowd was used to watching the play of the great Tom Gola, a forward for La Salle University who was then in his second season with the Philadelphia Warriors. The home fans turned in Jerry's favor. That game is when we basically realized what a great player he was." West finished with 37, his high for the season. More impressive, his team had opened the schedule with a fifteen-game winning streak.

The Mountaineers would lose a close game to Duke University in Durham, North Carolina, at midseason, then take off on another run. They won six straight, including a strong road win over Penn State, before everything came to a sickening halt. Schaus's wife, Barbara, suffered serious injuries in a toboggan wreck. Doctors weren't sure she would live. The Mountaineers, meanwhile, faced a good University of Detroit team that week, on February 17, but basketball wasn't really tops among their thoughts. Barbara Schaus would recover fully, but at the time, that was far from clear.

"Looking back on it, the players didn't know what to say," Schaus said years later. "The best way for them to show me that they cared was to go out and play a heckuva game, and that's what they did."

They smashed Detroit by 32 points and kept right on rolling through the rest of the schedule with three more wins in the Southern Conference tournament for Schaus's fourth straight conference championship and fourth straight NCAA tournament bid. Best of all, the Mountaineers were ranked at the very top of the final Associated Press and United Press International college basketball polls that season. In those days, neither poll took a vote after the NCAA tournament.

The Southern Conference championship, however, cost them heavily. Don Vincent, the team's number two scorer behind West, broke his leg and was finished for the season. Jolted by the news, West Virginia entered the NCAA field that year with a 26–1 record, the top ranking in the polls, and an opening round date in Madison Square Garden against Manhattan College.

"We had fourteen thousand people at the game, which was a good crowd," remembered Manhattan star Jack Powers, who scored 29 points that night. "A lot of the rooters from West Virginia didn't think they would lose . . . There were quite a few Jaspers fans."

It wasn't unusual that West Virginia fell behind. They had come roaring back so many times before that season. But there was no grand comeback this time. The game was tight, and as it went on, the crowd grew rowdier as the Jaspers closed in on a stunning upset, 89–84. "They stormed the court like they do now," Powers recalled. "It was a tough, physical game. It was a great upset with Jerry coming in with all the publicity. It was probably the worst nightmare for Jerry West."

West finished with just 10 points. Looking back on it years later, he scoffed, saying he was hardly Mr. Clutch that night. "We were overconfident," he remembered.

"The reason we didn't win the title was because Don Vincent broke his leg in the Southern Conference tournament," Barrett offered.

The Mountaineers had lost in the first round of the tournament for the fourth straight year under Fred Schaus and closed the season with a 26–2 record amid bitter disappointment. West earned second-team all-American honors from the Helms Foundation and from the Converse sports shoe company for averaging 17.8 points and 11.1 rebounds per game. Regardless, it was an extremely unhappy process for West, watching as Kentucky, a team that West Virginia had beaten handily on the road, went on to claim the national championship that spring in its home state. There was a strong sense that the Mountaineers had just wasted a tremendous opportunity with their best team ever.

KEEPING UP WITH OSCAR

The season may have ended in a shocker, but West had established his ability for clutch play at the top levels of the college game. Soon people were comparing him to Oscar Robertson, the great sophomore guard at the University of Cincinnati who had owned the 1958 season from tip-off on opening night. Over the three varsity seasons of his college career, Robertson averaged 33.8 points and 15.2 rebounds per game while shooting a whopping 53.5 percent from the floor. He was the NCAA scoring leader for three straight seasons as well. As a collegian, Robertson scored 50 points or more in six games. He scored 62 in one game, against North Texas State, and 56 in another, against Seton Hall University, in which he outscored the opposition all by himself.

Media coverage of basketball in that era was spare, but his special abilities meant that a lot of people had quickly become aware of Robertson. With Cincinnati just a short drive from Morgantown, West was among them. In fact, they were keenly interested in each other.

As for West, over the course of his three varsity seasons, he would average 24.8 points with 13.3 rebounds while shooting 50.8 percent from the floor. Just as he would later in pro basketball, West upped his scoring in play-off games considerably—to 30.6 per game in college. He became the only player in NCAA history to score at least 25 points in eight consecutive games, a record that would later be eclipsed, by Pete Maravich at LSU.

To some of those around him, it was obvious that West was keenly pursuing Oscar, although West himself said or indicated little about the subject.

Robertson's success served to motivate Barrett, who labored mightily over those three varsity seasons to get the national sports media to recognize that West possessed similar brilliance. Barrett was particularly frustrated with *Sports Illustrated* college basketball writer Jeremiah Tax. Barrett could not persuade Tax to write a feature on West, although Tax gave Robertson substantial ink. In fact, *Sports Illustrated* would not publish a feature on West until 1965, well into his Lakers years. As frustrated as Barrett was with Tax and other national media, the publicist was even more irked with Schaus.

"Jerry was kept under wraps," Barrett said, his irritation flashing five decades later. "He would be taken out of games early. Jerry went to Schaus to complain about it, and Schaus said, 'Jerry, you're going to be an all-American, but I need to develop these other guys and have a good bench.' That was his explanation. Robertson, of course, played just about all forty minutes each game, and that's why Robertson had such high scoring games. Oscar was like a potentate at Cincinnati. He not only dribbled the ball up the floor, nobody else on his team saw it. Oscar had the ball all the time."

Even without inflated statistics and the attention of *Sports Illustrated,* West would get his share of media and attention over his three seasons of varsity ball. His hunger was the basic hunger of most competitors. Acclaim was nice, West said many times, but the only way to really establish anything was on the court. This was especially true in an age when racial perception defined so much of what was printed and published. West simply knew that Robertson was a great player, which meant West wanted to get on the court to see how he matched up, if his team could beat Robertson's.

"I didn't score a lot of points in college," West would explain later, an obvious reference to Robertson. "You know, I scored a lot, but not any astronomical game. And I was pretty consistent throughout my college career, almost every year I was there."

West had gotten the sense that whatever the challenge, he had the ability to rise to it. And he would do so based on the unusual way he approached the game. "I always did better against the better teams than against the poorer teams," he observed much later. "Some nights I didn't do very well, from a scoring perspective. But my first year as a sophomore it was all defensive oriented and rebounding. That seems very strange for someone who's six three and a half to do those kinds of things. But that was the way I was gonna play, and that was the way I was gonna have a chance to prosper."

The circumstances meant that Robertson became a target, for Jerry West and for Barrett, his team's publicist. Like any competitor would, West longed to compete against Robertson to measure up, to settle the issue of who was better. That became part of his huge drive, his unspoken agenda, for his final two college seasons.

THE MOUNTAINEER PRINCESS

Many others players might have been elated by the unfolding events of the 1958 season. West was made miserable by them. The season had brought the first of his many battles with himself, fighting the profound disappointment of his perfectionism. Asked many years later if his perfectionist tendencies had made him too hard on himself in college, West replied, "Well, you know, I've always been that way, but I think that's probably the thing that's driven me in my life. People use the word *perfection* a lot, and I don't think you can be perfect in sports at all, because it's just not possible. But at that point in my life, there were just so many things that I knew I could do, that I hadn't worked on enough. If I'd miss two or three easy shots, it just . . . it made you tighter, it made you more tightly wound. And for some reason, maybe one of the demons that's been with me forever, has been that."

The thing that drove him also had the great potential to paralyze him. If he didn't see that at age nineteen, others certainly did, including his teammates and coaches. Fred Schaus would have his detractors over his seasons of coaching West, but the coach attempted to deal with this problem the best he could. And it was not a problem with an easy answer. Gaining better control of his emotions would prove to be a long-term project for West, one that would involve teammates and coaches on every team he ever played on.

"At times, Jerry tended to brood over the flaws in his game," Schaus later explained. "When he was not playing well, he'd kind of go into a shell. He wouldn't talk to anybody, not the coaches or his own teammates. If he wasn't playing well, he was tough to live with."

Even reading his moods presented challenges for teammates. He tended to be quiet anyway. But there was no mistaking when his perfectionism drove him off the deep end, as it did for a two-week stretch during that first varsity season in 1958. Schaus would swear later that during that time, West spoke to no one, not a single person. Joedy Gardner, his teammate and roommate, would later reveal that West was mute and extremely withdrawn, a silent presence caught deep in disappointment and frustration. Later, on the 1960 U.S. Olympic team, coach Pete Newell would be shocked to see the same thing. To see such debilitation in a star player who had such an ability to hit big shots and win games was truly surprising, said Jack Ramsay, who coached against West in both college and pro basketball.

West began to get a sense of how to deal with his emotions during his college years, but it was a problem that would surface, then mysteriously go away, only to resurface again and again, giving the impression he had a measure of control over his emotions but could never conquer them.

"One of the things he has beaten is his depressions," Schaus told

Sports Illustrated several years later. "It used to be a big problem for Jerry. He'd miss two or three shots, and he'd start to press. He'd get down on himself—never on anybody else, or even the officials—but his depressions would last as long as a week or ten days."

It was true that West had perhaps gotten better at staying away from the depths of the extreme lows that competition and perfectionism brought him. That was far from his only problem, however. As he gained more confidence and took on more responsibility with his team, West became wracked by incredible game-day tension. He would become a pacing, nervous animal each game day, with the tension building moment by moment until he was absolutely beside himself with anxiety over his coming performance. It was a condition that threatened to take down his legacy before it ever got started. "I've always been a nervous person," West admitted many times.

Maturity would provide part of the solution that junior season. And moving into Ann Dinardi's house also helped stabilize his sense of well-being. But the real tension relief came naturally in the form of a pretty coed. West found a romantic interest, although drawing the romance out of him proved to be quite arduous for Martha Jane Kane. She already had quite a debutante's resume when she sat next to West in a class midway through his time at West Virginia. She came from a prosperous family in nearby Weston, West Virginia, where her father owned a hardware store. She was the May Queen at her high school and later won a statewide essay contest. At West Virginia, she was named a Mountaineer Princess during her freshman year. She was elected as a representative to the WVU student legislature and appointed an associate editor of the student yearbook. She was also tapped to join an elite women's junior honorary society at the university, and in 1958 had been named a maid of honor to the Strawberry Queen.

She had a 4.0 average as an English major and played the organ beautifully. Her list of accomplishments would have made Howard West green with envy. She had been named the queen of all the right courts, had joined all the right clubs, and had collected all the right honors. She was a stylish and attractive brunette with confident eyes and a soft, pretty smile. All of this might have added up to the perception that she was a bit much, but she soon revealed an impressive depth to those who met her. Martha Jane Kane displayed spunk and class and character, all of the good attributes.

She also had quite a time getting any words whatsoever out of Jerry West. She would say that when she first saw him in class, she wasn't aware of just who he was. She later confided to *Sports Illustrated* writer Frank Deford that it took weeks "of passing notes back and forth and doodling on each other's paper" before she could entice the silent young star to ask her out on a date. Then once out on that date, she found that she needed a chisel to get any sort of conversation out of him. Unfortunately, it would take Martha Jane Kane years to learn that first impressions meant so much. Eventually, after much effort and heartache, she would come to see that it was virtually impossible to get Jerry West to share much of anything about what he was feeling.

For the longest time she accepted that being along for the wild ride of Jerry West's life would have to be enough. Then again, things would be plenty entertaining over those final two years in Morgantown. And far more than the public could ever fathom, female companionship was a critical factor for West in controlling his game-day tension.

West was learning that he would either control this tension or it would control him. He was coming to an understanding, a view of himself, that would serve him throughout his college career and on into his professional life. If he wanted to ensure that he was collected enough to perform on the court at game time, then he had to have something to calm him, something before each game. He began to think that he had to have something that came quite naturally to any red-blooded American male.

He had to have a woman's touch.

How did we win? Guts, heart, bench, hustle, and Jerry West.

—Fred Schaus
Charlotte, North Carolina, 1959 East Regional

THE MOUNTAINEER

Morgantown, West Virginia, 1958 to 1959

IRONY BECOMES A FACTOR ONLY WHEN YOU LOSE. WIN, AND AFTER-
ward there are no little details to ponder, no nagging thoughts to
drive you crazy. That's why summers always presented such a hurdle
of misery for Jerry West. The twist, of course, is that those anguished
off-seasons also drove him to keep getting better and better.

Every summer it was either go crazy or work on your game. Time
would reveal that West did a lot of both. That rhythm of loss and recovery began in college and then played like a bad joke year after
year over the course of his pro career. A case can be made that no
other player pushed to improve as much as Jerry West because no
other player—with the exception of Lakers teammate Elgin Baylor—
was so teased by fate.

"The closer you get to the magic circle, the more enticing it becomes," West said, looking back. "I imagine in some ways it's like a
drug. It's seductive because it's always there, and the desire is always
there to win one more game. I don't like to think I'm different, but I

was obsessed with winning. And losing made it so much more difficult in the off-season."

His sophomore year had brought the genesis of this miserable cycle. In terms of talent and national ranking, the 1958 campaign was easily West Virginia's greatest. The team had a deep roster and in the heart of the season spent seven straight weeks ranked as the number one team in the country. Then the Mountaineers went and spoiled everything by losing in the opening round of the NCAA tournament for the fourth straight year.

Pushed by the disappointment of that loss, West emerged as a different player the following fall. Beyond playing in the summer league in Charleston, he spent much of the off-season working on his left hand. It would take years to develop, but his summer work brought substantial improvement. That in turn meant that the entire floor opened up for him. He stepped onto the court in the fall of 1958 as a much-developed offensive player. No longer was he mainly a rebounder and defender who scored mostly in the flow of the game. He had made the big early steps in becoming a willful and determined scorer who forced opponents to take drastic measures to stop him. With the new season, it quickly became clear that West Virginia's offense would be in his hands much of the time.

And it wasn't simply because Fred Schaus had finally decided that it was West's turn to take over. In fact, that had little to do with it, said teammate Lee Patrone. "Schaus didn't design the offense to just go to Jerry. But we went to him anyway. He was just so darn quick. There was a comfort level when the ball got in Jerry's hands. He was just such a natural."

Even though he was a forward, still unpolished in handling the ball, his teammates instinctively looked to West, Patrone explained. "All the talent was there. Jerry was admired by all of the team. He could make you look good. He had that knack. And if you were open under the basket, or somewhere else, he made sure you got it."

The Mountaineers had shed much talent from the previous season, and that too factored into West's opportunities.

"He didn't have to play second banana to somebody like Lloyd Sharrar," Barrett explained. The six-foot-ten Sharrar was gone, and Schaus had replaced him with six-foot-six Bob Clousson. "Schaus saw Clousson walking down High Street in Morgantown," Eddie Barrett said. "He stopped him and said, 'What are you doing? Why don't you come out for basketball?'"

Clousson had played in high school, and Schaus had some scholarship money available. That's how the Mountaineers filled their hole at center, which says something about how their prospects were viewed heading into the 1958–59 season. Don Vincent and Joedy Gardner had moved on as well, which meant there were open spots to fill in the frontcourt and backcourt.

Willie Akers joined West as one of the forwards, making the frontcourt one of the smallest in major college basketball. When Schaus wanted to go "big," he turned to six-foot-five sub Jim Ritchie in the post.

The six-foot-four, 180-pound Bobby Joe Smith was back to play guard, and one-eyed Bucky Bolyard replaced Vincent as the other guard. The reserves included Lee Patrone, a smooth-shooting guard who had spent nine days at Ohio State as a freshman before transferring to West Virginia.

There was some question about how the Mountaineers were going to score enough. "There was a bit of hype because Jerry was an all-American," Eddie Barrett remembered. "He was the returning star, and Bob Smith was happy to be the number two guard. Smith was no slouch; however, he didn't have the ego that you need . . . He didn't say, 'I want the ball,' even though he was quite a competitor."

In his preseason comments, Schaus cautioned fans that his team had lost both quickness and size. His players responded by winning their first five games and moving to the fourth overall ranking in the national polls. They averaged better than 85 points in those first five wins. It was clear they'd find plenty of ways to score.

Schaus himself was due for more than a little of the credit for the rebuilt team's fast start. "Fred was a big guy," Lee Patrone said. "It was his stature and his belief in you. Schaus brought the best out in you. That man had a way of making you perform above and beyond your talent."

Yet the coach's approach was hardly all pep talks and motivation. No longer was he a rookie coach vulnerable to the grandstanding of a star player like Hot Rod Hundley. In fact, Schaus had gotten a firm grip on the program. One rival coach even described him as the last of the old-school disciplinarians. Schaus had matured as a coach. He

didn't tolerate foolishness. "We were scared to death of him," guard
Bobby Joe Smith recalled years later.

THE ALPHA MALE

As much as anything, those early wins presented clear evidence that
West had begun his emergence as a top-tier offensive talent. But as
the season wore on, it wasn't just his new skill that was evident. His
willful displays of heart at the end of games began to define him. West
Virginia fans were witnessing the early form of the persona that
would come to be known during his Lakers days as "Mr. Clutch."
West has often since acknowledged his mixed feelings about that persona. The name itself, devised by broadcaster Chick Hearn, was more
than a bit cheesy, but fans thrilled by West's heroics quickly identified
with it. West was partly embarrassed by the silliness of it but also
elated by the recognition, the status, the identity—the power, even—
that came with it. Such status has long been the guilty nourishment
for those select few supremely talented players.

"I just want to be the man," a twenty-year-old Kobe Bryant would
offer in 1999 in explaining the urges he felt as a player of unique ability. It's no accident that Bryant became West's greatest protégé. Forty
years earlier, West himself had the same overwhelming urges, although they were left unarticulated. Time and again over the remaining games of his college career, twenty-year-old Jerry West would
show that he too very much wanted to be "the man," especially in a
tight game's closing moments.

"We talk about the clutch baskets he made so many times over the
years where he scored the winning points or tied the game," Willie
Akers observed. "If the game was tied or we were one point down, he
would say, 'Just give me the fuckin' ball,' and he'd win it. He wasn't
afraid to take the shot, and very few people are able to do that. And
he was exceptional at it. When it came to those moments, he was better than anybody that has ever played the game with the exception of
maybe Michael Jordan."

Years later, in dealing first with Jordan and then Kobe Bryant,
coach Phil Jackson would sometimes use the term "alpha male" in explaining the force of personality of such a superior player. Asked once
to explain the special sway Jordan held over the game, Jackson

thought a moment and replied, "It's an amazing feat this guy has been able to accomplish. But I think his power is very addictive. You know the fans were there looking for him. Everybody was waiting. They loved it. He had this tremendous vision of basketball. He was this tremendous entertainer."

Yet the alpha male, the dominant dog in the pack, has a demanding and competitive nature that tends to grind up those around him, Jackson observed. "That attitude, that tremendous competitiveness, sometimes makes it tough to be a teammate, because you see that tremendous competitiveness is gonna eat you up everywhere. It's gonna eat you up playing golf with him next week, playing cards with him next month. That attitude of arrogance is gonna be there. It's not always the best for personal connections and friendship. But it certainly makes for greatness."

Fans in more recent seasons have been afforded a better understanding of the raw drive for dominance of Jordan and later Bryant. West and Oscar Robertson operated decades earlier, in a more obscure era, but they possessed that same rare personality type, restrained only by culture and perception. West was an alpha male wrapped in the cloak of his Southern Appalachian ways. A North Carolinian, Jordan possessed similar cultural influence. He and West benefited tremendously from this in their relations with the public. Until he was charged with rape in 2003, Bryant, a child of wealth, enjoyed a similar public appeal. In fact, he was able to regain much of that public goodwill despite his legal troubles. Oscar Robertson, on the other hand, came to maturity in Indianapolis, a witness to the ugly racism of the 1950s, and he never had the benefit of the media and cultural influences that made life easier for the other three.

The four of them, however, remain linked by the same uncompromising nature. Just like Bryant, Jordan, and Robertson, West wanted to consume every game ravenously. He wanted to play every minute, compete at every turn, and leave nothing to question. "Those are the frustrating things about basketball, especially for someone like myself, " West would say later. "I never wanted to come out of a game, never. They could have played me every minute of every game, and I would have been fine, because I had a lot of energy. I didn't get tired."

If there was some element of the game out of his control, he would study it and practice it relentlessly until he mastered it. Then he would employ it. It's no coincidence that Jordan and Bryant became known for pushing themselves through grueling routines to compete, just as West and Oscar Robertson did in their own fashion in their day.

Unfortunately, the gears of such a competitive machine never seem to stop grinding. Record producer Lou Adler recalled playing with West in one of those silly celebrity charity games in 1978 after West had finished his playing career. Whoever was coaching West's team had removed him from the game at one point. Adler remembers sitting on the bench with West and watching him grow increasingly irritated as the action went back and forth without him.

The game was a pointless and vapid affair, yet the frown on West's face deepened each time the action traveled up and down the floor. "He was getting really nervous because they were keeping him out," Adler said. "Finally he just went to the scorer's table and checked in."

West was incapable of viewing the game as just a bunch of goofy fun, Adler remembered thinking. "He could not take it. That's his life. That's the way he's always played. He doesn't know any other way."

Years later West was helping Chick Hearn with the broadcaster's fantasy camp at a high school gym in Maui, Hawaii. The participants were fifty-year-old fat guys who had paid thousands to be there. West was coaching one team, Magic Johnson the other.

For some reason, the officials didn't show up for a game scheduled one day at the camp, and Kurt Rambis, the longtime Lakers player and coach, was drafted as a volunteer to referee. The action started, and Rambis began officiating, stopping the action with routine calls mostly aimed at preventing the fat guys from hacking and hurting each other. From the first whistle, West was up on the sidelines, vociferously fussing at every call Rambis made.

"What did you make that call for?" West screamed at one point.

"Like I need this," an increasingly annoyed Rambis muttered to a spectator.

"It was these fifty-year-old guys out there playing, and West was going nuts," the spectator said. "If he felt this way about this, imagine how he felt about real games."

Finally, West became so upset at the calls Rambis was making that he stormed off in anger, leaving jaws sagging in disbelief.

For some reason, fantasy camps always seemed to set him off, which left other people shaking their heads. At another camp, he supposedly arranged extra practice sessions at a private gym to get his team ready for a championship game. The summer he turned seventy, he was working a fantasy camp in West Virginia and was trying to show a basic move to an older gentleman who had signed up to play. Associates told of watching West grow increasingly irritated at the camper's inability to learn the move. Sensing a scene brewing, those running the camp apparently knew to move things along before West boiled over with frustration.

High school teammate Joe Chrest spent some time in Los Angeles when West was the Lakers GM and had occasion to visit with him and observe West's difficulties in simply watching his own team play a game. West had gotten Chrest some tickets for a game, and Chrest asked his old friend if he was going to be there. West replied that he would probably watch the game later on tape because seeing it live upset him too much. "I can't stand to sit there and watch," West told his old teammate.

"He was such a perfectionist he just couldn't stand watching guys make mistakes," Chrest said. "He just couldn't take it."

Basketball guru Hal Wissel, a scout and shooting coach who worked with the Memphis Grizzlies teams that West ran, was asked what set him apart. "The number one thing is intensity," Wissel said immediately. "It made him great as a player, and that's the way he was as a GM. It made it tough on him, though. He put pressure on himself all the time, huge amounts of pressure."

So if West was like this at age sixty, what was he like at twenty, with testosterone coursing through his veins? How tough was it to be his teammate? Articulating that answer would prove difficult for Lee Patrone even years after the fact.

And that is another definitive characteristic of alpha males: While their specific brands of intensity differ, the teams they anchor are put under great pressure. Jordan, for example, seemed always to look for new and different ways to heap pressure on himself. And often he would treat his own teammates quite ruthlessly if they couldn't stand up to the pressure he placed on them. Robertson, who was known to be harsh with teammates, seemed to employ a similar strategy, and Bryant pushed himself with an unimaginable work ethic that frequently annoyed teammates and left them feeling inadequate.

West, for his part, saved all the pressure for himself, but that made it no less difficult for his teammates. In his years with the Lakers, he would be known for offering rambling complaints in off-the-record conversations with the media about his teammates' shortcomings, but that wasn't the case at West Virginia. In college he had yet to leave behind his reserved manner, off the court or with the media. "Jerry kind of kept to himself," Lee Patrone remembered. "He had a girlfriend, and in his spare time, he was with her. He was quiet and reserved and withdrawn."

Around the game and around his teammates, he was more animated. "He was pretty upbeat most of the time he played," Patrone remembered. "He was a perfectionist, though, and he could get down about things."

The more he developed as an offensive player, the more pressure West put on himself. As the season unfolded and West was pushing himself and the team, it was obvious to Eddie Barrett, Lee Patrone, and others that West was driven to keep pace with Oscar Robertson and the University of Cincinnati Bearcats. Averaging better than 30 points a game, Robertson was again leading the nation in scoring and racking up amazing totals in rebounds and assists as well.

That push to keep up with Robertson and Cincinnati would set the agenda for a fairy tale season for West and his team, with a dramatic climax in the national championship game in Louisville, Kentucky's Freedom Hall. How epic was the tale? West would achieve consensus status as an all-American, he would average 26.6 points per game, and he would carry his team toward the dream of meeting Robertson and the Cincinnati Bearcats in a titanic showdown. And that was what everybody seemed to want that season: a championship matchup pitting two great players against each other.

"The whole thing going toward the Final Four that year was to see that Jerry West–Oscar Robertson collision," Patrone recalled. "Everybody was waiting for that to materialize."

John Havlicek was a freshman at Ohio State that season, and when the Final Four was set at Louisville with a field that included West's team, Robertson's team, hometown favorite Louisville, and an unsung little team from the University of California, Havlicek managed to wrangle tickets from his high school coach to go see the affair. He traveled to Louisville, where he discovered there was hardly any room at the inn.

"We stayed in a hotel room that only had one bed and a common bath used by everybody on the floor," Havlicek would recall years later. "Everything was booked, so we just took what was left." Despite the unsavory accommodations, Havlicek got to witness a most un-usual weekend of championship basketball. Havlicek himself would scale the heights of college basketball over his varsity seasons, would win a national championship at Ohio State, then would go on to a seventeen-year career with the Boston Celtics and claim a wealth of championship memories. He would experience as a player some of the greatest moments in basketball history. Yet his memories as a spectator watching Jerry West that weekend and the surprises that unfolded were something he would treasure among his greatest moments, especially the 1959 NCAA championship game.

"That," he would say years later, long after his own playing career was finished, "was one of the most fantastic games I've ever seen."

HOME

In many ways, West Virginia's path to the 1959 national championship game started with athletic director Red Brown, the thoroughly ingra-tiating man with the big smile and the big vision.

"Red Brown scheduled West Virginia into the big time," Eddie Barrett explained. Brown, a former English teacher, had the polish and people skills that allowed him to forge relationships around the country when he was WVU's head coach. He knew everyone in col-lege basketball and would sit each year at the Final Four with NCAA commissioner Walter Byers. Brown's move to athletic director proved ideal, for him, for WVU, and, ultimately, for Jerry West. Brown knew that the Mountaineers had to reach out to find big-time athletics, since they played in the second-tier Southern Conference. Earlier in the century, the Southern had been the original power conference. It included many of the big southeastern universities, Georgia, Kentucky, Alabama, and most of the schools that would become the Atlantic Coast Conference, including Duke, North Carolina, North Carolina State, Virginia, and Wake Forest. But as many big schools got aggres-sive in pursuing major college athletics, the early Southern Confer-ence, headed by Virginia Tech athletic director Clarence Paul "Sally" Miles, sought "amateur athletic purity" and prohibited schools from broadcasting games on the radio or raising athletic funding from alumni. In 1932 a group of big schools broke off from the conference to form the Southeastern Conference. Two decades later, in 1953, another group of Southern Conference schools broke away to form the ACC.

So by the 1950s, the Southern Conference was no longer powerful. Yes, it had George Washington University, where Red Auerbach's old coach, Bill Reinhart, still produced strong teams. It had Chuck Noe building a decent program at Virginia Tech. But it also had William & Mary, Richmond, Washington and Lee, Virginia Military Institute, and the Citadel, schools with far less of an athletic focus. (Schaus used to swear that he would immediately retire from coaching if one of his teams ever lost to VMI, for example.)

In its entire history, the conference had only sent one team to the NCAA championship game: North Carolina in a 1946 meeting with Oklahoma State. With the departure of the North Carolina schools to form the ACC in 1953, the Southern Conference began slowly downshifting its expectations.

West Virginia remained in the conference, but it was a school with bigger athletic ambitions. Those ambitions had been ignited in 1942, when West Virginia won the NIT with a team of local boys who weren't even on scholarship. The very next season, WVU began offering basketball scholarships because its alums and fans hankered for a higher profile and more success.

By the time Jerry West finally got to wear the fancy long socks on the WVU varsity, Brown had assembled just the schedule to showcase a special young star. The Jerry West Mountaineers would play games in Madison Square Garden, in the brand-new Los Angeles Sports Arena, in Philadelphia's grand old Palestra, in Kentucky's Memorial Coliseum, in Chicago Stadium, in Louisville's shiny new Freedom Hall—just about all the sports palaces of the era. More importantly, that meant West played in front of the media in those cities, in games covered by AP and UPI representatives. And even more important, West played games against much of college basketball's top competition.

Those things were vitally important in an era when there was no ESPN to broadcast the top games, no talk radio to pump out opinion about the top players, no Internet sites to drive fan interest. Brown's scheduling ability meant everything to West Virginia, a state that had long battled its "backward" image, and it meant that some opposing teams would agree to make the difficult trip to Morgantown to play in the WVU Field House. Like a good alpha male, West had marked his territory well at the on-campus arena. He and his Mountaineers would not lose a game in the field house over his three varsity seasons.

"We had great home court advantage. It was so loud in there because the fans were right on top of the court," Schaus once explained.

"I always thought that playing in the field house," West told Charleston sports columnist Jack Bogaczyk, "it was sort of like you were in the Colosseum, and you were a gladiator, with the people right on top of you."

The opponents were often left feeling like the early Christians in that scenario, like they were about to be devoured.

Brown's scheduling and West Virginia's ambitions also factored into the construction of the Charleston Civic Center, which gave the state a bigger, better facility for events. The civic center had opened by West's junior season, and on December 13, 1958 the Mountaineers played the first college basketball game in the building against lightly regarded Virginia.

"I think if you look at the state back then, there really wasn't any kind of grand facility like the civic center," West said. "It was a very neat place, very clean. There weren't a lot of buildings of stature around then. It was a rarity." The game also would mark the first time that West had returned to play in his native Kanawha County. This time there would be no rowdy fans sitting right on top of the court. "This was a different feeling completely," West remembered.

The night before their first game in the civic center, the Mountaineers had played a contentious game against Duke in Morgantown. The year before, the only loss in West Virginia's regular-season run had come in a close game against Duke in Durham. Schaus didn't only hate to lose, he also hated whoever he lost to, and Duke coach Hal Bradley was on that list. WVU was scheduled to play Duke in Morgantown on December 11. But Bradley chose to wait until the day of the game to fly his team there. They encountered weather delays, and the game had to be moved to the next night, December 12. Barrett recalled that Schaus was so infuriated by Bradley's arrogance and late travel plans that he ran up the score on Duke that night. The Mountaineers won, 101–63, and West and the starters played long minutes to build that big lead.

West, too, would later recall the team's eagerness to avenge that

1958 loss to Duke. The big margin of victory seemed so satisfying that night, but the leg-weary Mountaineers had to get up the next day and ride down to Charleston, where they were somewhat listless and got beat by Virginia, 75–72. "We'd run out of gas," Barrett recalled, "because Schaus had expended everything against Bradley and Duke."

It would be the only time in his 93 college games that West lost in his home state.

The Mountaineers quickly recovered with a win over Richmond, then traveled to Lexington for the second straight year to play in the Kentucky Invitational. There they were paired with Oklahoma State, coached by the great Hank Iba. They handled OSU easily but lost by 6 to the defending national champion Kentucky Wildcats the next night in the championship. A week later, after the Christmas holidays, they traveled to Chicago Stadium to take on Northwestern University and lost yet again, 118–109, in double overtime.

From there, they flew down to Knoxville to face the University of Tennessee, a burly team that struck West as more of a football squad. He withstood a physical challenge that night to score 44 points, hitting 17 of 25 shots from the floor and 10 of 11 free throws.

The 44 points would be West's career high in college, but more importantly the 76–72 win turned the tide for the Mountaineers. They were 7–3 going into the contest, but the victory launched them on an eleven-game winning streak that would include their rallying from a 20-point deficit against William & Mary to keep alive their unbeaten streak in the Southern Conference.

Their momentum carried right through January into a February 7, 1959, home game against Holy Cross, the first college game in the state of West Virginia to be nationally televised. Such telecasts are a routine feature of the modern game, but in the 1950s, TV exposure—national or even regional—was extremely rare. Sensing the mood and the pressure building on West and on his team, Schaus sought to keep things light heading into the game. "He reminded us not to be scratching and picking and digging at ourselves during the game, because we were going to be on national television," Patrone remembered with a laugh.

The humor was to no avail, however, as West slipped deeper into a funk as the Holy Cross game approached. Schaus called West into his office and tried to address his problem. West told him he was brooding over the losses to Kentucky and Northwestern. Schaus was flabbergasted. Those games had happened nearly two months earlier. His team had won ten straight games since then. He told West it was important to care about winning, but that he was taking things to an extreme. Afterward, Schaus wasn't sure that the meeting had helped to keep West from dwelling on mistakes made weeks earlier. It was enough to make the coach think something else must be the problem.

"I was really concerned," Schaus later recalled. "He'd been moping around for I don't know how long, and we had a game with Holy Cross coming up that was going to be on national television. Two days before the game, I had George King take him to lunch, but George couldn't find out a thing. When the game started, we controlled the tip and quickly got the ball downcourt to Jerry for an easy layup. He missed it. I almost died. Right there on the bench, I almost died. I thought we were finished for sure. But then, hardly before you knew it, he straightened himself out. I don't remember how many points he scored, but it was plenty and we won."

Unfortunately, a basketball schedule is always ripe with opportunity for more unhappiness. The next game brought them back to Madison Square Garden. West had started to think of the building as a place where he didn't play well. Sure enough, they lost to Satch Sanders and New York University in overtime, 72–70.

Whatever West's problems, the Mountaineers closed out the season with four straight wins and headed to the thirty-ninth annual Southern Conference tournament in Richmond. They had dominated the field for four straight years, but the level of play was improving. And West Virginia's success had brought the event more fan interest and more media coverage. Reporters soon discovered Cecile West staying at the Hotel John Marshall in downtown Richmond, where the team also was staying. "Mr. West would be here too," she told a reporter from the *Richmond Times-Dispatch*. "But work hasn't been too good, and he couldn't afford to take off."

Howard West's work schedule was at the mercy of the wildcat strikes at the coal mine, but Eddie Barrett recalled that West's father and brother Charles often made appearances at home games. "I never saw Jerry with either of them," Barrett said, adding that West always seemed to have the attitude that his father and brother were hitching a ride on his fame. Barrett said he never saw that in the father or the sibling. They attended games but pretty much kept out of the way and never made demands or requests of the athletic program.

"Jerry's father, I never saw him in anything but a suit," recalled Barrett. "He had savoir faire, always smiling. Jerry had a chip on his shoulder about a lot of things."

Years later Charles West would bristle at the suggestion that he and his father were being anything more than supportive relatives. It was nearly impossible for the entire family not to be enthused by Jerry's success, he said, but no one ever attempted to capitalize on it in any way.

"That simply wasn't the case," Charles West said.

Reporters asked Jerry if his mother's presence would make him even more nervous than usual. "Nothing makes me nervous once a game gets underway," he replied. "But if I know where my mother is sitting, I can usually spot her." With all six thousand seats sold out for the tourney, West had no idea where his mother was during the event, and Cecile West made sure not to trouble her son during the weekend.

West Virginia stormed past Davidson in the opening game, but William & Mary proved to be much more of a challenge in the second round. West fouled out in the second half and watched as Patrone came off the bench to lead a come-from-behind win, 85–82. Over three tourney games, Patrone would score 54 points in fifty-six minutes of playing time and become the first sophomore sub in many years to make the all-tournament first team. After the William & Mary game, reporters wanted to know why Patrone hadn't seen more action in earlier games. Schaus seemed to struggle a bit for an answer before saying, "He hadn't been playing much in practice."

"That's when I took over," Patrone said of the conference tournament. "Jerry looked at me in the locker room afterward and said, 'You're the best damn shooter I've ever seen.'"

The moment, however, marked the first sign of a conflict that would resurface again the following season. As both Patrone and Barrett explained, the team was divided into cliques, with Patrone and players from the northern part of the state forming one group, while West, Akers, and players from the southern part of the state formed another. "Him and Akers were thick as thieves," Patrone said of West. "Everywhere you'd see one, you'd see the other."

"I don't think Jerry liked Lee," Barrett recalled. "Jerry was all for the team. Lee was much more about himself."

"Jerry was used to getting all the glory," Patrone said.

Patrone denied any selfishness or hard feelings on his part, but he acknowledged a division of sorts hung over the team. Internal competition has long been a fairly common feature of talented basketball teams, and sometimes the competition within a team can be greater than the competition against other teams. West had come to be worshiped by the press and by the public at large, and some players had more difficulty than others dealing with that, Barrett pointed out.

Fortunately, guard Bucky Bolyard had the ability to lighten the mood of his teammates, including West. Charles West recalled that Bolyard loved to needle Jerry about all the praise heaped on him by *Morgantown Dominion Post* columnist Mickey Furfari. Schaus loved Bolyard. The one-eyed guard not only kept the team loose, he helped keep West from getting too uptight, Barrett remembered. "Fred said you had to have a guy like Bucky around a team," Barrett said.

He was valuable for other reasons as well. "Bolyard was so quick, nobody could guard him," Patrone remembered.

"Some teams tried to work the fact that he just had one eye," Barrett said, "but they never seemed to get anywhere with it. Bolyard was a great athlete. He trained on candy bars and pop. They were worried about it and had him tested for diabetes and all that, but it didn't faze him."

The Mountaineers faced the Citadel for the championship that Saturday night, February 28. The Citadel had bused two hundred cadets north from Charleston, South Carolina, for the championship. To counter their noise, a West Virginia supporter had gone to a hardware store in Richmond and purchased dozens of cowbells to pass out to fans in the Mountaineer cheering section, which turned the championship into one hot, noisy contest. The Citadel generally got most of its scoring from hulking Art Musselman, but West took on the chore of defending him and held him to 3 of 14 shooting. Frustrated, Musselman knocked West to the floor and opened a gash in his head that would require stitches. West came back in the game to finish with 27 points, 19 rebounds, and 6 assists, as West Virginia claimed its fifth straight Southern Conference title, 85–66, and yet another automatic bid to the NCAA tournament.

One of the first things that Schaus did after claiming the trophy and the NCAA bid was to guarantee that this time around his team was going to win a game in the big tournament, "regardless of our opponent." A string of teams from the Northeast—Lasalle, Dartmouth,

Canisius, and Manhattan—had each whipped West Virginia in the first round for four straight years. Given the previous season's over-confidence, the guarantee by Schaus seemed rash. However, it was an age where coaches routinely predicted the outcomes of their games before they were played.

West was dressing for practice the week of the first-round game, when Mickey Furfari came into the locker room with the news that he had been named first-team all-American by the Associated Press. "It's the greatest honor I've ever had," West said, adding that he was surprised and had thought he might be a second-team selection. Over the days and weeks ahead, consensus honors from every news organ-ization and magazine would roll in. Oscar Robertson, with a scoring average of 34 points per game, claimed all the player of the year hon-ors, but West wasn't that far behind in the voting. Robertson had topped the AP team with 1,288 votes, while West polled 1,029.

Led by the bony West with his flattop haircut and his fashionably skinny ties, the Mountaineers repaired to the Hotel Manhattan on Eighth Avenue to stay for yet another date in Madison Square Gar-den. The event's game program featured West's smiling face, just as it had for the February Garden game against NYU. Dartmouth was led by the roughhousing forward Rudy LaRusso, who would later be West's longtime teammate with the Lakers. Schaus got those old feel-ings of dread when West injured his leg just above the knee in the early going, but he stayed in the game and posted 25 points and 15 re-bounds and delighted the crowd of 14,526. This time West Virginia handled the first-round challenge easily with an 82–68 win. Back home, the West Virginia newspapers proclaimed the victory with huge headlines.

The second-round regional finals were again in Charlotte, North Carolina, where the University of North Carolina looked to be the fa-vorite in the field. West Virginia faced Saint Joseph's University out of Philadelphia, a team with a 22–3 record, St. Joe's had an erudite young coach named Jack Ramsay who would become a Hall of Famer, highly successful at both the college and pro levels, and after that would spend years providing media commentary. He was armed with a PhD in education and his pregame analysis of his opponent presaged his future as a broadcaster. His opinion was widely sought because his team had played Robertson and Cincinnati during the regular season.

"West is the best all-around player in the country today," Ramsay told reporters, establishing an opinion that would be repeated many times over the coming weeks. "I have a lot of respect for Oscar. He got forty-three against us. But West'll get thirty-three and hold his man to two. He never neglects defense. He's the biggest six-three in perform-ance you'll ever see. He goes above the rim and sweeps the ball with one hand."

It was the dawn of modern basketball, with coaches, fans, and play-ers themselves beginning to see that African-American athletes were bringing overwhelming amounts of talent to the game. Not even two decades earlier, John McLendon, the first black coach to be voted into the Hall of Fame, was building tremendous teams at North Car-olina College for Negroes, later to become North Carolina Central. McLendon had studied at the University of Kansas under Dr. James Naismith, the inventor of basketball. McLendon then went on to the University of Iowa to earn a Master's degree. He recalled that his great challenge as a college coach in that heavily segregated era was to convince his own players that, contrary to popular belief, they were not inferior athletes. The silliness of such racist thinking would be-come apparent over the ensuing years as Bill Russell, Elgin Baylor, and a host of other players established the idea that African-American athletes might have a legitimate claim of ownership of the sport. Eddie Barrett pointed out that by 1959 West was already bur-dened with the perception that he was the "great white hope."

Like many others of that era, West was immensely curious about race, just as he was curious about the outcome of his competition with Robertson. But he clearly established his thoughts on the issue when Villanova University's George Raveling became one of the first African-Americans to compete at the field house in Morgantown. By West's junior year, he had become quite the adored figure. Before each home game, a long carpet was unrolled onto the court, so that West and his teammates could charge onto the floor like royalty. When they announced West in Morgantown "they might as well have said, 'Jesus Christ, number forty-four, from heaven,'" Rod Thorn joked. The atmosphere, then, was understandably tense when Ravel-ing leveled West with a hard foul. Years later, Raveling would recall the sudden quiet that descended on the arena as West lay on the floor. After some very long moments, West rose and went immediately to Raveling and shook hands and embraced him, a move that defused the anger in the building. It was a gesture that rang loudly across college basketball in that era before the civil rights movement had gained traction.

For his part, Jack Ramsay had also established his progressive mind-set. His comparison of Robertson and West was based on clear-eyed observation. Robertson had displayed great offensive abilities, and as a pro he would establish his defensive prowess. But there were times in college where his defensive play simply lacked enthusiasm. Unfortunately, he played in an era where African-Americans not only had to be exceptional in their play, they had to be far superior to whites merely to overcome long-ingrained perceptions and racial attitudes. This perhaps explains why West, Robertson, and the rest of the country wanted so badly to see the two great players meet on the court. That was the only place to find out how West and Robertson measured up.

But the odds were long against that for the Mountaineers, ranked tenth in the AP poll. Tex Winter's Kansas State team, with its triangle offense and a 25–1 record, was number one in both polls. Kentucky, the defending champ, looked strong at number two, as did Michigan State University, which was ranked in the top five along with Robertson and Cincinnati. But unranked Louisville, with a big frontline and a mediocre record, took out first Kentucky and then Michigan State in the Mideast Regional. That would get the West Virginia coaches talking with reporters about their chance to "win it all."

To do that, West would have to find a way to get his team past Saint Joe's, a deceptively good but undersized club that was riding a twelve-game winning streak. Of West Virginia's poor tourney showing in previous years, Ramsay observed, "In the past, when they had Hot Rod Hundley, they were always looking past the early rounds and got knocked off." Ramsay said that wouldn't happen this time around with his club, but, sure enough, Saint Joe's quickness and aggressiveness wrapped up the Mountaineers right from the opening tip, and with thirteen minutes left in the game, Saint Joseph's led, 67–49.

"We were beating them decisively throughout the game," Ramsay recalled five decades later.

The coach had turned the chore of defending West over to one of Philly's forgotten but all-time great players, Joe Spratt.

"Joe Spratt was a great defender. He was very quick; he had great hands and feet," Ramsay recalled. "He was about Jerry's size and had the quickness to match it. Joe was special. But Joe Sprat fouled out. When that happened, Jerry West just took over the game."

West scored 21 points in nine minutes. He recalled that the key factor was Schaus's moving him into the post, where he began scoring in bunches. Ramsay, though, remembered the game turning on Schaus's working the officials.

"I knew Fred," Ramsay said. "I liked Fred. He was a whiner, always berating the officials. At that game, he was constantly after the officials to call fouls on my guy, Joe Spratt, and finally they did and got him out of the game. Fred knew the game and coached Jerry very well."

The officials called 32 fouls against Saint Joe's, but Ramsay's team also turned the ball over repeatedly and fouled after the turnovers, according to press accounts of the game.

"I scored fourteen points in less than four minutes," West recalled. "I kept getting the ball and putting it up, and it kept going in."

"Once Joe Spratt went out, Jerry became possessed," Ramsay said. "I remember on one occasion he shot a jump shot from the left side of the floor that missed. He rebounded it on the right side and scored it. I don't know how you do that. Jerry was the first player I ever saw that would trail his man, and when the player went up to shoot the jump shot, he'd take the ball off his hand from behind. He did it repeatedly in the NBA. I've seen guys go through the shooting motion and find they didn't have the ball, and Jerry's going the other way with it and this guy's finishing his shot without a ball in his hand."

WVU supersub Ronnie Retton, all of five foot seven, Bolyard, and Patrone all played key roles in the comeback. "Bolyard and Ronnie Retton used to come off the bench and bring the house down with their defensive pressure," Patrone recalled.

Akers hit late free throws to cut the lead to 1, and West scored off a steal but missed a free throw. Saint Joe's had the ball down by 1 at the end, but Retton stole the ball on the inbounds to save the win.

West was fouled flagrantly at the end and made both free throws to finish with 36 points in carrying the Mountaineers to a 95–92 miracle win. Akers and Patrone scored 13 each. Hundreds of West Virginia fans, who had driven through a snowstorm down to Charlotte, celebrated wildly.

In the other semifinal game, Boston University, which had upset Navy in the first round, pulled off yet another stunner and beat North

Carolina. Reaching once more into their bag of dreams, the Mountaineers stretched past BU in the East finals, 86–82, to earn their first trip to the Final Four—except that the event wasn't called that then; it was known only as the NCAA championship. West scored 33 with 17 rebounds. North Carolina coach Frank McGuire later confided to a friend that he had stopped watching play just to focus on West.

Clemson University coach Press Maravich was likewise impressed. "Jerry West's all-around play makes him the game's outstanding player," Maravich wrote in a guest column for the Charlotte newspaper. "His rebounding, his ball-hawking, flashy shooting, and stellar defensive play make him basketball's great attraction."

All the praise didn't help boost confidence in the Mountaineers. Bookmakers installed the unranked University of Louisville Cardinals, who would be playing in their home city, as four-point favorites in the national semifinals.

Back in Morgantown, a crowd of five thousand greeted the team at the airport. The university band played "Hail, West Virginia," and the entire state seemed pumped with the same kind of pride that Howard West felt for his youngest boy. In fact, fans and coaches across the country raised their eyebrows. Oscar Robertson and his Bearcats had upset Tex Winter's top-ranked Kansas State team featuring Bob Boozer in the Midwest region. It looked like that showdown between West and Robertson just might happen after all.

FREEDOM HALL

If only the Louisville Cardinals hadn't upset their way to the Final Four, the facilities manager for the city's exposition hall might have kept his job. He was in charge of tickets for Freedom Hall, and suddenly there was lots of pressure. It was the twentieth anniversary of the NCAA championship tournament put on each year by the National Association of Basketball Coaches. With college basketball becoming more popular in the 1950s—better than fifteen million people had paid to see college games in 1958–59 alone—tickets to the 1959 Final Four were very tight. The top priority had always been the nation's basketball coaches, because in those days before videotape and televised games, scouting was minimal, and the trip to the championship afforded coaches the opportunity to watch the games and study first-hand the most innovative things happening in the sport.

The prized tickets were supposed to be reserved for the members of the NABC. Instead the facilities manager had succumbed to pressure and sold the tickets to local brokers and scalpers. The four finalists—West Virginia, California, Cincinnati, and Louisville—were told they would be allotted only 250 tickets each, news that infuriated fans at the three eastern schools. It wasn't long before hundreds of NABC coaches realized that their tickets had been sold too. The facilities manager would be fired over the outrage, and the coaches association would be profoundly embarrassed. Local officials tried to recover some of the wayward tickets but had little luck. When Freedom Hall's managers tried to tell the coaches, "Sorry, but we don't have any tickets for you this year," the NABC threatened to cancel the entire championship weekend. The compromise was to seat the coaches in the aisles of the 19,000-seat Freedom Hall. It's a good thing the basketball was great. Otherwise, it would have been a thoroughly miserable March weekend.

The ticket situation got out of hand in Morgantown as well, Eddie Barrett recalled with a laugh. "Our athletic ticket manager, who was kind of a notorious guy with money, went on television during the East Regional finals and said, 'I will have two hundred fifty tickets at my house Sunday at six p.m.' This guy wanted to make sure he sold them all. That night the cars were backed up on the street outside his house, and he had to escape the crowd out the back door."

University of California coach Pete Newell was hardly concerned about tickets with his team coming all the way from the West Coast. He did want to make sure that the school's pep band—known as the Straw Hat Band—had a place in the building. Those darn kids had followed his club all year long. It didn't matter if the Cal Bears were playing in Idaho, members of the pep band would jump in their cars and show up to raise a ruckus, so Newell made sure there was room for the band in Louisville. Beyond that, he even made arrangements for the pep band to eat the pregame meal with his players. In a way, the bright and personable Newell foreshadowed the age of Phil Jackson. He was a coach who not only studied Xs and Os, he took great care of all the little details around the game and was keenly aware of the psychology of his players.

A reporter had asked Kansas State coach Tex Winter who he thought would take home the trophy that weekend. Winter replied that California would win the title because its defense was so good. Newell had armed his Bears with a clawing, pressing defense that was ranked tops in the nation, holding opponents to just 51 points per game. Cal was unranked in the AP poll, put together by the media, but in the United Press poll, which reflected voting by the coaches, his Bears were ranked tenth. They faced Robertson and the Bearcats in the other semifinal.

"We were totally the dark horse," recalled Darrall Imhoff, a junior center on the '59 California team and the only player from the club who would go on to play in the NBA. "They figured West Coast basketball was out where the stagecoaches were."

"It was comical," Jack Grout, a reserve Cal forward, said later. "They didn't give us any chance. We weren't supposed to be there."

Asked about Robertson and West, Imhoff recalled, "It was like looking down two barrels of a shotgun. We had Oscar one night, Jerry the next."

Actually, Newell's players had no real idea who West was at the time. The Bears got their first look at the skinny forward while watching West Virginia during a Thursday practice at Freedom Hall. Unlike the modern Final Four, a weeklong media event with games played on Saturday and Monday night, the championship then was crammed into a quick weekend with games Friday and Saturday. West Virginia had flown in that Wednesday morning, March 19, and had gone immediately to the arena from the airport for practice. The Cal players sat and watched, trying to size up the Mountaineers.

"We couldn't help but notice this one guy who never missed," Grout recalled. "He shot and shot and shot, all the way around the perimeter. He was the real deal. But we weren't intimidated."

Even Newell himself had little idea of what to expect from the Mountaineers. The first time he would see West play was that next night in the semifinals against Louisville, Newell recalled some years later. "We didn't have TV like now, when you can see every team in the country four or five times just by flipping a few dials."

The fans from the schools were stuck high in the rafters in the four corners of the arena for the semifinals, but the West Virginia contingency managed to hold its own in a building dominated by the Louisville crowd. Many Mountaineers fans had begrudgingly ponied up the outrageous $50 scalpers wanted for a ticket to the semifinals and championship game.

Led by six-foot-eleven Fred Sawyer, the Cardinals were the tallest team at the Final Four, and the Mountaineers were the shortest. That seemed to define the contest in the early going. Battling on the boards, West collected his third foul with eight minutes left in the first half and West Virginia leading, 28–27. Schaus faced a choice. Figuring that West was smart enough not to foul again, he decided to leave his star in the game. By the half, West had 27 points, and West Virginia had stretched out a lead. After the break, the Mountaineers' quickness dominated the affair. The shorter boys from West Virginia outrebounded the Cardinals 49–37 and held them to 33 percent shooting from the floor. West left the floor to a thunderous ovation with fifty-nine seconds remaining. He finished with 15 boards to go with his 38 points as West Virginia advanced easily, 94–79.

From there, West figured he only had to wait for Robertson to close his half of the bargain. He didn't realize then, of course, just how fine a coach Newell was.

"That great matchup never materialized," Lee Patrone said.

Instead fans and coaches alike were left to wonder just how hard West and Robertson would have battled each other for supremacy. "It probably wouldn't have been much of a showdown," West said later. "He was so much more accomplished than I was." Still, West added, he would have liked the opportunity to meet Robertson on the floor, and he was pretty sure the fans would have liked it too.

Asked in 1987 to compare Robertson and West as college players, Newell said he'd have to give the edge to Robertson. "I think Oscar was probably tougher," he said. "What a lot of people don't know is that they were considered our two best forwards in college ball. They both played forward. Oscar handled the ball more. Oscar played forward more like Larry Bird played forward, you know, where he had to have the ball. He was such a great passer . . . you wanted the ball in his hands. Jerry was more strictly a forward. He was so tough when he got the ball. It was a little easier to play Jerry because he was generally down near the forward spot. Oscar didn't bring the ball up the floor, but he would go and get it. Then they'd clear out for him, and he'd just take it on his own. There was no way you could stop Oscar in a one-on-one from penetrating and getting his shot. Jerry, later, when he became a guard and he learned the guard play, he really improved his game. Then he was like Oscar. When he played out on the court like a guard, you couldn't stop him in a one-on-one. You couldn't stop either one of them. Because Oscar was going out and getting the ball in college, he was a little harder to defend."

To counter Robertson in the 1959 semifinals, Newell played a mind game worthy of Phil Jackson. "I had a player by the name of Rob Dalton," Newell remembered. "He was about six-foot-three, and he looked like the results of an X-ray. On the third day, you could see through him, but he was really a competitive kid."

Newell said he went over defensive assignments just before the big semifinal against Robertson and Cincinnati. "The last player assigned was Oscar," the coach said. "Well, Oscar was *the* player in college basketball. He was in every magazine that had anything to do with sports. He set all kinds of records and was truly one of our all-time great players. So when we got finished—I called this Dalton kid 'Thunderbird' because he was the only kid I knew rich enough to own a Thunderbird—so I said, 'Thunderbird, I'm going to give you Oscar.' And I can see him tense up. He's all ready for this. It's what he wanted. So we get out before the game, and you know how players shake hands? Well, Bobby walks up to Oscar before the game and puts his hand out and says, 'My name is Dalton. What's yours?'"

Robertson sort of stared at Dalton in disbelief.

"A year later," Newell recalled with a chuckle, "when we're in Rome for the Olympics, Oscar says to me, 'You know that guy you had guarding me there in Louisville? He knew what my name was, didn't he?'"

Dalton, with help from Grout, limited Robertson to 19 points, and the Bears upset Cincinnati, 64–58. A 6-point favorite, Robertson and his teammates had led 33–29 at halftime. But the Bears stayed true to Newell's defensive principles. They shut down Cincinnati's famed fast break by pressuring the defensive rebounder and not letting him make a quick outlet pass. "We made Oscar work like dickens for the ball," the coach recalled.

Cal's upset of Cincinnati proved to be one of college basketball's all-time biggest surprises. "It was because Pete was such a great coach," Cal guard Denny Fitzpatrick said years later. "It wasn't because we were such great players."

Newell himself seemed to think the difference was the music. "The only thing we had going for us," he said in 1987, "was the Straw Hat

Band. They were worth their weight in gold because they proceeded to start off the festivities by playing 'My Old Kentucky Home,' and all the Kentucky people adopted us. They became our rooters, and so even though we didn't have any California people there, we had a lot of Kentucky rooters and a lot of Kentucky support."

They would need that support in their showdown with West Virginia for the championship.

Newspapers called the championship match-up "racehorse West Virginia versus plow horse California." Indeed, the Mountaineers had the second most productive offense in the country, at 84 points per game, and the Bears plodded along to the tune of Newell's defense. But the contest had other cultural significance. "That was the last all-white Final Four," Eddie Barrett pointed out. "With West Virginia and California, all ten starters were white. California had one black player who came off the bench." Louisville, perched atop Dixie, also featured an all-white roster.

Looking back on it, West thought his team got off to a bad start, although West Virginia opened up a 23–13 lead. The game presented a battle for tempo from the very beginning, and the six-foot-ten Imhoff lorded over the game. He would later be West's Lakers teammate and a mediocre pro, but his size allowed him to dominate inside in the championship game. The Mountaineers had only the undersized tandem of Clousson and Ritchie as an answer.

"We were getting unbelievably easy shots," Newell recalled of the early going. "The shots were so easy that we were losing the tempo of the game. We were making one pass and getting practically a layup or getting an open shot eight feet from the basket."

Newell substituted, looking for better ball movement, and he got it. Suddenly Cal surged on three straight West Virginia turnovers that fed a 16–3 run by the Bears.

"We had to have the tempo," Newell explained. "They were a fast-breaking team and they could really run. But we were going up and shooting so fast that we got a pace that we weren't comfortable with. But we were kind of trapped into it. So I wanted to reverse the ball . . . We ended up going down the floor about five straight times and scoring and got control of the game. We ended up at the half in very good shape."

West had 15 points at the half, but Cal was up 57–44. A 13-point lead usually meant game over for Newell's patient teams.

"We were really good at holding leads," he said, "but I'll tell you what happened. They played a really good side-court trap press. It was something that we had not seen. I'd heard about it, but in those days, you really didn't have a chance to practice for it . . . We'd played side traps before, but I'd have to say not as special as this one."

West got his fourth foul with 15:38 still to play in the second half and had to sit for about three minutes. He was the key to West Virginia's zone press, so Schaus was forced into a race with the clock. He went back to West, who had decided he had no choice but to keep gambling. The fifth foul never came, yet West Virginia's press suddenly became very effective.

"They got back in the game," Newell recalled. "Jerry was such an electric player. He made two or three hoops in a row. The next thing I know, that thirteen-point lead is down to about five. But we never lost the lead. People seem to remember that we slowly lost it, but we didn't. We lost the lead in a fairly short time."

The noise in Freedom Hall was deafening. Cal's ball handling had broken down as West Virginia extended the press, which allowed West to feast. At one point, Imhoff was called for goaltending on a Bolyard shot. "Too bad, big boy," West told him. "That was as clean a block as I've ever seen."

With 5:40 left, West Virginia had cut the lead to 4, 65–61. At 3:35, West was fouled and made one of two free throws to narrow the lead to 3.

With 46 seconds left, West tied up Imhoff for a jump ball, but California controlled the tip. The key sequence came seconds later on a put-back by Imhoff. "Imhoff made that hoop with about twenty seconds left," Newell said. "He ended up right under the basket by himself. He missed the shot, but he found it and put it back in."

It was the bucket that Cal needed to survive West Virginia's rally, 71–70. "We're champions, but we had to stagger home to win," Newell said afterward.

Time and again over the years, West would recall the Imhoff put-back and become quite angry. The big left-hander had knocked the ball in with his right hand. The winning basket seemed almost accidental, freakish. For years, West would be troubled by the idea of the left-hander scoring with his right hand. It just wasn't natural, didn't make sense. He wanted a perfect game. This had nothing to do with perfect. This was dumb luck.

West thought he had one final shot.

"I had my hands on the ball about midcourt with no time left on the clock," West remembered years later, "and I said, 'If I could have just gotten one more shot . . . ' But it wasn't to be. Those are the things, frankly, that stay with you more than the wins. Those are the things that really are wearing. My basketball career has sort of been on the tragic side of everything. It hasn't been on the positive side. It was so close, yet so far away."

West had scored 28 points and pulled in 11 rebounds against the Bears. He had tied the NCAA five game tournament record with 160 points. He received forty-five votes in being named the tournament's Most Outstanding Player. The next closest vote getter was Imhoff with seven. Oscar Robertson was named on just three ballots.

"Maybe we got outcoached," Barrett said. "I don't know. Clousson was barely six-six, and we didn't have a good defensive player except West."

"We keyed our entire defense to Jerry," Newell said much later. "That first time we played him, we didn't know as much about him. We knew he was great. He had an MVP performance, which kept them in the game."

"John Wooden," then in his eleventh year as coach of UCLA, "went back to Los Angeles after the tournament," Eddie Barrett said, "and told the publicity man Dick Kelley that every coach in the arena would have picked West over Robertson."

West Virginia had scored 428 points in five games, more than any team had ever scored in NCAA tourney play. The team returned to Morgantown to find a massive crowd waiting at the airport. The university band again struck up "Hail, West Virginia."

Schaus spoke, saying that he was sure the Mountaineers could have won with just a few more seconds. Then West, who had made 52 percent of his shots that season, addressed the crowd and talked of his teammates, "great guys who gave us much to cherish this year."

That was patently untruthful, of course. There was nothing he could cherish about such a loss. The experience would hang there as he made his way through the personal hall of basketball horrors that lay ahead. As he explained, his career would always seem to cant toward "the tragic side," one disappointment after another festering in his mind. Yet he would choose to serve time with these memories, fully aware that it was no way to live a life.

I've always felt I've been different. I've probably been too competitive in my life for my own good.

—Jerry West

THE HOPEFUL

Morgantown, 1959 to 1960

AT THE 1959 FINAL FOUR IN LOUISVILLE, A REPORTER HAD ASKED Oscar Robertson about West. "He's tough, man," Robertson replied carefully, wary of a question that seemed loaded with racial implications. "Everybody knows that."

The reporter then asked if West was the second best player in college basketball.

"He might be the first, baby," Robertson said.

Having eyed each other from afar, West and Robertson became acquainted that spring of 1959 after the championship. In late March was the East-West Shrine All-Star Game, with Kentucky's Adolph Rupp coaching an East team that included both players. At first it was announced that West and Robertson would both start, but then Rupp, without explanation, moved West to the bench and in his place started WVU teammate Bobby Joe Smith. West scored 8 points in the game.

Next up in April were the tryouts for the U.S. team in the Pan American Games. Red Brown was on the U.S. Olympic Committee

and helped make arrangements for Schaus to coach the team. The format would be similar to that of the tryouts for the U.S. Olympic team
the following year. A group of college players coached by Schaus
would compete against AAU teams. These AAU teams featured former college players and were sponsored by business and industry. The
winning teams would contribute the majority of players to the national teams. Schaus would have to guide a group of college players
who had not played together against pro-level AAU teams that had
been playing together for an entire season. Besides Robertson and
West, the roster included Michigan State's Johnny Green, a muscular
leaper. Even though they hadn't played together before, that trio
would prove too athletic for the AAU teams to handle.

North Carolina coach Frank McGuire told reporters that West
had "the biggest heart I've seen in twenty-five years of coaching."

Apparently all the praise heaped on West began to have an effect
on Robertson. Schaus told reporters covering the team that Oscar
was showing much more interest in playing defense than he had at the
NCAA championships. Schaus moved both West and Robertson to
guard, which made defending them difficult for the AAU teams, just
as Pete Newell had predicted it would.

"Fred was always conscious that Jerry was going to play in the
pros," Eddie Barrett said. "Fred told him he was going to be all-
American. Secondly, he told him that in the pros he would be a guard
but that West Virginia needed him under the basket or closer to the
basket. So Jerry understood that. Then the Pan American Games
came along at the end of his junior year, and he and Robertson both
played in the backcourt for the first time."

Freed from their chores at forward, both players responded.
Robertson had 23 points and West 22 as the college team upset the
premier AAU team of the era, the Phillips Oilers, from Oklahoma.
West had blocked a shot, retrieved the ball, and scored to break an
81–81 tie and clinch the hotly contested game. Playing together, the
two rivals made for a formidable backcourt. Robertson has said many
times since that he liked and respected West immediately upon meeting him. They were both silent types, but Robertson said, "West was
even quieter than I was."

WVU's veteran trainer, Whitey Gwynne, was serving the college
team and, like everyone else, was curious as to how the two would
mesh. He watched them closely, then told a reporter, "Jerry and Oscar

got along famously together. Each showed a great respect for the ability of the other."

"Just to be on the same court with Oscar was important to Jerry," Eddie Barrett said. "He wanted to show he was the better player . . . He wanted to be the best six-foot-three player that ever played."

West would say repeatedly over the years that Robertson was the better player. Barrett disagreed. "That was only on offense, and that's because Robertson had the ball," the publicist argued. "Sure, Robertson had the talent; he didn't have Jerry's heart. I hate to say that. Robertson hogged the ball. On the court, Jerry was clearly better."

Both players looked forward to the international competition, although the games would be held in Chicago. They breezed past Mexico, Cuba, Canada, Puerto Rico, and El Salvador, but the Brazil team was big and strong enough to control the boards and the tempo. The Americans escaped, 45–43, and it would prove to be their only real test in international competition, including the 1960 Olympics the following summer.

THE SENIOR

West returned for his senior season as a consensus all-American. It seemed hardly possible, but his team got even shorter. Schaus moved six-four Willie Akers into the post and Jim Ritchie in as a forward. West stayed at the other frontcourt slot and helped make up for any rebounding difficulties by averaging 16.5 boards a game. He pulled down 31 in February against George Washington University to tie the WVU single-game record. His scoring continued to rank among the best in the country, at better than 28 points a game, and he again made better than 50 percent of his shots from the field. Jim Warren and Lee Patrone were the guards. Together they all shot better than 46 percent from the field and averaged just under 90 points a game.

West Virginia opened the 1959–60 season with ten straight wins, and with that momentum came a season-long stream of praise in the press for West, from opposing coaches and players. The Mountaineers were again ranked among the top teams in the country and played a schedule that reflected that status. The week before Christmas they returned once again to Adolph Rupp's Kentucky Invitational Tournament in Lexington, where they had to battle to get past a good Saint Louis University team, 87–86. Billikens coach John Bennington liked to keep his team in a stifling man-to-man, but he had to shift to a zone in the second half because he couldn't find a way to contain West. "He ruined us to the bitter end with his brilliant passing," Bennington said. In those days, the teams were seated along the end lines behind each basket. West could dunk easily, but dunking had yet to become a part of the game. It was still perceived as showboating. However, West had his momentum in that first game in Lexington and took the ball to the rack.

"He was following the break, and he stuffed the ball," Eddie Barrett recalled, "and he said, 'Boy, that's the best damn feeling I've ever had, stuffing the ball in front of Saint Louis's bench!' "

Rupp's club upset a top-notch North Carolina team in the other bracket, and suddenly the Saturday championship featured a rowdy, rollicking crowd cheering on the Wildcats. Rupp's teams always posed a physical challenge, and this time that challenge was even rougher than usual. West's nose was shattered by an errant elbow in the early going. Blood flew everywhere.

"Kentucky broke Jerry's nose three times, and they stopped the game to pack up the nose," Barrett said. "He kept playing."

Ron Green, sitting courtside for the *Charlotte News,* described the scene: "West, wiping blood from his face, took rebounds off the boards in bunches, fired baskets from every angle, and put up a steel defense, although he had three fouls riding him."

Most angry players execute poorly, but West's opponents said he was one of those players you never want to make angry. It only made him play better, with even greater fury. He played very angry that night and finished with 33 points and 18 rebounds as West Virginia won, 79–70, for its second Kentucky Invitational title in three years.

"Rupp said, 'Mr. West, we'll gladly give you an honorary degree just to get you out of our hair,' " Barrett remembered. " 'You are one of the best I've ever seen.' Jerry later said that was the greatest compliment he had ever gotten."

With his face heavily bandaged, West retreated to Chelyan for a few days at Christmas. He was in pain, but all the folks at home treated him like a hero. The pain subsided with some rest before the team loaded up and headed west to play in the Los Angeles Classic at the new Sports Arena. The field featured all the West Coast heavyweights, including Stanford, UCLA, and Cal. In the Stanford game, West rose up above two opponents, took a rebound, whirled in midair, and whipped an outlet pass the full length of the floor to a streaking Patrone. As he threw the ball, he tumbled, but when Patrone missed the layup at the other end, West was somehow there to finish the play. "I've never seen a player with such a continuous effort," said a dazed Howie Dallmar, the Stanford coach, after West Virginia whipped his team handily.

Next up was John Wooden's good UCLA team, against whom West put on another show. "There just aren't any better players than West," Wooden told reporters. "He's one of the greatest of this or any other era."

The two victories put West Virginia in a rematch with Pete Newell and Cal. This time his club was totally prepared for West. They allowed him just five shots, snaring him in a defensive web all night. He scored 8 points, and West Virginia lost by 20.

Denied by Cal's defense, West competed to the end. "Never did he allow himself to lose the wonderful court composure we all admire and start to play for himself," Newell said afterward.

"It was my worst college game," West said.

"We set our whole defense just on him," Newell explained. "That allowed us to do some things, and we beat them pretty good. We were successful against Jerry because we were playing five against one."

West and his teammates left the warmth of the West Coast to head back to the snowy cold of Morgantown. He sensed things weren't right with his team. There were rumblings that Patrone and his friends resented West shooting so much. He was concerned enough to stop by Schaus's office to talk about things. The coach said he didn't think there was a problem. The team was ranked second nationally with a 10–1 record.

"I do recall that there may have been just a little bit of resentment," Patrone recalled. "While we were in California for the holiday tournament, there was a newspaper headline that said, 'West Is Best, But Lee's No Breeze.' Willie Akers picked up the paper and said, 'Jerry, look at this.' He was used to getting all the glory. The next year, after Schaus left and George King took over as our coach, George told me, 'Lee, I don't think you got all of the attention you deserved.'"

"Lee Patrone was from Ohio, and he had a strong sense of self-esteem," Barrett said. "Jerry was courteous, polite to the other teams.

Jerry had his flaws. He knew how good he was, and he wanted to show it. One of the greatest things about him, like Schaus said, was his killer instinct. He always scored lowest against teams like VMI."

These traits made West immensely popular with the fans, Barrett explained. "He looked modest. He didn't swagger. He paid attention to the coach during the time-outs. He was set on winning, and he was all business. He didn't go around bragging about himself. He let basketball do the talking for him."

While all the parties apparently sensed the conflict, it wasn't something that was addressed openly. The Mountaineers moved through six more wins in January and added to their Southern Conference win streak all the while. The schedule also included a rematch with Virginia in the Charleston Civic Center, where West had 40 points and 16 rebounds as West Virginia whipped the Cavaliers, 102–81.

When visiting Villanova and George Raveling came to the field house January 16, 1960, with their Philadelphia media entourage, the writers were awed by the crowd and the thunderous ovation West received. First the WVU cheerleaders unrolled a one-hundred-foot carpet as West emerged, cradling the blue and gold ball and leading his team down the carpet and onto the floor. The PA announcer introduced him first, and the prolonged applause drowned out the names of the other starters. West was furious. "There are four other guys on that starting team," he fussed afterward.

At the end of the month came a road game at William & Mary. Now 16–1 and holding on to the number three spot in the national polls, West Virginia didn't want to play at William & Mary's Blow Gym, so the game was set for the old Norfolk Armory. Mike Strickler, who would later work as a sports publicist for VMI, was in the crowd that night. "There was this guy sitting down on the court who had been ragging West all night long," he remembered. "West was fouled and went to the line to shoot free throws. This guy really got on him. He said, 'West, you're nothing but a damn prima donna!' West was at the line and just paused and looked at him and winked at him and smiled. The guy never said another word the rest of the night."

West scored 40 points—the fourth time in his college career that he'd scored 40 or more—even though he fouled out with more than six minutes left in the game. With West gone, William & Mary was able to get control of the contest and win, 94–86. The loss brought to an end West Virginia's NCAA record of 44 consecutive conference wins, dating from the 1955–56 season. But the Mountaineers followed the loss with three blow-out victories, including a 98–69 win over NYU and Satch Sanders in Morgantown.

"Jerry was Jerry that night," Sanders recalled. "We couldn't stop him."

From there, West Virginia went 2–2 down the stretch, with road losses against St. John's University in Madison Square Garden and against George Washington University.

Once again, the Southern Conference tournament in Richmond became the focal point for the team's internal struggles and drama. West Virginia was 21–4 and ranked seventh in the country, but the late losses had given Southern opponents hope that they could deny the Mountaineers a sixth straight conference title. When they beat Virginia Military by a mere 7 points in the first round, the hopes soared. They blew out William & Mary in the semis but quickly ran into trouble against Virginia Tech in the championship. West Virginia hadn't played the Hokies during the regular season. Tech's star player was Charleston's six-foot-six Chris Smith. West would say many times over the ensuing years that if only Schaus had been able to sign Smith, they just might have been able to win that elusive national title. Smith was an active and athletic frontcourt player, and he was on his way to posting 73 points and 70 rebounds in the three games of the conference tournament. The battle had intensified in the second half of the championship when West fouled out with 14 points and 20 rebounds and 12:31 showing on the game clock. At the time, West Virginia held a 49–48 lead.

In that era, if you lost in the conference championship, there was no at-large bid to the NCAA tournament. West Virginia's season appeared to be in serious trouble. Barrett was sitting beside the West Virginia bench and witnessed a scene that rocked the team.

"Lee Patrone said, 'Now we can go to work, Coach.' Jerry took offense to that. Jerry regarded that as disloyal and not in the best interest of the team."

Patrone, however, was on his way to yet another outstanding tournament. In fact, he would again be named to the all-tournament first team.

The play of Akers, Patrone, and Jim Warren bailed the Mountaineers out just when their season seemed lost. "Schaus picked up this guy off the bench named Jim Warren and shook him by the shoulders," Barrett recalled with a laugh. "He said, 'Son, I want you to play the best goddamn game you've ever played!' Warren hit three shots from about thirty feet, and West Virginia won by ten."

The victory brought the Mountaineers their sixth straight conference championship, but the team had sustained some damage. In the aftermath of the Virginia Tech game, there may have been some negative vibes from other players, Patrone said. "Out of Jerry's mouth, he never said anything to me."

Whether there was a confrontation or not, there was a clear perception that Lee Patrone was the player who had challenged and insulted the great Jerry West. After West left Morgantown, Patrone played another season for West Virginia and earned a third team all-America recognition from the Helms Foundation. Although several lesser players have been voted into the school's athletic Hall of Fame, Patrone has never been selected or even nominated.

"That's the one thing I do resent, not being selected for the Hall of Fame," Patrone said.

"He should be in the Hall of Fame," Barrett agreed. "He was a great player." But Barrett said that Patrone, who was a low-round draft pick of the Detroit Pistons, never returned to the school for reunions and other player gatherings, and apparently had distanced himself from his former teammates. "No one has really stepped forward to nominate him," Barrett explained.

Patrone later earned further distinction by winning a hero's medal from the Carnegie Foundation for going into the Ohio River to rescue a person who had jumped from a bridge near Wheeling. In addition, Patrone spent years as a high school teacher and coach in Ohio.

Was Patrone ostracized because he was the teammate who challenged and insulted Jerry West? That appeared to be the case. Even fifty years later, Patrone seemed to challenge West's status as an icon. "I don't think Jerry was any more dedicated than the rest of us," he said.

As for the Mountaineers in 1960, they again headed to Madison Square Garden for a first-round game in the East Regional, with their ultimate goal being a return to the Final Four to challenge Oscar Robertson and the University of Cincinnati Bearcats. This time the first-round opponent was Ben Carnevale's Navy team. West Virginia won, 94–86, and again headed to the regional finals in Charlotte. Schaus and his team arrived back in Morgantown to find a snowstorm blanketing the East Coast, realized they had to alter travel plans, and, after spending just four hours at home, hopped a train that carried them first to Washington and then on to Charlotte.

There they took on Satch Sanders and NYU, a team they had beaten by 29 points a month earlier in Morgantown. This time the game was extremely tight. In the final seconds of overtime, NYU led, 82–81, and West, who would finish with 33 points and 16 rebounds, had the ball for one last shot. Schaus called for West's teammates to circle him on the floor, so he could get off a shot. He attacked the goal, defended by Sanders.

"The other eight players on the court cleared out, and it was Jerry against Satch," Barrett remembered. "Jerry went to his left—which was his best side, since he had worked it so much—and Satch, of course, was right-handed. So Jerry went to Satch's strength, and Jerry missed the shot."

The next night, West Virginia beat Saint Joe's, 106–100, in what might have seemed a meaningless consolation game. West fought furiously, scored 38 points with 16 rebounds, and afterward wiped away tears as he and Patrone (who had 42 points, 17 rebounds, and 11 assists in the two games) were named to the all-region team with Sanders.

"It was tough, especially in that Jerry wanted to appear in the same league as the Big O," Barrett said. "That was what broke him up about his senior year when we got beat by NYU in the regional. He wanted to go to the Final Four and show he was better."

Robertson and the Bearcats did make that appointment at the NCAA championships, where they were again defeated by Newell's California team, which then got hammered by John Havlicek, Jerry Lucas, and Ohio State in the national championship game.

In his four college seasons, West and his Mountaineers played 93 games and lost just 12 of them. West set a bevy of school records, including prodigious records for most points and rebounds in a career, records that will likely never be broken even though he set them in only three seasons.

The end to West's college career had come abruptly, as it always does for seniors in the NCAA tourney. But it's not surprising that

West had little time to ponder it. At the moment, he had what you might call a preoccupied mind.

THE CHAPEL OF LOVE

Upon returning home, West informed his parents that he was getting married in a matter of weeks. He had dated Martha Jane Kane for better than two years, but he had never introduced her to his family. So it came as quite a shock when Cecile learned that Jerry and the young woman planned to get married in early April, with the ceremony to take place at a small chapel in the Catholic student center on WVU's campus.

There was hardly time to make plans. First West dashed off to Madison Square Garden, where he finally competed on the floor against Robertson in an East-West college all-star game. Robertson scored 20, but West finished with 23 and helped lead his team to victory. However, the outcome hardly allowed anyone to draw any sort of conclusions, especially since Lenny Wilkens of Providence College was named the game's MVP.

From there it was on to Denver for the U.S. Olympic team trials. Pete Newell, who had retired from college coaching following his team's loss to Ohio State, coached the group of college stars who would take on the various AAU teams for the right to represent America in the games in Rome that August and September. West shot the ball terribly in the first game, and his confidence plummeted.

"In the first session of tryouts, Jerry didn't play well," Newell recalled. "Afterward he came to see me and said he didn't think he was playing well enough to help the team. He said, 'Maybe I don't belong here.' I told him, 'Listen, Jerry. If you don't go to Rome, I don't go.' The next day, he had a great practice. He was never a person to seek adulation . . . But he was driven for it, driven for greatness. His drive was greater than his fear of not succeeding. It's just that he's never been one to sing his own praises, to laud himself."

West's nature as an intense perfectionist had already been established. He demanded perfection from himself every night and was inconsolable when he failed to deliver. "As a player, he would get down on himself," Newell said, a phrase often repeated by West's teammates and coaches.

"I was nervous all the time," West explained. "But then again, I was a nervous player. That's where I got my energy from."

"Jerry was never a very secure kind of person," Newell said. "Believe it or not, he has never had great self-esteem. Everybody thinks more of Jerry than he does of himself. That's the West Virginia in him."

Told of Newell's appraisal, Eddie Barrett said, "I think that's an outsider saying that. I think it's more like Jerry expected to make every shot . . . I think Jerry had plenty of sense of self-worth. When Newell said that, I think he was thinking as a Californian."

In the championship game against the AAU national champs, the Peoria Caterpillars, West scored 39 in a big victory that established that the college players would make up the bulk of the U.S. team.

West returned to West Virginia with both his wedding and the NBA draft looming in the coming week. He hoped to go to New York to play for the Knicks. The Cincinnati Royals would pick first, and it was clear they were going to exercise their territorial rights and draft Robertson. Picking second were the Minneapolis Lakers, once the league's dominant team but one that had recently fallen on hard times. Speculation stirred as to whom the Lakers would take. Lakers guard Hot Rod Hundley was in West Virginia for an appearance that week and told a local newspaper, "Jerry's just too good to pass up, no matter how bad we need a big man." An NBA All-Star in 1960, Hundley laughingly acknowledged that West just might be taking his job.

The Lakers had finished 25–50 in 1960. They had acquired six-foot-eleven Ray Felix to help their undersized center, Jim "Boomer" Krebs, in the post, but the combination was barely adequate. "We still needed a center," Jim Pollard, the Lakers coach at the time, acknowledged in a later interview. "But all of our informal scouting reports came back the same. They said Jerry West is the best white player available. I watched him play and said, 'Forget white! Outside of Oscar Robertson, West is the best player, period.'"

As expected, the Royals took Robertson with the first pick. So West fell to the Lakers and began contemplating the idea of spending his winters in Minneapolis and playing guard in the NBA.

"West was lightning quick and he could score," Pollard said, "so we figured he would make the adjustment to pro guard."

The weekend of April 8–10 brought with it an insane schedule. That Friday, East Bank was renamed West Bank for a day. A motorcade came to the house in Chelyan and picked up West and his parents for the ride over to the high school, where West was presented the key to the town by the mayor. Roy Williams and Duke Shaver, his old coaches, were there, beaming. "He's East Bank's first and only all-American, God bless him," Williams told the crowd. That night West played in a tournament in nearby St. Albans and scored 41 points. Then Saturday night, the night before his wedding, he again played in St. Albans and scored another 41 points.

On Sunday morning, Cecile, Howard, and the family rose early, got dressed in their best, packed into Charles's car, and drove to Morgantown for the affair. On the way up, they stopped off in Weston to meet the Kane family in their finely appointed home. While the rest of the family gathered in the living room, Cecile West went into another part of the house to meet the bride.

Cecile admitted to the Charleston paper that "I didn't expect a wedding so soon. But she's a nice girl."

The wedding was held that Sunday, with Willie Akers serving as best man. When Charles West got to the chapel, it became apparent that his wife was wearing the same navy blue suit as the bride. Jane Kane decided to make hurried, last-minute alterations. "She ripped the cuffs out of her outfit," Charles remembered with a chuckle. "She didn't want to be duplicated."

Despite the circumstances, the West family took an immediate liking to Jerry's new bride. Yes, she was from a prosperous family, her parents weren't exactly happy about the circumstances, *and* they were less than taken with the groom. But Jane didn't have a condescending bone in her body. The West family soon began calling her "Janey," and West's siblings would retain an affection for her that lasted over the decades, regardless of what happened between her and Jerry.

As Jerry darted about the country playing basketball and preparing for the Olympics, Jane moved to Chelyan to take up residence in the Wests' humble abode. "My mother liked Janey," Charles West recalled. "She was around my mother on a daily basis for three months. There was a bonding there. That's remarkable in itself, because, as I've said, my mother wasn't the lovey-dovey type. If it was a difficult adjustment for Janey, we never knew it. Janey was always a lady. I never saw her lose her cool. Now, she came from an upper class family, so you might have expected otherwise, until you got to know her. Let's put it this way: She was certainly used to better accommodations."

Jane West spent her days helping out with the family chores, as much as Cecile would let her, and writing letters to her new husband as he flitted first around the country and then around the globe playing basketball for the good old USA.

The time in the West household certainly afforded Jane West the opportunity to watch her new father-in-law in full political mode. In fact, the entire state that spring was abuzz as Senator Hubert Humphrey of Minnesota and John F. Kennedy came down to the wire in the Democratic primary. Senator Kennedy had enjoyed a substantial lead in the campaign until his Catholicism became an issue that spring. Suddenly Humphrey went from far behind to leading in the polls in West Virginia. The state would prove to be critical in deciding the Democratic nomination, so Kennedy began pumping substantial amounts of money into West Virginia, and both campaigns spent considerable time there.

Howard West didn't support Kennedy because he had read about father Joseph Kennedy's checkered past.

"My dad came home one day and said he had his picture taken with Kennedy," Barbara West recalled. "I said, 'Oh, wow, are you going to get a copy?' He said, 'No, I told him I wasn't going to support him, I was going to support Hubert Humphrey.' I said, 'How could you do that?' "

As Charles West remembered, his father always seemed to have a knack for supporting the wrong faction of the party.

Patricia West Noel was at work in the post office when Kennedy came through campaigning. Local school officials had let the children out of school so they could attend the event. Patricia remembered walking across the street to get a better view.

"He was a nice-looking man," she remembered. "He came to Cabin Creek, and there was a lot of resentment. *Catholic* at that time was a dirty word. I can remember him coming down there to this little area. He had a microphone and stood up on top of a car. He knew that a lot of people were against him. He said he'd make the same moves as almost anyone does. He was sort of defending his positions. I don't think Dad voted for him because he had read a whole lot about Joe Kennedy and his maneuvers. Hubert Humphrey come up to the same place later. Another lady and I went out to see him. He shook hands with us. That tickled us to death."

"The secretary of agriculture came through to speak for

Humphrey," Charles West recalled. "He told the crowd that Hubert Humphrey was going to sweep West Virginia the way Jerry West swept the backboards."

Ultimately, West Virginia Democrats supported Kennedy in overwhelming fashion, and Humphrey withdrew from the campaign the very next day. By the time it was over, many people in the state had grown weary of the politicking and alleged vote buying. A letter writer to the Beckley paper expressed a popular sentiment of the day when he stated that the voters should ditch all the politicians and elect Jerry West president. That way, he said, we'd at least have someone who worked hard and told the truth.

In April, the WVU Touchdown Club, an athletic booster group, had a banquet for the team at the Hotel Morgan in Morgantown and brought in Boston Celtics coach Red Auerbach as the speaker. Auerbach praised West, then called Schaus "a bad loser. And I like bad losers. If I lose, I don't talk to anybody." Little could anyone have imagined on that happy night that Schaus would lose so many championship series to Auerbach and that the two men would end up despising each other.

The Lakers, meanwhile, badly wanted to hire Bill Sharman as coach. Auerbach told them he would release Sharman from his contract if they would give him the rights to West. The Lakers scoffed and went looking elsewhere for someone to lead their team.

GOLD

In November 2008, Jerry West set out at age seventy to talk to the important people who influenced his rise in the game. Even though his years in pro basketball had led West to certain beliefs about coaching and talent, few people were higher on West's list than Pete Newell. West made an appointment to visit the ninety-three-year-old Newell, who had long been known as one of the most generous men in the game, always eager to share his time and perspective with other coaches and sportswriters. He had readily agreed to sit down with West to reminisce about their days together on the U.S. Olympic team and the battles between Cal and West Virginia. But on the drive to visit Newell, West had become distracted and missed an exit. He took longer to get there and arrived at Newell's residence ten minutes late,

THE LAKER

Los Angeles 1960–1961

JERRY WEST HAD JUST RETURNED HOME FROM THE ROME OLYMPICS in September 1960 when he got an urgent message from Fred Schaus telling him to get to Los Angeles ASAP. The Lakers had lots of work to do. West barely had time to pack up his cherished Olympic medal and USA uniforms, which he'd left in the safekeeping of his mother. Then he grabbed his young wife — who was now obviously pregnant — and their belongings and said good-bye to his parents in their white frame house in Chelyan.

He and Jane jumped on a plane headed into a bright future, to Hollywood, land of movie stars and such. As they neared the West Coast, flight attendants came through the cabin, passing out pillows and nervously explaining that there was some trouble; that the passengers needed to brace for a crash landing.

The incident proved to be only a scare, but it would portend the turbulence ahead for West. He would later call that first year in Los Angeles the worst of his career, as he adjusted to a world of changes.

He and Jane moved into a small apartment and began sorting out their new lives. A creature of intense habit, West settled into a pattern of life that would define his existence for the next dozen years. And that November, as his tension-filled rookie season took flight, Jane gave birth to a fine baby boy. They named him David. Soon a parade of relatives and in-laws made their way to Los Angeles to inspect the newest West. In what seemed like no time, the young couple would produce two brothers, Michael and Mark, and the household came alive as the chipper Jane West raised her trio of boys while her husband came and went according to the odd cycles of pro basketball.

Game days at home would always be the roughest, as West would be wracked by anticipation, anxiety, sleeplessness, and finicky eating patterns. He would later, tongue in cheek, accuse his wife of understanding that he played his best basketball annoyed, just on the edge of true anger. She could find ways to set him off, such as cooking him hamburger when he wanted steak, he once observed. Jane had quickly learned that any little thing could discombobulate her uptight perfectionist. West himself understood this as well as anyone. He could have attempted to rein in the rough edges to what he readily acknowledged was his uneven personality. But he had come to see that these tendencies toward annoyance and unhappiness were the keys to his highly competitive nature, so instead of trying to quell them, West nurtured them. He wanted to be the way he was. He *had* to be that way. For him, there was no other way to compete, no other way to win, no other way to be Jerry West, this extraordinarily driven person.

In that and many other ways, Jane was the perfect wife for him. She embraced her role as part of this complex, competitive partnership. From his first games as a rookie, she sat in the stands and kept running totals of his stats, going so far as to check in with the scorer's table to make sure her husband got credit for his assists and rebounds. And she did so in the great hope that he would somehow learn to share more of what he was feeling.

"She liked very much being Mrs. Jerry West," his brother Charles observed. Even so, it must have been difficult in those early years, being constantly pregnant in and around Hollywood's overwhelming stock of beautiful people. In West Virginia, she had been the prize, attractive and smart. Hollywood was the kind of place that magnified even the tiniest blemishes, and like anyone, she had some. The cir-

cumstances had played on the insecurities of many a spouse and destroyed more than a few marriages. Jane West, though, was confident
and grounded. She enrolled in classes at UCLA to finish her degree,
even if that sacrifice meant she wasn't the world's greatest home-
maker. She was no petulant young thing. She had pluck, and she had
about her a way that allowed her to quickly adjust to the crazy life of
an NBA star in Los Angeles.

Ah, Los Angeles.

West had traded the wind and cinders of Chelyan, population
about five hundred and dwindling, for the smog of LA, population
about six million and booming. If the smog wasn't too heavy, the days
were so sunny and bright they seemed wrapped in cellophane. At
night, the eerie orange glow of the city left the palm trees that
presided high over the streets to repose in silhouette against the sky-
line.

"I liked Los Angeles," West said in an excellent use of understate-
ment.

The big city, with its laid-back beach culture and well-groomed
golf courses, would offer just enough to distract him a little from his
brooding. But only a little. The rest he wanted to hold on to.

THE GAME

On the court, West faced much uncertainty that rookie season. He
quickly learned that he was stepping into a faster, stronger league that
put unimaginable physical and mental demands on its players in the
days before it became a big-money lifestyle. The hotels were seedy,
the commercial flights cramped, the food mostly bad. Not only was
West in a new game, but he was moving to a new position, from forward to guard, and he already had an idea of what all the changes
would mean for his game.

"Coming into the league, I really had to change positions, even
though I was six-foot-three," he explained. "I played a lot up front,
mostly up front, in college, except defensively out front, pressing and
stuff like that. When they needed it, I'd bring the ball up the floor, but
I really didn't do that a lot. Basically, defensively, the adjustment
wasn't a problem for me. But offensively, instead of starting out nine-

teen or twenty feet offensively and taking one dribble to the hoop or one dribble to get a shot, I had to start out twenty-eight feet, which required a lot more finesse in getting where you wanted to go."

As far as the offensive style of the game, of course, West Virginia had prepared him well, with Schaus running that pro-style offense, a style that very much suited celebrity-crazy Los Angeles. Schaus's Lakers offense would focus on getting the ball to the star players, with everyone else basically getting out of their way. West had enjoyed his share of that in college, and he figured that Schaus would immediately turn him loose in the pro game.

West would have to adjust to a host of new teammates, including the resplendent and mercurial Elgin Baylor, already a dynamic new presence in the league, who had a biting wit and a forceful personality. Then there was the somewhat desperate Hot Rod Hundley, who was on his way to partying himself out of the game. Hundley lived a lavish lifestyle way beyond his $10,000 contract, wore bright colors, prowled the clubs, and practiced pool and table tennis—anything but basketball.

Beyond that, the roster was extremely young, with athletes trying to find a place in a sport that employed just eighty players. Those numbers reflected the difficulties of the team itself. Hanging by a thread financially, the Lakers had moved to a brand-new city, many miles and two time zones removed from the rest of the NBA. It was an eight-team league in 1960 and far from healthy. The Boston Celtics, Syracuse Nationals, Philadelphia Warriors, and New York Knickerbockers made up the Eastern Conference. The Western Conference had the St. Louis Hawks, the Cincinnati Royals, and the Detroit Pistons, with the Lakers now stretching things all the way out to the West Coast. On many nights, it seemed like they might as well have been playing on the Moon. West and his teammates soon realized they were an alien presence in their new city. In time, that new world would prove to be especially fine, but in 1960, pro hoops was a decidedly odd fit for LA.

"When the Lakers first came to Los Angeles from Minneapolis, they were terrible," West would remember. "They didn't have a lot of very good players. But things changed. When they came to Los Angeles, it seemed like the team was invigorated."

First the club would have to survive indifference to feel that way. Basketball was an indoor game, and Los Angeles was an outdoor city.

For years the game had existed merely as a sideshow. John Wooden was putting together good teams at UCLA, but the Bruins played some of their games at Venice High School and others at a little gym on campus. And the hoops program at the University of Southern California fared as well as it could at a football factory. Beyond that, the attraction was a mishmash of AAU and junior college teams, none of which could manage more than an occasional back-page paragraph in the local newspapers.

Yet like everything else on the West Coast, the culture of spectator sports had evolved, beginning with the first Tournament of Roses in 1890. Pasadena's Valley Hunt Club had hatched the idea of the Tournament of Roses to make folks buried in snow back east aware of Southern California's charms. The Hunt Club staged a host of sporting events over the first dozen years: races, jousting, tugs-of-war. Nobody paid much attention until the tournament committee set up a football game in 1902 between Stanford and Michigan. It wasn't the best situation for the region's foray into spectator team sports. New Year's Day 1902 was hot and dusty. The traffic headed toward the Rose Bowl field at Throop Polytechnic Institute (now the California Institute of Technology) was a mix of wagons and coughing automobiles festooned with blue and gold pennants (the official colors of the tournament). Sadly, the park had only one gate, which created first a massive traffic jam, then a depressingly long line into the stadium, and, finally, an angry, frustrated mob of a crowd.

From that uneven beginning, Southern California blossomed into quite a spectator culture, with sporting enthusiasts turning their focus to boxing, horse racing, college football, track and field, and minor-league baseball over the first four decades of the twentieth century. The competition of big-time professional sports didn't reach LA until reigning National Football League champions the Cleveland Rams grew tired of cold weather and sparse crowds and moved there in 1946. There was even a fling with pro baseball in 1946–47 when Maury Winston, who owned the Chicago American Gears, founded his own league and helped launch the Los Angeles Red Devils, a team that featured Jackie Robinson, who was about to make history by integrating baseball in 1947 with the Brooklyn Dodgers. The Red Devils posted a 13–3 record but the league folded within months, and with it went the Red Devils.

Then came the Dodgers from Brooklyn in 1958. When they won

the World Series a year later, LA fans suddenly realized that their town, with its sparkling afternoons and balmy nights, made a perfect stop for the big leagues. Both the Rams and Dodgers regularly drew large, enthusiastic crowds to the Los Angeles Coliseum and then Dodger Stadium.

All of this served to give the Lakers hope. Perhaps the newness itself offered one of the big positives. There was hardly any fan pressure at all, because there were hardly any fans. Then again, pressure for West was hardly ever external. No pressure from an outside source could ever match that which he placed upon himself. The real pressure was on the team to meet payroll and pay bills. The owners, Bob Short and Frank Ryan, planned to stay in Minneapolis while running a team 1,500 miles away, which meant they needed someone on site to manage things. Broadcaster Chick Hearn recalled, "When Bob Short bought the Minneapolis Lakers for a nickel on the dollar and brought them out here, he sent a fellow out here with fifteen thousand dollars to get them set up, to get the franchise started. He was supposed to buy basketballs, suits, stationery, all the equipment to get everything going. But this guy, whom I won't name, spent all the money entertaining people such as myself and the press. And so they still didn't have anything started."

Short's answer to the disaster was to hire an old friend, Lou Mohs. A Minnesota native, Mohs had starred in athletics at St. Thomas College.

"Lou Mohs was tall and broad shouldered, with a mane of striking white hair," Fred Schaus remembered. "He was in his sixties and had worked for years as a newspaper circulation director. He knew how to work long hours, and he loved basketball."

Mohs enjoyed having his players come to his office, where he could measure their wingspans and mark it on his wall. He was astonished at the eighty-eight-inch spread that West—like some sort of basketball crucifix, noted one reporter—threw up on the wall, and thereafter Mohs liked to boast about it to guests.

Mohs had jumped at the chance to get out of the newspaper business and into sports, Schaus explained. "It was Lou Mohs who talked me into leaving West Virginia to coach the Lakers. They had tried to get me to take over the team when it was in Minneapolis. But I turned them down. I knew they weren't very sound financially. But things changed when they moved out to Los Angeles. The place had a great climate, and the team had just drafted Jerry West. And Lou Mohs offered me $18,500 a year in salary. That was pretty good money in 1960, so I accepted the offer. If I had known how bad their cash flow problems were, I would never have taken the job. Right after I got out there, I knew we were in trouble when all the equipment suppliers were sending their packages COD."

While in the newspaper business, the GM had reveled in his love of sports, going to games whenever possible, even scouting talent for his coaching friends, Schaus said. "Lou was so happy to be involved, he didn't care that the franchise was broke. They ran out of money not long after he got to California, so Lou had to call Bob Short for cash to pay some bills. Short told him, 'Call me for anything, but don't call me for money.'"

Somehow Mohs took that directive and made it work.

"That son of a gun came in with literally nothing to work with," Hearn remembered. "He worked out of a desk and did it all. Tickets. Money. Everything else. He saved the franchise, no question about it. Literally threw his heart and soul into it."

One of Mohs's first ideas was an unfathomable sixteen-game exhibition schedule between the Lakers and Bill Russell's Boston Celtics, played all across Massachusetts and California that October. Crowds reached as large as 5,000—puny by modern standards, but absolutely inspiring in 1960. (In cold Minneapolis, the Lakers had left behind an average game attendance of 2,700.) A few of the exhibition games were even broadcast on local television.

The schedule meant that West's introduction to the NBA was Celtics, Celtics, Celtics, and more Celtics. "My first year in the league in 1960, I believe we played the Boston Celtics twenty-five times," West recalled in 2008. "I hated green. Not because it was the people wearing the uniform, but because I couldn't stand to look at that color anymore that year. So I don't have a lot of green in my wardrobe. We played them sixteen exhibition games, starting in Bangor, Maine, and ending up in San Bernardino, where there was a fight before they even tossed the damn ball up."

That sort of familiarity had to breed some contempt. The rookie got an early lesson in the dominance of Russell and Company. "By the time I first played against him in 1960, Bill Russell had already demonstrated his greatness very effectively by leading the Celtics to three championships," West said. "I'll never forget the circumstances when I played against him as a rookie with the Lakers. We played them in something like twelve to fourteen exhibition games that year and then in another ten regular-season games. I had my fill of seeing Bill Russell at an early age."

The series likewise gave the Celtics a good early look at West, who had several big games against them. Boston's Bob Cousy ruled the league with his fancy passing, but he soon saw that he couldn't cover the Lakers' rookie, Hot Rod Hundley remembered. "Jerry was too quick, too big for Cousy. He could shoot right over him or go right around him. They had to get the Jones boys, Sam and K.C., to cover him. Jerry was the quickest guy I'd ever seen at that time, and he had great basketball sense."

"It was obvious from that first year that Jerry was a superstar," Cousy agreed. "He had tremendous speed and quickness and explosiveness."

Tough-to-impress Celtics forward Tommy Heinsohn saw that West was different. "You knew he was going to be a solid pro," he recalled. "West was just inexperienced, that's all. He had these long arms—he had huge arm length. So he could shoot over guys who were taller than him, and then if you tried to match him sizewise, he'd beat you with his feet. That's what made him such a great player. Plus, he was fiercely competitive."

West, in turn, got a lesson in the Celtics' unique fast-breaking style, led by Cousy and ignited by Russell's ferocious defense and rebounding. The Celtics were the perfect team to educate and entertain California crowds. After all, they had come to the West Coast first in a 1957 exhibition, after winning Russell's first NBA title. Californians had lapped them up.

"The things that saved the game of pro basketball were the twenty-four-second clock and Bob Cousy," Chick Hearn offered. "Cousy introduced to the game the style that the Globetrotters had made famous around the world, the fancy passing and behind the back and so forth. And the crowds loved it."

The series was key that first year in Los Angeles, and it ran for several years afterward, Hearn recalled. "Boston used to come out in the exhibition season, and we'd travel with them for thirteen games in the preseason. It was a caravan of cars. It was an experience. It was like the old barnstorming days of basketball. The teams were all in rented cars. One night we'd play in Santa Barbara. The next night we'd play in San Luis Obispo. We played everywhere. In high school gymnasiums. This was all Lou Mohs's work. He was a hustler and a good promoter. He got the thing going, and it worked. They had Cous and Russ and Sharman and Heinsohn and Frank Ramsey and the Jones boys, K.C. and Sam. It developed into a good rivalry. Some of the games were very intense. Very intense. Every morning, we'd get out of the hotels and motels and get into those cars, and here we'd go. We did that for several years in the preseason. That helped expand the NBA to communities that had never seen a game. Basketball on TV wasn't prevalent at the time. And even when basketball got on TV, the league didn't always make wise choices about which teams would be on. They always did what was cheapest."

AT LAST, THE BIG O

While the exhibition games packed high school gyms, the start of the regular season brought a different story. West's new basketball home would eventually become the fourteen-thousand-seat Los Angeles Sports Arena, built in 1959 near the Coliseum. Funded by public bonds, the facility transported basketball into the modern age, as if a giant flying saucer had landed in the neighborhood near University of Southern California on a mission to show Los Angeles the future. Other arenas in the country couldn't compare to this strange oval. With its space-age decor, the Sports Arena featured elevators to lift spectators to the seating levels and electric fans to keep the flag waving gracefully during the national anthem. Even the turnstiles were electronic, keeping a running tally of the crowd size on a scoreboard as each spectator entered. Both UCLA and USC scrambled to play their games there, leaving the Lakers to settle for an unusual number of Sunday and Monday dates. Otherwise the Lakers had to search for local venues to play on their other game days. That, strangely, would prove to be something of an early boost. Small venues cloaked dismal crowds better than the cavernous new arena.

"They were drawing nothing," Hearn said. "They would play one night at a high school gym. They played the Shrine Auditorium on a stage! If you fell off the side, you dropped six feet. They played at the

University of California, wherever its various locations were. They just couldn't build a following. Wherever they played, the thousand people who lived in that area might go. But the newspaper coverage was very, very slim. It wasn't very easy elsewhere either. In the East, they were playing doubleheader games at neutral sites, trying to find a crowd."

Owners Bob Short and Frank Ryan, though, were just happy to be there, after struggling to survive in the antiquated auditorium in Minneapolis. They negotiated a three-year lease with a series of seventeen one-year options to follow, providing security through the 1980 season—what seemed like a distant signpost. In a matter of months, the Lakers had moved from the past to the future.

The team was hopeful that West would develop into a second star to play alongside the superb Baylor. On the eve of the season opener, Schaus boosted West to the Los Angeles press. "Jerry should make it big in the NBA," he predicted. "The average backcourt man gets about three hundred rebounds a season. I'll bet Jerry comes up with at least five hundred. He's the tallest six-foot-three-inch player I ever saw. He can go right up there with the biggest of them to dunk in the ball. He's a tremendous passer, a deadly shooter from anywhere. Most of all, he has the timing, coordination, and sixth sense to be at the right place at the right time."

But in talking to the Charleston paper, Schaus offered a more serious assessment: "Jerry's so nervous, he's not eating anything. I'm not going to start him. I'm going to let him sit there on the bench awhile."

The Lakers opened the season October 19 on the road, as the NBA quickly showed that it could accomplish in a matter of weeks what college basketball had failed to do in three years: get West and Oscar Robertson playing against each other in a game that mattered. But was it the case that West was finally going to get to play against Robertson and he wasn't going to get to start?

Much to Robertson's dislike, he would spend his career being compared with West. Thirty years later, during the 1990 NBA All-Star Weekend in Miami, a reporter would nonchalantly ask Robertson about West. The retired star would erupt in anger. "All of you media guys are racist," he said loudly. "You can't ask me a question without asking about Jerry West."

The moment was decidedly uncomfortable but entirely revealing in terms of the intensity of the public debate over the two. They had been compared since their college days right through their Olympic experience and every step of their pro careers.

West had long conceded that Robertson's skills and ability made him the best player in basketball. In fact, the NBA had never seen a guard like Oscar Robertson when he entered the league in 1960. At six foot five, he was tall and strong, a demanding teammate, and a floor leader with tremendous skills; plus, like West, he saw and understood the geometry of the game at a rare level. Don't even think that Robertson was ever a rookie, West said later. He was too good, too mature, too strong. But, like many of the black athletes who emerged during the bitterly racist 1950s, Robertson had developed an edge, a hard exterior, to endure the incessant indignities foisted on him by a relentlessly prejudicial culture.

Where West could pursue his basketball agenda within the narrow parameters of his obsession, Robertson was forced to carry the baggage of the broader, segregated world in his approach to the game. And this was the infuriating irony for Robertson. He knew he was the better player, but that wasn't really the issue. He saw a huge problem in a white-dominated media intent on playing up their competition simply because one was black and the other white. Asked by writer Scoop Jackson years later about his rivalry with West, Robertson said, "That was only because one of us was white and one of us was black. We had two totally different games. It was unfair. It was unfair to Jerry and also to myself, because we didn't play the same type of game. Jerry was the shooting guard, and I was just the opposite: ball-handling, setting up everything." Two decades later, Magic Johnson and Larry Bird managed to have some fun with similar circumstances. West and Robertson, however, saw their thing play out in the early 1960s, as people were getting killed in Mississippi simply because they wanted to register to vote.

The perception of the two players—among both black and white athletes—was that both had their athletic advantages: West his quickness, and Robertson his strength. And while many of their peers rated them equals in terms of intelligence and game smarts, West was portrayed as caring more, which in many eyes made him the better player—just another huge insult in Robertson's eyes.

"Oscar's approach was to try to get his own shot first," observed the Celtics' Tommy Heinsohn, who played and coached against both. "If he couldn't get his own shot, then he'd pass it to someone else."

"Oscar always got the credit," said Kareem Abdul-Jabbar, "but Jerry got a lot of credit too and deserved it. I wouldn't say that Oscar was absolutely the better player. They were like neck and neck, and they neutralized one another."

That first night, the Cincinnati Gardens was packed with its largest crowd ever, 8,176. West spent long stretches on the bench as he watched Robertson work his all-around brilliance: a triple double — 21 points, 12 rebounds, and 10 assists — and a 140–123 win over LA. It was an all-time high team point total for the Royals, which suggested the depth of the Lakers' early defensive problems. West finished with 23 points, but he was not happy at all. His team had lost, which always made him miserable. But worst of all, Schaus was not going to make West a starter. The intensely competitive rookie could think of nothing more abominable.

The writers covering the Lakers in the early days still chuckle when they recall West's indignation over not starting. "Jerry is still mad that Schaus didn't start him as a rookie, and part of it, I suspect, was Jerry was jealous of Oscar," said Mitch Chortkoff, an early Lakers publicist who later covered the team for years as a reporter. "Oscar started immediately, and here's Jerry sitting on the bench."

And so, in a season where the die was cast for West in so many ways, this running tally with Robertson got the competition off to a royal start. The problem became getting Fred Schaus to go along with it. Schaus was determined to shelter his rookie to begin the season.

"Fred Schaus was somebody who was familiar with me, who knew me as a player and someone who knew me pretty well as a person," West said. "The negative factor was that I almost felt I had to be so much better than the other people I was playing with that it was frustrating. I started out with the Lakers in Los Angeles, and we had a real poor team. No matter how I played in games or in practices, it seemed like my playing time was almost being handed to me in a different manner."

"It was because Jerry saw Rod Hundley as a playboy," Eddie Barrett observed, "and Jerry was dead serious, and he really resented Schaus starting Rod ahead of him."

Charles West brought his father to that first game, as Cincinnati became a regular destination for the family each time Jerry came through. That first night, Howard West wasn't quite prepared for the fast-paced style of pro basketball, Charles remembered. "His appearance wasn't the best. We were going to see Jerry play basketball. He had on a brown coat and blue pants and a dress hat that had seen better days. I got on him and said, 'Dad, why don't you wear your blue pants with your blue coat and your brown coat with your brown pants?' He said, 'Now, look here, son. Your thoughts don't rule the world.'"

Now sixty, Howard West was both amazed and immensely proud of his youngest son's climb in the sports world. After the game, Jerry stayed in his hotel room, talking to Jane on the phone. Down in the hotel bar, Hot Rod Hundley, who would have his best season as a pro, was holding court, Charles remembered. Jerry would hold to that reserved approach in the early days of his career, but Hundley would later boast to the sportswriters covering the Lakers that it was he who eventually lured West out to taste the night life that only an NBA player could enjoy.

From that first night in Cincinnati, the entire state of West Virginia seemed to hang on the early returns of West's pro career, especially in Cabin Creek. Later that first season, Patricia West and her husband, Jack, figured out a way to follow Jerry on the radio when the Lakers played the St. Louis Hawks, whose games were broadcast by a radio station in St. Louis. "We would go down to Cabin Creek, across from the Appalachian Power plant there, and park under the telephone wires, where we could pick that signal up," she recalled. "One night, my husband and our two children, we were down there in the car, listening to it, and a deputy sheriff's car pulled up. Jack got out of the car to speak to them and told them, 'Well, we're just listening to the ball game.' They said, 'So are we.'"

In Los Angeles, such enthusiasm would take longer to build. A gate of 4,008 paying customers turned out on October 24 to see the Lakers lose their first home game to the Knicks, 111–100. The next night, the teams played again and the Lakers won, with 3,375 watching.

At least those were the numbers Lou Mohs reported. "Every day Lou would phone Bob Short in Minneapolis to report the ticket sales for each game," Schaus recalled. "After one of the early games, Mohs told Short that four thousand seats had been sold. Short asked him,

'Can't you double that when you give it to the press?' Lou said, 'You mean double it again?'"

ELGIN

If Los Angelenos didn't yet realize what had landed in their midst, Baylor gave them the first big clue that November 15 when he scored 71 points, a new NBA single-game record, against the Knicks in Madison Square Garden. The news would hit Los Angeles like a lightning bolt, giving sports fans the idea that they needed to get out and see this talented Lakers team.

The veterans around the league weren't surprised by anything Baylor did. "You couldn't defend Elgin," explained Detroit guard Gene Shue. "He had such a good outside shot. He could stare you down. He had a quick jab step. He would catch the ball at the top of the key or further out, and he'd get you going back and forth. He'd just explode by you. He had a nervous twitch. He was very, very hard to defend. Not only was he a good outside shooter, but he had a good deceptive first step. He had incredible strength and could hang in the air with the ball. When you put all those things together, you couldn't stop him."

Baylor supposedly had gotten his surname at birth when his father glanced at his wristwatch and liked the sound of the name on the face. And later, his college coach, John Castellani, would say, "Elgin has more moves than a clock." Driving to the basket, he would leave the floor, often not quite sure what he wanted to do, simply relying on his hang time to open his options. Because he was an excellent passer, he could usually find someplace to put the ball for a teammate. Failing that, he could resort to a layup, as he seldom chose to dunk. Even so, Baylor was no gliding featherweight. He was six foot five and 225 pounds, a powerful rebounder with another special gift for following his own shots and correcting the misses.

"Baylor was really the first to have body control in the air," Hot Rod Hundley said. "He'd hang there and shoot these little flip shots."

"He just might be the best player I ever saw," Chick Hearn offered. "He was doing things that Dr. Julius Erving made famous twenty years later, the hang time and so forth. But Elgin didn't have the TV exposure. Nobody did in those days."

C&O STA. CABIN CREEK JC., W. VA.

The railroad terminal at Cabin Creek Junction
during Jerry West's youth.
The West Virginia Collection

Hot Rod Hundley was the
Mountaineer star who preceded
West as a West Virginia favorite.
The West Virginia Collection

West handling the ball as a West
Virginia Mountaineer in the late 1950s.
The West Virginia Collection

West, at left, leads his teammates onto the floor for a game at the WVU field house in Morgantown.
The West Virginia Collection

West, shown here absorbing a physical blow against Holy Cross, was quite the ball hawk in college.
The West Virginia Collection

West broke his nose twice during the 1960 season, his senior year at West Virginia.
UPI Photo/Corbis

The 6'3" West was a frontcourt player in college. He's shown here rising up to defend against William & Mary.
The West Virginia Collection

West is shown here with the wife of Sen. Hubert Humphrey and her son during the 1960 Democratic primary campaign in West Virginia.
UPI Photo/Corbis

West is shown on the medal stand with teammate Oscar Robertson during the 1960 Summer Olympics in Rome.
UPI Photo/Corbis

Elgin Baylor with Fred Schaus and West in a Los Angeles Lakers publicity shot from the early 1960s.
UPI Photo/Corbis

Rod Hundley starred at West Virginia, then joined the Minneapolis Lakers as the top overall pick in the 1957 NBA draft.
Full Court Press Collection

Jerry West guarding Oscar Robertson in the 1964 NBA All-Star Game. Robertson was the MVP of that game.
Full Court Press Collection

West looked to Elgin Baylor as a teammate who could teach him much about playing pro basketball.
Full Court Press Collection

Rudy LaRusso provided rebounding and scoring for the Los Angeles Lakers in the 1960s.
Full Court Press Collection

From his earliest days in the NBA, West, shown here against Hal Greer, was known for his defensive prowess.
Full Court Press Collection

Chick Hearn, the broadcasting
voice of the Lakers, lauded
West's play for the team's fans.
Full Court Press Collection

Fred Schaus coached West at West
Virginia and then with the Lakers.
Full Court Press Collection

Wilt Chamberlain lorded over the NBA statistically in the 1960s and '70s.
Full Court Press Collection

West as a mature player in the 1970s.
Getty

Jerry West as general manager of the Lakers in the 1980s.
Full Court Press Collection

Bill Bertka, longtime Lakers assistant coach and scout, had an up-close view of West's career.
Full Court Press Collection

Jerry Buss, not long after he purchased the Lakers in 1979.
Full Court Press Collection

1980-81 LOS ANGELES LAKERS

Dr. Jerry Buss
Owner

Bill Sharman
Gen. Manager

Paul Westhead
Head Coach

Pat Riley
Asst. Coach

Mike Thibault
Asst. Coach, Head Scout

Jack Curran
Trainer

The 1980–81 team photo sheet with photos of Buss, Bill Sharman, and Pat Riley.
Full Court Press Collection

West was particularly close with Lakers sixth man Michael Cooper.
Full Court Press Collection

Nothing is more emblematic of the Logo's legendary career than the sight of West attacking the basket guarded by Boston's Bill Russell during the 1965 NBA Finals.
UPI Photo/Corbis

Added to Baylor's dynamic mix was the curiosity of his nervous tick, a twitching of his face, leaving defenders confused as Baylor headed around them to the basket. "We used to kid about it," recalled Johnny "Red" Kerr, a highly regarded center for the Syracuse Nationals–Philadelphia 76ers franchise. "If he gave the nervous tic to the left, he was going left. If he gave it to the right, he was gonna go to his right. But when he shook both ways, that's when you fell on your ass, and he was gonna go around you."

The Minneapolis Lakers had made him the first pick of the '58 draft, and Baylor, a Washington, DC, native, sent his uncle to negotiate the contract, a $22,000 deal. As a rookie, he averaged 24.7 points and 15 rebounds in 1958–59. He was second in the league in the most minutes played and led the Lakers in assists, scoring, and rebounding. Midway through his rookie season, he scored 55 in a game, the third highest total in NBA history. The team clunked along to a 33–39 record while the other Lakers learned to play with Baylor. By the play-offs, they had gotten the hang of it, first dumping Detroit, then defending NBA champion St. Louis to meet Boston for the 1959 league title. The Celtics promptly swept the Lakers. "Baylor was clearly the most exciting player in the league," said his coach, former Lakers great Jim Pollard.

The Lakers quickly hustled to increase his salary to $50,000 a year, huge money at the time. Baylor opened that next season by scoring 52 against Detroit. A few nights later, on November 8, 1959, he rang up 64 points against the Celtics, breaking the league's single-game record set a decade earlier by Jumpin' Joe Fulks.

"Elgin was very strong," said John Radcliffe, the Lakers' longtime scorekeeper. "He would get bumped all the time, but it never seemed to throw him off stride. Even in the air, he would get bumped a lot, but his concentration was so good that the shot would still go where he wanted it to go. He used the glass a lot. I never saw him dunk. It wasn't the thing to do in those days."

"Some players, they struggle when they score," Shue said. "Elgin, his instincts were so good. He kept you off balance. There wasn't one forward in the league that wanted to play Elgin. Elgin was one of those players that could embarrass you. He could do sixty on you. And you couldn't stop him."

The opportunity to play with a talent like Baylor was one of the major strokes of good fortune in West's career, something he would genuinely cherish. West came to rely on his multitalented teammate that first year.

"It was an honor to play with him," West said later. "I never considered Elgin Baylor as someone I competed against. He is without a doubt one of the truly great players to play this game. I hear people talking about great players today, and I don't see many that compare to him, I'll tell you that. He had that wonderful, magical instinct for making plays, for doing things that you just had to watch. I learned from him, from watching him. I was young, wanting to learn. I had an incredible appreciation for other people's talents. It was incredible to watch Elgin play."

Baylor's performances seemed to entrance his less-talented Lakers teammates, especially the forwards, Tommy Hawkins and Rudy LaRusso. Which left little doubt that the Lakers were Baylor's team, on and off the court.

"Tommy Hawkins was the hardest worker on the team, but he always had trouble getting the ball to go in the hole," said John Radcliffe. "He was a tremendous leaper, but he had small hands. He and Rudy LaRusso worked so hard for Elgin. They'd battle and battle, setting picks, getting rebounds, whatever it took."

Baylor's mastery extended far beyond the floor with those young teams in Los Angeles, explained Merv Harris, who covered pro basketball for the old L.A. *Herald Examiner:* "It was fascinating to see the domination of his personality over that team. Elgin was the boss. He was the most physically dominating player, and his status began with that. Whenever Elgin wanted to play poker, they played poker. Wherever Elgin wanted to eat, they went to eat. Whatever Elgin wanted to talk about, they talked about."

And in that age before trash talking became an art in the NBA, Elgin pioneered that element of the game as well. "Elgin knew he was good, and he'd let you know," Gene Shue recalled with a chuckle. "He did it out on the court. He was really an unstoppable player."

"Our nickname for Elgin was Motormouth," Hot Rod Hundley said. "He never stopped talking. He knew everything, or he thought he did. We had a lot of fun."

In 1960–61, a lot of that fun came at Jerry West's expense. The TV sitcom *The Beverly Hillbillies* wouldn't air on CBS until September 1962, but by then West could have written the episodes all by himself.

He had come to Los Angeles with a flattop haircut, skinny legs, and a high-pitched mountain twang, like he had just fallen off the turnip truck. His looks and wardrobe would pass the early test, but the dead giveaway came any time he spoke. Baylor first called him "Tweety Bird" because of the high-pitched voice and the skinny legs. West hated it.

"He's as easy to understand as a beagle with a sore throat," Baylor quipped.

Then Baylor came up with another name: Zeke from Cabin Creek. West tried to no avail to explain that he wasn't even from Cabin Creek. He was from Chelyan, and he hated the nickname Zeke from Cabin Creek.

"Hey, Zeke," Baylor said to West within earshot of reporters. "They tell me when the scout came for you, the folks came from miles around to look at his shoes. I hear tell one guy said, 'Hey, Mirandy, lookie here, here's a guy with feet that got two toes!' That right?"

Catchy as the name was and eager as the team was to build a following in Los Angeles in the early years, broadcaster Chick Hearn took to referring to West as Zeke on game broadcasts, until Jane West quietly asked him to quit using it. Hearn obliged, but it was a name, an image, that would not die.

There was backstory to Baylor's constant teasing, an ugly incident that happened in Charleston, West Virginia, in January 1959. Baylor had visited the city with the Minneapolis Lakers to play a regular-season game against the Cincinnati Royals; an attempt by the team to seize on Hundley's statewide popularity. When the Lakers went to check into the Kanawha Hotel, the desk clerk refused to give Baylor and two other black teammates a room. "You can't stay here," he told Baylor. "We run a respectable hotel." Baylor was furious. A similar incident had happened in Charlotte, North Carolina, earlier in the season. Baylor told his teammates then, "I'm no dog; if this ever happens again, I won't play."

The entire team moved to a different motel downtown—Edna's Tourist Court on Lewis Street—but he was also denied access to a local restaurant and ended up staying in his room and eating food from a grocery store. True to his word, Baylor declined to play that night, a stand for which he was roundly criticized, especially because the Lakers fell to Cincy, 95–92.

"The big colored boy from Washington, DC, who played at Seattle, was irritated over racial discrimination," the *Charleston Daily Mail* explained the next morning.

Keenly aware of the incident, Schaus regularly assigned black and white players to room together on the road, which meant that West and Baylor sometimes shared quarters, which might have been a bit of a challenge. "When you room with Baylor, he's talking when he goes to sleep and talking when he wakes up," LaRusso said. "Maybe he never stops."

It stands to reason that Baylor wanted to test West. Besides, hazing, then as now, was a key part of NBA life. Rookies carried team luggage and even paid their teammates' cab fares to and from arenas, duties that West carried out that first year.

"The first time I saw Jerry, I knew he was going to be a good one," Baylor recalled for a Los Angeles reporter a few years later. "I have also learned he's one of the finest guys I've ever met. We've never had any troubles. When he's hot, I feed him, and when I'm hot, he feeds me. I'll tell you something else, too. He hates to lose."

Even so, the stereotyping and lampooning that first season deeply offended West.

"For one thing, no one could understand him," Jim Murray, the *Los Angeles Times*'s great columnist would write, inspired by Baylor's humor. "He had an accent that was three parts sweet potato, one part magnolia, two parts coonskin, and a sprinkling of Elizabethan moonshine English strained through a broken nose."

Baylor was his roommate and friend. Murray was an admirer. West laughed with them in fun. But he hated that their talk provided grist for all the people he didn't know, strangers who felt free to address him in such terms.

"I've never seen Jerry walk by an autograph yet," Pete Newell would later recall. "He signed because he believed he owed it to the fans. But when people would ask him to sign 'Zeke from Cabin Creek,' he'd refuse."

Hundley was his teammate, but Hundley had several years' experience in the league and was far more worldly. Where he could laugh off the constant references to hillbillies, West took it personally. Already prone to harboring resentments, West added it to his long list, not against Baylor, but against the mind-set in general. Hundley once remarked that West accomplished "ten times as much as I did in my career, but he's about a tenth as happy as I am."

Being lampooned added mightily to that misery.

West wasn't in Los Angeles long before folks back home began to detect a strange new diction. Eddie Barrett noticed that West was trying hard to pronounce his *g*'s. There was no more talkin' and jokin' like folks in Chelyan. In time, it would contribute to the impression back home that Jerry West had turned his back on West Virginia.

Such complex issues remained in the background in West's early days with the team. The rookie reserved his true anger for where things really mattered: on the court. Schaus persisted with the idea that Hundley and Frank Selvy remain as his starting guards, and he left the perfectionist West on the bench for long stretches.

"That was a frustrating period, because I could not learn sitting on the bench," West recalled. "The only thing I could learn were bad habits, with the things that I saw. I had to get out there and get over those first-year jitters—and the time in my career where I wasn't a real good player—to get to the point where I could be competent enough to compete on a higher level with these other players."

It would lead to West's long-term resentment of Schaus, although he never made those feelings known until years after the fact.

Rene Henry, a close friend of Schaus's and Hundley's, said the situation proved difficult for Schaus. "Fred didn't want to choose," Henry offered. "He's from West Virginia, they're from West Virginia; and if they lost, it's because they're West Virginia guys. They did play together sometimes, but not a lot. Rod felt that with Jerry's moves off the ball and the way Rod could handle the ball, he could have gotten ten assists a game."

"Schaus wasn't a bad coach," Hundley observed. "He was just mechanical and predictable. He'd take Jerry West out of games with two minutes left. It didn't matter if he was shooting the ball great. It was automatic. Schaus wouldn't ride a hot hand. Most coaches will, but Schaus wouldn't. Hell, Jerry made the All-Star team, and he wasn't even a starter."

"He was old school, no nonsense, no sense of humor," Red Kerr, the former NBA center and coach said of Schaus. "Tolerance for mistakes? None. Guys didn't like Freddie Schaus."

Schaus may have had his detractors, but he understood an important part of West's personality: the self-destruction and paralysis brought on by his perfectionism. West himself would admit later that he had important lessons to learn that first year. "One of the biggest," West conceded later in the decade, "was that I was too much of a perfectionist. I had to realize that every pass couldn't be perfect and every shot couldn't go into the basket. I used to get angry at myself every time I made a mistake. The anger would make me lose my concentration, and then for a few minutes I would play poorly. A mistake doesn't bother me anymore. It's just part of the game.

"I think there was a lot of pressure on me when I first came here. I had been a big college star, but I didn't score too well when I joined the Lakers. Of course, I hadn't played guard before, but that was only part of the trouble. In college you had two or three games that were important, but all of them are in pro ball. Then there was the traveling. I couldn't sleep after a game for hours. That problem I never have conquered, but the schedule was much tougher then, because we were the only western club. Believe me, with the long trips, I lost weight."

Hundley has said many times that it was silly not to start West and play him more. Yet Hundley, with about a dozen points a game, was off to his best year as a pro since the Lakers had drafted him as the number one overall pick in 1957. He was named to the All-Star team for the second straight year. Still, the Lakers weren't performing up to their potential, which fueled West's unhappiness.

"I felt after twenty games that I had earned more playing time because the team was doing so poorly," West said. "The one thing I always felt, if the team is not winning, you have to be free to make changes."

Surprisingly, Los Angeles placed three players on the Western Conference All-Star team. The game was played in cold Syracuse, and in those days it was a far cry from the fancy international event of the modern era. It would be the first of West's fourteen consecutive appearances.

"There were times when I thought I'd never make it pro," he told the *Los Angeles Times* in 1965. "I was quite discouraged until they selected me for the All-Star Game. That was the lift I needed. I still would play a good one, then a poor one. But by play-off time, I felt I could become an outstanding player."

After the All-Star break, Hundley went to the bench. It was an embittering experience, and it would take him years to forgive Schaus for the move. He felt that Schaus should have kept him in the lineup instead of Selvy, the Lakers' other guard. It was the moment that signaled Hundley was moving toward the end.

Asked about it later, Schaus was frank. Hundley wouldn't have been good to start alongside West because Hundley was a ball hog and he wasn't steady. West had to have the ball, and Selvy would pass it to him. Plus, Hundley was in poor shape and suffering from bad knees that slowed him considerably.

"Rod was fun, and he did a lot of funny things," Schaus said. "But he was a fine player, too. He was a great dribbler and passer, and he played pretty fair defense. He was a great scorer, but he was not the great shooter that Jerry West was."

"All of a sudden, things weren't very good, and I had a chance to step in and start, and I never gave it up," West said. "It was a struggle, and then things changed. Then it got to the point where I didn't come out very much. That felt good, because I believe basketball players need to play more, particularly if you can play at a higher level. Getting to that level is the hardest thing. You can't do it unless you have ability and you get the opportunity."

The Lakers began a turnaround with West in the lineup, although it was nothing that the rookie guard engineered by himself. Baylor was in his prime, playing the forward spot in spectacular fashion. He led the team offensively and finished second in the league in scoring behind Wilt Chamberlain at a 34.8 points per game pace.

"They were only drawing about three thousand that first year," said Mitch Chortkoff. "But Baylor and West made it into something. Baylor was so spectacular he could sell tickets with the way he played."

The team may have started winning more games and doing better at the gate, but that didn't change its sorry financial state that first year.

"The worst thing was, they charged Jerry for extra tickets," Hundley remembered. "They took money from him. I was standing right there. Jerry wouldn't say a word. He just sat there and turned red."

The Lakers finished second in the Western Conference with a 36–43 record, just enough to make the play-offs. But the Sports Arena wasn't available, so they moved one of their first-round games with Detroit to the local Shrine Auditorium, where they played on a stage.

"That's the closest I've ever been to Broadway," quipped Gene Shue, who starred for the Pistons. "That was strange."

By the end of the year, West was showing his greatness, Shue said. "Jerry didn't have to beat you with quickness. He could take you to a spot on the floor and shoot over you. He was very, very good at that. He got the ball way back on his shot. You had a very tough time guarding him. He was very good at catching the ball and backing you down. He didn't have to back you down too far, and then he'd just rise up and shoot the ball.

"Jerry was never like the point guard on a team," Shue added. "He was mostly a two guard. He could beat you with quickness, he could beat you with his outside shot. He could dribble you down and just shoot over you. I played Jerry all the time when I was in the pro leagues, and I could never get his shot. The only way you could bother Jerry was to try to be on the side of him when he went up to shoot. You're up not as high as he is. When you're going body to body, with Jerry he'd just bump you, go up, and have that high release. He was just unstoppable. Jerry was such a clutch shooter, and Elgin was as well. When the game was on the line, these were the guys that always had the ball. They produced."

On the backs of Baylor and West, the Lakers overcame Detroit, then took on St. Louis in the Western finals. The Hawks were on their way to their fourth trip to the championship series in five seasons. They would be the only team to beat Russell's Celtics in an NBA championship series, and they did that only after Russell was injured, in 1958.

The Lakers beat the Hawks the first game in St. Louis and later claimed another at home. Suddenly the series was knotted at two all. Bob Short and Lou Mohs were ecstatic. This was the turnaround they'd been looking for. They knew it was time to do some serious promoting. And maybe even spend a little money.

"The Lakers couldn't get anyone to carry their games," Chick Hearn recalled. "No radio station would take them, so they didn't have any broadcasts the first year, despite West and Baylor, guys who made a pretty darn good team. After they made the play-offs that first year, I got a call one night asking if I would go to St. Louis to do a play-off game. Bob Short was the guy who called me at two a.m. and asked me if I'd go to St. Louis the next night to televise the play-off game. I said, 'You can't get a TV station by tomorrow night, Bob.' This was after midnight on Sunday. I'm talking to him lying on my bed. We didn't have satellite trucks in those days like TV has today. So I said, 'You're not gonna get a TV station that can get it together for tomorrow night. Why don't you go on the station I'm working for here, KNX radio? We can go all over the country, particularly at night.' They had a fifty-thousand–watt clear channel. And so he did that."

The Lakers had tied the Hawks in the Western finals and were set to play the fifth game in St. Louis that Saturday, March 27, 1961. Hearn arranged a KNX broadcast of that game, which the Lakers won 121–112.

"I went to St. Louis and did a game," Hearn said. "It happened to be an overtime game in St. Louis. The Hawks had the likes of Cliff Hagan and Bob Pettit and Lenny Wilkens. A very outstanding team. The Lakers beat them in overtime. It was a well-received game, and they came home to fifteen thousand in the Sports Arena. And that's when it really took off."

Indeed. The packed house saw the Lakers fall in overtime that Monday, then the Hawks took the seventh game and the series at home, 105–103. But Los Angeles had discovered the Lakers, and the team would never again go begging for a broadcast or a broadcaster. Hearn was hooked for good. And his swift, smart delivery was perfect for selling Southern California fans on Baylor, West, and the Lakers.

"That started it," Hearn said. "That was the turning point."

And yet West was anything but pleased. Yes, he had gotten a taste of success, but he hated to lose. He wanted to get better. And he was going to do something about it.

The Celtics played as a team. That's the thing that the Lakers never did do. They played as individuals.

—Tommy Heinsohn

THE HORROR

Los Angeles, 1961 to 1965

THE NUMBERS WOULD HAVE BEEN ROUGH FOR ANY ORDINARY JOE, SO try to imagine what they have meant to an intensely competitive perfectionist. From April 1962 to May 1969, Bill Russell's Boston Celtics defeated Jerry West, Elgin Baylor, and the Lakers six times in six NBA championship series. That's six times in seven calendar years. The only two springtimes the Lakers failed to reach the championship round in that period, in 1964 and 1967, it was due to serious injuries.

Even after Russell finally retired, following the 1968–69 season, West, Baylor, and the Lakers lost a seventh time in 1970 to the New York Knicks, in the most celebrated and talked-about NBA championship series of all time. That made for seven championship losses in eight calendar years if you're counting—and everyone was, especially Jerry West. At the time, though, his competitive motor just kept grinding, trying to find a winning gear.

"He was then, and still remains, the single most revered Celtic opponent of all time," wrote longtime *Boston Globe* columnist Bob

Ryan. "No Celtic opponent has ever had more fans wishing he would switch uniforms, and that includes Michael Jordan. 'Noble' doesn't begin to describe the level and style of his performances against the Celtics in the '60s. His LA teams lost Finals series to Boston in '62, '63, '65, '66, '68, and '69. His scoring averages in those six series were 31, 29, 34, 35, 32, and 38."

"West was West," Hot Rod Hundley pointed out. "Jerry burned the Celtics every time he played them. He killed the Celtics; really played well against them every time. He loved playing against Boston."

In his last game against the Russell-led Celtics, West registered what may well be the most impressive triple double in league history— 42 points, 13 rebounds, and 12 assists—in game seven of the 1969 championship series. And still the Lakers lost.

And it's not as if losing was West's only trauma. During this same period, his father suffered a serious heart attack and spent several years in convalescence. And the family's house in Chelyan burned down, taking West's cherished mementos, Olympic gold medal, and uniforms along with it. And his father eventually died of another heart attack. And although only West knew it at the time, he was also watching his marriage come apart before his eyes.

Whenever tragedy and disaster strike around sports, there always seems to be the inevitable talk about these things "putting the game in perspective." For West, there never was such perspective. Basketball was everything.

"There weren't any funny stories with Jerry," observed Lakers broadcaster Stu Lantz, who played against West for six seasons. "Everything was business with Jerry. Everything was business. That's why he didn't stay a coach very long. He was so intense all the time."

To go with this intensity, West was cursed with an elephantine memory. The games, the defeats, rarely left his thoughts. Ever. Nearly forty years after his battles with the Celtics ended, West and Baylor were interviewed by HBO for a documentary on classic sports rivalries. Later, HBO interviewed the Celtics' Tommy Heinsohn. To prep him for the interview, HBO producers allowed Heinsohn to see what Baylor and West had to say, and the former Celtics forward and coach was stunned by the animosity and hard feelings expressed in the interviews. "I couldn't believe how much they were against us," Heinsohn said, "because we had the utmost respect for them as opponents. They were just . . . I couldn't believe it. Yeeesh."

West has acknowledged that the championship losses controlled his life and took his inclination toward unhappiness to dark, dark places. But Heinsohn said that the Celtics were structured as a true team, while the Lakers seemed to build everything around their two stars, Baylor and West. It always came down to the Lakers' two great players—and Heinsohn, who has spent decades playing, coaching, and broadcasting the sport, contends that Baylor and West were two of the five greatest players ever—battling Boston's immense depth and team play.

"We ran things, and we moved without the ball. If we were open, we got the ball. We played basketball. They were playing on the school yard."

Heinsohn said he had no idea if the lack of team play was a function of the personalities of Baylor and West, or if that was the way Fred Schaus coached them. "I just know what we were doing," he said. "We were all involved in how we played." For his part, Schaus once indicated that he used West and Baylor so much because he believed that provided him the best chance to win. "In all honesty, we had no post game," Schaus said. " . . . We survived on what West and Baylor did. They were fearless."

Heinsohn explained that the Celtics were focused solely on taking advantage of their opponents' weaknesses. One night, that might mean that a certain Celtic had the advantage. On another night, someone else from the team would be the star. "There was nobody that felt they had to defer to anybody," he said of the Celtics teams that won eleven championships in thirteen seasons from 1957 through 1969. "On any given night, you would take advantage of a weakness on the other team. A particular guy might take advantage. I don't think that was ever in the Lakers' game plan."

Actually, most NBA teams approached the game the same way the Lakers did. It's just that the Lakers seemed to take the matter to extremes, and they did so with great intent. Mitch Chortkoff, who covered the team for years as a reporter, first worked for the Lakers as a publicity assistant in 1962–63. He recalled noticing the trend then. "I asked Lou Mohs, 'Why do those two shoot all the time?'" Chortkoff recalled. "Lou Mohs said that in baseball every player comes up to bat four times a game. By virtue of baseball's rules, every player gets to bat. He said, 'We don't have such a rule in our sport. Those two guys are going to take all the shots.' "

In all fairness, the league's illegal-defense rules created a playing format where the secondary players would "clear out" and move to the other side of the floor so that the most talented offensive players could attack the basket in a one-on-one or two-on-two format.

Such an approach had been the standard in pro basketball for decades. "I thought Fred Schaus was a good coach," said newspaperman Mike Waldner, who covered the Lakers during that era. "He isolated Elgin and Jerry on the weak side. It was always like, 'You three get over there and let them play two on two.' And then they played two on two. He took advantage of the rule."

Yet even old NBA hands scoffed at the absurd extremes to which the Lakers took things. "When I was coaching the Bulls," Johnny Kerr recalled, "we were playing against them in LA. We were up by 1, if you can believe this, and I'm over in the huddle during a time-out. There's about ten or fifteen seconds left in the game. They've got the ball. I've got all my players around me, everybody listening. I'm saying what we're gonna do. I look down at their bench and at Freddie Schaus. All their players are sitting on the bench. And Schaus is talking to Elgin and Jerry. He's talking to two guys."

"Those two guys were going to beat you," Heinsohn said. "I mean, we never even had a guy who was a top-ten scorer. They just never trusted their team members, just never trusted them," Heinsohn said finally. "They were going to go and win it by themselves, and our approach was completely different."

In the modern game, when critics took issue with the play of alpha males such as Michael Jordan and Kobe Bryant, that issue was most often selfish, individualistic play. The phrase often used to describe this selfish play was, "They never trusted their teammates."

Asked about Heinsohn's pointed criticism, West said, "That's the way we were encouraged to play. That's the way we were gonna play, the way the coach wanted us to play. It had nothing to do with selfishness, by the way."

In his 1969 autobiography, *Mr. Clutch,* West told coauthor Bill Libby, "The Celts never had two scorers like Elg and me. Schaus always taught a freewheeling game which stressed the contributions the top individuals could make. Very often the game the Lakers have played has just been to get the ball to Elg and Jerry and let us work for our shots. But Elg and I made our shots. Would it have been smarter basketball to let others who can't shoot as well shoot more?"

Heinsohn said the Lakers finally became a team in 1971 when former Celtic Bill Sharman became their coach. Sharman moved a thirty-three-year-old West to point guard almost exclusively for the first time in his career. That move was made to open up the team's playing format. It was a dramatic shift for an aging star, but Sharman confirmed that West made the move and sacrificed his own game without the slightest resistance.

"Jerry was just great," Sharman said. "I couldn't have asked for more cooperation from any player. And Jerry was a star. He did everything that I asked him to do."

Even as a point guard distributing the ball, West averaged better than 25 points that season. More important, the Lakers ripped off the league's all-time winning streak, thirty-three straight games, then closed the season by winning the NBA championship.

A long list of former players and coaches have said that while the Lakers under Schaus did go to great lengths to emphasize their stars, the defining issues of the era were the play of the great Russell and Boston's amazing depth. Boston clearly was superior, said Hall of Fame coach Jack Ramsay. "Two can't beat eight. I don't care who they are, and the Celtics were superb."

"Russell is the most dominant individual who ever played a team sport," Schaus said later.

Around Bill Russell, Boston Celtics coach and general manager Red Auerbach fit an array of spectacular players, including Hall of Famers Heinsohn, Bob Cousy, Sam Jones, K. C. Jones, John Havlicek, Bill Sharman, Frank Ramsey, and Bailey Howell.

"They had two great players, and we had eight great players," Heinsohn acknowledged. "It's tough to beat. In the early years, Baylor would have sixty [points], West would have thirty, and we'd still win the game. Our team was very diversified and very focused on winning. With Cousy and Russell, their personalities demanded that they win, and we went out there and played to win. We lost one year when I played and that was against St. Louis [when Russell was injured]. Besides that we were in the finals all the time, so it was fun to play."

The architect of these great teams was Red Auerbach, the brash and brilliant coach and general manager, an immensely competitive and polarizing figure in the game. "I didn't like Red Auerbach," a rival NBA coach once said. "But in time I grew to hate him."

"Red was hated around the league," said the late Paul Seymour, a former NBA player and rival coach. "He wasn't a very well liked guy. He always had the talent. He was always shooting his mouth off. If you walked up to him in the old days, he was more than likely to tell you to get lost."

Schaus was one of those said to hate Auerbach, although he would never admit it publicly. "Red was a very astute judge of talent," the Lakers coach said. "When you have a lot of stars, you have to keep them happy and playing as a team. Red did that. I didn't like some of the things he did and said when I competed against him. Some of the things he said would bother me. But the guy who wore number six out there bothered us more. You had to change your complete game because of Russell."

Yet there is little question that it was singularly Auerbach who recognized Russell's brilliance at a time when other coaches and general managers seemed to be more focused on a player's skin color. Auerbach, on the other hand, was almost wholly consumed with winning basketball games, so much so that he left his wife and two daughters in Washington, DC, eight months out of each year and lived in an efficiency apartment in Boston while he coached the Celtics.

The son of a Russian immigrant, Auerbach had grown up in Brooklyn, where his father operated a small laundry. A man steeped in work ethic, his father frowned upon time wasted with athletics. But the young redhead played high school basketball well enough to earn a junior college scholarship, then went on to play for Coach Bill Reinhart at George Washington University. After a stint in the navy, Auerbach talked his way into the head coaching job of the Washington Capitols when the Basketball Association of America, the forerunner of the NBA, formed in 1946. Though only twenty-nine, Auerbach immediately directed the team to a regular-season divisional crown. The Caps lost in the play-offs, but Auerbach's reputation had been established. Across the league, opponents quickly learned that his wavy red hair was true to the stereotype.

"He was flamboyant, gutsy, on top of everything. And fiery. I mean really fiery," Celtics radio announcer Johnny Most said of the young Auerbach. "But the important thing about him was that he knew the

rules better than the officials. And he pulled the rule book on the officials all the time because he knew them. And he had the bite of intimidation. Like, when his team was not playing well or playing lethargically, he'd go out there and start to scream at the fans or the referee and get them on him."

After a falling out with the management in Washington, Auerbach coached the Tri-Cities Blackhawks for 1949–50, then moved to Boston for 1950–51. The Celtics had been losers in their first four seasons of operation, and team founder-owner Walter Brown figured that Auerbach was gritty enough to change that. It was a perfect marriage: Auerbach had found an owner who wanted to win as badly as he did.

"Walter Brown was one of the pioneers of professional basketball," Auerbach said. "He was a true sportsman. His word was his bond. He gave his whole material being and everything else to basketball . . . He mortgaged his house and everything else. He was a great man. I always compare people to Walter Brown by saying, 'Yeah, he's got some of Walter Brown's traits, but he's no Walter Brown.' Which means he's no sportsman. Walter Brown dedicated his life to sports. He used to subsidize it out of his own pocket, and he was never a real wealthy man."

Auerbach pushed Boston to a 39–30 finish that first year, but the job of building the Celtics had just begun. New Englanders cared little about basketball in the early fifties, choosing instead to spend their time with hockey. To lure them to basketball, it would take a player like Bob Cousy, the so-called Houdini of the Hardwood. Cousy, a six-foot-one all-America guard at nearby Holy Cross, came to the Celtics in an expansion draft. Auerbach believed deeply in the running game, the strategy he had learned while playing under Reinhart at George Washington. And Cousy wasted little time proving he was just the player to take the running game to a new level. That first season, Cousy averaged 15.6 points on his way to winning NBA Rookie of the Year in 1951.

"He was the greatest innovator of the game," Most said of Cousy. "He had such a fabulous imagination. I think the greatest passer who ever lived. He could throw any kind of pass. The minute he touched the ball, his head was up and he was looking downcourt looking for the open man. It was his philosophy to do it with the pass rather

than the dribble. But if he had to dribble, if they forced the dribble, he could make you look like a fool. He really could. He had all the moves of a Globetrotter. And he never was lacking in confidence."

Just before hiring Auerbach, Walter Brown had signed Easy Ed Macauley, the six-foot-eight, 190-pound center. Macauley was no intimidator, but he had a graceful offensive style and could run the floor. The next year, 1951–52, Auerbach added Bill Sharman, the sharpshooter and defensive hawk out of USC who was playing baseball for the Brooklyn Dodgers. With this cast as the core of the franchise, the Celtics finished at .500 or above each season. But they never could make it past the division finals.

Then for 1954–55, the NBA adopted its twenty-four-second shot clock, and to Auerbach's liking, the game became much speedier. Yet the new tempo made the Celtics' weaknesses even more glaring. Boston had the greyhound guards in Cousy and Sharman to run other teams off the floor, but they didn't have a powerful rebounding center who could pull the ball off the defensive boards and throw the outlet pass to start the fast break. Macauley was a fine shooter, but he simply didn't have the muscle and inside knack to fill that role.

Auerbach had begun looking for that special inside player, when his old college coach, Bill Reinhart, told him of Bill Russell, then a sophomore center for the University of San Francisco. Because he competed on the West Coast, Russell was largely unknown to the eastern basketball establishment. Plus he was an unusual package. He was six foot ten and exceptionally athletic (he could run the 440 in forty-nine seconds), and his sense of timing made him an excellent rebounder and shot blocker. Yet his offensive skills were unrefined to the point that much of his scoring came from guiding his teammates' missed shots into the basket. His knack for this led to the development of offensive goal-tending rules in college basketball.

Russell's reputation improved in 1955 as he and guard K. C. Jones led San Francisco to the first of two consecutive NCAA championships. His lack of offensive polish left most pro teams skeptical of his potential, but Auerbach knew that Russell was just the player he was looking for.

"I had to have somebody who could get me the ball," Auerbach recalled. "I'd been tipped off about Russell by my college coach, Bill Reinhart. Bill said Russell was the greatest defensive player and greatest rebounder he'd ever seen."

The Rochester Royals had the first pick in the 1956 draft but planned to select Sihugo Green of Duquesne University. To get the second pick in the 1956 draft, the Celtics traded Macauley and former Kentucky star Cliff Hagan to the St. Louis Hawks. The trade went through smoothly, the only hitch being that Russell had made clear his intentions to play with the U.S. Olympic team in the Summer Games in Australia. He wouldn't join Boston until late December, and because of Olympic rules in effect then, he wouldn't be able to sign a contract until after the Games were over. The Celtics, however, weren't exactly shorthanded. A year earlier, they had drafted "Jungle" Jim Loscutoff, a muscled six-foot-five forward out of the University of Oregon. And Frank Ramsey, a six-foot-three forward drafted out of Kentucky in 1954, was returning from a year in the service.

In addition, Auerbach had picked up two other strong players in the 1956 draft: Tom Heinsohn, a six-foot-seven forward out of Holy Cross, and K. C. Jones, Russell's teammate at San Francisco. Jones, a third-round pick, would do a stint in the army and try pro football before joining the Celtics in 1958. But Heinsohn would become an immediate factor, and all three from that 1956 draft would eventually wind up in the Hall of Fame.

With Loscutoff and Heinsohn working the defensive boards, the Celtics got the ball out on the fast break that fall of 1956 and ran their way to a 16–8 record, three games ahead of the NBA's defending champions, the Philadelphia Warriors. Then that December 22, after having helped the U.S. win the Olympic gold, Russell joined the Celtics. (The young center had been offered $35,000 by the Globetrotters but turned that down to accept a $20,000 contract with Boston.) After getting stuck in his first Boston traffic jam and arriving late for the game, Russell scored only 6 points, but he pulled down 16 rebounds to help Boston beat St. Louis. Maybe it wasn't obvious that first night, but the NBA would never be the same.

The impact on the Celtics was almost immediate. Russell struggled a bit the first few games, but his presence unshackled the rest of the team. The rookie center was such an effective defensive rebounder that Heinsohn's and Loscutoff's roles shifted from battling on the boards. The forwards merely boxed out their men, then released quickly for the fast break while Russell was snaring the rebound and whipping the outlet pass to Cousy.

Sharman and Cousy, meanwhile, were ecstatic with this development, after having spent the previous seasons frustrated by the team's lack of inside power. Plus, Russell's intimidating presence at center allowed them to gamble on defense. If they made a mistake, Russell proved to be the kind of center who made opponents stop and think before they moved. He interrupted the sense of timing of the entire league.

Auerbach considered Russell's shot blocking to be one of the major innovations in the evolution of the game. The young center exuded a confidence that bordered on arrogance, to some observers. As he later revealed in his book *Second Wind,* Russell was far more insecure about his offensive skills than he let on. He was aware of his detractors. Across pro basketball, the coaches, the players, and the writers all believed that the ideal big man was an offensive force.

But when Russell arrived, Auerbach called him into his office and told him not to worry about offense, that his primary responsibilities were rebounding and defense. The coach also promised that statistics, particularly scoring averages, would never be a part of contract discussions. Auerbach's understanding of Russell's unique skills was the single most important element in the genesis of this dynasty.

Like Auerbach, Russell really cared only about winning. Player and coach didn't have to spend much time together to sense this in each other. "He was the ultimate team player," Cousy said of Russell. "Without him, there would have been no dynasty, no Celtic mystique."

Beginning in his college days (he received little playing time until his senior year in high school), Russell had made shot blocking a science. By the time he reached the pros, he possessed a very special skill. He never swatted the ball so that it went out of bounds. Instead he brushed it, or caught it, or knocked it away, so that most times it remained in play and became a turnover, sparking the Celtics' fast break the other way. Such a defensive presence sent shock waves across the league.

"Nobody had ever blocked shots on the pros before Russell came along," Auerbach said. "He upset everybody."

The often-cited example is that of Neil Johnston, the Hall of Fame Philadelphia center who dominated NBA scoring with his rather flat hook shot. Russell was so effective in blocking Johnston's shot that the three-time NBA scoring champion became ineffective and tentative on offense. Because Johnston was basically a one-dimensional player, he was unable to adjust. He was out of the NBA just two seasons later, at just age thirty. It was said that Russell's presence drove Johnston from the league, a claim that the Philadelphia center vehemently denied. Yet after the 1956–57 season, Johnston ceased to be a dominant offensive power.

Two weeks after Russell began play, Philadelphia owner Eddie Gottlieb protested that Boston's center was playing a one-man zone and goaltending. Other coaches and owners around the league joined the chorus. But Auerbach fended them off. "When we made the deal for Russell, nobody thought he was going to be good," the Boston coach told reporters. "He has far exceeded everybody's expectations. None of his blocks of shots have been on the downward flight. He has marvelous timing. He catches the ball on the upward flight."

When the league supervisor of officials said Russell's play was clearly within the rules, Gottlieb dropped his complaint. The age of a new athleticism had dawned, and everywhere, coaches looked for a way to counter it. Mostly, other teams tried to muscle and bang Russell, but Boston's new weapon wasn't about to back down. In time, his opponents came to appreciate his intelligence as a player and his gentlemanly approach to competition.

The Celtics finished the regular season 44–28, six games ahead of Syracuse in the Eastern Division, as Russell averaged 19.6 rebounds. Cousy led the league in assists and was voted the NBA's MVP. As the play-offs began, Heinsohn was selected the Rookie of the Year. In the locker room before the first play-off game, he opened the envelope containing the $250 rookie prize. Always a needler, Russell eyed the money and said that at least half of it should be his. Time would prove his needling a huge understatement. Having led his San Francisco team to two straight NCAA championships in college, Russell would then carry Boston to the 1957 title his first year in the league.

About the only thing undermining the glorious beginning of Boston's dynasty was the undercurrent of race. The NBA and the Celtics were integrating ahead of society. There were few, if any, problems on the team. But Boston was a racially troubled town. Some sportswriters in Boston made little effort to mask their contempt for Russell. And road games were sometimes rough, particularly in St. Louis, where the fans weren't averse to shouting racial epithets. As with the rough play on the court, Russell wasn't about to back down. "Russ has always been extremely militant, and he is to this day,"

Cousy said. "He came into Boston with the proverbial chip on his shoulder. His militancy had been honed before he arrived. Of course, there were good reasons for the way he reacted, and I've said many times I would have been far more radical than he was. He couldn't play golf at the local courses. At one point, vandals broke into his house and defecated in his bed."

Russell's anger was justified, broadcaster Johnny Most agreed. "I knew where he was coming from deep down. And for a lot of it, I didn't blame him. He faced a lot of irritating, irritating prejudice."

But his private manner with his teammates was as playful as his public face was scowling. In Auerbach's system, winning was the only priority. For that system, the coach sought players who wanted to win as badly as he did. They weren't about to let racial differences interfere with that. Russell has said many times that above all, he knew he could trust his coach not to be petty. A master psychologist, Auerbach created an atmosphere of give-and-take—a unique mix of toughness and fun, where pranksters thrived amid grueling practices, an atmosphere that allowed exploding cigars and other silly gags to bring a soft edge to Auerbach's hard drive for winning. Within this system, the Celtics liked one another and got along. When Russell arrived, Boston's veteran center Arnie Risen took him aside and talked about the ins and outs of the competition around the league. Another veteran on another team might not have imparted knowledge to a rookie about to take his starting job, Russell later noted, but Auerbach surrounded himself with people who cared only about winning.

That's not to say there weren't problems. The white press had no sophisticated knowledge of basketball in those early years, and the reporters fawned over Cousy, the local hero, while virtually ignoring Russell's brilliance. Auerbach, however, sensed these injustices and constantly raved about Russell and other unrecognized players to reporters.

It was in this spirit that Frank Ramsey, the first of the Celtics' sixth men, grew in the public mind. Auerbach didn't invent the idea of the sixth man, but he tirelessly touted and promoted it to the writers covering Boston's games.

Then, at the end of each of his many victories, the Boston coach would light up a cigar, an act soon despised by opponents, especially Schaus, as arrogant and taunting.

"Anytime you're winning, you get criticism," Auerbach said years later. "Nothing instigates jealousy like winning. When you're winning, they look for a thousand reasons for taking potshots. You don't pay attention. You just keep doing what you're doing."

BREAKOUT

In retrospect, the horror for Jerry West is that he and Elgin Baylor became locked in as the foils to Russell, the great hydra of basketball, year after year. After all, they too played for a dynasty that rivaled the Celtics. Before moving to Los Angeles, the Minneapolis Lakers dominated much of the first decade of the NBA. They won five championships in pro basketball's new league, plus another championship in the older pro circuit, the National Basketball League. But the Lakers had slipped and struggled after winning their sixth championship in 1954. By 1958, the franchise was deep in debt, but it had the good fortune to draft Baylor that spring. Even though they had a losing record his rookie year, the Lakers upset their way into the 1959 NBA finals, where they became the first team to lose the series without winning a single game. The victor in that 1959 championship, of course, was Russell and his Celtics.

But in the summer of 1961, West's battles with Boston lay in his future. His concern then was only to get better. If there's a part of his journey that West later looked back on with a sense of delight, it was perhaps in measuring his work and the progress he made as a player. He and Jane had an infant at home, and she was busy as a young mother. Still, she allowed for his intense focus in her daily schedule. She made his meals, communicated with his family, and slowly made their home in Los Angeles. Summers were easily the best part of their lives. No grueling travel for her husband. No tension driving him to distraction on game days at home. Yes, West worked hard in the summers. But his efforts weren't tied to wins and losses, to those peaks and valleys in his mood. Plus, his personal demeanor was changing. He had begun filing away the harsher edges of his accent, and he was becoming quite the Californian: tanned, fit, and busy. The summer of 1961 may have been the most dramatic in terms of his self-improvement, and he would emerge from it as one of the top players in the NBA, capable of averaging 30 points a game.

"When Fred [Schaus] talked to me after that first pro season, he told me the things I must work on to become a star," he recalled. "Actually, they were such fundamentals as dribbling, ball handling, and passing."

Part of West's secret was that he didn't confine his work to just the off-season. He understood that playing with Baylor presented a rare opportunity. "My best teacher was Baylor," he said. "I owe so much to him. Elgin taught me how to get in the open for shots. Just watching him. The important thing is to get in position for shots. I spent the summer after my first season at camp, and I worked many hours improving my game. I was really enthusiastic about starting my second season."

With their success in the '61 play-offs, the Lakers gathered a quick following in Los Angeles, and they soon became popular with the Hollywood crowd. They had two exciting young stars, and Hollywood had learned long ago to love its stars. Lakers games became a place to be seen, and soon Lou Mohs was fielding regular requests from stars for complimentary tickets.

"Back then, if a celebrity wanted a ticket, he had to come see Lou personally," Mitch Chortkoff recalled. "I remember he got a call from Peter Falk, and Lou had never heard of him. This was before the *Columbo* TV series. The secretary explained that he was an actor, and Lou said, 'Well, he must be a bad actor if he can't buy his own tickets.' Then we convinced him that this was someone you should give tickets to."

Once Lakers management understood the value of the Hollywood connection, games at the Sports Arena became a parade of stars. Doris Day, Danny Thomas, Pat Boone, and other celebrities moved into regular courtside seats. "The celebrities had tremendous impact," Chick Hearn explained. "Put a guy like Jack Nicholson in the front row, and people will come to see the game and the star. Doris Day was a real heartthrob and a real star on the screen. Others would come occasionally. But she was a regular in those early days."

And it wasn't only Elgin and Jerry attracting them. Hundley turned on his flair for the Hollywood crowd as well.

"Doris Day and Pat Boone were big fans, on the sideline all the time," recalled Red Kerr. "She liked Rod very much. They all did. Before Pete Maravich, Rod was Pete Maravich. He did all that stuff behind the back, that razzle-dazzle stuff. Rod was great."

West could have played the part and probably could have been a very affable Beverley Hillbilly, but he had little stomach for the celebrity scene. "I have never been enamored with that part of Los Angeles," he said later. "I don't view those people as stars. I view them as people. That never affected me. I was not close with any of them. I know a lot of those people today. I was so shy at that time, and almost painfully shy. Even doing an interview was a chore for me. I never felt comfortable with publicity. Was never interested in it. Some people seek it. Some people like it. That was uncomfortable for me. What I did was just something I loved to do. If people liked to watch it, fine. But they sure didn't like to watch it much when we first started."

The entire NBA, however, seemed to enjoy a chance to go to Southern California for a few games and enjoy the sun. Before long, the weather, the Hollywood atmosphere, the beautiful women, all added up to a Lakers home court advantage.

"It was like a vacation for us, coming out of Syracuse, Boston— snow up to your ass and everything else," Kerr said with a chuckle. "All of a sudden you go out there, you gotta go buy some sunglasses to put on. Movie stars. That was their home court advantage. You'd go out, and you'd play the Lakers twice. You go out and play them maybe on a Tuesday and maybe on a Thursday. So you're out there for three, four days, and you'd just forget that you were there on business . . . We'd always head down to San Pedro; great wine and food. We're out screwin' around, and the Lakers were over at their place practicing."

For the Lakers, 1961–62 was one of those golden, fun-loving seasons in which almost everything seemed to go right. Even their only real setback during the regular season had its advantages. After opening the season on another scoring tear, Baylor was called into reserve duty with the army near Fort Lewis, Washington. As a result, he was able to appear in only forty-eight regular-season games. He made the lineup mostly on weekends or with an occasional pass, and when he did, he was fresh, ready, and virtually unstoppable. His 38.2 scoring average was second only to that of the prodigious Wilt Chamberlain, who averaged better than 50 points per game that season.

When Baylor wasn't there, West had to carry the load, which pushed him to do more with his game. West himself averaged 30.8 points per game that second year, an indication of just how much of the offense was in their hands. The schedule was dotted with games where he scored 40, even 50, points, but even that didn't please him.

"I didn't feel I was competent enough to be consistent," West explained. "I would have outlandish scoring games, but maybe the rest of my performance would not be what it should. That was such a unique learning experience for me, and I was nervous all the time. That was a time when I would defer more to other players on our team, to Elgin, because of his greatness. I didn't view myself as being in that category, even though I had started to make inroads into being a real good player. I had the ability to score, and I also had flaws in my game."

As his confidence grew, West began demanding the ball in the closing seconds with the game on the line, just as he had in college.

"I always thought that if we needed a basket, I could score," he said. "I didn't care who was guarding or what the defense was."

Noticing this late-game trend, Chick Hearn came up with a new name for the second-year guard: "Mr. Clutch." West didn't complain; he scored better than 30 points over the first four games of the season and that set the pattern. But hidden behind those numbers was West's defense.

"We didn't keep steals in those days," said the Lakers' longtime scorekeeper, John Radcliffe. "But if we had, Jerry probably would have led the league. He used to take the ball away from everybody. He knew how to time it just perfectly, taking it down low off the floor."

Against the Knicks on January 17, 1962, West hit for 63, his career single-game high, by making 22 of 36 shots from the field. He'd lay awake late that night, still buzzing over the game and feeling the electricity generated by his accomplishment.

"I had nights where you just couldn't guard me," West recalled. "I was making them from everywhere. If I made it from the outside, it was an impossible task for the defensive player to guard me. Quickness and the ability to draw fouls is an art. There are people who have great quickness who don't know how to draw fouls."

"It seemed Jerry could always get a shot," remembered Radcliffe, who watched all of West's home performances. "All he had to do was have the defender moving. Then he could get his shot off. It was a flat one. That's how he shot the ball back then. Flat. You could hang your clothes on the line."

Part of West's off-season labor had been to add arc to the shot. He wanted to perfect the ellipsis. In the meantime, even the flat ones seemed to go in, as his scoring average soared.

"I wasn't a point counter," West said. "One time I scored sixty-some against the Knicks. Either sixty-one or sixty-two, I'm not sure. I only played thirty-nine minutes in that game. It was one of those nights. I had other nights. I wasn't even a real solid basketball player at the time. There were things I could not do. But I had that huge night. There were other times I could have done the same thing if I had been playing in different circumstances with another team, a poor team."

The game, though, revealed that the Lakers still weren't an every-day item in Los Angeles: Only 2,766 fans were in attendance at the Sports Arena. Still, the team's second star had come into his own. In that regard, the Lakers' looseness made them the perfect team for West, particularly in 1962.

"It was an enjoyable year," Elgin Baylor remembered. "Our camaraderie was great. On and off the court, we did things together. We enjoyed one another. As a team, we gave the effort every night."

"The players then were closer," West said. "There was no reason to be jealous of anyone. No one was making any kind of money at all. Nothing like it is today. The money was so minute, and every day you didn't know if you were going to be there. There was no players' association, nothing to protect your rights as a player. You played for what those guys wanted you to play for. Period."

Even if you were a bit uptight, it was hard not to enjoy time with the likes of the wisecracking Hundley, Tommy Hawkins, and Rudy LaRusso. Known in Boston as "Roughhouse Rudy" (the nickname courtesy of Celtics radio man Johnny Most), the six-foot-eight, 220-pound LaRusso had developed into a tough-minded forward, able to rebound in traffic and hit his jumper from the key. He was a Dartmouth graduate, yet nothing about him suggested Ivy League.

"Rudy was good," Johnny Kerr recalled. "He was a defensive player. He was the banger on the team. A guy you didn't respect sometimes during the game; a guy who did the dirty work for them. When it was all over, you'd say, 'You know, that guy killed us.' He was a hard worker, very much a background player."

When the game ended, you could also count on LaRusso for a little entertainment, which made him a fitting partner for Hot Rod Hundley.

"One time in the Detroit airport, Rudy pulled this stuffed tiger off the shelf in the gift shop and started wrestling it," Hundley recalled.

"He fell down on the floor and was rolling around. We were crying, we laughed so hard. Rudy was a crazy man. When we went back up there on another trip, he figured it was time for a rematch with that tiger."

"Back then, you almost felt like you were a traveling freak show," West said. "You traveled with five people getting into a cab. Nothing was first class. Some of the hotels we stayed in were embarrassing. There were probably more characters associated with basketball because of the way you traveled. You had to do things to keep it lighthearted. It was hard." Schaus kept this chemistry going by rotating the road rooming schedule without regard to race, a major issue at the time.

Even with Baylor's intermittent schedule, they won the Western Division with a 54–26 record, 11 games better than Cincinnati, and whipped Detroit 4–2 in the division finals series. For the league championship, they faced the Celtics, who had ousted Chamberlain and the Warriors in the Eastern play-offs. West faced his first championship test as a pro, and he was excited. "Too worked up," he would admit later. But you had to be stoked to take on fire-breathing Bill Russell, whose team had taken four titles in five years. To match him, the Lakers had their usual solution: six-foot-eight Jimmy Krebs and six-foot-eleven Ray Felix. Krebs could score but didn't like to work in the post. A former rookie of the year, Felix could muscle around, do a little rebounding, and play whatever offense he could muster. "In one game, Ray took four shots, and Bill Russell blocked all four," Hot Rod Hundley recalled. "Finally, Ray backed in and tried to surprise Russell by flipping a shot over his shoulder. The ball went up over the backboard. Ray pointed at Bill and said, 'You didn't get that one, baby!' Bill looked at him like, 'You're crazy, Ray.' Ray was a little nutty. He had strange habits. Like, he'd eat his dessert first. We called him Baby Ray, because he called everybody baby."

Krebs, on the other hand, remained a limited player. "Krebs was effective against the Celtics because he was a perimeter pivot man," Schaus recalled. "When we sent him outside to shoot, he brought Russell away from the basket."

With Russell unable to hang in the lane, the Lakers worked their offense and sometimes got decent shots, but that wasn't their only reason to be hopeful. That Boston had defeated Philadelphia in the Eastern finals left the Lakers drawing a sigh of relief in Los Angeles. Chamberlain had averaged better than 50 points per game that season. "We couldn't stop Chamberlain on offense," Schaus recalled. "He was too dominant. Russell was dominant on defense. But he didn't present the same problems that Wilt did."

The series opened in dank, smelly Boston Garden, where the smoky haze hung over the floor. In that diffused light, the air took on a green hue. It was clearly Russell's lair, and the Celtics emphasized that in game one with a 122–108 victory. The Lakers' edge was that their legs were younger, and they used that the next night to deliver a 129–122 upset. A record crowd of 15,180 packed the Sports Arena for game three on April 10. West had never seen the place so crazy. All night the noise fed his adrenaline — as if he needed the boost. In the closing seconds, the Lakers were down 115–111 when West scored 4 points to tie it. Then Boston's Sam Jones tried to inbound the ball to Bob Cousy with four seconds remaining. Guarding Cousy, West laid back, then surged into the passing lane, stole it, and drove thirty feet for the winning layup, 117–115. Red Auerbach complained to the refs that it was impossible for West to dribble the distance to score with only four seconds left. The Lakers bench had feared as much. Everyone there shouted for West to pull up and shoot. But he kept digging for the goal and laid the ball in. It fell through the net as the buzzer sounded.

"I had deflected the ball on the run," West recalled. "I knew I would have enough time. Most things in my life have been instinctive. I played basketball that way. I always knew what the clock was."

All across West Virginia, radios were tuned in to the moment. Joe Chrest, West's high school teammate, was working the night shift as a dispatcher for a grocery chain. He listened to the game, amazed at the territory West had covered since those days when they imagined he was Easy Ed Macauley of the Celtics.

"It was a pretty amazing moment," Chrest remembered.

The crowd erupted into celebration with the play, and West went home that night buzzed like he'd never been buzzed about a game in his entire life. His greatness had revealed itself to him, and he took the luxury of lying there that night thinking long and hard about it. Unfortunately, the Celtics never allowed dreams to linger. They promptly killed any thoughts of prolonged jubilation in LA by taking game four, 115–103, and headed back to Boston with the series tied at two. There, it was all Baylor. Despite fouling out, he scored 61 points (an NBA finals record) and had 22 rebounds, while the Celtics' defensive specialist, Satch Sanders, contemplated another line of work. "Elgin was just a machine," Sanders said later.

Boston attempted to double-team him, but Baylor passed the ball too well for that to work, and he carried the Lakers in that fifth game, 126–121.

"It was one of those nights where his every effort seemed to guide him to just the right spot on the floor," West recalled. "He had that wonderful, magical instinct for making plays and doing things that you had to just stop and watch. He is without a doubt one of the truly great people who played this game. I hear people talking about forwards today. I don't see many that can compare to him. He wasn't unconscious that night. He just could do those things. It just happened. It's like when everything is perfect. You wake up in the morning and you feel so good. Your day just goes perfect, not an upset along the way. You just have those days. Your instincts to play the game are one thing. But your instincts to be in the right place are greater than the average player. His instincts to be in the right place probably got him five more baskets that night. Instead of having fifty-one, he had sixty-one. People can say, 'Oh, he scored fifty-one.' But sixty-one? That's a special night."

From the high of that game five win in Boston, the Lakers headed home with a 3–2 lead. The title lay right there before them. Win at home, that's all they had to do. The Celtics, though, again doused their hopes by tying the series with a 119–105 win in the Sports Arena. It was a huge loss, because they had to load back onto an airplane for yet another cross-country flight. Because they never had home-court advantage, the Lakers always needed more air travel to play in the championship series, with the wear and tear always a factor in the outcome.

On Wednesday night, April 18, they faced off in game seven in that hazy green air of the Garden, with its cramped dressing rooms and miserable facilities, the smell of piss hanging in the hallways. Auerbach may have had trouble drawing crowds in the early days—Boston never sold out even a season opener during Russell's great run. But you had to give the locals credit: Every sort of soul came out to pack the place for the play-offs. Where the LA crowds were too often imbued with that Hollywood cool, the New Englanders spent their pregame hours crowded into the city's bars. Then they'd pack onto the

Green Line, chug up the hill to North Station, and pour into the Garden with a hungry snarl.

The Celtics took a 53–47 lead at the half, despite the fact that their main offensive player, the magnificent Sam Jones, only netted 1 of 10 from the floor. The Lakers knew that a prodigious night from Baylor had delivered them earlier, and to win, they would have to have another. He took 18 shots in the first half and made 8.

The Celtics maintained their lead through most of the third and were ahead, 73–67, heading into the period's final minute. But West then scored 7 in a row to help tie the game at 75, setting up a fourth quarter that would haunt the Lakers for decades.

The Celtics first rushed up by 6, then fell back into a tie at 88 with six minutes left. Then Boston went back up by 3 again. Then the Celtics' Tommy Heinsohn fouled out, joining Satch Sanders and Jim Loscutoff on the bench; all had gone down trying to stop Baylor, who already had 38 points.

But Russell scored on a stickback seconds after that, and Boston breathed a bit at 96–91. West canned a jumper, and Baylor hit one of two free throws: 96–94. Boston then added two Russell free throws, and West answered with another jumper: 98–96. Then Sam Jones blocked Lakers guard Frank Selvy's shot and hit two free throws at the other end: 100–96. LaRusso picked up an offensive foul with a minute to go, and the Lakers seemed doomed.

Selvy, though, saved them momentarily by getting a rebound and driving the length of the floor for a layup. Seconds later, he repeated the act; this time, however, he missed the shot, but nabbed the rebound and scored to tie the game at 100.

The Celtics got the ball back with eighteen seconds left. Ramsey tried a driving hook shot in traffic and missed. LaRusso clutched the rebound, and the Lakers had a shot to win it. Schaus called time-out with five seconds to go.

"Schaus set up Elgin as the first option, and Jerry was the second," Hundley recalled. "If that failed, he said to get it to whoever else was open. I was in the game to handle the ball. In practice the day before, I fantasized that I made the winning bucket, a set shot. Once I got the ball, I moved right where I dreamed I would have the ball. Jerry and Elgin were covered, but Selvy was open on the left baseline."

Cousy, who was guarding him, had gambled for a quick double-team on West. "I passed it to Selvy," Hundley remembered, "and Cousy rushed back over to cover him. He got an open shot. It was about an eight-footer, the kind that Selvy always made."

It hit the rim and fell away, to be known forever as the shot that could have ended Boston's dynasty and the Lakers' agony before it ever began. "I would trade all my points for that last basket," Selvy told reporters afterward. "It was a fairly tough shot. I was almost on the baseline."

The ball came off the rim, and Russell, who would finish with 30 points and 40 rebounds, wrapped it in his arms for overtime. During the break, West looked down to the other bench, where Russell sat, dripping in sweat, seemingly exhausted. In the darkness, West wondered if the center had anything left. In time he would learn that the answer would always be, *just enough.*

The Celtics escaped with their fourth straight title in the extra period as they built a 5-point lead and won, 110–107. The Lakers could only think of what might have been.

"The major lesson was that you have to play every minute of a championship series," West said later. "That was the first time I ever felt that maybe good fortune was not on our side. Of all the ones we played, even though we didn't deserve to win that one—they were better than we were—good fortune almost let us win that one. It kept us close, but it didn't let us win it."

"Selvy thought Bob Cousy fouled him," Baylor recalled. "I thought Cousy fouled him. He took the shot from a spot where he was very proficient. Cousy said he never fouled him. I was in a position to get the offensive rebound. But somebody behind me shoved me out-of-bounds right into the referee. There was no foul call there, either. I looked around and saw Russell and Sam Jones were behind me. Some years later I got a copy of the game film. It was just what I suspected: Sam Jones had shoved me out-of-bounds."

"There's been a lot of publicity about Selvy missing the shot," West said. "But he made a couple of baskets to get us there. I never really talked to Frank about that. Then again, there was no tendency to blame people for things. Frank Selvy happened to miss the shot that we could have won a championship with. I think there's been too much said there in a negative way. There should be more positive. We were real fortunate to get there."

"It was tough in the locker room," Hundley remembered. "I was wishing I had taken the shot just like I had dreamed. Selvy felt really bad. He was sitting there with his head hanging down. I told him, 'Don't worry. You only cost us about thirty thousand dollars, you bastard.'"

"That's all right, baby," Ray Felix told them. "We'll get 'em tomorrow."

Tomorrow, of course, never quite came for West and the Lakers. Or for Ray Felix. The team released him after the season and employed two six-foot-ten rookies, Leroy Ellis and Gene Wiley, to share time in the post. To the backcourt, Los Angeles added veteran guard Dick "Skull" Barnett. "Dick Barnett was 'Fall back, baby!' That's what he said after his shots," John Radcliffe remembered. "He'd shout it out and hold up his follow through a little extra long. He was the only person in the NBA over six-four who couldn't stuff. Dick had some hang time, but he couldn't dunk." Still, when Barnett's confidence was high, he showed that he could aid the core of Baylor, West, and LaRusso as another scorer.

On the negative side, the Lakers traded Tommy Hawkins to the Royals for a draft pick. They would soon realize how much they missed his athleticism and smarts.

CHELYAN AGAIN

Only summers allowed time for Jerry West to make short trips home. And anyway, the world was just so big and bright in Los Angeles in the early 1960s that it was hard for West Virginia to compare.

Still, home had a way of coming to him when he least expected it. In late 1962, his father had a major heart attack, one that would require months of medical care. It was while Howard West was in the hospital that the next round of hard luck paralyzed the lives of his family. Cecile was cooking with oil in the kitchen one day in early 1963 when someone came to the door. She went to answer, delayed a moment too long, and suddenly the grease fire took up the kitchen and then shortly thereafter the entire frame house.

Barbara was the only child living in the household at the time. "It was devastating because we knew my father could not go back to work, and the house burned to the ground," she recalled. "We lost everything except my parakeet and an aluminum stepladder. My dad always wanted a house with a big front porch. We had a huge front porch, and we had put a hook in the ceiling. My bird was sunning himself, and I think I climbed up on the ladder and got the bird down."

The incident brought yet more humiliation for Cecile, and tremendous trauma for Howard, who wept in his hospital bed over the loss. All of Jerry's keepsakes had been lost. Contributors from the West Virginia University fan base later helped replace some items with reproductions and copies, but many special things were gone forever. Then again, West himself often seemed to have little sentimentality about the artifacts of his career. In Los Angeles, when he would be awarded game balls commemorating his milestones as a player and scorer, he would take them home and let his young sons play with them and ruin them. Other items he would simply throw away because he could not stand the dust they collected.

Rebuilding the home and lives of Howard and Cecile would take time. Fortunately, Charles West said, there was insurance. It provided coverage for their older home, but that money was not enough to cover the cost of building a new brick home. "They took out a mortgage to cover the difference," he said. And soon enough, construction was under way.

"We had a neighbor who had a bedroom in the corner of a house that was across from our property," Barbara recalled, "and he was kind enough to let us move into that house while we were rebuilding our house. By that time, my dad was up and about, and he enjoyed going over and watching the progress every day and talking with the workers and thinking he was contributing with the construction."

These events brought minimal coverage in the newspapers around the state; mainly a paragraph or two. And in Los Angeles, where West was busy playing his way through the 1962–63 season, the incidents rocked him but hardly drew any public notice or comment from him. Actually, the first edition of his 1969 biography and even subsequent printings, written with Bill Libby, strangely lists 1963 as the year Howard West died, but Jerry's father would not pass on until a second major heart attack on his birthday in 1967.

Some of West's confusion could perhaps be attributed to the dizzying pace of pro basketball travel. By his third season, he was finally getting accustomed to it. Many nights he was lucky to get two hours of sleep, especially with his fretting over and replaying games in his mind and the early departure dates on commercial airlines.

"We put up with it because we loved the game," West said.

The season was also remarkable in the dramatic decline of Hot Rod Hundley's skills and career. By the 1962–63 season, Hundley's partying had caught up with his basketball. His skills declined to the point that he became almost exclusively an end-of-game show.

"If they were way ahead or far behind, Schaus would put Hot Rod in to entertain the fans with his clowning and dribbling," Mitch Chortkoff recalled. "When they won, Hot Rod was the sign that the game was over, like Red Auerbach lighting up his victory cigar."

"I'd pull up beside Doris Day, where she was sitting at courtside," Hundley said. "I'd wink at her and tell her, 'This one's for you, baby.' Then I'd shoot a thirty-foot hook. She was gorgeous."

And the fans loved it. Opposing teams, however, weren't so amused, particularly if Hundley worked his act on their home floor.

"Rod had more than a little showboat in him," Johnny Kerr recalled. "Cousy would go behind his back and make this great pass and do a lot of stuff. But it wasn't showboat. It was innovative, before anyone else had done it. Hot Rod got to the Lakers, and he was Broadway. He was Showtime before they had Showtime. I remember we played against the Lakers one time, and he was doing a couple of things like that. I remember my best friend and roommate, Al Bianchi, was guarding Rod, and Rod came by him and went behind his back with the ball. And Al just knocked him on his ass, stood over him, and said, 'I fouled him.' Going behind the back in those days was greeted about like a dunk. We dunked some, but if you did, guys asked, 'What are you doing? You're really showing off, aren't you?' Today the NBA has packaged these things to be part of the high-wire act. But people didn't like it if Rod showed off too much."

St. Louis Hawks coach Harry "the Horse" Gallatin hated the clown game.

"One night I told Harry, 'Don't get too far behind tonight or it'll be Showtime,' " Hundley said.

Ultimately, Hundley himself picked up the tab for all the fun. "Rod was the only guy who came into the league making ten thousand dollars and left making ten thousand dollars," Kerr, a Hundley friend, explained. "The Lakers had made a huge trade to get Rod as their number one draft pick. They had traded Clyde Lovellette. It was a blockbuster."

"There's no question that if Rod had worked harder, he would have had a more productive NBA career," Schaus said later. "But he grew up under difficult circumstances. Considering that, he accomplished quite a bit."

With his lust for partying, Hundley saw his skills decline to the point that he would retire from the NBA at age twenty-seven, although he would remain a part of the team as a broadcaster with Chick Hearn.

CELTICS REDUX

The 1962–63 season brought major changes to the league. The Warriors and Chamberlain packed up and moved to San Francisco, giving the Lakers some company on the West Coast. The shifting of the divisions created a new rivalry for Los Angeles, although the Warriors' introduction to the new time zone would prove a bit rough. Wilt's scoring average dipped to 44 a game, and they lost a lot of games making their adjustment.

As usual, West had his eyes on the Royals back east. Cincinnati had added Ohio State's Jerry Lucas, West's brilliant and superbly skilled teammate from the Olympics. Suddenly there was speculation that the Celtics were aging and Oscar Robertson now had the team around him to hasten their decline. As the best team in the West, the Lakers rode that notion through an eleven-game winning streak, a club record, dotted with 30- and 40-point games by West. Indeed, there was some hope all around the league. Bob Cousy, whom West called the best he ever saw at lacing long passes down the floor and at running the break, had announced that he would retire after the season. Observers saw his leaving as a major loss to the Celtics, but they didn't see the wheels of Auerbach's mind turning. The previous spring, he had drafted John Havlicek out of Ohio State after the Lakers had drafted Leroy Ellis. Auerbach had seen Havlicek play in camp that summer. "I remember I was stunned," the Boston coach recalled. "All I could think of was, 'Ohh! Have I got something here! Are they going to think I'm smart!'"

Havlicek was just one of several new faces in the Celtics' locker room. Later Auerbach would get Don Nelson and Bailey Howell and several more key pieces to the puzzle. Plus Cousy's leaving meant that the Jones duo of K.C. and Sam would become a larger factor. Most important, though, was Russell.

Boston again claimed the Eastern Division with a 58–22 record in 1963, then faced Oscar Robertson and his new and improved Royals in a seven-game shakedown in the Eastern finals. Russell's team survived a game seven shootout in Boston Garden, 142–131.

West had suffered a painful torn hamstring muscle while diving for a loose ball in Madison Square Garden. He missed the last twenty-four games of the season but managed to return for the play-offs. The Lakers beat St. Louis in a seven-game Western final when West drove the Lakers to overcome a 7-point lead over the final minute of one game, then got one final steal and hit the game-winning jumper at the buzzer. Although he was back in rare form for the play-offs, the Lakers still hadn't worked out all the kinks as they endured another long plane ride east to face Boston in the championship series.

Auerbach allowed that his team was tired and ripe for plucking. The city, though, was pulsing with energy in anticipation of Cousy's last game. In reality, it was one of Boston's best clubs, with a deep, deep bench that helped form a perfect picture of team play. The Celtics eased by in game one in the Garden, 117–114. Game two wasn't much different. Boston took a 2–0 series lead, 113–106.

Back at their Sports Arena, the Lakers retaliated with a blowout, 119–99 (West scored 42, Baylor 38), only to see the Celtics take firm command by sneaking away with game four, 108–105, as they tied up West in team defense and held him to 18 points. Up 3–1, Auerbach was as confident as ever. "We've never lost three games in a row," he told reporters.

The Lakers headed back to Boston and found the stuff to survive. Tommy Heinsohn was ejected, Cousy fouled out with 12 points, and the LA duo went wild. Baylor had 43 points, West 32, as LA took one back, 126–119.

The loss fueled speculation that the Celtics had run out of gas, that the younger Lakers were about to surge ahead. In Los Angeles, a throng estimated at more than five thousand converged on the Sports Arena hoping to buy play-off tickets. When they found there were none, the scene turned angry. The Lakers quickly calmed things by offering closed-circuit TV seats at $2.50 a head. By game six, more than six thousand such theater seats had been taken, to go along with the fifteen thousand arena sellout. "We were aware we were testing the future of pay television," Lakers general manager Lou Mohs told reporters.

But that paying crowd saw Bill Russell dominate game six. And Havlicek had the hot hand, scoring 11 straight points to put Boston up by 14 at the half. The lead had dipped to 9 with eleven minutes left in the fourth period when Cousy tripped and sprained his left ankle. He didn't return until the five-minute mark. By then, the Lakers had cut the Boston lead to 1. At 2:48, the Celtics were holding on, 104–102. Then Heinsohn stole a West pass, drove and scored. From there, Cousy worked the clock as he had in the old days. He dribbled out the last seconds of his career and threw the ball high into the rafters of the space-age arena. Then he and Auerbach hugged as the final touch on a 112–109 win.

"The Lakers never seemed to be able to muster a center to match with or even come close to matching up with Bill Russell," Heinsohn said. "And, of course, we had a great team, and they had two great, great players. That was the measure of why that rivalry went that way all the time. We at times could shut them down. But then they'd break loose, they'd win some games. At times they'd shut us down. But the difference was that we had more guys who could pop out and score. So they always had difficulty playing against us. We knew we would always be involved in a terrific game . . . Elgin Baylor as forward beats out Bird, Julius Erving, and everybody else. A lot of people don't remember him, but he had the total game: defense, offense, everything, rebounding, passing the ball. And Jerry West played the two guard; what you call the two guard now. And he played the point guard, what they call the point guard now, and he was tough. West was what I call a freak. He had these long arms, and if you tried to match up to him and bring size into the situation, he would out-quick that guy. And if you matched up speed against West, West would shoot over that defender."

Cousy's career ended, and yet the Celtics got even better. Cousy's retirement opened the door for Sam Jones and K. C. Jones to play more minutes, and that only increased the complications for the Lakers.

For 1963–64, Los Angeles ran up a 31–19 record before West broke his thumb trying to steal the ball from Wilt Chamberlain. The Lakers went 11–19 afterward. West missed nine games and returned to the lineup as the Lakers finished 42–38 for 1964 and were eliminated by St. Louis in the first round of the play-offs.

Baylor had been troubled much of the season by leg and knee troubles, which brought West to realize just how much it meant to have him on the floor. "There's really a big difference playing with a healthy Baylor," West told the *Los Angeles Times*. "It helps my game and everyone else's too. You know I get just as many shots—many of them easier ones—when Elgin's playing as when he's not."

The next season, West would gain a full understanding of what Baylor meant to the team. With Wiley and Ellis maturing, the Lakers came back strong for 1964–65 and reclaimed the Western Division title with a 49–31 record. But Baylor suffered a severe knee injury on April 3 in the first game of the Western Division finals against the Baltimore Bullets.

"I went up for a shot, and my knee exploded," Baylor recalled. "I could hear a crack and a pop and everything else."

West and LaRusso were left alone to lead Los Angeles. They got help from their teammates, but it was impossible to replace Baylor. Gone were Selvy and Hundley and Krebs, who was killed in May 1965 in a freakish tree-cutting accident. Wiley and Ellis moved into the starting frontcourt together, and the Lakers also got 14 points per game out of guard Dick Barnett. Jim King, a second-year guard out of the University of Tulsa, rounded out the backcourt. Also filling out the roster were Don Nelson, Darrall Imhoff, and Walt Hazzard.

With Baylor out, the load fell on West, who responded by averaging 40.6 points over ten play-off games. In fact, over the six-game Western Conference play-off series with the Bullets, West averaged 46.3 points per game, a record that has withstood the test of even Michael Jordan's best. In one game against Baltimore, he scored 52 as Bullet guard Kevin Loughery struggled to stop him.

"I had to guard him when he averaged about fifty a game in the play-offs," Loughery recalled with a laugh, "so I had too many battles with him. I hated to guard him, I really did, because of his quickness. I'd rather guard Oscar Robertson, because Oscar just backed you down and beat you with strength. But Jerry embarrassed you. He was just so quick, one of the quickest guys for that size who ever played the game. In the old days, which is different from today, we didn't have help defense. You were on your own. You were out there on a lit-

tle island by yourself playing great players. That was a tough assign-
ment because he was one of the first players that had tremendous,
tremendous quickness but also could take the ball over the rim. Plus,
he was a great defensive player. Terrific competitor."

West's heroics proved good enough to take the Lakers back to the
finals for yet another meeting with the Celtics. But with Baylor out,
Boston waltzed through game one in Boston, 142–110, as K. C. Jones
held West to 26 points.

"K. C. Jones used to tackle West rather than let him get off a jump
shot," Schaus recalled.

"K.C. was a dog," Heinsohn said. "He'd go after you; he'd hang on.
He'd bite your pants leg and never let go. He was doing those kinds of
things. He was one of those guys."

"I absolutely hated playing against K. C. Jones," West said.

"You're guarding Jerry West, a guy who can shoot the ball *and*
drive to the basket," K. C. Jones remembered. "He's gonna have the
ball fifteen seconds of any twenty-four second period. There's pressure in that. So then he hits a couple on me from outside. I say, 'Uh-
oh.' So I get up on him, and he drives by me. So now I get scared. And
every guy playing defense gets scared, but it depends on how long it
took you to come out of it. With West, I had to come out of it in a
hurry."

"K.C. was aggressive, quick," West said. "Great lateral quickness,
and on top of it he had real quick hands. He fouled a lot. He got called
for some, but he fouled a lot. The great thing he did was that he tried
to get you to take shots in areas where you were not used to taking
them. At that time in my career, I had just started to develop an ability to take the ball to the basket, particularly to my left. And the one
thing he would do, particularly early in my career, he would sort of
funnel you to Bill Russell. Again, if your abilities are not good enough
to get away from that—and mine weren't at that time—you have to
play at a very high level. You had to be so good, and physically I
couldn't do those things sometimes. If I was best going to my right,
then I had to be really good that night going right, or really quick. As
I went along, I had a lot better success against him, because I learned
how to do everything. I learned how to handle the ball. I learned how
to go to my left a lot better. It was an adjustment, a growing adjustment in meaningful games. I think that's the one thing I was able to do

best. I was able to improve my game in a different phase year after year. And that's what helped me."

"We threw people at Jerry, too," Heinsohn said. "One, two, three people and worked him up the floor. He was a great individual player, but, Jesus Christ, he was entitled to get tired. That's the theory of all the Celtic victories . . . One guy can't beat you. We shut out the other four, and then that guy has to be superhuman, and it's easier to shut out the other four."

"West would go up for the jumper, and I'd charge him," K. C. Jones said. "Then he might give a head and shoulders fake—he was amazingly quick—and I'd go after him, from the side. Then another time, I'd be ten feet away from him. I'd approach slightly differently and jump straight up in the air. It seems impossible, but the anxiety we had created by our constant pressure made him waver, and sometimes I'd block the shot."

West didn't waver in game two of the championship series, scoring 45. But Boston still controlled the outcome, 129–123. Wounded as they were, the Lakers managed a home win in game three, 126–105, as West hit for 43 and Ellis, 29. The Los Angeles crowd celebrated by pelting Auerbach with cigars. Game four, though, was another Celtics win, 112–99, as Sam Jones scored 37. They went back to Boston to end it, 129–96, with the Celtics outscoring the Lakers 72–48 in the second half. At the outset of the fourth period Boston ran off 20 unanswered points. At one stretch, West, now thoroughly exhausted, missed 14 out of 15 shots.

"Jerry just carried that team out of sheer will," recalled Merv Harris, who covered the Lakers for the LA *Herald Examiner.* "By the fifth game of the finals, he was just a bundle of raw nerves, a wreck."

For Frank Ryan and Bob Short, the championship loss hardly mattered. As the sole owners of the Lakers, after having bought out numerous Minneapolis investors, they had hit the jackpot. The team had turned a whopping $500,000 profit for the 1964–'65 season. Suddenly they had leverage to strike new deals, the biggest being a proposed merger between the Dodgers and Lakers, with Short and Ryan owning 20 percent of the new sports conglomerate. But that deal was delayed while Dodgers president Walter O'Malley negotiated a broadcast deal for his club. In the interim, Jack Kent Cooke, a Canadian millionaire living in Pebble Beach, California, inquired about buying the Lakers. Cooke owned a minor league baseball team in Canada and one-fourth of the Washington Redskins football team.

"I had never heard of the Lakers or even seen a pro basketball game, when one of my investment advisers suggested I purchase the team," Cooke recalled. "The more I looked into them, the more I liked them."

At first Short declared that the team wasn't for sale, until his financial advisers suggested that he at least hear Cooke's offer. The Boston Celtics had recently sold for $3 million, so Short reached for something excessive.

"He said he wanted five million for the Lakers," Cooke said. "I asked to see a profit and loss statement and told him I'd think about it. The P&L Short gave me was just thrown together. I couldn't make any sense of it."

Cooke, a self-made man who had begun his career selling encyclopedias and soap, decided to buy the team anyway. Suddenly there was yet another strong personality calling the shots in Jerry West's professional life, someone who understood very little about basketball.

"He thought he knew," West said. "He didn't know."

It got to the point where Jerry hated anything green. Jerry told me, "I couldn't even wear a green sport coat or a green shirt for a lot of years." Green really rubbed him the wrong way.

—Bill Sharman

MISERY

Los Angeles, 1965 to 1969

THE SELLING OF THE LOS ANGELES LAKERS FOR $5 MILLION SENT shock waves across the NBA in 1965. Just eighteen years earlier, a group of Minneapolis investors had purchased the franchise for $15,000 from a Michigan jewelry store owner who had operated it for one miserable year as the Detroit Gems. A decade later, Bob Short and Frank Ryan diluted the stock of the Minneapolis Lakers investment group and ended up getting the shares for just pennies on the dollar.

Then Short and Ryan had packed the club off to Los Angeles while they remained back in Minnesota. To the players and to the people actually running the Lakers, it seemed almost obscene that these absentee owners could sell the franchise for such a huge profit.

As longtime NBA hand Marty Blake pointed out, Lou Mohs labored uncountable hours trying to keep the cash-strapped Lakers afloat. Although Bob Short made millions in selling the Lakers, he never gave Mohs a bonus for working so hard to build the investment,

Blake said. Blake, himself a former St. Louis Hawks GM, got a $100,000 bonus when owner Ben Kerner sold the Hawks to Atlanta investors in 1967. Mohs died just months after retiring from the Lakers that same year.

"All Bob Short did was cash the money," Blake said. "Louie never got a dime of it."

Perhaps no one was more shocked by the sale price than the players, especially West. Certainly the players weren't going to get anything out of the deal, even though they created value in the team. At least Baylor was one of the best-paid players in pro basketball. West's pay was still hindered by the fact that he had agreed to an inferior contract when he came into the league. In 1964, West took a hard line in negotiating his own contract and finally pushed his pay to $30,000 per season, still far short of other major stars. However, it was the stardom of Baylor and West that connected with the fan base in Los Angeles and drove the huge profits for the 1965 season; many felt that Short and Ryan were simply two distant figures who'd waited for the right time to profit. What made this even more difficult for those involved was that the management by the absentee owners seemed to be the cause of the team's financial troubles in the first place. Short was liked by some of the players, but he was rarely around. This fact was far from lost on West, who, like his mother, kept a keen eye on finances. It angered West that the owner had operated it from afar and didn't want to put anything into it. And then there was their personal chemistry. "Bob Short seemed to blame me for every loss, and I resented it," West told Bill Libby.

The idea that Short would profit so handsomely was almost too much to take, except that West welcomed the arrival of an owner who was going to be around the team. At least that was the way his relationship with Jack Kent Cooke started.

West had turned twenty-seven at the end of the 1965 play-offs. His time in the league had changed him. "When he first came to the Lakers, West was very quiet; not articulate at all," said Merv Harris, who covered the team. "As he came on as a player, he became more at ease, more articulate. But he still had that West Virginia twang. He was always disgusted with many players in the league who weren't dedicated to the game."

"I love basketball, now as much as ten years ago, so I'm not letting up any," West said at the time. "I want to do well so much it makes me sick. To me, the hardest part of the game is sitting around waiting. I'm just awful to my wife and kids on game days, and I'm just real glad when I can get the heck out of the house and into the arena. I get this nervous stomach, this awful feeling, before games, but, to me, this is a good feeling, because I know I'm ready to play. When I don't feel it, I worry, because then I know I'm not up for the game, and I have to figure out something to rouse myself."

"Jerry seems to feel as if the whole burden of each game is on his back," Jane West observed in early 1965. "I try to tell him there are four other players, but he seems to have the desire for everyone. When he makes a clutch play, I figure it's because he wants it so very much. If he doesn't have a good game and the team loses, he blames himself. If the team wins, he doesn't care what he did. Remember, in college at West Virginia, the team always seemed to win every game. Here, in pro ball, the best teams lose twenty or thirty games a season, which has been hard for Jerry to get used to. He takes it all so seriously.

"There are things a wife can do to help," Jane said. "He is just awful on game days. I let him have his way. I send him on errands. I tell him to save his haircuts for those days, anything to pass the time or get him out of the house. But, the truth is, the more worked up he gets, the better he seems to play. The night before he scored 63, he got hardly any sleep, the kids acted up, and we fought all day. And once the game is over, he's just Jerry again, a wonderful guy. Even when he loses, he's Jerry again. So I can put up with the rest of it. In fact, I love it all. We spend a fortune in baby-sitter's fees so I can go to every game. They say you shouldn't, but we're always talking basketball around the house. It may be a hard life, but it's a very exciting life and I know we'll miss it real bad when it's all over. I'm very proud of Jerry. He's come a long way, and I hope we can stay here a long time."

As West entered the prime of his career, the forces that shaped and controlled his professional life began to shift. Perhaps it's no coincidence that West, looking back, thought his ability to shoot a basketball had peaked with the 1965 season. Perhaps the circumstances had begun to wear on him. The run of three losses in the championship series certainly had worn on Fred Schaus. He would eventually leave the bench to become general manager of the Lakers, thus holding sway over West's life until Mr. Clutch was well into his thirties. Eventually their relationship would descend into bitterness and alienation.

The same was true for West's relationship with Jack Kent Cooke, although at first Cooke's presence brought much-needed attention to the franchise, as West explained. "He was a different kind of owner. Completely. At first it was tremendous. Jack Cooke was a much more dynamic man in the sense that he wasn't an absentee owner. An absentee owner like Bob Short has a hard time really looking at what he had there, except for what it does financially."

But as West came to realize, the remarkably forceful personality of Jack Kent Cooke soon had control of the basketball decisions, even though he knew little about the game. He would turn the team upside down with a series of coaching hires until he finally found someone who could do the job.

As the 1965–66 season opened, the new ownership set a different agenda. Among Cooke's biggest moves was merely capitalizing the team. A brusque, efficient executive, he immediately set out over the summer of 1965 to transform the Lakers from a small, haphazardly run venture into a sound business. While the Watts riots, which left thirty-four people dead and more than one thousand injured, horrified the city that summer, Cooke charged into the task of transforming the Lakers with a flurry of memos and acerbic reminders to employees. Nothing escaped his view, from an occasional Chick Hearn mispronunciation to a receptionist's tardiness in answering the front office phones. If the memos didn't get the job done, Jack Kent Cooke tended to shout.

"Mr. Cooke brought immediate change to the atmosphere around the team," remembered John Radcliffe, longtime Lakers scorekeeper. "Everybody was on eggshells. We were afraid to make a mistake, because we were gonna get yelled at. He yelled at Fred Schaus too. It was his style. He didn't hold anything back. He always seemed to imply that people weren't bright."

"Mr. Cooke shouted and screamed at anyone who didn't give him perfection," explained Bill Bertka, longtime Lakers scout and assistant coach. "He was interested in the bottom line, in success, in winning. That's all he wanted."

"The Lakers had been a mom-and-pop organization until Cooke arrived," said Merv Harris, the veteran Lakers beat writer. "Pro bas-

ketball was getting bigger in the midsixties, and Cooke was the kind of guy to help it get bigger. He was a very complex man. He could be extremely charming, extremely unreasonable, extremely cold."

"He was the number one asshole that ever lived," said Hot Rod Hundley. "He was totally, absolutely, unbelievably wrapped up in himself and had no respect for anyone but himself."

There were exceptions to his exactness. Cooke could let an employee's honest $50,000 mistake go by without comment, then explode over mere pocket change. Because he knew business and possessed a flair for marketing and promotion, Cooke concentrated there in his first months with the team. "Jack Kent Cooke was basically a salesman," said Robert "Jake" Embry, former owner of the old Baltimore Bullets. "He was a pretty good one."

After acquiring the Lakers, Cooke turned his focus on a National Hockey League franchise for Los Angeles. To get that, he had to have a place to play. But the commission for the city-owned Sports Arena turned back his attempts to secure an agreement there. The commission debate went back and forth until Cooke grew frustrated and decided to finance and build his own building. He wanted to call it the Forum, and Chick Hearn thought that was a fabulous name. Soon the new owner had located a piece of land, and before long, crews had begun constructing the Lakers' new home.

RECOVERY

West may have been masterful in the 1965 play-offs, but the experience had mostly stressed just how valuable Baylor was to the team. Unfortunately, doctors had told Baylor that his knee injury had ended his playing career, and for a time he believed them.

"The main ligament in my knee had been damaged, and my kneecap was split, almost in half," Baylor recalled. "When it first happened, I was worried that I'd never even walk again."

But after a time, the pain subsided, and Baylor found he had some mobility. "The more I thought about it, the more determined I became to prove the doctors wrong," he said.

"Afterward to watch the slow, painful process of him getting better and improving and never really getting back to where he was, that was the thing that was difficult for the rest of us to accept," West re-

called. "We wanted him back having all his greatness. He came back and played, and played incredibly well. But he wasn't the Elgin Baylor of old."

By training camp that next fall, Baylor was able to see limited action. Eventually he would return to full speed, but never again would he be the dynamic player he had been. Before, Baylor had dazzled opponents with a fearless approach to driving and rebounding. After the injury, that part of his game diminished. "It was very, very difficult," Baylor recalled. "I would try to do a lot of things that I just couldn't do. It was frustrating. But it made me more determined, too. Before I was injured, I loved to penetrate and create, to pass off or take the shot. At times after I returned, I just couldn't do it. My knee wouldn't respond. I couldn't rebound as well. It just wasn't there. I just couldn't run the same. I had to rely more on perimeter shooting and posting up occasionally."

He played in sixty-five games the following season, 1965–66, and averaged 16.6 points. West, meanwhile, scored at a 31.3 clip and became the top option in the Lakers' offense. He also averaged 7.1 rebounds and 6.1 assists, a sign of just how much of the team's offensive burden had fallen to him. But Baylor's mere presence made them stronger, and he and West remained very much a superstar duo.

For 1965–66, the Lakers had also picked up excellent guards from John Wooden's first national championship teams at UCLA. Walt Hazzard came in the 1964 draft, and Gail Goodrich arrived a year later. With the picks, the Lakers obviously hoped to draw on the growing UCLA mystique in Los Angeles. With the young guards on the payroll, the Lakers opted to ship veteran Dick Barnett to New York for forward Bill Bridges, who would be lost to the Chicago Bulls in the expansion draft less than a year later. The net of those moves left the Lakers short on experienced guards. West was dismayed by that, feeling it subtracted from their ability to win.

"I always thought Dick Barnett was a very underrated player," West said. "Defensively he never got his just due. He had a reputation for being a scorer, a reputation for being a character, but he was a very good defensive player. He got traded in a move that was not very popular among the players."

For 1966, they not only faced a deficit in the post but in the backcourt as well.

"I'm prejudiced," West observed. "I think guards have to do more

on the court than anyone . . . Sometimes it's more difficult for guards to do it. My gosh, you get defended here. You get defended there. So it's a more wearing, more difficult job than playing up front. So I'm prejudiced. I love to have great centers. But the most frustrating thing in the world is not to have someone competent playing alongside you as a guard."

As a guard, West's top challenge remained Robertson. He continued his streak following the 1965 play-offs with what seemed like a personal battle with the Big O that December. Twice within a matter of weeks West scored 51 points against the Royals during a stretch of six games where he scored more than 40 points.

On Christmas Eve 1965, he scored 51 while Robertson scored 48 in leading Cincinnati to a win. A week later, West outscored the Big O 51 to 31, and the Lakers won by nineteen. During that period, West had another game where he scored 46 against Robertson and the Royals, leaving little question that he coveted the opportunity to compete against his old rival.

"It's hard to separate them," Lakers GM Lou Mohs said at the time.

"But Oscar is bigger and stronger and dribbles better. Jerry has other qualities."

In many respects, West had the perfect coach for accommodating such battles.

Schaus, heading into his ninth year as West's coach, had fallen into a different role as his friendship with his star player had grown. It was clear that Schaus had come to view West as his coach on the floor. In time-outs, he offered suggestions rather than ordering changes. Schaus considered West an almost perfect embodiment of a guard. "He has everything," the coach told the *Los Angeles Times*. "Long arms, a fine shooting touch, speed, quickness, all the physical assets. In addition, he has the greatest temperament for basketball I've ever seen. He has a tremendous dedication to the game. Moreover, he conditions himself to the game and the situation. If he has a bad one, you know he'll come back and tear you up. He's smart and has great basketball sense. He used to get mad at himself, but he's gotten over that now, and his mental approach is perfect. The reason he's so good in the clutch is that nothing bothers him. He remains cool because he's concentrating to the utmost. Even if he's hurt, he can come through in the clutch because that's all he's thinking about. Another thing about him is that he works on his weakness. I knew when he was a youngster and he was practicing on those hot summer days in West Virginia that he was destined for greatness. He is dedicated. In my nine-year association with him, he's never presented a problem. If the Lakers were to get rid of Jerry, they might as well send me along too, because I'd be lost without him."

Schaus's last comment remains curious, even decades later. In a 1992 interview, West revealed that he had harbored hard feelings toward his coach since his playing days.

"When Fred Schaus was the coach, it got back to me that he wanted to trade me," West recalled. "He wanted to trade me for Walt Bellamy because he needed a center. I said to myself, 'I have performed for him in college. I have performed for him as a professional better than he ever dreamed I could perform.' And his teams won. To trade me for Walt Bellamy, I felt, was a real slap in my face. I know it had been talked about, and to this day, that's the one thing that really rankles me. It wasn't that I felt that I was too good to be traded, but to be traded for something of that nature I thought was a real slap in my face. I almost wish in some respects I had been traded, because I would have had an opportunity to come back and play against his teams. That always gives you some sort of tremendous emotional lift. I had never thought of myself as not being expendable, even as a player. But I think when you are put with a group of people that seems to work well, any thought of that group getting separated by a trade or whatever, those are the things that really stay with you."

Asked at the time about West's charge, Schaus seemed truly surprised. "We would never have considered trading Jerry West," he said.

Mitch Chortkoff, the veteran LA sportswriter and West's friend, agreed, "I don't think they were trying to trade him. That's just the perfectionist in Jerry West, somehow projecting that."

"There was a trade being considered for Walt Bellamy at one time," recalled Merv Harris. "West was not involved. West was the on-floor tactical key to the Lakers' success. They weren't thinking about trading him."

Why would West harbor such notions? Why did Michael Jordan hold similar dubious grudges? The best answer is that highly competitive, alpha-male types often seize on any detail to blow it up in their minds as a source of motivation, as a means to push themselves further. They have to believe such details for them to be effective. That seems to be the best explanation that any of West's longtime associates can come up with to explain the supposedly phantom trade.

CIGARS, AGAIN

That spring of 1966, the Lakers won the Western with a 45–35 record and eliminated the Hawks in a seven-game conference final series. Once again, the issue fell to contending with the Celtics for a championship.

The 1966 championship series quickly turned into another Celtics-Lakers scrap. The Celtics had a 38–20 lead in game one in Boston Garden, but the Lakers fought back to a 133–129 win in overtime. Baylor scored 36; West, 41. But instead of the glory and the psychological edge falling to the Lakers, the attention shifted abruptly to Boston. Red Auerbach craftily announced that forward Russell would replace him as head coach. Working as a player-coach, Boston's center would become the first black head coach in a major American sport. The announcement made headlines the next morning, while the Lakers' upset became a secondary story. Observers would hail it as Auerbach's brilliant mind game to diminish the importance of a big Lakers win in game one, and the Celtics coach didn't discourage such talk.

With the future of the team settled, the Celtics bore down on the Lakers, winning the second game in the Garden, 129–109, then adding two more victories in Los Angeles for a 3–1 lead. The major problem for the Lakers was Boston's John Havlicek, who could swing between guard and forward. Schaus had tried to play Rudy LaRusso, a forward, on Havlicek, but it hadn't worked. "No one in the league his size is even close to Havlicek in quickness," Schaus told reporters.

So the Lakers coach used the rookie Goodrich on Havlicek. West moved to forward, and this three-guard lineup left Los Angeles weak on the boards. But it worked. West, Baylor, and Goodrich lashed back and won games five and six to tie the series at three apiece. Once again the championship had come to a seventh game in Boston Garden. The Celtics took a big lead, as Baylor and West were a combined 3 for 18 from the floor in the first half. As usual, the Lakers cut it close at the end, paring the Boston lead to 6 with twenty seconds left. Massachusetts governor John Volpe figured it was time to light Auerbach's victory cigar. The Lakers took exception to that, cutting the lead to 95–93 with four seconds left.

The fans always rushed the floor to celebrate Boston's championships and chose to do so with time remaining in 1966. Russell was knocked down. Orange juice containers on the Celtics bench spilled across the floor, and Boston's Satch Sanders lost his shirt to the crowd. Somehow K. C. Jones got the inbound pass to Havlicek, who dribbled out the clock for Boston's ninth championship.

No one was more angered by the early cigar than Schaus. "I would have loved to shove that victory cigar down Red Auerbach's throat," the Lakers coach recalled years later. "We came awfully close to putting that damn thing out."

Auerbach's cigar smoke would roil through the decades for the Lakers, and there was nothing they could do about that. But Russell's first year on the bench had finally opened the door for someone else to win a title. The Celtics faltered, and Wilt Chamberlain and the Philadelphia 76ers stepped into the gap in the Eastern Conference. West was in his prime and seemed a likely candidate to succeed. Instead he was met with a plague of injuries and hard times. He had missed two dozen games with a torn hamstring in 1962–63, but other than that had enjoyed relative health despite his slight frame. The Lakers' lack of frontcourt depth meant that more and more he was back playing the forward position, where the game's big men seemed infuriated every time he claimed a rebound from them. As a result, he finished the season quite battered.

He opened the 1966–67 campaign with a painful foot injury that cost him the first nine games. The Lakers, as a result, got off to a slow start. West rounded into form by December, and for the next two months he impressed observers as perhaps the best player in the sport. On offense, he produced a run of 30- and 40-point games. On defense, he brought to mind a miniature Bill Russell with a flurry of blocked shots and steals. The trouble started in early February when he banged his hand trying to steal the ball from Chamberlain. West shook that off and watched his team take off on a winning streak. The club had traded for center Darrall Imhoff, and the extra frontcourt help (they also added smooth-shooting big man Mel Counts) started to make a difference.

As February closed, the Lakers were making their way through yet another East Coast road trip when West learned that his father, who had been back in the hospital, had died. "He passed away on his sixty-seventh birthday," Barbara West recalled. "He had his second heart attack, and I guess he had congestive heart failure, and that killed him."

That night, the Lakers played Detroit in a doubleheader in Madison Square Garden. West hit the winning jumper in the last seconds, finished with 34 points, then got on a plane and headed home to Charleston for two days for the funeral. The family buried Howard with the military honors that he had so often bestowed on others, and he was laid to rest just as David was, in the Memorial Gardens at London Memorial Park cemetery. Always comfortable in the public eye, Howard would have liked that the wire services noted his passing in brief stories that ran in newspapers across West Virginia and even in California.

Afterward West boarded a plane and caught up with the team. The Lakers had been behind all season, and with the play-offs just ahead, there was still much catching up to do. West rejoined them for a home game the next night and scored another 34 points in defeating the Knicks.

Less than a week later, in a game at Madison Square Garden, West's nose was broken for the seventh time in his career. Jim Murray wrote that the Lakers star arrived back in Los Angeles with "two black eyes and a nose so broken he could breathe better through his ears." Their next game with the extremely physical St. Louis Hawks was only six minutes old when bruiser Paul Silas knocked West to the floor and opened a gash in his eyelid that required stitches.

The injuries seem to follow in one bad flush of karma after that. Playing with his swollen eyelid still in stitches, West then severely pulled his hamstring and missed four games, only to return and immediately suffer a badly sprained ankle.

The Lakers limped to a 36–45 finish and faced the Warriors in the play-offs. West missed the first two games, both home losses, but managed to make an appearance in game three in San Francisco's decrepit Cow Palace. There he played a matter of minutes before breaking his hand. The Warriors swept the series, 3–0, to end an eerily frustrating campaign. The loss was enough to convince Schaus that he needed a break from coaching. "It was a good time to let someone else try their hand at it," he recalled. "I moved to the front office."

"Most of our players responded very positively to him early on,"

West said of Schaus's years on the bench. "Obviously, later in their careers, when a coach has been around a few years, they've heard all of his stories. Frankly, it wears out. He did a very competent job with our team. We played hard all the time, and I think that's a tribute to the coach."

IN DUTCH

Schaus replaced Lou Mohs as general manager and began fielding questions from Cooke about a coaching replacement. Schaus put together a list of five candidates.

"Mr. Cooke read in *Sports Illustrated* that Butch van Breda Kolff had coached Bill Bradley at Princeton," Schaus recalled. "So he was on the list. Butch interviewed extremely well. Mr. Cooke liked his decisive style."

"Butch was a strong personality," the Lakers' Bill Bertka recalled. "They called him the Dutchman. They also called him bullheaded and stubborn."

A former drill instructor in the military, van Breda Kolff brought a major change in style to the Lakers. He stressed conditioning and wanted to get the rest of the team involved in the offense along with West and Baylor. For years, teammates had complained that Schaus wanted only West and Baylor taking shots, which left him open to criticism that no one else had confidence in the clutch. Van Breda Kolff took the ball out of West's hands, used him even more at forward, and told reporters that pro players, especially West, weren't fundamentally sound.

"When van Breda Kolff came in, he brought an eastern style of play, with all five men moving and everybody sharing the ball," Bertka explained.

"Oh, Lord, was there ever changes," West recalled. "Not only in style but also in the attitude surrounding the team. There was a volatile person who pretty much said what he thought. He felt that was the way to do it. You cannot do that at the professional level. He was a purist. But on the professional level, it won't work."

Schaus had blended his pro experience with the running game to fashion a pro style for his team. But van Breda Kolff's approach was a profound departure from that, and it took the players a half season to adjust. Beyond style, he treated his pros like college boys, going so far as to institute a bed check. The only problem was, van Breda Kolff would make the check but wind up visiting with his players, sipping beer in their rooms and talking basketball for hours until they begged *him* to get some sleep.

"Some coaches want to win every game," West said. "In the NBA, you can't do that. It was difficult for him, because it's no fun to lose. As a college coach, he might have lost five games in a season. On the pro level, he might lose five in a row over a two-week period. It's more difficult, because coaches have to be able to handle losses."

Still, it was quite a change for West to have someone actually coaching him again. And certainly West taught his new coach a thing or two as well. Van Breda Kolff didn't like the way he played defense, then watched him in action, and thought better of trying to get him to change. West had worked out his own system that fared quite well against opponents, the new coach acknowledged.

In December 1967, just eighteen months after breaking ground, Jack Kent Cooke's Forum opened for business. Throughout construction it had been referred to as "Cooke's Folly," which only steeled the owner's determination to make it a structure that would stick in the Sports Arena Commission's craw for a long, long time. He had looked across Los Angeles and the San Fernando Valley before settling on a twenty-nine-acre site in Inglewood, at the intersections of West Manchester Boulevard and South Prairie Avenue, next to Hollywood Park. Built about the same time, the Spectrum in Philadelphia cost approximately $5 million, but Cooke plowed $16 million into his Forum. No expense was spared. Each of the eighty columns supporting the roof stood fifty-seven feet high and weighed fifty-five tons, so large that they had to be formed on the work site.

Construction crews worked double shifts under giant lights to make sure that the building was finished on the date Cooke had promised the NHL. The owner painstakingly oversaw every detail of the process. His building would set the standard for ultimate ambience, with unique, fully upholstered, extra-wide theater-style seats, and rows spaced to provide more legroom. It opened on December 30, 1967, with Cooke beaming as his Los Angeles Kings defeated the Philadelphia Flyers in a nationally televised hockey game.

The next night, New Year's Eve, the Lakers played their first game there, blasting the San Diego Rockets, who had a young sub named Pat Riley, 147–118.

"I was just so proud," Cooke recalled. "It was a special night."

A press release boasted that his Forum would "be in essence a modern version of the greater Colosseum of ancient Rome."

The Roman motif set Cooke's creative juices to flowing. A former bandleader, he wrote fight songs and cheers for both his hockey and basketball teams and authored nicknames for his hockey players, which he instructed his broadcasters to use on the air. And he designed uniforms for both hockey and basketball. No longer did the Lakers wear their traditional blue and white. Cooke outfitted them in purple and gold, only he hated the word *purple* and insisted that the team call it Forum blue, which left Chick Hearn advising television viewers not to adjust the color on their sets. In the Forum, the Lakers wore gold, the first time in NBA history that the home team didn't wear white.

"Mr. Cooke called them Forum blue, but they were purple," Bill Sharman said. "At least *we* thought they were purple. Everybody said, 'That's purple, that's not blue!' But he wanted to make it different."

"Mr. Cooke dressed the ushers in togas, with slacks for the men and short pants for the women," John Radcliffe remembered. "The ladies did not like 'em, to say the least. The male staff were issued purple blazers with gold patches, to be worn with white dress shirts and black ties. One night I wore a gold turtleneck with my blazer, and the next day I got a memo from Cooke reminding me of proper dress. Rod Hundley looked at my blazer one night and said, 'John, you ought to have that thing cleaned and burned.'"

The new building meant a realignment of celebrity seating. When Doris Day and her husband asked to have their seats moved, Cooke learned that they weren't paying for them. So he informed Day's husband that they would have to start paying, leading Day to decide that she wouldn't be attending any more Lakers games. Cooke didn't care. All of Los Angeles seemed to want seats, including Walter Matthau and Jack Nicholson, who gladly paid.

In his last game at the Sports Arena, West made a point of saying good-bye to the building where he had faced the Celtics in so many battles. He wondered if the change of scenery would change the Lakers' luck. It couldn't make it worse. His plague of injuries had picked up immediately with the start of the 1967–68 season. West had broken his hand again in the exhibition season, then added back troubles and a hip pointer. "Sometimes injuries lead to injuries," he said when reporters asked about his run of bad luck. He would miss thirty-one games over a season and a half. He reminded the media that even with those missed games, he had still logged more court time than any other NBA guard over the seven seasons he had been in the league.

"It's been discouraging," he admitted when asked about the injuries and revealed that they had even driven him to thoughts about retiring as he neared his thirtieth birthday.

That February, a year after his father died, West got news that Roy Williams, his high school coach, had succumbed at age sixty in a Charleston hospital. The smoking, it seemed, had finally caught up with him.

The new building to his liking, West was playing well in February when he again injured his hamstring. He missed games, then fought back and again started playing well. He was engaged in a furious battle one night with Oscar Robertson in Cincinnati when the Royals' hulking Connie Dierking broke his nose yet again. Finally, West missed the last two games of the regular season to have surgery on his nose. Even though there were dangers involved, he launched right into the play-offs after a brief convalescence. Van Breda Kolff's Lakers had struggled along until January, when they acquired Erwin Mueller and Fred Crawford, who gave them quickness off the bench. From that point, they rolled through a 38–9 run, good enough for a 52–30 finish, second place in the West behind the Hawks.

"That second half of the season, the team realized van Breda Kolff's vision," Bill Bertka recalled. "They were really a happy bunch. They shared the ball and moved it around."

Guard Archie Clark, out of the University of Minnesota, proved to be a fine addition, with quickness, strong defensive desire, and an ability to score. He was one of the few players who could carry the team offensively as West had. And Gail Goodrich, now in his third season, had come into his own.

"They called him 'Stumpy' because he was only about six feet, but he had the longest arms in the NBA," Lakers scorekeeper John Radcliffe recalled. "Goodrich was left-handed and fearless going to the basket. He would disappear into a crowd of big men; then suddenly the ball would kiss off the glass and fall in."

At center was Darrall Imhoff, short on talent but long on willing-ness to sacrifice. He set scores of picks for Baylor, West, and Clark.

From the bench, van Breda Kolff urged this group with an anima-tion never seen before in Los Angeles. "Butch was just all over the place," Radcliffe remembered. "It was amazing how he would just throw himself down on the seats. The body language alone was enough to get him technicals."

Though he racked up the technical fouls in bunches, the Dutch-man drove his Lakers through the play-offs. They nailed the Chicago Bulls, in just their second season, 4–1, then swept the Warriors in the Western finals. Disposing of their postseason opponents so efficiently left them eight days of watching the Celtics and 76ers battle in the Eastern finals. The Lakers worked to stay fresh, but practices couldn't approximate the intensity of games. As van Breda Kolff feared, they grew stale.

The Celtics had finished second in the divisional standings at 54–28, eight games behind the 76ers, who won 62 games. Philly took a 3–1 lead in their play-off series, only to watch the Celtics come back. The Lakers followed the games on television and pulled for Boston, figur-ing that player-coach Russell would be easier to beat than Chamber-lain. Boston did come back to whip Philadelphia, advancing to the championship round for the eleventh time in twelve years. "If we can rebound, we can win," West told the writers. "We're little, but we match up well with Boston. We're quick, and we shoot well, and that can be enough in a seven-game series."

They alternated Mel Counts and Darrall Imhoff in the post, and Mueller's quickness helped out on the boards. Archie Clark joined West in the backcourt, with Goodrich and Crawford coming off the bench. Baylor was still the man in the corner, but Tommy Hawkins had returned to the team to provide depth at forward.

By now, the championship series had become a comfortable stage for West. "I never looked at it as pressure," he recalled. "During the season, you didn't worry about things like that. But when the play-offs start, you always have your goals and aspirations of winning a cham-pionship. We were pretty consistent in getting there."

And always consistent in creating early trouble. The Lakers opened the series with a not-too-surprising split in Boston Garden. They lost the first, 107–101, when West shot only 7 for 24, and Baylor 11 for 31. But they pulled their usual surprise and won the second,

123–113. The Celtics returned the favor when the series switched to the Forum, winning game three, 127–119. Then West scored 38 points and Baylor added another 30 as Los Angeles evened the series with a 119–105 win in game four, after van Breda Kolff had been ejected. West, however, sprained his ankle in the closing minutes, dampening the victory. It appeared serious enough to keep him out of game five back in Boston. He played anyway and scored 35, but it wasn't enough to counter the Celtics, who jumped to a 19-point first quarter lead. By the third quarter, the lead was still 18, but LA came back to tie the score at 108 in the fourth. The Lakers were down four with less than a minute to play when West stole the ball and found Baylor downcourt for a layup. The Lakers then tied it when Clark got another steal and West scored. But in overtime, Russell blocked a Baylor shot, and Nelson hit a late free throw to give Boston a 3–2 series lead, 120–117.

Just as the series returned to Los Angeles for game six, with the tension turned high, things went terribly awry for the Lakers. It began with the national anthem. Johnny Mathis, the featured vocalist, launched into "God Bless America," then realized his mistake and switched to "The Star-Spangled Banner." The best switch of the day, though, was made by Coach Bill Russell, who moved Sam Jones to forward, where he scored over Goodrich and forced van Breda Kolff to go with a taller, slower lineup. The Lakers never could get it together defensively. Havlicek scored 40; Bailey Howell, 30. The Lakers trailed by 20 at the half, and Boston danced to its tenth title.

"He is an unbelievable man," West said of Russell afterward. "To be frank, we gave them the championship. We gave them the first game, and we gave them the fifth. But I take nothing from them. There is something there, something special. For instance, twice tonight the ball went on the floor, and [Larry] Siegfried dove for it. He didn't just go for it hard, he dove for it. And they're all that way on the Celtics, and you can't teach it."

"We weren't a dominant team," Bailey Howell said of those teams that Russell coached. "Unless everyone was playing well and together, we couldn't win."

"I don't really dwell on any part of my basketball career," West said. "That is a part of my life I'm very proud of, but I don't really like to talk about it very much. We never really seemingly had the right mix. I believe in chemistry very, very much. Without chemistry, talented teams can fail. We always were close, but we always were a body with chemistry short. It's not easy to find the right people in this league."

In the aftermath of yet another Lakers loss in the championship round, the team's management began pondering the next move. It didn't have to wait long. "That May," Jack Kent Cooke recalled, "Philadelphia 76ers owner Irving Kosloff phoned me in my Forum office and asked if we would be interested in Wilt Chamberlain.

"Struggling to speak in measured tones, I said that we certainly would be."

GIANT EXPECTATIONS

Wilt Chamberlain had long ago learned that it wasn't easy being the giant, especially in a five-man game. "I felt that I was gifted enough to do some things on the basketball floor," Chamberlain said. "I couldn't do everything I wanted to do, because if that was the case, I'd have won every game."

As big and talented as he was, Chamberlain's career progress had often been frustrated by the presence of Boston's Bill Russell. Whereas Chamberlain struggled most of his career, seemingly out of context, Russell always seemed to have the right coach, the right teammates, and they got the right results. On the other hand, Chamberlain's career was a profound contradiction. For him things were wonderfully easy and terribly difficult all at the same time.

"The world is made up of Davids," he once explained, "and I am Goliath."

"Wilt was my greatest opponent," Russell said years later. "It's not even close. There's no doubt about that."

As a six-foot-eleven ninth grader in Philadelphia, he led his undefeated Overbrook High team against West Catholic High in the finals of the city championship, where a scenario developed that would become miserably familiar to Chamberlain over the years. West Catholic packed four players around him inside, but his teammates couldn't make the open shots. Overbrook lost its only game of the season. Over the next three years, his teams won fifty-eight games and lost just three, while Chamberlain averaged 36.9 points (he scored 90 in

one game). His junior and senior years provided a study in dominance, with Overbrook claiming consecutive city titles. A friend in the
NBA public relations office got Chamberlain a summer job as a bell-
hop at Kutshers Country Club in New York's Catskill Mountains.
There, while still in high school, he played against the best talent pro
and college basketball had to offer, humbling Philadelphia Warriors
center Neil Johnston in one game. The pro scouts knew Chamberlain
was ready then, but NBA rules forbade drafting a high schooler. So he
chose the University of Kansas, where the Jayhawks' offense focused
on his towering presence.

Which meant that opposing defenses did the same.

"That was always the problem when Wilt was playing with us,"
said former Kansas coach Dick Harp. "The defense was always going
to concentrate on him. Teams would rig zone defenses around him
with three and four men, making it impossible for him to move, particularly around the basket."

"You know, basketball is a team game, played by positions, played
in different times," Chamberlain said. "I was fortunate to come along
at a time that was great basketball, a different kind of a game, played
a little bit more technically. I was a different breed of athlete at that
particular time."

As a result, defenders became quite physical with him. "It was difficult for the officials to be objective about Wilt," Harp said. "There
were numerous opportunities for officials to call defensive fouls. But
most of the time, they didn't. Wilt, though, always managed to keep
his composure and managed to power through our opponents."

But as Chamberlain himself noted, his frustrations led to errors in
his method. When he rebounded, he liked to take the ball in one hand
and slam it against the other, making a gunshot of a sound that startled the smaller players around him. What he should have been doing
was whipping a quick outlet pass downcourt. When he blocked shots,
he liked to smack the ball loudly and violently and usually out of play.
So opponents retained the ball and another chance to score. This
habit would later hurt him when he faced Russell, who always brush-
blocked the ball, often creating a Celtics fast break.

"Wilt understood the game of basketball," Harp said. "He had an
opinion about the game and was bright about it. He wanted to use his
size in close proximity to the basket. But he didn't develop his skills

beyond that. If he wanted to, he could have been a significant play-maker. Wilt had demonstrated he could have shot the ball and been an effective passer."

Over his sophomore season, Chamberlain averaged 30 points, 19 rebounds, and 9 blocked shots. And Kansas was clearly the best team in college basketball. But in the finals of the 1957 NCAA tournament, the Jayhawks lost in triple overtime to North Carolina, an outcome that set the cornerstone of Chamberlain's frustrations. He returned to Kansas the next season, but the Jayhawks lost in postseason play to cross-state rival Kansas State, a team coached by Tex Winter.

Disgusted, Chamberlain decided to leave the University of Kansas. Because his class had not graduated, he was still ineligible for the NBA draft. So he played a barnstorming season with the Harlem Globetrotters, made a good sum of money, and waited his turn. That arrived the following season, 1959–60, when he made a heralded return to Philadelphia to play for the Warriors. His presence had an immediate impact on the league's statistical races. He led the NBA in scoring (37.6 points per game) and rebounding (27 per game). The next season, he became the first player in league history to shoot better than 50 percent from the floor. For the 1961–62 season, Chamberlain maximized man's potential for forty-eight minutes of basketball by averaging 50.4 points per game.

"For accumulating numbers, there's not anybody to even come close to that," Bill Russell recalled. "I'll just say that he played forty-nine minutes a game or something like that. I think that's absolutely incredible. And we won the Eastern Conference by eight games that season."

"One thing about him, he always thought he was the best at everything he did," West said. "That simply was not the case. If that was the case, he would have been an eighty percent free throw shooter."

The next season, Chamberlain scored a mere 44.8 points per game and won the league rebounding title for the fourth straight season. He made each season his statistical fiefdom, and yet they all ended in bitter disappointment. The reason, of course, was the Boston Celtics. Quite often, Chamberlain would dominate Russell statistically, but he could never vanquish the Boston center and his teammates in the big games. Chamberlain was actually taller than his listed height of seven foot one, and he towered over the six-foot-ten Russell, which caused the public to marvel at the smaller man's success. To the basketball public's way of thinking, Russell had a winner's heart, while Chamberlain certainly had to be lacking in something.

"Most people couldn't relate to what an imposing physical thing Wilt was," Russell explained. "The first time you see him, it's like you're standing in his shadow. He's so big. Then he was really smart and a really great athlete. The only saving thing is that he was not me. He was not me."

"A lot of people over the years have said that Bill Russell had more heart and desire than Wilt," Bob Cousy observed. "That wasn't it. Russ was simply quicker than Wilt, and he knew how to use that quickness. That was obvious from the first time I ever saw the two of them on the court together. This is a tremendous advantage Russell had on Wilt. He didn't give him the offensive position he wanted. Russell kept him from overpowering him and going to the basket. Russell had better speed and quickness, so he could always beat Wilt to the spot. He pushed Chamberlain out a little further from the basket, forcing him to put the ball on the floor once or twice. We always felt Russell could handle him one-on-one."

As a result, Chamberlain was forced to develop and shoot a fallaway jumper that was far less effective than his dunks and his short bank shot. His critics, meanwhile, saw Chamberlain as a giant fascinated by his own statistics. "I've always felt that that part of him people misinterpreted," West said. "They would say, 'He's a selfish guy, he doesn't care, he's not a team player.' That's simply not the truth. It really bothered him, all the negative publicity he received, which, frankly, was not justified. It was really pretty ugly; it really was. He's like all of us. No athlete wants to fail. Wilt Chamberlain certainly didn't want to."

The Warriors moved to San Francisco for 1963–64, and Chamberlain again led the league in scoring. He also broadened the scope of his game by finishing fifth in assists. It didn't matter. The Warriors lost in the NBA finals that year to Russell and the Celtics.

San Francisco traded Chamberlain to the Philadelphia 76ers in the middle of the next season. "Chamberlain is not an easy man to love," Warriors owner Franklin Mieuli said later of the trade. "I don't mean that I personally dislike him. He's a good friend of mine. But the fans in San Francisco never learned to love him. I guess most fans are for the little man and the underdog, and Wilt is neither. He's easy to hate, and we were the best draw in the NBA on the road, when people came to see him lose."

Chamberlain quickly made the 76ers into a title contender, but that spring they lost a seven-game series to the Celtics again. The following year, 1965–66, Philadelphia actually beat out Boston for the Eastern Division's regular-season crown but got caught flat-footed in the Eastern play-offs and lost to the Celtics, 4–1.

Chamberlain's frustrations were no deeper than those felt by West, Baylor, and the Lakers. Bill Russell had simply built a wall around the NBA title. He had made it his personal property, or so it seemed until 1967, when Chamberlain finally led the 76ers to a 68–13 record and the league title, leading many observers to call them the greatest team of all time.

"I think Wilt's best season was in '67 when the Sixers won it and Alex Hannum was his coach," said former 76ers general manager Jack Ramsay. "He became more of a team player that year than ever before. Wilt was very stats conscious. He wanted to lead the league in scoring, rebounding; lead the league in everything. And he was capable of doing that. But that year Alex convinced him to be more of a team player. That year he averaged about twenty-four points, twenty-four rebounds, about eight assists. He was terrific."

But Boston's comeback victory over the 76ers in the 1968 Eastern finals soon quieted all the "greatest team ever" talk, and Wilt—again voted league MVP—decided he wanted out of Philadelphia. Jack Kent Cooke was only too happy to help him find a ticket.

"Wilt demanded a trade, and we gave in to him, which is how he got to the Lakers," Jack Ramsay explained.

Cooke gave him a five-year deal at $250,000 per season, making the thirty-one-year-old Chamberlain what was believed to be the highest-paid athlete in any pro sport. In return, the Lakers shipped Archie Clark, Darrall Imhoff, and Jerry Chambers to Philadelphia. The deal was announced in early July, setting off immediate speculation about Chamberlain, West, and Baylor on the same team. Could they share one ball?

"We'll simply have the best team in basketball history," Chamberlain replied.

Seeing an opportunity to tweak the Lakers, Red Auerbach told reporters, "I wonder if Jerry West and Elgin Baylor are going to be willing to be underlings to Wilt Chamberlain?"

Cooke and Chamberlain were infuriated. "A statement like that is typical of Mr. Genius," Cooke shot back. "It's preposterous."

"Butch van Breda Kolff was at a party at my house in Santa Barbara when he heard that Chamberlain was being traded," Bill Bertka recalled. "He was upset by the trade. Butch didn't have anything against Chamberlain or his effectiveness. But you had to have Chamberlain in the post, and that dictated a style of offense that Butch didn't particularly like. He'd rather have all five men moving, all five men interchangeable and sharing the ball. Van Breda Kolff had had the great Princeton team. Schaus coached fast-break basketball. When van Breda Kolff came in, he had a great first year, the second year was even better, and then they acquired Wilt. He wasn't an admirer of Wilt's game and how he could fit in."

Within hours, the trouble started. First Chamberlain read in news accounts that van Breda Kolff said he "could handle" his new center, who'd make a great rebounder for the Lakers. Who needs *handling*? Chamberlain wondered. At a charity game later that summer at Kutshers, van Breda Kolff asked Chamberlain to don a Lakers T-shirt and pose with him for a photo. When Chamberlain refused, the coach fumed.

In training camp, the tension increased a notch. Van Breda Kolff thought the center gave him one good day's practice, then began slacking off. Chamberlain thought the coach was trying to run a pro team with college rules. Then came a season-opening loss to the 76ers in which Chamberlain concentrated on defense and rebounding. The next game, Chamberlain scored big points, and the Lakers beat New York, 118–96. Afterward, when writers asked about the difference in the two games, Wilt replied, "Tell the coach."

A few games later, van Breda Kolff angrily benched Chamberlain when rookie Wes Unseld of the Baltimore Bullets outrebounded him, 27 to 21. The newspapers enjoyed the proceedings immensely, questioning Chamberlain's $250,000 salary and his sinking scoring average (20.5 points per game). "There are certain deficiencies with every club," Chamberlain replied. "Here with the Lakers, I've tried to blend in, lend myself to the deficiencies, try to help overcome them. Here with the likes of Jerry and Elgin, we have people who can score. So

I've simply tried to get the rebounds, get the ball to one of them, so we can score."

The questions about Chamberlain's salary were pointless, Atlanta Hawks general manager Marty Blake told reporters. "There's no athlete in the world worth two hundred fifty thousand, or even two hundred thousand, unless you can take it in at the gate. In LA, they take it in at the gate."

Lakers beat writer Doug Krikorian recalled, "In *Sports Illustrated,* they wrote about how the *Herald Examiner* was Wilt's paper and the *LA Times* was van Breda Kolff's paper. Wilt was feuding with van Breda Kolff throughout the season."

The fans, however, embraced the giant in gold. For the first time in his career, Chamberlain encountered a warm crowd. "Wilt was always the villain," Bill Bertka said. "Wherever Wilt went in those days, he was always booed and unappreciated. But, in tribute to the Lakers fans, from the day he stepped on the Forum floor, he was never booed, never shown disrespect. He was only appreciated. But it took him about a year here to realize that."

Some observers, however, questioned whether Chamberlain's presence hadn't weakened the team. He often set up on the left low post, dead smack in the way of Baylor's drives.

"Wilt was in the post, so it shut the lane down," Bertka explained. "That somewhat affected West's game, too, although West was one of the greatest pull-up shooters to ever play the game. Elgin liked to take it all the way to the basket, so it affected Baylor more than Jerry West or Gail Goodrich."

Van Breda Kolff sought to move the center to a high post, but Chamberlain figured that only took him away from rebounding. Privately, Chamberlain told friends that the coach favored West and Baylor and blamed him for the losses.

"What a lot of people forget is that they gave up some pretty good ballplayers to get Chamberlain," Atlanta forward Paul Silas observed at the time. "For example, Archie Clark. Guard is where they are hurting this year with Archie gone. You can concentrate a little more on West now, and that is something you couldn't do last season. Also, their style of play is slower."

The conflict raged on. Player and coach began shouting at each other during games. "I finally had to call the two of them in for a peacemaking session," Schaus recalled, "and I tried to lay down some new rules. No more bashing each other in the press. Van Breda Kolff is the boss . . . Those two guys just couldn't agree on anything. Six weeks later, I had to fly to Atlanta for another meeting. After that meeting, I told the players to have their own meeting. Baylor was the captain, so he ran it. Wilt was told to stop frowning at his teammates on the court when things went wrong. The players told him to stop being so aloof, that he needed to socialize more."

That helped, but after an early February loss to Seattle, van Breda Kolff and Chamberlain screamed at each other for twenty minutes and would have come to blows in the locker room if Baylor hadn't stepped in. "It was embarrassing for everyone to hear them screaming like animals," one Laker confided to a writer. "It was ridiculous. The guys wanted to hide."

"Wilt being the dominant personality that he was and Bill being the dominant personality that he was, there were sparks," Bertka explained. "Wilt had definite opinions about how the game should be played and how he should be used. So did Butch. Yet they both wanted to win in the worst possible way."

"After that Seattle blowup, we had yet another meeting and another truce," Schaus said. "Wilt asked Butch, 'What do you want me to do?' Butch told him, 'Play defense and rebound.' "

Chamberlain complied, and the Lakers won the conference title. "Wilt's skills had diminished by the time he got to LA," Jack Ramsay recalled. "They were on the downside. By that time, I don't think he was capable of scoring at the same level that he once did."

By the 1969 play-offs, the Lakers were a picture of team defense, giving up just 94.7 points a game. Baylor, Chamberlain, and West were the heart of the lineup. But there was more. There was Keith Erickson out of UCLA, recently acquired from Chicago, as sixth man. There were John Egan, the veteran guard, to boost the backcourt, and Mel Counts, the seven-footer and former Celtic, to do the same up front. With Counts playing alongside Chamberlain, Los Angeles could close the lane and make opponents live off of jump shots. "Mel Counts was another character who would try his very, very best," West recalled. "And a good guy to have on your team. The bottom line was, he cared."

On the strength of their defense, the Lakers advanced to the most disappointing of their finals meetings with the Celtics. As hurt as the previous losses had left him, Jerry West justified them each year by re-

membering that Boston had the better team. But that was no longer
the case in 1969. Los Angeles had taken the top seed in the West with
a 55–27 record and thus had home-court advantage over the Celtics,
who had finished fourth in the Eastern Division.

In particular, the 1968–69 season found Bill Russell struggling with
leg injuries that forced his hospitalization briefly. With Sam Jones also
hurting, Boston came to rely on John Havlicek and Bailey Howell
again.

"His knees really bothered him," Howell said of Russell. "So he
didn't even practice. He just played the games. But once he got his
knees warm, he was all right until the game was over. Then they were
stiff and sore again."

The play-offs became a moment of urgency for the Celtics, particularly Russell, who had privately thought about ending his career.

"He didn't tell us," Howell said. "But he knew he was gonna, so he
had an extra incentive to go out as a champion."

A week before the season ended, Los Angeles flattened Boston,
108–73, on national television, emphasizing that the Lakers now had
a center and a real shot at winning. With both Russell and Jones limp-
ing, the Celtics had slipped by, hoping to stay healthy for the play-offs
and a shot at one final title. The Lakers were favored, but they didn't
have many young legs either. Baylor, in particular, had begun to show
his age. "I don't have to take his fakes as I always did before," Howell
told the writers. "And he is not as quick on the drive or following the
shot."

West, though, was determined not to face another championship
loss. He scored 53 with 10 assists in the first game, which Russell
called "the greatest clutch performance ever against the Celtics." It
was just enough for a 120–118 Lakers win. Afterward West was so
tired that he iced down his arms. Boston had opened with Emmette
Bryant covering West, but he was too short to stop West's shooting
over him. When the Celtics tried to play West close on the perimeter,
he drove right past them for a variety of layups. In years past, Russell
had always dropped off his man to stop those drives, but Wilt's presence meant the Celtics center couldn't get away with it anymore, West
said. "I know he scares a lot of people, but if you're looking for Russell, you're not playing your game."

West cooled down to 41 points in game two, while Havlicek upped his total to 43. Very quickly the series became a shoot-out between the two of them. Chamberlain scored only 4 points, but he countered Russell on the boards. Even better, the sluggish Baylor came alive to score the Lakers' last 12 points for another win, 118–112.

Up 2–0, the Lakers had private thoughts of a sweep as the series headed to Boston.

In game three, Russell decided to double-team West. The Celtics took a big early lead but lost it after Keith Erickson accidentally poked a finger in Havlicek's left eye. The Lakers tied the game heading into the fourth and seemed poised to break the Boston curse and go up 3–0. But Havlicek, with his left eye shut, hit several late free throws to keep Boston alive, 111–105. Game four provided yet another opportunity for the Lakers to strike the deathblow. The two teams combined for 50 turnovers and enough bad shots and passes to last a month. The Celtics slowed the Lakers' scoring by double-teaming West, forcing him to make the pass rather than take the shot. Over the final four minutes, the two teams had one basket between them. But with fifteen seconds left, the Lakers had an 88–87 lead and the ball. All they had to do was get the pass in safely and run out the clock. Instead Bryant stripped the ball from Egan, and the Celtics raced the other way. Sam Jones missed the jumper, but Boston controlled the rebound and called time at 0:07. On the inbounds, Bryant threw the ball to Havlicek, then set a pick to his left. Boston's Don Nelson and Bailey Howell followed in line to make it a triple screen. At the last instant, Havlicek passed to Jones, cutting to his right. Jones stumbled to a halt behind Howell, who cut off West. There, at the 0:03 mark, Jones lofted an eighteen-footer. He slipped as he took the off-balance shot, and it just cleared Baylor's outstretched hand. Jones knew it was going to miss and even tried to pull it back, he explained afterward. The ball went up anyway, hit on the rim, rose up, hit the back of the rim, and fell in. Chamberlain leaped up and lorded over the basket, his face a picture of anguish as the ball came through the net.

"They had the fourth game won and had the ball with about eight seconds to go," Doug Krikorian recalled, "and the Celtics stole the ball from the Lakers. It was a foul, but they didn't call it, and Sam Jones just threw the ball up, and it hit the backboard and went in. They lost by a point. It was the damndest game."

Boston had tied the series with the 89–88 win, and a dagger in West's heart wouldn't have felt any worse. "The Lord's will," he said later.

"I thought to shoot it with a high arc and plenty of backspin," Jones told the writers. "So if it didn't go in, Russell would have a chance for the rebound."

Russell wasn't even in the game, a writer pointed out. "What the hell," Boston's Larry Siegfried said. "You hit a shot like that, you're entitled to blow a little smoke about arc and backspin and things like that."

The Lakers regrouped and headed home for game five. "Coming back, no one was more depressed than West," recalled Krikorian. "Of course, you could see the stuff that was playing on his mind. He had already lost five times to the Celtics. How could that have happened? There's no way Sam Jones should have hit that shot. Baylor was all over him. How did he make it? He just threw it up, and it went in. West was depressed, and it was like an omen of things to come."

In Los Angeles, the Celtics just didn't have it. Russell scored 2 points with 13 rebounds. Chamberlain owned the inside, with 31 rebounds and 13 points, while West and Egan struck from the perimeter with 39 and 23 points, respectively. Boston fell, 117–104, and trailed 3–2.

"They're winning easily, and I think they had a fifteen or eighteen-point lead," Krikorian recalled, "and for some inexplicable reason van Breda Kolff kept West in the game. Guess what happened? He pulled a hamstring and couldn't play defense in the last two games."

Jane West wept after the game. A hamstring injury? After all these years, it seemed he was truly cursed.

West clearly was hobbled by the hamstring. He scored 26 in game six, but the Lakers could get no more from him. Chamberlain scored a measly 2 points. Boston won, 99–90, to tie the series. "West shouldn't have even played in that sixth game," Krikorian offered. "Should have conceded it anyway because it really wasn't that close of a game. That was a game where the Celtics absolutely dominated."

Once again a Celtics-Lakers championship series had come down to a seventh game. Only this time, game seven was in Los Angeles. This time there wouldn't be a Garden jinx. Or would there? West's hamstring had worsened. It was wrapped, and he declared himself ready to go, but everyone wondered. Everyone except Jack Kent

Cooke, who began planning his victory celebration. He visualized the perfect finale for a championship season. He ordered thousands of balloons suspended in the Forum rafters, and team employees spent hours blowing them up. According to Cooke's plan, they would be released as the Lakers claimed the title. With the balloons raining down on the jubilant Lakers and their fans, the band would strike up "Happy Days Are Here Again." Cooke could see it all clearly.

And so could Bill Russell. Lakers legend has it that Red Auerbach walked into the Forum that May 5 and gazed up into the cloud of balloons in the rafters. "Those things are going to stay up there a hell of a long time," he supposedly said. But Hot Rod Hundley recalled that Russell, not Auerbach, made the comment. Auerbach later agreed, saying that the balloons angered him, but he'd said nothing.

Bill Russell said, "I was the coach, and I said to my players, 'It may be a better show to watch them take those balloons down one at a time.'"

No one was more infuriated by the balloons than West. The thought of them made him sick with anger. The Celtics, always looking for that extra little boost of emotion, found it in the Forum rafters and in a Lakers memo outlining plans for the celebration, which was passed around the Celtics' locker room before the game. They hit 8 of their first 10 shots on the way to a quick 24–12 lead. The Lakers charged back to pull within 28–25 at the end of the first. At the half, the Celtics were up 59–56.

"In that last game, Bill Russell not only outplayed Wilt, but Sam Jones went wild and West couldn't guard him," Doug Krikorian recalled. "West scored forty-two himself, but West couldn't guard him with the bad hamstring. He couldn't play defense anymore."

The Lakers tied the score in the third before going strangely cold for five minutes. West, playing brilliantly despite his heavily bandaged leg, finally hit a shot to slow down the Celtics, who led 71–62 with about five minutes to go in the third. Then, with 3:39 left, Russell took the ball inside against Wilt, scored, and drew Chamberlain's fifth foul to round out a 3-point play: 79–66, Boston. Chamberlain had never fouled out in his entire 885-game NBA career. Van Breda Kolff decided to leave him in. With Chamberlain playing tentatively, Boston moved inside and took a 91–76 lead into the fourth, and the balloons upstairs weighed heavily on Cooke's team.

The lead went to 17 early in the fourth, but both Russell and Jones picked up their fifth fouls. In the void, West went to work. A bucket. A free throw. Another bucket. The lead dropped to 12. They traded free throws. Then Havlicek got his fifth foul, and moments later, Sam Jones closed his career with a sixth foul. He had scored 24 on the day. After a Baylor bucket, and 3 more points by West, the Celtics answered only with a Havlicek jumper, and the lead dropped to nine, 103–94.

At the 5:45 mark, Chamberlain went up for a defensive rebound and came down wincing. His knee. He asked to be taken out, and van Breda Kolff sent in Counts. West hit two free throws, and the lead was 7. Russell and his teammates were out of gas, hoping to coast. Another West jumper. And moments later, two more free throws from West, cutting the lead to 103–100.

Three minutes to go, and Counts, who shot 4 for 13 on the afternoon, surprised everyone by popping a jumper: 103–102. Chamberlain was ready to come back in.

"We're doing well enough without you," the coach told his center.

"I just thought he was hurt," West recalled. "Not till afterward did I know that he should have been back in the ball game, that he asked to go back in the ball game. I didn't even know that. But if people thought we were better off with Wilt Chamberlain sitting on the bench, that's a bunch of bull. We were better off with him on the court. It's just another annoying thing with something that's already very annoying. All it does is annoy you."

"Boston dominated the seventh game except the last seven minutes," Krikorian remembered. "People forget that game was the microcosm between Wilt and Russell, because Wilt absolutely disappeared for three quarters. Russell totally outplayed him. Where was Wilt? He'd get psyched out and couldn't play. You look at the stats of that game, Russell had twenty to twenty-five rebounds. Wilt had nothing."

Boston and Los Angeles traded missed free throws. With a little more than a minute left, West knocked the ball loose on defense. Nelson picked it up at the free throw line and threw it up. It hit the rim, rose several feet, and dropped back through. The dumb luck of it would play reruns in West's mind for decades to come.

"People don't realize there's so much luck involved," West said in 1992. "If games are close, luck plays a factor. They say luck is an element of design. Bull. It's luck involved. You might shoot a ball from the right side of the basket that one hundred percent of the time if shot from that angle will bounce back left. And then one time it will someway somehow bounce back right, and there will be no one but the other team in position to get the thing."

The balloons were all but popped. The Lakers missed twice, and the Celtics committed an offensive foul, all of which an angry Chamberlain watched from the bench. After a few meaningless buckets, it ended. The Celtics had hung on to win their eleventh title, 108–106.

The debate began immediately afterward: Chamberlain versus van Breda Kolff.

"Jerry West's hamstring injury was the key to me, not van Breda Kolff benching Wilt in the seventh game," Krikorian offered. "Wilt deserved it in that seventh game. He was playing horribly. Russell completely outplayed him that game. Wilt was like he was in a fog in the first half when the Celtics built an eighteen-point lead. Bill Russell was dominant in that first half, in that last game. He was dominant. People said that Wilt tended to choke; well, he did. This is not revisionist history, this is reality. People never want to bring that up about Wilt, just like the year before Wilt had a three-to-one lead with the 76ers against the Celtics and blew that one too. So there was something to the saying that Wilt chokes in the big ones. I saw it in that seventh game. His teammates talked about it later. They couldn't believe it. It was like his feet were encased in cement. Russell was scurrying around the court in his final game, and Wilt was doing nothing."

"The Lakers should have been better," Tommy Heinsohn said. "They had Wilt . . . That was Russell; that was the epitome of Bill Russell. He was a winner, and the whole team was a very focused team."

"People always say, 'You beat Wilt. You beat Wilt. You beat Wilt.' We beat everybody," Russell recalled. "I loved that."

Although they had been friendly through their careers, Russell criticized Chamberlain for leaving the game. Perhaps a broken leg should have taken Chamberlain out, Russell said, but nothing less. The comments caused a rift between the superstars and strained their friendship. Some observers later commented that perhaps Russell had only feigned friendship during their playing days to prevent Chamberlain from becoming angry and playing well against the Celtics.

All of this mattered little to Jerry West. He was merely disgusted with another loss. He had finished with 42 points, 13 rebounds, and 12 assists. Over the seven games, West had averaged nearly thirty-eight points. The Celtics went to the Los Angeles locker room immediately after the game. Russell took West's hand and held it silently.

"Jerry," Havlicek professed, "I love you."

"He is the master," Boston's Larry Siegfried said of West. "They can talk about the others, build them up, but he is the one. He is the only guard."

West was named the MVP, the first and only time in NBA finals history that the award went to a member of a losing team. The gestures were nice, West said, but they didn't address his agony.

"Most of the years we played, they were better than we were," West said. "But in '69 they were not better. Period. I don't care how many times we played it, they weren't better. We were better. Period. And we didn't win. And that was the toughest one."

"I remember him crying, literally tears in his eyes, after the Celtics beat them," Krikorian said. "He took it as hard as any player I've ever seen. But he always talked to the reporters. He never refused to talk. He was high strung, obviously. He was a marvelous player; just marvelous."

"I really have blocked almost all of that stuff out of my mind," West said. "The only ones that have any clarity to me are the first one and the last one. Those are the only two, the first one because of the excitement, how the game ended, what the locker room was like. The last one, with the ugly feelings I had. I didn't want to ever play basketball again. I didn't want to ever see another basketball game again. I was furious with our owner for putting those balloons up there. It made *me* mad. I didn't like it. That wasn't my style. That was awful. I just had had it. When you feel like you compete and there's not an ounce of energy left in you. When you go to take a shower and feel like you can't even take a shower. I was spent after that last one. In the years since, I have blocked everything out. I can't tell you. I don't even know. It's something to me that has nothing to do with not being willing to talk about it. Some players can tell you every shot they made. I have no idea how many points I scored in my career. I know the most points I ever scored in my career. I know that. But I don't remember what I should remember about my career, because consciously I have erased the slate."

"I think losing that series should disturb Jerry West and the rest of the Lakers," Sam Jones said frankly. "They had a great team, but I still felt we were better. That whole year we had a lot of injuries, but we found our way again in the play-offs. We were a team that didn't feel we had to have home court advantage. Bill Russell was our advantage. I think he's the greatest player ever to put on a uniform. He wanted to win. It's nice to have a center that played defense the way that he did. I knew I could gamble. I knew there was not gonna be any layups. So we did pretty well."

"In a lot of ways, Wilt was actually better off than West," observed longtime Lakers beat writer Merv Harris. "They both had pride and ego. When the game was over, Wilt could leave basketball behind. He had a much broader range of friends and interests than Jerry. His personal prowess was so important to Wilt. Jerry was such a purist, to the point of a mania about the game."

Cooke, in the aftermath, was left with the task of figuring out what to do with all the balloons. He finally decided to send them to a children's hospital. For years they would hang metaphorically over the Lakers' heads, the victory balloons that never rained down.

"It was a challenge to play against Russell and the Celtics," Baylor said. "It was fun. It was disappointing to lose. But it was the ultimate challenge. They were a proud team, and they had reason to be. Some people thought they were proud and arrogant. But I enjoyed playing against them. They were the best."

"We lost six world championship play-offs with the Boston Celtics, the difference being Bill Russell and whoever the Lakers' center might have been," Chick Hearn said. "But they were very closely competed series. The Celtics were a great ball club. If Russell had been the Lakers' center, they would have won all the ball games that the Celtics did. That was the big difference. Two or three times, they went to overtimes in those series with Boston. Three of them went seven games. The Lakers had a nice ball club. They had LaRusso and Selvy and West and Baylor and whoever the center was, and Leroy Ellis. Actually, the real center was Ray Felix, God rest his soul. And Jimmy Krebs, too. We had Gene Wiley. None of them the caliber of Russell. That's not a shot at them. That's just a fact."

He is a very complicated, wound-up spring, a bundle of nerves. He is so high strung that in all the time I have known Jerry, I have never once seen him fully relaxed.

—Fred Schaus

THE LOGO

Los Angeles, 1969 to 1974

SO MANY GAMES, SO MANY OF THEM PLAYED SO WELL, SO MANY BAT-
tles, one after the other, night after night, traveling that old pro circuit,
a blur of airports, cabs, hotels, late games, early flights. New York,
Boston, Atlanta, Milwaukee, Chicago. The long pull back to LA for
three or four home games, then start the whole thing over again, all
the while fighting to stay tensed up enough to compete at that highest level through every sort of complication. The hamstrings and the
broken noses, the painkilling shots so that he could keep playing
through injury, the anxieties and superstitions, the quirks of the game,
the personalities—all of those things had marked him, but nothing
touched and changed Jerry West as did the lack of fulfillment.

Somewhere along the way, defeat began to warp him.

Jerry Sloan, another sort of competitive standard-bearer like Bill
Russell and West, developed a creed in his years as Mr. Chicago Bull
during the 1960s and 1970s. Sloan saw the game as simple enough if
you went out and laid your heart on the line every single night. West

certainly did that, pushed every limit that he could identify, accepted every challenge, asked every question. His perfectionism wouldn't allow him to approach it any other way. Yet not one bit of it could ever be described as simple. Not for Jerry West.

"I didn't think it was fair that you could give so much and maybe play until there was nothing left in your body to give, and you couldn't win," West said, looking back. "I don't think people really understand the trauma associated with losing. I don't think people realize how miserable you can be, and me in particular. I was terrible. It got to the point with me that I wanted to quit basketball. It was like a slap in the face, like, 'We're not gonna let you win. We don't care how well you play.' I always thought it was personal."

The defeat West met was not the run-of-the-mill, grind-you-up sort of losing that left lesser men dispirited. West and his teams won and won and won, only to suffer ultimate denial almost every season, to the point that West achieved a rare and unwanted distinction in popular culture as a valiant figure marked by fate. West became, in essence, the great, great loser. In the South, after the Civil War, such a status was conferred upon General Robert E. Lee, who lived on in legend as a revered figure. West's career had absolutely nothing to do with defeated Confederate generals, and there's nothing on or off the record to suggest that he ever cared even a whit about such things. But in a very different setting, in a very different way, he came to be seen as this uncompromising figure, immensely noble in defeat, a Jesus of sorts in short pants. That's why the Celtics were so eager to enter the Lakers' locker room and worship him after the seventh game of the 1969 series. They felt it as well as everyone else. West tried to be polite and appreciative, but the whole thing nauseated him.

"We all have our own little particular feelings when we lose," he explained. "There's no gratification. When other people come in and express their condolences—and basically, that's what it was—it's nice from people that you really respect. They paid their gratitude, I guess. It became personal in the sense that I didn't think I was doing enough. I was searching everything that I'd ever done in my life for the reason, looking for an answer why. Why can't we get a bounce of the ball? And that's what it came to personally. It almost controlled my life. It was a controlling factor in my play. When we played against those guys, I didn't care what it was, I wanted to play my very best. I didn't want any friends on the other team."

The very competitive NBA was a business that bred contempt on a nightly basis, yet virtually everyone connected with the league seemed to hold Jerry West in esteem. This admiration could be seen in the other players, coaches, team owners, and even their fans. They regarded him with awe. Even the officials. Some would say *especially* the officials. Norm Drucker, known to run a fairly tight ship as a referee, once remarked, "If someone like Jerry West, who usually never says a word, wants to discuss a call, I let him have his say."

Such elevation had its complicating elements, especially for West's own teammates. His popularity ate at Wilt Chamberlain, who had battled image problems for much of his career. Like Russell, Chamberlain had faced the issues of a black giant dealing with an entirely white press corps during a blatantly racist era. With West in California, however, Chamberlain found few of the old problems. Instead he soon became distrustful of what he saw as Chick Hearn's hero worship of West. The Lakers broadcaster had come to have an amazing influence over Southern California radio audiences. In the 1960s, Hearn's radio broadcasts brought to life the adventures of West and Baylor for a generation of young Californians.

"It's all Chick Hearn. I mean, that's the guy," recalled Hall of Famer center Bill Walton, who grew up in La Mesa, California. "I started playing basketball when I was eight years old in 1960, and we didn't have a television. We couldn't afford one. When we finally could afford one, my parents said, 'There's nothing on, so why do we need one of those?' I bought a $9.95 transistor radio and listened to Chick Hearn on the radio. Chick Hearn taught me how to play basketball, how to think about basketball. He taught me how to *love* basketball. I lived for Chick Hearn on the radio every day. Jerry and Elgin and all the guys. Rudy LaRusso. The endless list of characters. But it was always Chick. The love affair with basketball in Los Angeles and the Lakers is all about Chick Hearn. He is the guy who convinced so many millions of people that this is the greatest thing in the world. Once we came and saw what he saw, we could never leave. While Chick broadcast 3,300 games, or whatever the number is, I'm sure I listened to at least 2,500 of those games. I planned my life around Chick Hearn. I would sit there as a young boy and just be amazed. I would listen to this game, and I could see it all. I would laugh out loud at the things Chick would say."

In the process, Hearn drove a popularity for West that confounded

Chamberlain. Having witnessed just about every single game West had played in the NBA, Hearn had developed a tremendous regard for him, and that came through in every broadcast—too much so, Wilt thought. "Chick is an extremely knowledgeable basketball man and an exciting play-by-play announcer," the center explained. "But he has one problem: He thinks Jerry West is Jesus Christ."

Chamberlain complained that Hearn would gloss over any mistake West made while often pointing out those made by other Lakers. The center said that fans would write to the team sometimes complaining about the disparity and the West worship. "Jerry's a great player—maybe the greatest guard ever," Chamberlain offered. "He doesn't need someone like Chick trying to deify him every game. In fact, I've got a hunch there are times when even Jerry wishes Chick would let up some."

The West family was quite aware of the effects of Hearn's praise for "Mr. Clutch." "The word we got, not from Jerry but from others, is that Jerry pretty much owned California," Charles West recalled.

In California, as in West Virginia and New York and Boston and other NBA cities, he stirred a strong response in the people who saw him play or heard Hearn describe that play on the radio. It was the kind of thing fathers pointed out to their sons. "That's Jerry West," they would say. "Nobody cares more, tries harder, plays harder than Jerry West. If you're going to play basketball, play it like Jerry West."

The league discretely confirmed this lofty status in the months after the 1969 championship series. Charged with creating a logo for the NBA, designer Alan Siegel picked through many photographs before settling on a shot by photographer Wen Roberts of West pushing the ball along the baseline on a sortie to the basket. Siegel took West's balanced, graceful silhouette and reversed it out of a red, white, and blue background. The logo was an instant hit upon its unveiling. No one, not Siegel, not the league itself, certainly not West, announced that he had become the symbol for the game. Yet it was immediately recognizable and soon became ingrained in every phase of the NBA's daily operations. As the logo, West's specter began to pop up everywhere, looming subtly yet powerfully over a league that was seeking to leave behind the gritty image of its early decades. Once the NBA began to find a much larger audience in the 1980s, West's image would brand every backboard in every arena, every communication, every piece of the $4 billion in merchandise the NBA marketed globally each year. On satellite transmissions and websites and broadcasts and magazines and books and videos and DVDs and press releases, Jerry West would loom as the pervasive icon of the sport.

As such, the logo became perhaps the largest of many ironies in West's life. It meant that, as much as he sometimes wanted to forget it, he would be reminded of his playing career at every turn. It consecrated his status. West knew that. He was no fool. "I don't remember anything about my career," he would testily tell reporters and interviewers if they asked one question too many about his playing days. "I choose not to. I really don't live in the past. I really don't care about the past."

As a player and later as an executive, West slowly came to acknowledge the admiration of millions. Just as Mickey Mantle was the golden boy of baseball for a generation, West assumed a similar role in the NBA. *Sports Illustrated* senior writer Jack McCallum recalled that his youthful hero worship of West came up years later in an interview with his idol. "I told him, 'Growing up, you were the guy I sort of modeled myself after, like every white kid in America who had half a jump shot.' West, just totally without ego, looks at me and says, 'Yeah, a lot of guys have told me that.'"

Now one of the league's elder figures, West heard the same kind of talk from younger players who were trying to challenge him. "I'm really anxious to see these new kids come in every year, the ones I've read so much about," he said. "Of course, it kind of shakes you up when one of them tells you that you've been their idol since they were in tenth grade or something."

As he aged, he did manage to gain an occasional sense of humor about the circumstances. "The Lakers had a young PR guy who was just there for a year or so," recalled *LA Times* columnist Mark Heisler. "And West was introducing himself. He said, 'I'm the logo.' And he was kidding. The thing is about West, in one way, he's tremendously humble and doesn't think he's done anything. There's also another side of West where he knows he's Jerry Fuckin' West."

That iconic status registered clearly with the baby boom generation, but long after his playing days, West would still draw the admiration of younger generations. "I was born in 1970, so I never got to see him play in person," recalled sportswriter J. A. Adande. "But his son belonged to my Boys Club in Santa Monica when I was a kid. We played our biddy games on Saturdays, and Jerry would show up. All of us would look up when he entered the gym and say, 'There's Jerry West! There's Jerry West!' Years later, after I'd been in the newspaper business a long time, I'd interview him, then hang up the phone and say to myself, 'I just talked to Jerry West.'"

His image set the terms for his relationship with the media as well. So many of the sportswriters in Southern California came to idolize West. Even those who were his contemporaries sought to protect him, mainly from his own raw emotions. For the writers, the respect began with how he responded to their questions. "He's got the twang, when he got mad his voice would go way, way up," remembered Mike Waldner, who covered the Lakers for better than three decades. "He sounded like Tweety Bird. When the Lakers lost, the whole team, they were candid. Jerry would sit there and as long as people were asking questions, he'd answer them. They were easier to talk to when they lost than when they won. When they won, they didn't want to be bragging or anything, so they'd be ratcheting it down. When they lost, they were very candid about what they did wrong. Jerry never made excuses."

Even so, West was often overwhelmingly emotional, and writers would often find him growing animated at odd, awkward times. "There's four writers sitting together watching practice, and West's sitting with us," Mitch Chortkoff recalled. "Somebody knocks Happy Hairston," a forward for three teams, including Los Angeles, in the sixties and seventies. "They said, 'Happy Hairston hasn't guarded anybody in his life.' What he'd do is play off you, let you shoot, and if you missed, get the rebound. But he's giving you the shot. So somebody knocks Hairston. West turns around and starts chirping, defending Hairston. Then he goes down the entire rooster, player by player, and criticizes every player on the roster. Now he's out of players to criticize, so he starts cursing Hairston. And everybody's laughing in his face, because that's who he is. He's this ball of anger, energy, and intensity."

There was no question that this great wellspring of emotion left West quite vulnerable, and out of respect for him, the reporters covering the team routinely left these comments off the record. They did it to protect him and themselves, because the comments usually meant little to their stories. As a player, coach, and executive, West would become angry at some circumstance and claim he was prepared to quit or retire. As Mitch Chortkoff explained, woe to the reporter who took West at his word and wrote about his "retirement," because West was just blowing off steam and had no intention of walking away from the game he loved. Over time, his intensity and over-the-top competitiveness would contribute to the idea that West was more than a little crazy.

"Jerry West is one of the wackiest guys I've ever covered in sports," observed Mark Heisler, "and I've covered Al Davis," the volatile owner of the Oakland–Los Angeles–Oakland Raiders football team. "Jerry, as wacky as he is, can function in the world, whereas Al has to retreat to wherever and work from his cave. I'm a Jerry West guy. I thought he did an incredible job for the Lakers. But his nervous system, it's just wired a little tighter than most of them, or any of them."

"The lunatic part cannot be denied, because that was a part of him," Chortkoff said, "but all that emotion is what made him great."

Those emotions didn't just trouble the public Jerry West, they also played havoc with his private persona as well, as Jane West revealed. One of the conflicts at home had to do with the time he spent with his sons. He would return exhausted from the Lakers' whirlwind road trips with little stomach for taking the boys out in public, especially to baseball games and other places where people would pester him no end. He read the sports pages exhaustively and knew all the teams around Los Angeles in great detail. But if he went to a public sporting event, he usually preferred boxing matches, where the crowds tended not to recognize him as readily, or at least tended to leave him alone. It also helped explain why he increasingly sought the solitude of the fairways.

He was also much like his mother, strong in the basics but not much in the way of coddling or giving extra attention to his offspring. Just as Cecile West had her cleaning and cooking, he had his other interests.

"He's so antsy, he's always on the go," Jane confided to *Sports Illustrated*'s Frank Deford. "If you tried to keep up with him, you'd be going all the time, seven days and seven nights a week. When we belonged to a beach club, Jerry couldn't sit long enough to enjoy it. Here we are right near the ocean, and he can't stand it. He plays golf, and I take the boys to the beach. That may sound peculiar, but togetherness in the traditional way just hasn't worked for us. I've reached the point where it doesn't bother me."

As Jerry's salary increased, the Wests finally moved from the middle-class neighborhood they had inhabited for years in West LA and bought a fancy place in upscale Brentwood, complete with walk-in closets and sunken baths, considered luxury items in the early seventies. It was a time when his boys were clearly infatuated with sports cards and the trappings of their father's life.

"They come to me," West said at the time, "and they show me a card and say, 'Do you know this player.' And if I say I do, they get all wild-eyed. But they're not very excited about me. Maybe in another player's house, I'm very big. They get a certain excitement at the games, but I really don't know if they go for the game or the popcorn. Ah, they're front-runners. We're raising them just to be regular fans, I suppose."

Jane provided his connection to anything "regular," just as she provided his connection to his former life back home—the person who did much of the communicating with his mother and relatives. She remained much the same smart small-town girl who had been the daughter of the local hardware store owner. West may have ditched his hillbilly accent, but she hadn't bothered.

"Really, I had everything I wanted," she explained at the time. "A big, happy family. Good grades, cheerleader, May Queen, all that. I was always a very optimistic person. I always thought I was going to marry Prince Charming. I was always sure of that."

As it turned out, her Prince Charming could handle everything but losing, she learned, and it was through that that she painfully discovered they really didn't have that much in common after all. There was a part of his world—the part in which he nurtured the tension he needed to compete—that he could not share with her. She tried. She made every effort to be a part of his life, but there was a part of him, an important part, that she could not reach.

After one championship loss to Boston, West had packed up and slipped away to Palm Springs by himself. In 1969, after the humiliating seventh game, they drove away from the Forum together. When he said nothing for the longest period, Jane thought to bring up small talk, in hopes that she could divert him from the misery of his thoughts. He pulled into the driveway not having said a word the entire ride home, turned to her, and said, "Okay, get out."

She opened the door, got out, and watched him drive off.

"Jerry doesn't like to have anyone see him cry," she later explained. "When he came back, we had a big thing about, you know, me sharing the wins, me having to share the losses too, that sort of thing. My God, I tried to tell him, not just, 'Okay, get out.' Not just that. I was killed by that. Just killed."

SPRINGTIME IN NEW YORK

For a place that wasn't supposed to be a basketball town, LA had done all right for itself. Lew Alcindor, who was on his way to becoming Kareem Abdul-Jabbar, had just won his third straight NCAA title that spring of 1969, giving UCLA coach John Wooden five championships in six seasons. The Lakers, meanwhile, were in the midst of a run that would carry them to the NBA finals ten times in fourteen seasons. All of this, of course, was played out in relief to the city itself, which was being rocked by a stupefying turn of events, from the Watts riots in 1965, to the assassination of Senator Robert F. Kennedy in 1968, to the Charles Manson murders in 1969. In that era, it seemed the Doors' Jim Morrison, not Randy Newman, controlled the sound track at Lakers games. They were Strange Days, indeed.

Over at the Forum, the Lakers were brewing their own weird stew. Two weeks after the 1969 season closed, Butch van Breda Kolff resigned to become the head coach of the Detroit Pistons and was replaced by Joe Mullaney, the veteran coach from Providence College. After van Breda Kolff was gone, Chamberlain criticized his heavy drinking, his penchant for conducting farting contests, and his failure to prepare for games. The center swooned over his replacement. Mullaney was another practitioner of eastern basketball, but where van Breda Kolff was brash, Mullaney was mild. "Wilt is special and must be treated special," the new coach said with a smile.

"Mullaney is all right," Chamberlain observed. "He don't act like he wants to *be boss.*"

Mullaney asked Chamberlain to help trap the ball in the corners. The big center was willing to cooperate, and this defense quickly showed that it would be effective. Alas, the thirty-three-year-old Chamberlain suffered a knee injury nine games into the season. He had missed just twelve games in eleven years, but now the doctors said he would be out for the season. Chamberlain promised, "I will be back."

In the meantime, West again stepped into the void and produced a masterpiece of a season. Defense may have been his secret weapon, but his career had been measured in terms of the scoring onslaught. In 1962 he finished fourth in the league with a 30.8 average. In 1965 he finished second at 31.0 points per game, behind only Chamberlain, then followed it with the unprecedented and never equaled 40.6 points over eleven play-off games. In 1966, West upped his regular-season average to 31.3, and again finished number two behind the prodigious Wilt. In 1967 that dipped to third and 28.7, yet he always seemed to finish in the top five in assists. Even in his two injury-marred seasons of 1963 and 1968, he averaged 26 points a game.

But there was no doubt that 1970 was his statistical masterpiece. West led the league in scoring, with 31.2 points per game while averaging 7.5 assists and shooting 50 percent from the field.

"In 1969–70, Jerry should have been MVP of the league," said Lakers beat writer Doug Krikorian. "That's when Wilt went out, and Jerry, to me, was the best player in basketball that season. He was just tremendous."

Late that March, *LA Times* columnist Mal Florence pointed out that West had carried the Lakers to a divisional title despite the fact that the team had "no Chamberlain, two rookie starters, a rookie coach, and Elgin only part-time." Citing a recent game that West had won with a jumper in the final two seconds while scoring 42 points with 12 assists, Florence wrote, "Nobody has ever meant more to a team than West has to the Lakers this year." West, he added, had played three thousand minutes over the season, "and they can hardly find a bad or dull one among them."

But when it came to the MVP voting, the thirty-two-year-old West was outpolled, 498–457, by the NBA champion Knicks center Willis Reed, a twenty-seven-year-old who wasn't even in the top ten in scoring and finished only sixth as a rebounder, at 13.9. The MVP traditionally had been about big men far more than it was about guards. Yes, Oscar Robertson had claimed the prize in 1964, but it had required an overwhelming statistical season. And that perhaps emphasized the irony that West faced. The individual prize proved even more elusive than the championships, if that could be possible. In some years, the MVP was apparently about team success (when Russell won), while in other years it was all about stats (when Wilt won).

During the 1960s, Russell and Chamberlain won it four times each. West finished second in the balloting (based on votes by the league's players) on four different occasions; in 1965, and from 1970 to 1972.

John Hall, another LA writer upset by the outcome in 1970, said it was time to create two awards. One would be the MVP for centers, and the other, he said, would be the Jerry West Award, for the "most exciting all-around athlete and game-breaker in the sport."

Asked how he felt about not winning, West said he was "disappointed but not upset." Some said that Reed was simply the best player on the best team, but others argued that wasn't really the case. The most valuable Knick, they said, was guard Walt Frazier. At the least, the controversy made the play-offs a referendum on the voting outcome.

In Chamberlain's absence, Baylor had revived his career a bit. In recent seasons, with Wilt in the post, Baylor had given up his drives and taken up jump shots, which sent his scoring average and effectiveness plummeting. "It was a sad thing," explained Lakers beat writer Merv Harris. "The less effective Elgin was as a player, the more he felt troubled by it, the more the power of his personality over the team waned. The team developed its factions. There was one with Elgin and one with Wilt. You could almost see Elgin fade before your very eyes." He did have flashes, however. That February he and West each scored 43 against San Francisco, one of only eight times in league history that a pair of teammates had topped the 40-point mark.

Chamberlain, meanwhile, worked diligently at rehabilitation and, as the 1970 play-offs neared, announced his intention to return, surprising even his doctors. He played the final three games of the regular season and was enough of a force to help the Lakers thrive in the Western play-offs. They started off in trouble, falling behind the Phoenix Suns, three games to one. But as he gained momentum, they pulled a Houdini and advanced. The Lakers had finished second in the Western Conference regular season behind the Atlanta Hawks, led by forward Lou Hudson, but with Chamberlain back, they swept Atlanta in the divisional finals.

West would continue to carry the team offensively throughout the 1970 postseason, averaging 31.2 points, 8.4 assists, and a whopping forty-six minutes over eighteen play-off games. As always, he absorbed tremendous pressure to do so. "The play-offs are the toughest of all because of the mental part," he told the *LA Times*. "It means so much . . . I know I'm always tense. Very tense. And if I'm not, I don't think I play as well."

With Russell now retired, it was the Knicks and Reed the MVP who stepped in the path of West and his Lakers. At six foot nine and 235 pounds, Reed seemed no threat to overpower Wilt, but he managed to do so in dramatically symbolic fashion. Like Russell before him, Reed was quick and intelligent. Unlike Russell, Reed had a smooth shot with some range. Beyond all that, Reed had a presence that began with his physical power.

"As a player and a man, he was always on fire," said teammate Walt Frazier.

Coached by Red Holzman and led by Dave DeBusschere, Bill Bradley, and Frazier, the Knicks had clashed with Baltimore in the first round in a seven-game series. The Bullets had Wes Unseld at center, but the Knicks finally closed out Baltimore in the seventh game in the Garden, 127–114.

In the Eastern finals, New York defeated the rookie Alcindor and the Milwaukee Bucks, in just their second season, 4–1. By the 1970 championship series, Holzman's team had transformed the Madison Square Garden crowd into a loud, silly horde. Like the Lakers in Hollywood, the Knicks soon acquired their courtside attractions. Woody Allen, Dustin Hoffman, Diane Keaton, Elliott Gould, and Peter Falk were regulars. So was Soupy Sales. And author William Goldman. Suddenly it seemed that all of Manhattan wanted a seat in Holzman's Garden, and despite the Lakers' overwhelming edge in play-off experience, the Knicks were favored by the oddsmakers. Game one showed why. Although Reed had been worn down by battling Unseld and then Alcindor, he quickly ran circles around Wilt Chamberlain. Dick Barnett also was eager to match up against West, his former teammate. New York opened a quick lead and pumped it up to 50–30. The Knicks lost it for a time when West scored 16 points in the third quarter (he would finish with 33), but then they blew by Los Angeles rather easily over the last eight minutes to win, 124–112. Reed finished with 37 points, 16 rebounds, and 5 assists. Asked why he had left Reed open outside, Chamberlain replied, "I just didn't come out after him. Next time I will."

As promised, Chamberlain was much more active on defense in game two. He hounded Reed into missing 17 shots and blocked the New York center's shot at the buzzer to preserve a 105–103 Lakers win. Despite a badly bruised hand, West drove the offense with 34 points.

Back home for game three on April 29, the Lakers rolled out to a 56–42 halftime lead. Long-haired forward Keith Erickson, a local kid from nearby El Segundo and UCLA, raised on beach volleyball, helped West push the Lakers' offense along, while Chamberlain and Baylor ruled the inside. The Knicks couldn't seem to find a rebound. Erickson presaged a wild ending by hitting a forty-foot shot to close the first half. But the Knicks abruptly reversed that momentum in the third period. DeBusschere and Dick Barnett started dropping in shots from the perimeter in a scoring duel with West. The late scoring ignited a run that allowed the Knicks to tie it at 100 with thirteen seconds to go. The Lakers' defense forced New York out of a set play, but DeBusschere took a pass from Frazier, gave a head fake, and dropped in a neat little jumper for a 102–100 Knicks lead with three seconds left. The Lakers were out of time-outs. Chamberlain halfheartedly tossed the ball to West, who dribbled three times as Reed dogged him. Two feet beyond the key, just to the left of the lane, West let fly from sixty-three feet. Good! DeBusschere, underneath the basket, threw out his arms in disgust and collapsed.

Dr. Robert Kerlan, the Lakers' team physician, was excited enough to momentarily forget his arthritis. He jumped up from his courtside seat and began to celebrate, only to be shooed back by official Mendy Rudolph. Wilt was fooled too. He laughed and ran off to the locker room, thinking the shot had won it. But only the ABA had a three-point rule back then. The officials brought Wilt back out for overtime, 102–102.

West missed all five of his shots in the extra period. Barnett, the former Laker, clinched it for the Knicks with a bucket at the 0:04 mark. West and Erickson had no more miracles. It ended, 111–108. Reed had run up MVP numbers: 38 points and 17 rebounds. Most important, though, the Knicks had the big stat, a 2–1 lead in games.

West, who had contributed another 34 points, was taken aback by the almost celebratory approach to his shot in the locker room afterward. "The shot meant nothing," West told Bill Libby. "Afterward, when everyone kept asking me about the shot, I had to remind them that we lost the game."

A flow had been established to the series. Each side had an advantage: the Lakers, their inside strength; the Knicks, their running and quickness. One side would use its advantage to get a lead, then the other would come back. Injuries were beginning to play a factor as well. West had jammed his thumb, and both Chamberlain and Reed had aching knees.

Game four was another nail-biter. Barnett hit 6 of 7 from the field in the first quarter as the Knicks opened up hot. West was the answer for the Lakers. Despite the sprained thumb, he played fifty-two minutes and scored 37, with 18 assists and 5 rebounds. Still the game would come down to overtime and the hands of Lakers reserve forward John Tresvant, who would lead Los Angeles to a 121–115 win and a 2–2 tie in the series. Baylor did his part too, with 30 points.

Wilt came out strong for the fifth game in New York and was determined to cover Reed all over the floor. With a little more than eight minutes gone in the first quarter, Los Angeles had raced to a 25–15 lead. Then Reed caught a pass at the foul line, and Chamberlain was there to meet him. Reed went to his left but tripped over Wilt's foot and fell forward, tearing a muscle in his thigh.

"I drove past Wilt, and I just fell," Reed said. "I was having problems with my knee, and I tore a muscle in my right thigh."

With Reed out, Holzman employed subs Nate Bowman and Bill Hosket, a six-foot-seven forward, to hound Chamberlain. By the half, the Lakers led by 13. In the New York locker room, Bill Bradley suggested that the Knicks go to a zone offense, which would either force Chamberlain to come out from the basket or give them open shots. "When we saw Wilt not playing a man, it was like attacking a zone," Bradley explained. "Just hit the open spaces in a zone."

It began working in the third. The Lakers seemed almost possessed by the notion of taking advantage of the mismatch in the post. Time after time, they attempted to force the ball to Chamberlain, and the Knicks got bunches of steals and turnovers. The fourth period opened with the Lakers holding an 82–75 lead and a troubled hand. They were in obvious disarray. And the Knickerbockers were surging, cheered on by the awakened Garden crowd. At 5:19, Bradley dropped in a jumper to give the Knicks the lead, 93–91. That prompted a flurry of New York baskets to extend the lead to 8. After the final exchanges, the Knicks took the 3–2 edge, 107–100. Los Angeles had been forced into 30 turnovers for the game. In the second half, West didn't have a single field goal, and Chamberlain scored only 4 points.

"They blew the eighteen-point lead," Doug Krikorian said. "Basically, I look at that game as where they blew the series."

Later, West would acknowledge that the Lakers, himself in particular, had become victims of their mind-set. After so many championship losses, West had come to believe that they were unlucky; that something would always get in their way. He became a prisoner of his own expectations. They couldn't win that fifth game because they didn't believe they could, he would conclude later.

"I think maybe we felt we were jinxed," he said. "Maybe we didn't go into the game with enough confidence."

The Lakers returned home and corrected their mistakes in game six. With Reed out, Wilt scored 45 with 27 rebounds. The Lakers rolled, 135–113, to tie the series at three each. The stage was set in New York for the seventh game drama. Would Reed play? The Knicks left the locker room for warm-ups not knowing. Doctors had to place painkilling injections at various places and various depths across his thigh in an effort to numb the tear. Reed appeared on the Garden floor just before game time that Friday, May 8, bringing an overwhelming roar from the crowd. The Knicks watched him hobble out, and each of them soaked in the emotion from the noise. The Lakers watched too, and made no attempt at furtive glances. Once play began, Reed scored New York's first points, a semijumper from the key, and immediately Los Angeles sought to take advantage of his lack of mobility. Seventeen times the Lakers jammed the ball into Chamberlain in the post; Reed harassed him into shooting 2 for 9. Reed himself would finish 2 for 5 with 4 fouls and 3 rebounds, but it was enough. The emotional charge sent the rest of the Knicks zipping through their paces. They simply ran away from the Lakers. New York led 9–2, then 15–6, then 30–17. When Reed left the game in the third quarter, New York led 61–37. From there they ran on to the title, 113–99.

"The Laker dressing room later was a morgue, in which living humans were interred," wrote Bill Libby for the *LA Times*.

Drenched in sweat, Chamberlain sat and pondered his painful comeback from injury, now rewarded with yet another championship loss. "My knee didn't hurt much," he said, turning down an excuse. "We just lost, that's all. I didn't lose. We lost."

JERRY WEST NIGHT

Yet another championship loss brought new depths to the Lakers' emptiness. Baylor would miss much of the 1971 season with injuries, leaving West and Chamberlain as the focal points of the offense. Gail Goodrich, who had been lost to Phoenix in the 1968 expansion draft, returned to the Lakers and averaged 17.5 points per game. West showed a knack for finding him and Chamberlain with pinpoint passes. He moved into the league lead with 9.5 assists per game while still pushing his scoring average to almost 27.

For the 1970–71 season, the NBA realigned itself into two conferences (Eastern and Western) of two divisions each: Atlantic and Central, and Midwest and Pacific. The Lakers won the Pacific but lost to the winners of the Midwest division, the Milwaukee Bucks. The league also expanded from fourteen teams to seventeen by adding the Buffalo Braves, the Cleveland Cavaliers, and the Portland Trailblazers.

That March 2 West was trying to stop a fast break against the Buffalo Braves when he tore the medial collateral ligament in his knee and was pronounced done for the year.

On March 19, the Lakers held Jerry West Night at the Forum, and though the event had been planned long before his injury, it proved a perfect relief from the regimen of surgery, crutches, and rehab that he had begun. All the family, friends, and teammates were there as the applause rained down on West while he stood on crutches with Jane and the boys nearby. It felt very good, he would admit later. The surprise guest of the night was Bill Russell, who had flown in at his own expense and offered the most compelling words of the night.

Russell strode out to great applause and hugged West. Then the Forum grew silent as he spoke: "Jerry, I once wrote that success is a journey, and that the greatest honor a man can have is the respect and friendship of his peers. You have that more than any man I know. Jerry, you are, in every sense of the word, truly a champion."

Then he turned to West and said, "If I could have one wish granted, it would be that you would always be happy."

Of course, it was Russell, more than anyone, who had played the largest role in West's prodigious dismay. That disappointment was about to grow even larger. During the off-season, Oscar Robertson had been traded to Milwaukee, where he teamed with a young Kareem Abdul-Jabbar to win the NBA championship in 1971. For so many years, West had vied for the title while Robertson, saddled with inferior teams battling the Celtics in the Eastern Conference, had never advanced to the championship series. But now his old foe had snuck in and claimed the ultimate prize while West watched from rehab. It pained him no end, yet when Abdul-Jabbar won the MVP award for the championship series, West spoke up and pointed out that Robertson, though no longer the tremendous performer he once had been, had actually controlled the outcome by playing the kind of floor game that only Robertson could play. Robertson deserved MVP consideration, West said. "Even with a sore leg, he was masterful, quarterbacking the team, orchestrating the games, making the big plays, seldom shooting, but making good shots, proving himself under pressure and helping his team take the title I always wanted so much, and I'm sure he wanted just as much."

Kareem, Robertson, and the Bucks had already dispatched the Lakers, 4–1, a Western finals series that showcased Abdul-Jabbar versus Wilt. "You had a young player and an aging player in that series," West recalled. "That's pretty much what it was. The reigning monarch was paving the way for the arriving monarch. It was just a changing of eras. It was two completely different centers. Wilt was motivated by that matchup. He was a very proud man."

In the aftermath, Cooke wanted Joe Mullaney's job, even though the Lakers had won their division by seven games. "I hated to see it happen to someone as nice as Joe," Schaus said. "But when you're dealing with a guy like Jack Kent Cooke, when they've made up their mind, there's nothing you're going to say to change it."

If West hadn't gotten injured, Mullaney might well have kept his job. West still faced much rehab to get ready for the 1971–72 season. He realized that the injury and the night in his honor had renewed him. "I did not want it to be a farewell," he said.

But I got an emptiness deep inside

And I've tried, but it won't let me go

—Neil Diamond, "I Am . . . I Said"

THE LAST CHANCE

Los Angeles, 1971 to 1974

BY THE SUMMER OF 1971, JERRY WEST WAS OFF HIS CRUTCHES AND cruising around Hollywood in his yellow Lamborghini. Neil Diamond was his favorite music, but he had to turn it up to hear it over the car's "Megaphono" exhausts that announced his appearance well before he arrived anywhere. From the four Weber carburetors over the V12 engine, to the low-slung front end, the ride sported a mix of muscle and elegance that would have auto enthusiasts drooling for decades. West himself would soon dismiss it in favor of a white Ferrari, but in the meantime, it served well enough as an emblem of his success.

If Howard West could have looked in on his son's life, he might well have been agog, if for no other reason than the car itself. Howard had never even owned one, and then there had been the whole fiasco with the gas station in Mineral Wells. And now here was Jerry, tooling around exclusive Brentwood in a bright yellow Italian job. There were so many things that Howard had aspired to in his own life, but it was his children who had realized those longings. And Jerry had done so in unimaginable fashion. From the outrageously expensive sports cars and tailored suits to the golden tan and the shades, the thirty-three-year-old West had clearly checked into the Hotel California. He now had a personal manager and his own TV show on KTLA, plus a radio show, and he endorsed a host of commercial products: milk, clothing, razors, tires, basketball shoes. It all added up to make Jerry West very much a man of his times. Even the angle of his broken nose seemed to add just the right touch of angular ruggedness to his features.

His siblings had always seen so much of their mother in Jerry, but Howard would have recognized a surprising amount of himself. Jerry may have been Mr. Clutch (the name took on a new meaning with the high-performance manual transmission of his sports car), but he still kept to the small-town ways of his upbringing. His father had loved loafing at the gas station and smoking and joking with his neighbors. For Jerry, that same kind of fix came with hanging out at the West-wood Drug Store near UCLA, where his fishing buddy Hollis Johnson ran the lunch counter. If it was summertime, West might take Jane with him for lunch, and they'd grab a sandwich while perched on up-turned orange crates in the back room. If the arrival in the Lamborghini seemed incongruent with the orange crates in the back room, it's safe to assume that the drugstore provided ballast for the West Coast seventies chi that West had going on. Hollis Johnson's place was merely West's escape from the lifestyle he had created for himself. He most often went there alone, to talk sports or whatever with whoever happened by. West loved the Westwood Drug Store, and during the season, he'd get up early and head over before practice.

"I used to have breakfast on a regular basis with Jerry West at Hollis Johnson's Westwood Drug Store, right in Westwood," recalled Bill Walton, then a student at UCLA. "We'd go in the back door, and Hollis would bring out gigantic omelets and stacks of pancakes. I would be wolfing down this food. Jerry would be there eating. He'd be on his way to practice. He would tell me all about the NBA. It was just the greatest time."

Some observers figured that West used this time at Hollis Johnson's to claim the sort of closeness he increasingly found hard to achieve with his own teammates. West was a loner, even a narcissist, according to Charley Rosen's book *The Pivotal Season,* which did not attribute the dim view of West. Whatever the criticisms, most of them could be traced to his nature. "I'm too much of a perfectionist, too demanding, never satisfied with my own play or anyone else's," West would admit. Yet he continued to be as demanding as ever, and he continued to turn his harshest assessments on himself. No one disputed that. But as he would show later as a team executive, West remained quite disappointed with the level of commitment of players around the league. And he could still become quite angry at how the Lakers played. His standards remained very high. "That's what made him great," Mitch Chortkoff explained. It's what separates the alpha male from the rest of the pack. "If you didn't come into the game breathing fire every night, Jerry couldn't understand," explained former teammate Tommy Hawkins.

On the other hand, West had always enjoyed being a part of the group. He engaged in the small talk, the card playing, the routine camaraderie of the road, but he was also very aware that he was different. His teammates realized this as well, and some thought to keep their conversations with him to light talk, mostly because they didn't want to do anything that might set him off in one direction or another.

These complications of his team life made it easy to understand why West cherished the opportunity to get away with Johnson and go fishing, often in the High Sierras. They tried to do that at least four times a year, and if the season was over, those trips might last as long as a week. That's when West was really able to relax. That's when he could show something of his father's good-natured gift for gab.

"I've probably got more reels than anybody in the U.S.," Johnson once bragged. "But when it comes to passion for fishing, you have got to see Jerry to believe him."

The trout in the High Sierras took West about as far away from basketball as he could get in those dismal springs just after another season had ended with another loss. God, how he hated sitting in those silent dressing rooms after the final big defeat each year and listening through the walls to the noise of celebration in the other locker room. God, how he hated that. And to take him right away from it all, Johnson always seemed to know exactly where the trout were.

"One time Jerry drove three hundred thirty miles in a snowstorm just so he could be there when fishing season opened," Johnson recalled. "Twice he was stopped, one time when his windshield wiper broke, and then again when the cops said he couldn't go any further. He finally straggled in, and before you knew it, he was out there in the snow cleaning fish and telling me, 'Hollis, you're hotter than jailhouse coffee,' and 'Hollis, you're my man.'"

West's father would also have been proud to know that his son retained his old Democratic leanings, even when they bumped up against Johnson's substantial conservatism. "Hollis is a superconservative," West once explained. "We don't always see eye to eye. But I like and respect him just the same. I like a man with opinions. They're what make the world go round."

Howard West may have been more comfortable choosing his words, but he and Jerry obviously shared many of the same sentiments, just as they shared the same deep and very basic desire. In their own very different ways, they had both ached to be loved. Once again, it would be fair to observe that the son basked in the sort of approval that was well beyond Howard's wildest dreams. Jerry's female admirers were said to be legion, according to many sources who witnessed the way he lived outside of the spotlight's glare. When a group of NBA teams converged in Hawaii that September for training camp and a series of preseason games, the Phoenix Suns' young center, Neal Walk, made sure to hang in West's shadow. He figured that was the best way to catch one or two of the many ladies who always seemed to trail the legend wherever he went. *Sports Illustrated* reported that the throng would likely include a number of flight attendants, supposedly a crowd that doted on Mr. Clutch.

Heading into his twelfth season playing pro basketball, he had begun to ponder how he would feel when it came time to quit playing. The knee injury had helped ease the growing doubt that losing so many championships had brought to his life, and now he was clear on the issue: He knew he wanted to keep playing as long as he could play at a high level. He also knew that wouldn't be much longer.

"The toughest part of it," he said at the time, "will be having to leave the life, the trips, the laughs. I've been around so long. The greatest job in the world would just be to go along with the guys. Oh, I'm telling you, it's an unbelievable part of our lives. Unfortunately, it is our lives. It seems like basketball first, then family. When I leave, there'll be a void. It's going to bother me, I know . . . It's kind of sad when you think about it, because it's such a carefree life. Everybody always says it's a kid's game, but you see, it's a whole kid's life, too."

STAR WARS

Los Angeles had long been a city of divas. After a decade in town, the Lakers had begun realizing their full identity as Hollywood's basketball club, and they acted accordingly. The seventies found them still living just at the edge of true success as a loose alliance of green-eyed stars prone to bouts of jealousy and envy. Chamberlain later acknowledged that he and Baylor were too much alike, too competitive, too loudmouthed and opinionated, to ever be allies, much less friends. They spoke if they had to. Otherwise they kept their distance, fully aware that they were both huge know-it-alls. "Never in his life has Elg ever said, 'I don't know,'" West alleged. "If he doesn't know the facts, he'll make them up."

Chamberlain himself required little fiction, because at one point or another, everything people said about him became true. He was that much of a contradiction. Mostly, Wilt faced each day with the idea that he was the king of everything, contrary to whatever evidence popped up. West thought at least some of that was a defense mechanism.

His teammates liked to joke that you could smell Wilt long before you laid eyes on him. He wasn't fond of showers and hauled around a notoriously smelly gym bag stuffed with half-eaten sandwiches, uncashed checks from the Lakers, and fermenting undies. In those days, players were responsible for washing their own game uniforms. Wilt usually just peeled off his sweat-soaked garments, tossed them in the bag, then pulled them out and broke them of their stiffness for the next contest. If you wore your uniforms dirty, then you had to tape your nipples to avoid chafing. Wilt was a noted nipple taper, teammates joked. And showers? Not a necessity for Chamberlain, who was known to splash on a little water and move right along.

Just as he was aware that his smelly gym bag easily offended, the center knew that his presence constricted Baylor, but he didn't care. He believed that Baylor, now limited defensively with his bad knees, had come to the end of his effectiveness. Not long after he arrived in

LA, Chamberlain had begun sizing up the Baylor-West relationship. The center had quickly come to believe that the longtime Lakers duo had been competing against each other for years, always trying to outdo each other in status and statistics, perhaps even more than either had realized. They got along fine so long as the Lakers remained a two-man team, he deduced, because their issues were never really articulated.

In the name of truth, Chamberlain openly admitted he was envious of West's popularity. Still, the center and the guard had found a friendship of sorts, Chamberlain said, because they complemented each other quite well. West tended to gamble on defense, which worked nicely with Chamberlain's sitting in the lane protecting the basket. And West was largely an outside shooter later in his career and posed few intrusions on the center's domain.

He and West did have their conflicts, Chamberlain acknowledged. "We each had our habits and our way of doing things. I think Jerry probably envied all the records I'd set and all the money I made, and he was probably a bit sensitive to my 'invasion' of his turf; Los Angeles was 'his' town, and here I was, coming in to challenge him."

Chamberlain said that if anything truly irked him about Mr. Clutch, it was West's failure to speak out on team issues. In private, West would express his anger and frustration, but he always seemed too concerned about his goody-goody image to challenge anything publicly, the center said.

Wilt was building an exotic and expensive (a whopping $1.5 million) house, which he would proudly exhibit with a house-warming party in March 1972. He invited West, although Chamberlain had been wounded months earlier when he wasn't invited to West's own house-warming party.

"I really liked Wilt Chamberlain," West recalled. "If I didn't like him, I'd tell you. He was someone who helped prolong my basketball career. The ironic thing about Wilt was that he never seemed to be relaxed and fun. I think after he got out of basketball, he became much more relaxed, much more fun. Much of it had to do with the fact he was Wilt Chamberlain, and no one pulled for him. I think those things have really bothered him all his life. There's no question it was tough to be a giant."

West, of course, had his own problems with relaxing, even when he was relaxing. "You go out with Jerry, you hit eight places every five minutes," Hot Rod Hundley pointed out. "He comes in a place, takes a sip of beer, looks around, and says, 'Come on, let's go someplace else.'"

"Jerry West eats as if the twenty-four second clock extended to the dining room," Jim Murray quipped in one of his columns.

"He is a very complicated, wound-up spring, a bundle of nerves," Schaus said that year. "He is so high strung that in all the time I have known Jerry, I have never once seen him fully relaxed."

That seemed especially true if money was involved. Over his years with the team, West had been keenly aware of the contracts of other players around the league, and how they compared with his. In time, West had eclipsed Baylor in terms of salary, but neither of them made the cash Chamberlain did. Chamberlain had been the first NBA player to sign a $100,000 deal, although the center would later claim that for several years the owners paying him announced his pay as $75,000 to hold down demand from other players. In 1965, when it was finally revealed that Chamberlain had reached $100,000, Red Auerbach promptly raised Russell's announced pay to $100,001 a year. Chamberlain later claimed that even though his salary had been announced at $100,000, he was actually making far more than that. By 1968, when he arrived in Los Angeles, Chamberlain held a contract paying him $250,000 a year, supposedly the most in the league.

Chamberlain said of West, "He'd always been the highest-paid, most-popular Laker. I took one of those titles away from him before I played my first game."

West had welcomed Wilt and his big contract, not just for the basketball but because his big deal set the agenda for West to earn just as much. Unfortunately, Chamberlain also multiplied the team's already considerable complications. West, Wilt, and Baylor were all so talented, so opinionated about the process of competing, that they left observers in wonder. How could they spend so much time doing what they did and still have the basic truth elude them so completely? Over Chamberlain's first three years in LA, that mystery had only deepened. No one asked the question more often than West himself. "Why can't we win?" he wondered over and over.

No matter how many of the factors fell favorably, the three stars had managed to demonstrate quite effectively that they could make things impossibly difficult. "Egads, they were prima donnas," recalled Jack Kent Cooke, no shrinking violet himself. On the Lakers roster, even the role players sported big egos. "We had a lot of players who'd had personal success but hadn't enjoyed team success; a lot of very frustrated people," West said of the 1972 Lakers. "It had been frustrating to lose each year. It was terrible."

Chamberlain, now thirty-five, had his giant pride; West was sullen with frustration; and "Motormouth" Baylor, at thirty-seven, struggled with his declining skills and influence. To go with them were forward Happy Hairston, an irascible locker-room lawyer who chattered incessantly; Gail Goodrich, a determined scorer who liked to control the ball; and Jim McMillian, a chunky Ivy Leaguer pushing for a starting role. Among the bit players were Pat Riley, Keith Erickson, Flynn Robinson, and rookie Jim Cleamons, all of whom sported healthy self-concepts.

Who could possibly coach them? Who could help them to see beyond themselves? Who would want to?

REBIRTH

Cooke had tea with John Wooden and tried to talk the Wizard of Westwood into taking on the Lakers, but he declined. Fred Schaus then asked Cooke to consider forty-five-year-old Bill Sharman, who had just coached the Utah Stars to the 1971 American Basketball Association title. "I was intrigued by Sharman," Cooke explained. "He had that inner intensity." Time would reveal that of the many fine moves Schaus made as Lakers general manager, hiring Sharman was perhaps the most impressive.

Intensity had indeed been his trademark as a player for the Boston Celtics from 1951 to 1961. Off the court, Sharman was a pleasant sort, nicknamed "Willie" by his pals. Once the clock started, he was a demon, a transformation that amazed and amused his teammates. He soon became known for ending quickly what other people started. "A brutal fighter," Doug Krikorian remembered. "I saw him beat the shit out of Earl Lloyd, a big six-foot-six tough guy. Sharman was like a boxer."

"Willie didn't talk," former Celtics teammate Ed Macauley recalled. "When he'd had enough, you knew it."

The NBA had been started just after World War II by men who owned hockey teams. They thought a good fight added to the aesthetic of sport, not to mention the box office draw. The league in the early days presented quite a physical challenge to all newcomers. Sharman seemed to relish that.

"If you put a hand on him playing defense, he'd break your wrist," Hot Rod Hundley recalled. "He knocked it away with a hell of a chop."

"I was always kind of aggressive," Sharman admitted. "When we played in the fifties, pro basketball was still growing. It was kind of like hockey. The owners didn't say, 'Go out and fight.' But they didn't discourage it. Back then they didn't throw you out of games for fighting. They kind of let it go. If you backed off and didn't hold your own, other players kind of took advantage of you. I always feel I never started a fight, but I never backed away from one. If you did, they just kept pushing and grabbing at you. I saw a lot of good basketball players in those days get pushed right out of the league because they wouldn't push back."

As a coach, he paced the sideline, pushed by that same intensity. It never hurt that his players were always mindful of his reputation for toughness, although you'd never hear about it from Sharman himself. He knew how to give and receive respect. To go with that, he flat out knew the game. Sharman's 1967 San Francisco Warriors had reached the NBA championship series, where they lost to Wilt's 76ers. Before that, Sharman had made a winner of the miserable program at California State University, Los Angeles. He'd even coached the Cleveland Pipers of the old American Basketball League to a title in 1962, the ABL's only full season before it folded. His 1971 ABA championship simply emphasized the fact that as a coach Sharman knew how to assess personnel and how to get them to perform at a high level. That was why he, like John Wooden, would wind up in the Hall of Fame — that rare man to be elected as both a player and a coach.

The son of a newspaper circulation man, Sharman had lettered in five sports (football, basketball, baseball, tennis, and track) in high school in Porterville, California. After a stint in the navy during World War II, he played basketball and baseball at the University of Southern California. Sharman was a muscular freshman when Tex Winter was a senior. Winter recalled matching up against him once and then telling Coach Sam Barry that he had to move that guy Sharman up to the varsity in a hurry. From USC Sharman joined the NBA's Washington Capitols, then moved to baseball with the Brooklyn Dodgers

organization; he even earned a brief spot on their roster in 1951, although he never actually got to play in a major league game. But that
fall Red Auerbach coaxed him back to basketball. Sharman had been
a six-foot-two forward in a control offense at USC. He couldn't handle the ball too well, but he was a tough defender and he could shoot,
and Auerbach's freelance system required scorers. Sharman led the
Celtics in scoring for four seasons, 1956–59, and had the league's top
free throw percentage for eight.

Sharman's friends told him not to take on the Lakers. "Everybody
told me, 'You don't want that job,' " he recalled. "They said the Lakers
had not won a championship with Wilt, Jerry West, and Baylor for a
number of years. And now Wilt was thirty-six, and Jerry was thirty-
two or thirty-three, and Baylor was thirty-seven . . . On the other hand,
I wanted to live in Los Angeles. I thought it was a challenge. I was familiar with the Lakers, and I had known Jerry West. I had played
against him, played golf with him. And I had coached college in Los
Angeles, and in the ABA, so I was familiar with a lot of the players. I
had played against Wilt, too. I knew them."

He viewed the Lakers as a dream job and promptly accepted the
offer in July 1971. Mostly, Sharman jumped at the chance to coach
West. His regard for the player was immense, and it had begun the
very first time he had played against the rookie West in September
1960. "I'll always remember his eyes," he once explained. "They
darted from side to side while he was guarding you. He wanted that
ball."

Sharman told reporters that West was one of the few superstar
guards in the history of the league to play both ends of the floor so
competitively. Most star guards rested on the defensive end to save
their energy for offense, Sharman pointed out, adding that if West had
been more selfish and saved his energy for playing offense, he could
have easily averaged 40 points or more per game for several seasons.

Sharman thought it wrong that a player as great as West had not
won an NBA title, especially after trying so hard for so many years.
Asked his goal for the Lakers, the new coach answered matter-of-
factly, "the world championship." The team's fans and media had
heard that one before. Even West himself later acknowledged having
substantial issues in believing that it could be done. Bill Russell had
been out of the game two years, and still the Lakers hadn't found a

way to win it. West's negative thoughts about fate and luck had become entrenched.

Sharman, though, had a clear plan. He was going to remake the Lakers' collection of talent into a team. Insiders around the league smirked at the thought. "On that one team, you probably had more diverse, strong personalities than you had on any championship team in the history of the game," said longtime Lakers scout Bill Bertka. "But you had the strongest personality in Bill Sharman. He was on fire right at that time. He was at the peak of his career with his personal intensity as a coach. He was a great communicator. No frills. No bullshit. With Bill, it was all down to productivity."

In retrospect, his biggest asset was all the time he spent in the Boston Celtics backcourt with Bob Cousy. As a player, Sharman had been the epitome of an off guard. He circled in constant motion until he came open in the Boston offense, and just at that moment, Cousy always seemed to get him the ball right where he wanted it. As a coach, he knew what he wanted out of his guard combo. He wanted to move West to the point, where his passing could make the difference.

First he had to discuss this with West, which he did in late summer 1971 during a round of golf. The coach asked his star guard how much longer he thought he could play. As Sharman suspected, West replied that he didn't feel he could stay in the game too much longer. Since the 1970 season, he had labored under the load of scoring all the points necessary for the Lakers to win. "The pressure was really getting to me," West recalled.

Knee ligament surgery in that era was an iffy proposition. West was returning from his 1971 injury and clearly faced a fragile time. Scoring had been such a part of his identity. Knowing that all of this was preying on the guard's mind, Sharman proposed the move to point guard, where the scoring load would be a little lighter. He'd have to run the team and deliver the ball, something that West was already largely doing along with his other roles. With little hesitation, West agreed. In looking back, Sharman acknowledged that it would have been understandable for West to reject such a major move. However, he switched positions without complaint. "He was just so cooperative, so eager to do anything to help the team," Sharman recalled. "He had just a wonderful attitude."

While the idea seemed logical, West recalled that it was actually

Sharman's enthusiasm that sold him on the change. It actually made perfect sense. It was obvious he would still score plenty, but the primary burden for that would be distributed to the rest of the team. Scoring would become a team chore, no longer West's personal cross to bear.

"What it all amounts to is that Bill Sharman gave me a new lease on life," West would say later. "Basketball became enjoyable again."

CHANGES

Sharman wanted a five-man team that got out and ran much like Russell's Celtics, which meant that Chamberlain would have to focus on rebounding and blocking shots and playing more like Russell.

And Baylor? He'd have to move to the bench as a sub.

Wisely, Sharman didn't announce these plans all at once. He was much more tactful than that. Even so, the Lakers didn't quite know what to make of their new coach. They found him to be a strange mix of fight and quiet innovation. He was a Southern California boy, but he was also a Celtic. "It was difficult for us to relate to him in the beginning, because he was covered with Boston green," explained Pat Riley. "But in time, we came around. He was a low-key guy, but very competitive, very feisty."

It didn't help that Sharman added K. C. Jones, his Boston teammate and West's longtime foil, as the first assistant coach in Lakers history. "We've never had an assistant coach before," Cooke grumbled, "except, of course, Chick Hearn." Given the team's history, the move could have seeded some resentment.

"Not much was said to me or to K.C.," Sharman said of the Celtics issue. "Now, there might have been talk behind. The players were so cooperative, I don't think they resented it in any way. I wasn't a player for the Celtics for most of their finals losses, when they had lost for the sixth or seventh time. I wasn't playing against them when sometimes tempers can flare. I don't think there was any great resentment. K. C. Jones is a sweet person who gets along with everybody."

Sharman and Jones had seen Red Auerbach's running game work wonders, with Russell snatching rebounds and firing outlet passes on the fast break. Sharman had played in the "center opposite" offense at USC under coach Sam Barry. Tex Winter would fashion Barry's system into his highly effective triangle offense as a college and pro coach. In a 2008 interview, Sharman said that his approach had some similarities to Winter's and Barry's systems. Sharman thought the weakness of most pro offenses was that they left players simply standing around on the weak side. Winter's triangle would in fact attack from the weak side with a Michael Jordan or a Kobe Bryant. Sharman at least wanted to keep his players moving on the weak side, to keep things challenging for the defense. And like Barry and Winter, Sharman still employed a two-guard front. But the Lakers coach said his 1972 system was basically about "twenty-five percent Sam Barry and seventy-five percent Red Auerbach."

"Red Auerbach was not an Xs and Os man. But he had a great competitive spirit," Sharman offered. "He was a very smart coach. He knew how to substitute. He knew how to get a team in shape. He knew how to motivate 'em. Put all that together, he was a great professional basketball coach. Now, I don't know if all that would have worked in college, because he wasn't a fundamentals coach. But in pro ball, he was super. I got from him how he installed and encouraged the running game and the fast break. Then when you had a Bill Russell and a Cousy and a Heinsohn and the Jones boys and Ramsey—all these great players—naturally you're gonna have a great team. But you could see the advantages of a running team. We ran at every opportunity we had. We had the rebounding to run, we had the ball handler in Cousy, and we had the runners. The point I got from all of that: Even if you couldn't fast break and get a layup, by running and moving the ball downcourt, you could take advantage. If only one person was back on defense, your players could find each other. Of course, the Boston Celtics were the ones most responsible for starting the fast break, where you sustain it. You don't just do it once in a while. It was a running style. The first year in Los Angeles, I encouraged the running and the fast break because I felt we had the strong rebounding with Wilt and Happy Hairston. So I really pushed it to run at the other teams."

Sharman's announcement that he planned to make the Lakers a running team brought yet more snickers around the league. Use Chamberlain, the NBA's resident dinosaur, in a running game? Absolutely loony. Chamberlain was the premier post-up weapon. Sharman knew he would have to sell the key players on the idea, and no one was more key than Chamberlain. The coach knew the entire season rested on how the center responded. First, Sharman invited Chamberlain to a pricey LA restaurant for lunch. Once there, they discussed the need for Wilt, the greatest scorer in the history of the game, to focus on defense and rebounding. The big center had heard this line from other coaches. But Sharman was different. He listened to Chamberlain's opinions on the issue. Sharman had played the running game, and he knew exactly what it took. Chamberlain had his doubts but said he would cooperate fully.

Sharman was very much a realist. He knew that Chamberlain might have good intentions, but ultimately the center would respond to him as he had to all his other coaches. He would stare blankly as they talked, then do just what he wanted anyway. Sharman knew he would have to find a way around the old Chamberlain puzzle.

Sharman also asked Chamberlain to consider another of his new ideas: a game-day shoot-around in the mornings. As a player, Sharman had insisted on going to the gym each morning before a game for shooting exercise, running through exactly the shots he planned to take that night. As a coach, he required his players to go through these same routines. A notorious night owl, Chamberlain hedged at the idea. But Sharman was determined that his team embrace his approach.

"Jerry West was very eager," Sharman recalled. "He said he thought it would help. Gail Goodrich and the others all said they would try it. Then I got to Wilt Chamberlain. I knew this might be a problem."

Under pressure, Chamberlain reluctantly agreed to try it. He and other players often grumbled that season, but Sharman's game-day shoot-around soon became a staple of NBA preparation. So would his notions on diet and exercise. Beyond that, he required his players to become students of the game. His Lakers were the first NBA team to break down game film and study it like football coaches did. In that age before videotape, scout Bill Bertka would spend hours cutting and splicing film.

Sharman had hoped that the shoot-around might help Chamberlain's foul shooting, but that aspect of the big man's game proved to be an unconquerable mountain. An eight-time all-star, Sharman would later author an instructional book on shooting. As a coach, he used his understanding of the mechanics to improve his players' touch. In Los Angeles, however, he soon met his match. After years of trying everything, Wilt admitted he was befuddled at the line. Crowds at the Forum took to cheering wildly when he made one. "My embarrassing moment in basketball was perpetual, which I'm famous for," Chamberlain recalled. "That's my lack of ability to make foul shots."

"I never could figure out how to help him with free throws," Sharman conceded.

Regardless, the coach remained relentless in his agenda for change. Next he asked Happy Hairston to sacrifice his offensive game and concentrate on rebounding. Dominating the defensive boards was a two-man job. Every great center needs a tough power forward to help out. Hairston's sacrifice would be a key to winning the title, Sharman said. A muscular six-foot-seven, 225-pounder, Hairston agreed. (It helped that Cooke had just awarded him a new contract.) The new emphasis would cause his scoring to dip from 18.6 in 1971 to 13.1 in '72. But he would average 15 boards over the last half of the season and become the first forward to pull down 1,000 rebounds while playing alongside Chamberlain.

With Hairston and Wilt controlling the defensive boards, the Lakers had West and Gail Goodrich to run the fast break. Goodrich had started his career in LA but had spent lots of time sitting behind West. The Lakers had let him go to Phoenix in the expansion draft, then later brought him back. Goodrich, known for his cockiness, liked to control the ball. It was a major challenge sorting out the guard situation, Bill Bertka recalled. "When Gail was acquired, people said, 'You're gonna need two basketballs now. One for West and one for Goodrich. You don't have enough basketballs on that team.' That wasn't quite true. Bill Sharman, in his discussions with Gail, said, 'I want you to play without the ball.' Gail just snapped. When he was at Phoenix, he was a point guard, a high scorer. Gail took great pride in being able to play without the ball and moving without the ball. Gail was a master at it. He and West became one of the highest-scoring backcourts in league history that year. Gail was just so smart and a tenacious competitor. People liked to say 'Little Gail Goodrich.' He was six-one and very strong. Deceptively strong. And he had this ability to get his shot off, with the different moves that he had. Gail knew how to use picks, could curl off a pick, could deceptively backdoor his man. His man would lose vision on him, and Gail would find an open shot. He was a deadly spot-up shooter."

Goodrich was no great defender; however, he did share an attribute with West. "He had arms down to his toes," said Kevin Loughery, a former Baltimore Bullet. "He had that seven-foot wingspan. He could go to the basket because of that and take it over the rim."

Goodrich and West would each average 25 points per game over the season as they hauled in pass after pass from Chamberlain. West would run the break from the center, with Goodrich finishing from the wing. Opponents didn't realize how much Goodrich had improved when the season began. He had made himself difficult to defend, but early in that season teams thought they could lay off Goodrich and double-team West. "That left Gail open a lot of times," West said, "and I was able to pass to him for easy shots."

They quickly gained a sense for each other and soon knew when and where to deliver the ball to each other, Goodrich recalled. "Jerry was a great player, and I think we complemented each other. We blended and didn't hurt each other's games."

"It was chemistry," West said when asked about the 1972 success. "We had the right kind of chemistry. Bill Sharman treated us like we wanted to be treated. He was a very organized guy in the sense that there were certain things that he wanted to see. He let you play. We weren't encumbered by a hundred plays. We weren't encumbered by things that you see modern teams encumbered by. We weren't over-coached. Bill just had the right approach, said the right things. Maybe it was just our time to get through this past mess as far as winning a championship."

THE SWITCH

Baylor had always held on to the ball. You threw it to him, he was going to give it a feel. (That's how Adrian Dantley, another DC native, later worked his offense too.) But as he got older, the problem got worse. You threw it to Baylor, and ball movement froze in agonizing fashion. Sharman was all about ball movement, and the coach knew as the season opened that Baylor posed a huge problem. He had been the Lakers' dominant figure for most of his thirteen-year career. But he had missed all but two games of the previous season with an Achilles tendon injury. In the off-season, he had worked hard to come back and was now able to play again—only Sharman's new running

system required a very active, small forward. Baylor just didn't have the mobility. At first, Sharman wasn't sure exactly how to handle it.

Training camp opened first in LA, then moved to Hawaii, and Sharman saw what he already knew. Jim McMillian, Baylor's backup, was a fine defender and a deadly shooter along the baseline. But McMillian did have a tendency to gain weight. Baylor thought he looked like a chubby Floyd Patterson and dubbed him "Floyd Butterball," or "Butter" for short. But he had slimmed down and steadily improved.

"He came to epitomize what you wanted in a small forward," Bill Bertka explained. "He could run the floor. He could post-up. He could pass the ball. He had a nice medium-range jumper. He had a quick release on his shot. And he was smart."

By the opening of the 1971–72 season, McMillian was pushing Baylor for the starting role at small forward. Sharman might have moved Baylor to the bench earlier, but West suffered a severely sprained ankle in the fourth game of the season and missed four games. Once West returned and showed no ill effects from the injury, the coach decided to make a move. The Lakers had broken out to a 6–3 record that first month.

"Elgin started every game," Sharman said. "But Jim McMillian was coming on strong." He hustled and ran the break with West and Goodrich. Before practice one morning at Loyola Marymount in LA, Sharman informed his captain that McMillian would replace him as a starter.

"He just wasn't the Elgin Baylor of old," Sharman said. "I knew he felt bad, and I wanted him to keep playing. But he said if he couldn't play up to his standards he would retire."

Promised a PR role with the team, Baylor announced his retirement the next day, November 4, 1971, and their thirty-three-game win streak began that night.

THE STREAK

With Baylor's retirement nine games into the season, Sharman had asked West and Chamberlain to become team captains. West declined, but Wilt relished the leadership role. In the past, he had infuri-

ated Lakers coaches, sometimes snacking on hot dogs or fried chicken on the bench before a game. But now he was all business. He had 25 rebounds, 6 assists, and a dozen points in the first victory of the streak, at home over Baltimore. Next came the Golden State Warriors in Oakland and a 19-rebound effort, followed by 22 rebounds and 7 assists against New York in the Forum. In Chicago two nights later, it was 20 rebounds and 8 assists. Most of the assists came from his pulling defensive rebounds and hitting the streaking Goodrich, West, and McMillian for fast-break buckets. Yet even those statistics said little about the blocks and changed shots he forced on defense. Instead of smacking the ball out of bounds as he had in years past, he began brush-blocking shots and starting a fast break the other way.

For Sharman, persuading Chamberlain to play this way had become a matter of hinting at something and waiting for Wilt to come up with it as his own idea. If Chamberlain saw the value in things and considered them his own adjustment, he was perfectly willing to defend the high post and the screen and roll, just as he was willing to key the fast break with outlet passes. But they had to be "his" ideas.

West, meanwhile, flourished as the point guard. He was rusty the first game back from injury and made only 5 of 17 shots. But the next game, in Oakland, he led the team with 28. Against New York, he scored 29 and held Walt Frazier to 17. Against the very physical Bulls, it was 24 points and 13 assists, followed by 20 points, 10 assists, and 8 rebounds against Philadelphia. "West was totally unselfish," recalled Jack Ramsay, who then coached the 76ers. "He was so fundamentally sound that he'd throw two-handed bounce passes. With his long arms and his flawless decision making, West was absolutely the most important guy on the team."

The streak ran on, with West defending, piling up assists, and scoring as the team needed. Obviously the biggest question for West had concerned his comeback from surgery. Would he retain enough of his legendary quickness? "Jerry led the league in assists and still averaged about twenty-five points a game and played great defense," Sharman said. "I still say Jerry West is probably the greatest defensive guard who ever played. People don't realize this. They know of him scoring points and everything. He was so good on defense. Had quick hands and stole the ball. He stole more than anybody, although they didn't keep records on it then. And he'd come around behind shooters and block their shots from behind."

"In practices, they did a lot of scrimmaging in those days," Bill Bertka recalled. "Sharman's style of coaching, he had them play ten-point games, a lot of five-on-five scrimmaging and a lot of fast break drills. The thing I remember about the scrimmages was that West would never shoot in scrimmages. He would always pass, which made for great competition. Wilt didn't particularly shoot a lot in scrimmages either, but they all played hard."

Pat Riley figured into the mix as a seldom-used backup guard. "As a player, he played behind Jerry West," Bertka remembered. "Jerry played big minutes, so Pat didn't get a lot of minutes. Pat accepted that because he was a true professional . . . He was totally committed, always in condition. I mean, he used to get after West in practice. One of the reasons that West was the player he was is that he had a guy guarding him in practice who was going harder than most games. That's the way they competed in practice. I remember that so vividly, how hard they played against each other in practice. Riley would be playing maniacally out of frustration of not playing in games."

The season itself would be framed as a showdown with Oscar Robertson, Kareem Abdul-Jabbar, and the defending champion Milwaukee Bucks. Just six months younger than West, Robertson had accomplished much in his pro basketball tenure, including seven years as the NBA assists leader, his triple-double season of 1962, his 1964 MVP honors, the 1968 scoring title at 29.2 points per game, eleven All-Star Game appearances, and nine selections to the all-NBA first team.

"His greatness was his simplicity," West said, making a statement that revealed just how much of a goal Robertson had posed for West's own career. "He made every play in the simplest way because his skill level was enormous. It took me a long time to catch up with him."

Robertson's physical presence at six-five, 225 pounds, allowed him to use his great strength in his showdowns with West. To counter, West always relied on his quickness and leaping ability and defense. As Abdul-Jabbar pointed out, they always managed to cancel each other out in the Bucks' battles with the Lakers. But over the past two seasons, Robertson had used his strength to hold West to 38 percent shooting from the floor against Milwaukee. That again proved the case in their battle during the eleventh win of the streak, on November 21. West scored 22, but he made only 8 of 23 shots. The Lakers enjoyed a lead down the stretch, only to watch the Bucks pull close.

That's when West broke loose of Robertson's hand checks and grasp for a fifteen-footer. Then he drove for a layup to seal the win.

This victory over the league's defending champions caught the attention of the media in a big way. Sharman, too, took notice. His team now had a stretch where it could win some games. West himself would later observe that NBA teams had been unbelievably strong in the mid-1960s, but expansion of the league and the addition of the American Basketball Association had watered down the competition considerably. The Lakers sensed that with their new approach, they could keep on winning. Bill Russell saw them in Boston and recognized the old paradigm; he called them "Celtics West."

The victories rolled by. Seattle, Detroit, then Seattle again, to cap a perfect 14–0 November. December 1 brought the Lakers to Boston, and West was pumped as usual. He scored 45 against the Celtics. Next came Philly, followed by a win over Portland, where seven Lakers scored in double figures.

The perfectionists West and Sharman had found a nirvana. It included a system that worked, the highest level of talent, perceptive coaching, and a depth of experience—all of that, plus wisdom. Sharman took to reminding his team of the streak before each game, how it was changing basketball itself. Otherwise, few of them even talked about it publicly, except for Wilt, who joked that the Globetrotters teams he played on won more and so did his pro beach volleyball team. At first, the Lakers got little notice in the East because the late schedules meant that their scores seldom made the papers. But the more they won, the more it mattered everywhere. Deadlines or not, the results and the story kept growing. The Lakers streaking across the sports pages brought the NBA a new level of interest, and a growing media entourage with each passing game. The Knicks had won eighteen straight in 1970, only to watch the Bucks break their record with 20 straight wins during their championship drive in 1971. The Lakers tied the Bucks' mark with a win over the Phoenix Suns December 10, as West had 28 points and 11 assists. When they broke the record at home two nights later against Atlanta's big, strong backcourt, West had 14 assists and 26 points. Somebody popped the cork on a bottle of champagne in the locker room afterward, but he turned it down. "So many guys are contributing in so many ways," he said.

"All the pieces just fit," Sharman recalled.

Especially the big one, the Big Dipper. Their twenty-fifth straight came on December 19 in Wilt's hometown of Philadelphia, where he celebrated with 32 points, 34 rebounds, and 12 blocks in a 154–132 rout.

"Sharman has Wilt playing like Russell," Joe Mullaney said after watching the Lakers on television.

"Wilt should be the MVP in the league this season," Baylor told one writer, a sentiment echoed by Philadelphia's star forward Billy Cunningham.

Many observers rushed to credit Sharman for the "new" Wilt. "I don't think I should get the credit," the coach quickly pointed out. "He's always had a bad rap. Whatever they ask of him, he's done. He's just doing more things better now that he is not mainly a scorer. He must block a zillion shots a game. And he scares guys out of other shots or makes them take bad shots." Plus, the secret to the entire running game, Sharman added, "has been Wilt's rebounding and fast passes."

In addition to longest win streak, the Lakers seemed on the verge of becoming the all-time NBA lovefest. "I really like the man," Wilt said. "I've never had a coach as conscientious as Bill." Still, Chamberlain, always a stat freak, admitted feeling a twinge every time he looked at his drooping scoring average, down to 14.8 for the season. "I'm happy about it," he said of the streak, "but here I am the greatest scorer in the game of basketball, and I've been asked by many coaches not to score. Now, where else in a sport can you ask a guy to stop something he's the best in the world doing? It's like telling Babe Ruth not to hit home runs, just bunt."

Each win brought more notoriety for Sharman's shoot-around. Soon just about every coach in the league had instituted a game-day practice. Which was bad news for Wilt. "I'm still not for those eleven o'clock practices," he said as the streak rolled on. "I don't think they've done anything personally for Wilt Chamberlain except to make him lose some sleep. But we're winning, and I'm not going to do anything to knock the winning way."

West had 37 points in the twenty-seventh win in a row, over the Bullets in Baltimore, right before Christmas, and the run-up to New Year's brought three more for a second consecutive perfect month: sixteen wins in sixteen tries. Goodrich was third in the league in scoring at 26.7, West was seventh at 25.3, and he led in assists at 9.5, while Chamberlain owned the rebounding lead at 20 per game and topped the NBA in shooting at 63.8 percent.

The league's sportswriters selected all three Lakers to the All-Star team early in 1972. In a sure sign that the stars were aligned for the Lakers, the game was scheduled for January 18 at the Forum.

The streak ran through January 9, when they lost a road game to rival Milwaukee, 120–114. Bucks coach Larry Costello had scouted the Lakers' thirty-third consecutive win, a road victory over Atlanta, and quickly devised a defense to cut off their fast break by pressuring Chamberlain to slow down the outlet passes. West had 20 on 5 of 16 shooting; Oscar Robertson scored 17 with 9 assists.

Because West had missed the Lakers' first three losses due to injury, he had played in 41 consecutive victories, a record that surely no pro player can ever touch.

"We knew it had to end sometime," Sharman recalled. "When we finally lost, it was an opportunity to learn. You can learn from winning. You learn from losing. Of course, we didn't want to learn too much."

THE TOLL

Through each game, Sharman had been a fiend on the bench, shouting incessantly. "I was always a yeller," he said. "When I got back from Milwaukee, my throat was sore that whole week. It got to where I couldn't even be heard. I went to the doctor, and he told me I really had a bad case, and not to even talk for a week or ten days. I couldn't do that. We were in the middle of a season, a championship season.

"So I tried using one of those battery-operated megaphones. But in a game, I couldn't use it. So I just kept hollering. The doctors said I shouldn't do it. But I thought after the season it would come back. But the damage had been done. My voice never came back."

The voice damage suffered during the streak was permanent and would eventually force Sharman from coaching.

Played at the Forum, the 1972 All-Star Game proved to be Mr. Clutch's night. West hit a shot at the buzzer over New York's Walt Frazier for a 112–110 win for West. It was nice to be the MVP of a winning team for a change, West said. "I've played a lot of these games, and I've played pretty good in some and not so good in others. Suddenly I have a good game in front of my own home crowd and win the MVP award. It's an incredible thrill."

"Jerry deserved it," Wilt told reporters. "He's past due for the honor."

If nothing else, the award and the win streak were signs for West that things might be turning the Lakers' way. Still, he took no chances. His long-held superstitions took an even stronger hold. He had taken to wearing a pair of boots to games. He wouldn't polish them, wouldn't alter them in any way. When he wore out game shoes, he usually gave them to a ball boy, but he refused to give up on the pair that had sustained him through much of the season, even as they started to show signs of serious wear. It was the same for his routes to the Forum. He took one set of backstreets for practice, another for games. And he never altered the routine. Fearful of disturbing their fate, Sharman and the rest of the team all nurtured a similar array of enforced routines.

It all seemed to work as they began yet another win streak that would go eleven games, highlighted by a big win over the Bucks in which West scored 37 with 13 assists. Robertson sat down late in the third quarter with a strained stomach muscle after scoring just 13.

One of the secrets, West observed, was the running game, because it meant that the Lakers faced less pressure on offense. They got out ahead of the defense on many possessions. And if the defense did catch up, he was aggressive against the double-teams that invariably still came his way. He simply drove and found the open teammate.

The Lakers went 30–10 over the last half of the season, each win bringing them a little closer to that unreachable goal. But as the playoffs neared, the team sensed that old Lakers jinx hovering somewhere nearby. And West remained the personification of that bad karma.

"All told, he has scored almost 30,000 points," Frank Deford wrote in *Sports Illustrated.* "If in five particular games he had scored (a total of) 10 more points, he would have won one NCAA and four NBA championships. As it is, he is 0–8 in the finals, and five of those times it came down to one game, winner take all. In the history of sports, there has never been anything like it."

As March drew to a close, sportswriters in Los Angeles began talking about "rumors" that West might retire after the season, which was their way of writing about what West had told them off the record. They then asked him about it on the record. West boldly replied that it was about the money.

"The interest is universal in money," he said, adding that players' salaries around the league should be publicized because fans liked that sort of thing. Then he declined to reveal his own yearly contract, rumored to be about $300,000 a year. Whatever it was, he wanted a raise. "If Mr. Cooke is willing to pay, then I'm willing to play," he said. "This has been the happiest year I've ever had."

Then, as the team neared its record-setting sixty-ninth win, key sub Keith Erickson was lost for the season. Was it going to happen again? Lakers fans seemed to entertain that thought. Though the Lakers were closing out a season to remember—one in which they lost a mere thirteen times—they had sold out just a dozen home games, which kept Cooke worried and left West wondering if he weren't being played long minutes each game in an effort to boost fan support. What made it worse was that the fans who did show up often seemed encased in an impenetrable LA cool. It took a lot to get them excited, just one of the many little factors that played on the minds of West and his teammates as they faced yet another play-off.

"We had been so snakebit in the sixties," Pat Riley recalled. 'We could never, ever win. Always got beat by Boston in the finals. We won thirty-three games in a row, it was incredible. It was a storybook year. But even as we were winning the world championship, we were waiting for something to happen, something bad to happen again."

Chicago, their first-round opponent, had won fifty-seven games, but the Bulls had no center and were forced to play a control game led by Jerry Sloan's very physical defensive play. "Playing against Chicago is not exactly basketball," West told reporters after he scored 23 in the opener. "It's more like arm wrestling." He then hit for 37 and 31 as Los Angeles took a 3–0 lead in the series, which prompted Sloan to complain, "West gets to the foul line whether he's fouled or not."

The fourth game was another physical test in an extremely loud Chicago Stadium. West picked up three early fouls, and Sharman left him on the bench for a long stretch before the half. "I did not want to come out of the game. Definitely not," West said, setting off a small snit with Sharman by complaining that the bench time affected his rhythm. West then took off like a jet in the second half, scoring 23 points and closing out the sweep with a 10-point fourth quarter.

"The truth is that we can't stop West," Bulls coach Dick Motta admitted to reporters. "The only other player I've ever seen who can take over at the end of a game like that is Oscar Robertson. The difference is that West is even more dependable in the clutch than Oscar."

That view would be put to an immediate test. Next up were the Western finals against the Bucks. Chamberlain and Kareem would battle, as would West and Robertson. In game one at the Forum, the Milwaukee defense overplayed and double-teamed the Lakers, forcing them out of their favorite shooting spots and into a 27 percent performance from the floor. Los Angeles scored a mere 8 points in the pivotal third period, and the Bucks took away the home-court advantage, 92–73. Although Oscar was slowed by his persistently painful stomach muscle injury, he hand-checked West into a knot of frustration. West made just 4 of 19 attempts from the floor and afterward blamed himself, saying he had missed open shots.

"A lot of people were calling that the greatest team of all time," Sharman recalled of the Bucks. "They had swept Baltimore in the finals the year before. That was a major obstacle. We lost our first home game to them in the play-offs, which might have helped us. We had that wonderful record, and everybody was . . . not complacent, but we were on a roll. Losing our first game woke everybody up and got us going."

In practice before the start of the series, Goodrich had complained about the ABC television lights that had been added for broadcasts. Cooke asked the network to remove some of the lights, which it did. Cooke wanted even more removed, and ABC again complied. After game one, the Los Angeles owner wanted still more adjustments. But it wasn't the lights, Sharman finally said. "It was that our good shooters were all way off."

For so many years, West had come to believe that the Lakers were unlucky, but very late in the second game he got clear evidence to the contrary. The Lakers were up 133–132 when Robertson and Abdul-Jabbar sought to trap West as he brought the ball over the ten-second line. West reversed away from them but lost the ball. It bounced back toward the half-court line and struck official Manny Sokol, who was trailing the play. West scooped it up, Kareem knocked it away yet again, only to have West again retrieve it and help the Lakers hold on for a 135–134 win.

The Lakers had evened the series at one game apiece, but they were obviously shaky. West had shot 10 for 30 from the field and finished with 28. "I know what I'm doing wrong," he said afterward. "I'm turning my hand too much. But I can't get it stopped. It's got to go away by itself."

Game three took them to Milwaukee, a gloomy, dark city that annoyed West. So he drove frequently, drawing fouls and shooting free throws. On defense, Wilt overplayed Kareem to stop his skyhook, forcing him instead into short jumpers and layups. At one point, Chamberlain blocked 5 shots. In the critical fourth period, Wilt held Kareem scoreless for the last eleven minutes. Abdul-Jabbar still finished with 33, but Chamberlain had done the job. West got a key steal and assist to help the Lakers hold on, 108–105, and regain the home-court advantage. Somehow they had survived 61 percent shooting from the home team.

The Bucks finally took advantage of their home court in the fourth game, taking a 75–43 rebounding advantage and tying the series at two all with a 114–88 blowout. Abdul-Jabbar celebrated his twenty-fifth birthday with 31 points. West, on the other hand, was only 9 of 23 from the field. "I'm tired of shooting, I'm tired of doing everything," he fussed. "I'm supposed to score, and then I'm supposed to defend against the other team's high-scoring guard. I played too many minutes again this year. When there are seventeen thousand people in the Forum, for example, I have to play forty minutes whether the game is close or not."

The Lakers headed back to the Forum, where they ran away with the fifth game, 115–90, despite West's continued struggles. He scored 27 on another night of poor shooting, but the LA fans had awakened to make lots of noise, and the Lakers fed off that energy. The test of the series now became the sixth game in Milwaukee. All of the pressure from the sixty-nine wins came to bear. At practice, West kicked at a press table after missing an open jumper. Teammate Flynn Robinson frowned and told him to calm down, that he was going to hurt himself.

"Clearly, the perfectionist inside West was seething," wrote Peter Carry in *Sports Illustrated*.

"In the past—when we've always lost in the play-offs and I scored so many points—they always talked about why we lost and not about all the points I scored," West said. "Now we're winning, and they don't talk about that. All anyone seems to be concerned about are the points I'm not scoring."

Trying to calm his star, Sharman told the writers covering the series that people had failed to notice that West could virtually rule the floor with his defense alone. "Jerry does so many other good things for us that it makes no difference he's in a bit of a shooting slump," the coach said.

No one in the Lakers' entourage wanted to think of what a fold in this eighth attempt at a championship would do to Jerry West. But Robertson's stomach injury flared up, and he hardly played in the deciding sixth game. West hit the key shots down the stretch, as the Lakers vanquished the Bucks in Milwaukee, 104–100, to take the series, 4–2. Yet it was far from pretty. He had shot 8 of 29 for 25 points with 8 rebounds and 9 assists.

"I've been in slumps like this before, but it's been a long time — like, since the seventh grade," West said. "Still, I'm a confident person, and when you've got confidence like I do, you want to shoot at times when other guys might not care to. You expect to make shots when other guys don't. I guess I can't figure out much better than anyone else what's gone wrong with me. But I've got one thing all figured: This winning is beautiful."

LORD OF THE RING

As the league championship series opened, *Basketball Weekly* announced that West had pulled in the most votes in its annual all-NBA voting. The Lakers' opponent in the 1972 finals would be the New York Knicks, who had beaten a resurgent Boston club in the Eastern finals, 4–1. The Knicks, however, were not the team of old. Cazzie Russell had been traded away after the '71 season to get Jerry Lucas from the Warriors. And Mike Riordan and Dave Stallworth had been shipped to Baltimore in exchange for Earl Monroe. Willis Reed was out of action with his nagging knee injuries; his absence changed the entire nature of the team. "We operate on such a small margin of error," Bill Bradley told the writers. "We don't have Willis there to take care of our mistakes."

The Knicks, though, made no mistakes in the Forum on Wednesday, April 26. Jerry Lucas scored 26 points, and Bradley hit 11 of 12 shots from the field as New York shot 53 percent. They used a nearly perfect first half to jump to a good lead and won much too easily, 114–92. West finished with 12 points while shooting just 3 of 15. "I can't really explain what's going on," he said. He had watched hours of game film, taken hours of extra shooting practice, yet it all had worked to shovel him deeper in the hole. "I simply don't have any rhythm, not even in practice. Shooting has always been such a natural thing for me that I've never even had to think about it. Right now I feel like a hitter in baseball standing at home plate with a pencil in my hand instead of a bat."

Sharman told him to keep shooting, so long as he was open.

Early in the second half, the Forum crowd had begun filing out dejectedly, their awakening now apparently rewarded by what looked to be another Los Angeles fold in the finals. The Lakers had lost their home court advantage, sixty-nine wins gone up in smoke. But the gloom lasted only a few hours. Dave DeBusschere hurt his side early in game two and didn't play after intermission. With no one to hold him down, Happy Hairston scored 12 points in the second half, and Los Angeles evened the series, 106–92. West had 13 assists and 7 steals, but again shot just 6 of 21 from the field.

Luck had always been such a big factor for the Lakers, West said. Each of the previous finals, they were overcome with a sense that fortune had turned against them. But that all changed after game two in 1972. That night West lay awake wondering how he would act if they actually had a championship to celebrate. What would he do?

At Madison Square Garden for game three, DeBusschere tried to play but missed all 6 of his field goal attempts. The Lakers dominated the frontcourt and danced out to a 107–96 win. West took 28 shots and made just 10 of them.

"What's so ironic about '72 is that I played terrible in the finals," West said years later. "It didn't seem to be justice for me personally. I had contributed so much in years when we lost. And now when we win, I was just another piece of this machinery, so to speak. It's not that I felt so terrible. It's just that I had played so poorly."

But the Lakers' momentum was holding. Even when in the first quarter of game four Chamberlain fell and sprained his wrist, he decided to stay in. It would prove to be a crucial decision. The game went to overtime, but at the end of regulation, the Los Angeles center picked up his fifth foul. In 13 NBA seasons, he had never fouled out of a game, a statistic of which he was immensely proud. Immediately speculation started along press row that he would play soft in the overtime. Instead he came out in a shot-blocking fury that propelled the Lakers to a 116–111 victory. At three games to one, the Lakers' lead now seemed insurmountable.

"The patient is critical and about to die," Walt Frazier observed.

Here at last were the Lakers on the cusp of a title. "Somebody said, 'Are you putting balloons up this time?' " Sharman recalled. "We said, 'Nope, no balloons. You don't win till it's over.' They figured that was a jinx."

Back home, West rose early that Sunday May 7, 1972, and watched the Boston Bruins beat the New York Rangers in the Stanley Cup final on television. He could have suited up for the game and played right then, he was so psyched to close out the title run. The early word on Chamberlain was that he would be unable to play game five at the Forum. But West knew better. As game time neared, Chamberlain received a shot of an anti-inflammatory drug and took the floor.

Packed with energy and pressing through much of the game, West took another 28 shots and made just 10 of them for 23 points. But he hustled everywhere on the floor and refused to settle for jumpers. Again and again, he drove to the basket, knowing that would open up the floor for his teammates. And that proved to be plenty of help for Chamberlain, who ensured the title with 24 points and 29 rebounds as Los Angeles finally broke the jinx, 114–100. West and Chamberlain both left the game with time on the clock and the crowd caught up in a thunderous ovation. "Just to go over to that bench and sit down knowing you've won . . ." West said. "The team was ready. We just ran and ran and ran and played great team ball."

The effort earned Chamberlain his second finals MVP award. Afterward the Lakers sipped champagne and toasted one another quietly. There was no shaking and spewing, no riotous behavior. And certainly no rain of balloons from the Forum rafters. "Wilt," West said, "was simply the one who got us here."

As he spoke, he stood dripping with sweat, flanked by sons David and Michael and surrounded by reporters. Bill Russell, who had broadcast the game, came into the locker room and reached across the circle of reporters to shake hands with West. "I'm glad to see this finally happen to you," he said with a smile.

"Now I know what it feels like to be a champion," West replied. He held an open bottle of champagne from which he had yet to take a sip. He admitted that after so many years of inhabiting the deathly quiet locker room of the losers, he wasn't quite sure how to feel about this new experience. "I don't know where I'm going to celebrate," he said. "The feelings I have now are private ones. I'm going to go home and lock the door."

Over the three series, he had scored his four thousandth play-off point, making him the NBA's all-time leader in postseason scoring; in addition, he'd averaged 23 points and 9 assists but shot only 38 percent from the floor.

Asked about the moment years later, he replied, "Even though we'd won four games to one, I felt I hadn't been able to contribute what I normally did. In other years, I'd laid everything out there on the table. Then all of a sudden that year, I didn't play my best. I felt I hurt the team in certain ways."

"You could see what made Jerry great and what drove him," sports columnist Mark Heisler observed. "It was this nagging fear that he hadn't ever done anything. And then when he did do something, when they finally broke through in 1972 and won a title, he didn't know what to do. Pat Riley talks about how Jerry walked in and took a sip of champagne and just walked out. Didn't know what to do with victory. He was very comfortable with defeat, although he hated it and it made him miserable."

"When it came to Jerry," Riley said, "he hadn't shot the ball as well as he did in the past, but we were more of a team. We had a lot more pieces at that time, and we got the job done. We blew through the play-offs that year. That year, we weren't going to lose, unless somebody got hurt."

Sharman thought that West's own assessment was just him being a perfectionist—it didn't take into account all that he did to drive the team. "Jerry wasn't one hundred percent, but he was still fantastic," the coach explained. "He might have felt it wasn't one of his better years, but I thought he was sensational. He was so cooperative from a coach's standpoint. Anything you wanted to do, he'd go along with it or make suggestions. You couldn't ask for a better player, especially being a superstar. There are so many so-called superstars who have an ego problem or are hard to get along with. He was never, ever a problem."

"It was particularly frustrating," West said, "because I was playing so poorly that my team overcame me to win. Maybe that's what a team is all about. Maybe that's what I was missing all those years. I'm not sure."

PARTIED OUT

Jack Kent Cooke was quite taken with his team's championship. The owner wanted to kiss West, then thought better of it and wrapped him in a bear hug instead. "I remember Mr. Cooke walking in the locker room with the biggest smile on his face," Sharman recalled. "He was so happy, and he went around the room, talking to the players. Then all of sudden, in came the writers and the whole room was jammed, just jammed. It doesn't seem like they kept the writers or anybody out more than a minute. We didn't even have a chance to say, 'Okay, gang, we did what we wanted to do.'"

Those moments of joy, which had taken so many years to win, evaporated within hours. As a postseason bonus, Cooke gave each of his players $1,500—the only problem being that the previous season, when they hadn't even reached the finals, the bonus had been $5,000. The players were miffed and suggested that rather than take the money, everybody should just turn his share over to Sharman.

"At least that would have meant a fifteen-thousand-dollar gift for the coach," West recalled. "We figured that would be greater than the $12,500 share of play-off money."

What the players wanted was for Cooke to pay the coach's play-off share. Cooke, however, disagreed, saying that Sharman's money should come from the players' allotment. The morning of the team championship dinner, the LA *Herald Examiner* published a story saying that the players were trying to cut Sharman out of his play-off share.

"Cooke got [columnist] Melvin Durslag to write that story," West recalled. "Whenever he wanted something derogatory written about me or Wilt, he got Durslag to do it."

"The story broke the morning of the team banquet," Pete Newell recalled. "The players were furious with Cooke. They felt he was using the circumstances to picture them as selfish. That night of the team party was a tremendous brouhaha. It was worse than an Irish wake."

"An Irish wake would have been better," Cooke said. "An Irish wake at least carries a spirit of celebration."

"The players refused to speak to Mr. Cooke at the banquet," Newell remembered. "Wilt Chamberlain walked in, and Cooke rose to greet him. Mr. Cooke had Jim Murray, the great *LA Times* columnist at his table. He was trying to introduce Wilt to Jim Murray, but Wilt walked past as if Cooke wasn't there."

"I was just appalled by their behavior and very hurt," Cooke said. "It was just an air of sullenness. It was Jerry West again. He went up and down the hall sulking."

"That's not true," West said. "It's too bad that it got blown out of proportion. Everyone there that night felt bad for Bill Sharman. All the players loved him. One of the good things that happened to me in my career was having him as a coach."

The backstory to the disharmony included the deterioration of the relationship between West and GM Fred Schaus. Still angry over his treatment as a rookie and his belief that Schaus had tried to trade him, West had avoided Schaus for months. If he saw the general manager walking toward him, West seemed to always make a point to turn and head the other way. The situation apparently created some discomfort among West's teammates. Schaus himself had grown weary of the circumstances, and the uproar over distribution of the play-off money only made it worse. In the wake of the success of the team he had built, Schaus quickly resigned and took a coaching job at Purdue University. Cooke hired Pete Newell as the new GM and gave him a four-year contract. The owner also named broadcaster Chick Hearn as the team's assistant GM.

"The whole atmosphere of dislike had pushed Freddie Schaus to take the job as head coach at Purdue," Pete Newell recalled. "I replaced him as general manager. I know when I got in there, nobody was speaking to anybody. That was one reason Freddie Schaus wanted to get out. All the players were mad at him too."

For years, West had done a remarkable job of keeping his anger and resentment out of the public eye in Los Angeles, but this incident changed all that. His dislike of Jack Kent Cooke would first smolder and then burn in a fire so white hot that it ultimately consumed his playing career.

Jerry West, Jim Brown, O. J. Simpson—they all got married in high school or college. Then they get to the pros, they recognize they are a number one commodity out there in the women's world, and it's hard for them not to appreciate what's out there.

—Wilt Chamberlain

A "WEARING THING"

Los Angeles, 1972 to 1979

IN THE WAKE OF THE 1972 NBA CHAMPIONSHIP, JERRY WEST'S PLAY-ing career careened down a rocky path toward a rough ending, only to be followed by an equally messy transition. "Frankly, I've tried to block those years out of my life because they weren't real pleasant for me," he explained. The problem with that was that he was cursed with an exquisite memory and a tendency to dwell on events, the perfect formula for long-term personal torture. The circumstances left wounds that would hurt for decades.

West had pondered for years how the end would come, and those thoughts understandably increased as he sensed the moment approaching. There were some road signs as he neared the final act, and while a few of them had to do with his physical skills, most of them stemmed from the weariness brought on by his unfulfilling relationships in the game.

Number one on that list was his relationship with Jack Kent Cooke.

As if he didn't have enough conflict on his hands that summer of 1972, the team owner tried to promote another prizefight. He had co-promoted the first Ali–Frazier fight in March 1971. Over the spring and early summer, he labored to put together a Joe Frazier–Muhammad Ali rematch. That deal never happened, but it did provide the owner a much-welcomed distraction from the task of re-signing his championship roster. The players' differences with Cooke boiled through the hot season and well into the fall—though it could be argued that those conflicts never really ended. The owner did get some temporary relief in July when West agreed to a two-year contract extension worth an estimated $300,000 per year. As the newspapers quickly pointed out, about twenty NBA players made more than that, with Kareem Abdul-Jabbar earning $400,000; Walt Frazier, $350,000; and Pete Maravich, $325,000.

Wilt Chamberlain had a two-year deal in place, ostensibly for the same amount as West, but the center held out and refused to join the team for training camp because he wanted Cooke to renegotiate the second year of the contract. The disagreement dragged on through training camp, but eventually Chamberlain and Cooke worked out their differences in time for the first game.

West, now in his thirteenth season, played his one thousandth game (including play-offs) and soon passed Elgin Baylor's 23,149 career points to move into third place on the all-time career scoring list behind Chamberlain, who had just over 30,000 points at the time; and Oscar Robertson, in second place with 24,785 points. Against the Houston Rockets that fall, West also came close to breaking his own Lakers club record of 23 assists in a game, which he had set in 1967. He had 20 with almost eight minutes left in the fourth quarter, but Sharman benched him to protect against injury. West didn't complain; he was now thirty-four and frank about his limitations.

"There's no question that there are a lot of things I can't do that I once could, particularly on offense," he said.

On the downside, West was ejected from a game for the first time in his career that November when he launched into a vulgar tirade before a stunned crowd in Phoenix. He had stolen a pass but was called for a foul, which set off the outburst, and his language carried across the quiet arena. "I've never been so embarrassed in my life," he told reporters later. "I said something nobody should ever say. I felt like crawling in a hole after it happened."

It wouldn't be the last time fans saw a different side of Mr. Clutch. Most observers, though, still considered him easily one of the top guards in the league. He missed thirteen games in 1972–73, mostly with hamstring injuries, but battled back each time to compete at a high level. If he had played one more game, he would have been listed among the NBA's scoring and assist leaders for the season. As it was, over sixty-nine outings, he averaged 22.8 points and 8.8 assists (which would have been good for second in the league), while shooting 45 percent from the field. The numbers disappointed him, but just about any other guard then playing would have been thrilled. Most impressive was the fact that he still averaged thirty-six minutes a game. In the play-offs that spring, West averaged thirty-eight minutes per game, second on the team to Chamberlain's staggering forty-seven minutes.

Looking at his offensive statistics led people to miss the point about West, Sharman insisted yet again to reporters, explaining that even as a guard, he changed the outcome of games with his defense. "He intimidates people the way Chamberlain and Russell do," the coach said. The league did not officially keep steals stats until the 1973–74 season—West's final, injury-plagued campaign, in which he played only thirty-one games. Even in that abbreviated campaign, West registered 81 steals, a 2.6 average per game. Lakers scorekeeper John Radcliffe said that if steal stats had been kept for West's career, he would easily be the league's all-time leader, with little hope of anyone catching him. In his prime, there were many nights where he registered 6 or more steals, and many other nights where he had more than 10, explained Radcliffe, who closely observed nearly every home game that West ever played.

Wilt, meanwhile, remained a statistics monster in 1973. He led the league in rebounding (18.6 per game) and shot an incredible .727 from the floor, but that didn't stop critics from noting that Chamberlain seemed increasingly lethargic. Goodrich again played the off guard, and Keith Erickson and Jim McMillian worked from the corners. But Happy Hairston spent much of the season injured, and to man the frontcourt, the team picked up veteran forward Bill Bridges. Without Hairston's speed and rebounding, the Lakers' running game slowed to a walk on many trips up the floor.

Still, they had Wilt and West on defense, which allowed them to win a surprising sixty games and the Pacific Division crown. The Lakers tied Milwaukee for the best record in the Western Conference, and the league unceremoniously flipped a coin to decide home court advantage in the play-offs. The Lakers lost and took on Chicago in a bruising seven-game first-round series. With Bulls guards Jerry Sloan and Norm Vanlier battling him every step of the way, West had 30 points and tied the NBA play-off single-game record with 19 assists (a record shared by Bob Cousy, Walt Frazier, and Chamberlain) in game two as the Lakers took a 2–0 lead in the series.

The Bulls then upped the physical challenge in Chicago Stadium and managed to tie the series. In game five in Los Angeles, West answered with another masterpiece—36 points, 11 assists, 6 rebounds—and Chamberlain matched it with 26 points and 29 rebounds. The Bulls tied it again back in Chicago, setting up a game seven climax in the Forum, where it looked like the Bulls might finally break an eighteen-game losing streak in Cooke's palace. With 2:58 to go, Chicago led, 90–83, but West and the Lakers went on one of those trademark 12–2 runs to claim the series.

"We had a lead with about forty-five seconds to go in the game," former Bull Gar Heard recalled. "I remember one great play Wilt made. He blocked a Norm Vanlier layup that really turned the whole game around."

West would score 27 and hit 2 free throws at the end to lock up the 95–92 win. Chamberlain matched West's effort yet again with 21 points, 28 rebounds, and the key defensive play in the game's last minute.

"We just absolutely blew it," Vanlier recalled. "Turnovers. Missed shots. And they just came storming back. They had all but given up. That one was hard to take."

"I wake up in the summer thinking about West and Goodrich," Bulls coach Dick Motta said during the series. "Against us, they're the best pair of guards in the world."

It would prove to be the last great play-off series of West's career.

"I don't shoot the ball as much as I used to," he observed at the time, "and that may not be a good habit. I probably pass up shots when I should take them, but I believe the more I shoot, the more I would hurt the ball club, and the more inconsistent I would be because it's a wearing thing. As you get older, you have to compensate and do other things. One of the reasons I've been able to play so long is that Sharman hasn't made me shoot and has let me pass the ball. If

I were in another role as a scorer, I don't know if I could handle it every night."

In the second round, the Lakers brushed aside the surprising Golden State Warriors, who had upset Kareem and Milwaukee. West hit the winner in the first game with seconds left, and Los Angeles rolled from there. For the fourth time in five seasons, the Lakers of West and Chamberlain advanced to the championship round. And for the third time, they faced the Knicks, who had won fifty-seven games. New York had finished eleven back of Boston, which had topped the league with a 68–14 record, but the Knicks upset the Celtics at home in the seventh game of the Eastern finals on Sunday, April 29. Then they had to scramble to Los Angeles for a Tuesday-night game one with the Lakers. New York phoned to ask if the Lakers would consider delaying the series until Wednesday. No way, Cooke said.

Regardless, the players looked forward to this rubber match. New York and Los Angeles had won a championship apiece. Now they had an opportunity to settle the issue. "It will be nice to see Jerry," Walt Frazier said of West and his Lakers. "Between us it will be a battle of pride."

Not to mention age. West was days away from his thirty-fifth birthday, and Chamberlain was already thirty-six. The Knicks were just as long in the tooth. And while there was plenty of mutual respect, the feelings between the clubs weren't always warm. On that Knicks team was reserve forward Phil Jackson, who had been injured during the 1970 championship showdown. He had returned to become a key reserve and was known for his wicked elbows.

"I remember this one dubious moment Phil had with Jerry West," Walt Frazier recalled with a laugh. "I'm not sure of the exact game. It was during that '72–'73 era when we played the Lakers in back-to-back finals. It may have been during the regular season, even. The game was over. West was walking off the floor. Phil flared his elbow and broke the guy's nose. West was just walking off the floor! He was flabbergasted like everybody else. You see, West had already had numerous broken noses in his career. But he turned around and there were those elbows of Phil's. Phil was just that way, man. He was so awkward, and those arms were so long. In our practices, nobody wanted to get near him."

At least West knew to expect another physical challenge.

Exhausted, the Knicks arrived that first day of May and met a

well-rested Lakers team. Chamberlain blocked 7 shots and intimidated 5 others. Mel Counts, the Lakers' other seven-footer, had 9 rebounds. Los Angeles owned the interior, while the Knicks shot from
the perimeter and rebounded poorly. The Lakers jumped out to a 20-
point edge with 26 fast-break points. But then West, who had scored
24, fouled out of a play-off game for the first time since 1970 and
watched from the bench as the Knicks cut the lead to 115–112 in the
closing seconds. Erickson got a defensive rebound at the end and
whipped the ball out to Bridges to preserve the win.

However, that would conclude the highlights for the Lakers, as the
momentum abruptly shifted to the Knicks once they had rested. And
West was soon sidelined by hamstring injuries in both legs that rele-
gated him to watching the conclusion from the bench. New York
swept four straight to claim the championship. West grew furious
toward the end when he heard Chick Hearn comment on the radio
that the Lakers were showing their age.

"They were beaten in five games by the Knicks, but, again, Jerry
was hurt with a hamstring," Doug Krikorian explained. "Happy Hairston was out. Jim McMillian was hurt in that series. But the Knicks
had a very good team."

Afterward Chamberlain peeled off his soaked Lakers jersey for
the last time. Never close, this cluster of personalities had run out of
things to say to one another, and Sharman didn't have the voice to
keep them together another year.

What followed is a time West described as "the worst period in my
life." It is no coincidence that the same could be said about the entire
organization, starting at the top. Cooke had suffered a heart attack
that March, and just one month after that, the stock of TelePrompter
Corp., his cable television company in New York, plunged because of
huge losses.

With one year left on his contract and his desire wavering, West
entertained an offer from CBS to become the network's broadcast
analyst on NBA games. He wondered if he would enjoy broadcasting,
just as he wondered if he had enough desire to continue playing in
1973. Ultimately he turned it down and began thinking about another
season. Chamberlain had published a book that summer with writer
David Shaw that was critical of West, Hearn, Baylor, and other members of the Lakers organization. The media got excited about it, but
West insisted that the criticism really wasn't all that bad. "We may not

be the closest of pals, but we work well together," he said of Chamberlain.

One of their last joint projects would be a work stoppage against the team. West, Chamberlain, Erickson, and McMillian all decided to hold out as training camp approached that September. Newell vowed there would be no renegotiating of deals.

Chamberlain, whose contract had expired, was negotiating to become player-coach of the San Diego Conquistadors of the ABA. The center and West sat together in the Forum and watched a Lakers intrasquad scrimmage late that September. Afterward West talked to reporters. "It was awful," he said, apparently seeking to ramp up the stakes in the showdown. "Right now the Lakers are a last-place team."

"West hasn't driven this street before," the *LA Times* said of his holdout.

"Maybe I've gotten too sensitive," West answered, defending himself. "Maybe my ego has gotten to me. But I feel a principle is involved."

The Lakers were fining him $200 a day for missing camp, and he admitted that he hadn't heard from Cooke. He had hoped his ties with the owner would lead to a resolution of the situation. "We've had an incredible relationship," West said of the owner. "I admire him. He's been great to me. But then this is the first time I've tried to negotiate."

Hearn, Chamberlain, Goodrich, and Hairston had all renegotiated their deals in the wake of the championship season, and West clearly figured that now it was his turn. Newell, however, held fast, and on October 1, 1973—just a week before the season opener in Chicago— West announced that he was ending his holdout. Reporters noted that he looked "haunted." He was asked why he decided to come back. "Because I wanted to play," he replied.

In short order, the dominos fell. McMillian and Erickson were promptly shipped out of town, and Chamberlain took the San Diego offer and was soon trading lawsuits with Cooke. The season became a study in chaos as Newell hastily put together a lineup. Chamberlain's departure left the Lakers without a center, and the Buffalo Braves had twenty-three-year-old Elmore Smith, a seven-foot 250-pounder known for blocking shots. "To get him, we had to give up Jim McMillian," Newell explained.

The Lakers traded Erickson to Phoenix for the legendary Connie Hawkins, who would show great difficulty learning the team's plays. Newell also drafted a powerful but unpolished rookie, Kermit Washington. Sharman and assistant coach John Barnhill worked at getting the new faces introduced. West assumed the role of team captain for the first time, but as he explained to reporters, he was in "mental pain." He believed that he was underpaid and had been cheated by Cooke.

"What Cooke neglected to mention was that he was charging himself the second highest rent in the league behind Madison Square Garden," recalled Mike Waldner, who covered the Lakers at the time. "The arena was set up as a different company, so he's paying himself so much money at the end that both Wilt and Jerry accepted less than what they were asking. Jerry got really, really mad. He felt he was deceived. Erickson, who's just a warm body—he was a starter but not a top-of-the-line player—was holding out at the same time. He never signed, they traded him to Phoenix, and he got what he wanted. Jerry really got mad. He was mad at himself for accepting it. That was the start of him being mad at Cooke because Cooke faced him down. He got mad at himself because Cooke beat him."

Although angry, West played well, and in December against Phoenix he racked up 26 points, 14 assists, and 5 steals on the night he amassed his 25,000th point. His sons, David, thirteen, Michael, eleven, and Mark, ten, watched proudly from the stands.

As strong as the season looked in December, West was soon sidelined and wound up missing fifty-one games over the 1973–74 season with an assortment of stomach muscle and groin injuries, yet still he managed to average 20.3 points and 6.6 assists per game. He was voted to participate in a record fourteenth straight All-Star Game but declined so that he could continue recovering. His main encouragement in coming back from the stomach injury was that Oscar Robertson had done so, West told reporters. "And I've always been a Robertson fan."

All in all, it was a miserable year. Sharman's forty-year-old wife, Dorothy, was diagnosed with cancer and spent much of the season hospitalized in New York. "It was a tough period," Pete Newell recalled. "Jack Kent Cooke lost his health; Sharman lost his voice; then his wife, Dorothy, died of cancer."

"It was very difficult," Sharman remembered. "After the doctor told me she only had a few months to live, I wanted to be with her all the time. I'd go with the team for a few days, then fly to New York, then go back with the team again."

In his absence, John Barnhill ran the Lakers, and despite all the setbacks, they trailed Golden State by just three games with seven left on the regular schedule. From there they found a last burst of emotion and fought their way to the Pacific Division championship with a 47–35 record. But the effort left them spent, and they fell to Kareem and the Bucks in the first round of the play-offs, 4–1.

West played just fourteen minutes in the series and scored 4 points. The circumstances led to speculation that he would retire. Instead he negotiated a new, two-year deal with Cooke with just about all their talking coming over the phone while the owner was in New York. They even reached an agreement over the phone while West was on the fifteenth hole of the Bel-Air Country Club. In a statement to the press, Cooke said he expected West to remain with the Lakers for years in playing, coaching, and management capacities. But within a few short months, West's mental state had again deteriorated, and he fell into yet more bickering with Cooke over money.

"It started over money, but then it became personal," West said.

This time he learned that Cooke had deceived him on an even bigger matter of pride. West said the owner had told him that he and Chamberlain were making the same salary. West later claimed that his agreement with the team called for him to be its highest-paid player.

"I thought they were both getting $250,000 a year," Newell recalled.

But West learned over the summer of 1974 that Cooke during previous seasons had been paying Chamberlain $400,000 or more. The owner justified this by arranging a side deal with the center for other services. Angered, West told his agent to attempt to have his contract renegotiated. "He basically told my agent to go to hell," West recalled, "and that was as ugly, as bitter . . . I felt I was deceived. When you feel that you're deceived, you don't want any part of the organization that deceived you."

"Jerry wasn't upset that Wilt was getting the money," Newell recalled. "He was upset because Cooke had told him he was getting the same deal. It wasn't the money. It was the fact that he was told one thing, and another happened. Jerry is not petty, but he believed that he had not been given what was rightfully his. After all, Jerry had been with the team long before Wilt got there. Jerry was a superstar in his own right and a big draw. A lot of people had come to the Forum over the years to see him play."

"I always have viewed trust as an important factor," West explained. "Trust in a coach, trust in the people you've got around you. And I lost that trust with Jack Cooke. I just felt I wasn't compensated correctly."

"Jerry West was a brilliant young man in many areas," Cooke explained in a 1992 interview. "But he was very naive back then in the ways of the world. Jerry was obsessed with money. He's a very rich man now. He's been very careful in the handling of his money. From the moment I purchased the Lakers in 1965, it was a continuing battle every year between Jerry West and me as to whether Elgin Baylor got a penny more than Jerry. Jerry felt the amount of money he got should be greater than Elgin because he did so much more. As far as Wilt Chamberlain was concerned, I never made such a commitment to Jerry. I did, however, make a commitment to him concerning Elgin Baylor. But Wilt Chamberlain was an entirely different story. I should point out that I did not dislike this constant clamoring for equal financial treatment with Elgin Baylor. That revealed Jerry's spirit. It was part of the man."

West said that his rounds with Cooke had very little to do with other players' salaries and a lot to do with the owner's manipulation. The matter came to a head during training camp and the exhibition season in 1974.

"Jack Cooke used players' salaries to play mind games," West said. "No one ever had to pay me to play basketball. But Mr. Cooke's manipulation made me not want to play for him. My relationship with Mr. Cooke was acrimonious because the negotiations were a game to him. I knew that. It was very frustrating."

He knew he could have played two more years and wanted to play. But not for Cooke. "I could've played another very good year," West said. "Every athlete says that. But I could've, and I knew I could've. But I could never have played for the Lakers again, and I wasn't going to play for anybody else."

Newell went to work as GM trying to stave off disaster. "I begged him to change his mind," he recalled. "It just crushed me when Jerry phoned and said, 'Pete, I'm going to retire.'"

"There's no question about it," Chick Hearn recalled of the incident. "Jerry West should have played another two years."

West, though, was determined. He retired at thirty-six, walked away the day after a dazzling preseason performance against Portland. Newell recalled that the Trailblazers' Geoff Petrie was then touted as one of the league's top young guards, and the Lakers were eager to see how West played against him.

"Jerry had something like thirty-four points that night," Newell said. "It was just like Jerry to make a statement like that."

"Did you see what he did to Petrie?" Portland GM Stu Inman asked reporters. "Retire, hell, he's still the first- or second-best guard in the league."

West had focused his entire spite on that single preseason game. "I expended more energy in that game than I ever did in my life," he said. "I tried harder than I ever had."

"This is one of the most emotional moments I've ever known," Sharman told reporters. "Jerry is a personal friend. There has never been a guard who could do the things Jerry does."

West blamed his retirement on his disappointment in his declining skills, and said nothing publicly about Cooke. Reporters asked him why he was leaving the game now. "You have to want to play," he replied.

In April 1975, West filed a $6 million lawsuit against the Lakers, claiming that Cooke owed him for back wages and other losses, which set in motion an estrangement between West and the team. The suit claimed that Cooke had failed to live up to an agreement that guaranteed West $1 million for employment with the team in coaching, scouting, broadcasting, public relations, and other services for five years beyond his playing career. The suit also claimed that Cooke had promised West would be the highest-paid Lakers player.

Cooke quickly countersued. Neither party would fare well in this time of division. The Lakers would miss the play-offs for the first time in their Los Angeles existence, and West would find himself a lost man, explained his good friend Gary Colson, then the Pepperdine University basketball coach. "You hear about movie stars who have done it all and just go fruitcake? Here you go. I had this fear, you know, a Marilyn Monroe type of thing. What else was there? What would he do now that the cheering had stopped? He was searching for something. It was a depression that all great actors and athletes go through."

"He was pretty restless then," sister Patricia recalled. "He wasn't playing ball for the first time in a long time."

THE GREAT DIVIDE

Cut loose from Cooke, West then turned to the task of shedding many other things from his life. In the midst of all his turmoil, he separated from wife, Jane, and informed her that he wanted a divorce. The couple's three sons were all fourteen or younger. West moved into a Brentwood apartment, the first of a series of bachelor pads, and spent long hours on the golf course and running around with a small circle of friends that included Gary Colson. It was Colson who introduced him to a Pepperdine cheerleader named Karen Bua. For the introduction, West was seated next to her at a Pepperdine basketball event in 1974. They began talking, and suddenly he poured out his life's story. "I had never met the man, and he just basically told me everything," she recalled. "He was just starting a divorce and was not a happy person. Very famous, had done everything, and was just empty. I felt, what a sad human being."

The beautiful young cheerleader and the lost basketball star would become an item. West was infatuated, but even so, the relationship had to compete with his other new love: golf.

"I can't stand to sit still," he explained. "If you sit on a beach, people want to talk basketball. And I get a little tired of it. I've never known a golfer who would talk anything but golf. So that's the place for me."

It also provided a place to hide in that age before cell phones. His associates complained that all the time on the golf course made it difficult to find West and even more difficult to see him. "I like it that way," he replied.

In truth, he was almost as driven by the new game as he had been by the old one. In the summers, he held a basketball camp at Virginia Military Institute in Lexington in the lower Shenandoah Valley. There he was seen just about every day practicing for interminable stretches on the college's spacious green parade field. "He'd hit golf balls on that drill field for hours at a time," recalled Richard Gregg, who played against West in high school and later helped him with his basketball camps. At one end of the field would be a bag that West used for a target for thousands of iron shots. One VMI cadet recalled joining him on the field to hit shots. West was friendly, introduced himself as Jerry, and never mentioned a word about basketball or his past. He was happy to talk golf, though.

Word soon spread around the LA golf circuit that West had fashioned a scratch game and was angling for the pro circuit. Eddie Merrins, the pro at Bel-Air Country Club, watched West's progress. "I think he felt, in his own mind, that he'd just switch from one game to another, play professional golf," said Merrins. "He was a very good club golfer . . . Yet he was reluctant to enter competitions. He wasn't perfect, and it was as if he didn't want to embarrass himself with a poor round."

If perfectionism proved problematic for basketball, it was virtually impossible with golf. First, there was the sheer speed with which West played. He raced over the course, taking little time to set up shots or to obsess over placement, as did other golfers. He'd simply approach the shot, set up, and whack it, just about always with impressive results. While others began speculating on his attempts to turn professional, West soon came to realize that would never be the case. Golf provided some piece of mind and an escape from the basketball people trying to track him down, but he soon understood that this new game would provide no long-term answer to the nagging question "What am I going to do with the rest of my life?"

Besides, golf could take up only so much of his day. Much of the rest of the time, he seemed to spend brooding over his playing days. "The one thing that's bothered me more than anything, that hasn't set right with me, is that I couldn't stand anything less than perfect," he admitted in late 1975. "I was never satisfied with my performance, no matter how I'd played. And for years, I'd go home after a loss and blame myself. I've thought about it a lot the last year, and I guess I was trying to accomplish something unattainable. I think as I get older, you realize you can't be perfect."

In some ways he could come to terms with his perfectionist approach. What he couldn't deal with was how much he missed the game—the practices, the play-offs, being part of a team. How would he replace that in his life?

Some of his short-term answers flopped. He agreed to join a variety of big-name athletes to participate in a "Battle of the Sexes" for a CBS special. His challenge? A game of H-O-R-S-E with women's basketball player Karen Logan.

His friends whispered that he still had way too much time on his hands. He tried his hand at broadcasting, providing color commentary for pro games and some college hoops for UCLA, but even the local columnists who doted on him complained that he spent all his time as a broadcaster second-guessing the coaches. One account reported that he had even worn a tie for the broadcasts. "Who loaned it to him?" quipped a columnist in Long Beach.

Others thought he might make a nice college coach, but he couldn't see it being a good fit. "Recruiting is dirty," he responded in June 1975. "I've never liked recruiting, even when I was in high school being recruited. I think coaches sell their souls to recruit athletes."

If he wasn't going to sell his soul, he was going to have to sell something. Divorce will do that to you, friends advised him. His marriage remained a nagging question. What was he going to do there? West pressed ahead with the split, after a series of hearings in April 1976. "Jerry divorced her," Charles West said of Jane. "He gave up a lot to do it. He basically had to start all over again financially."

He signed over all his rights on their house, which was worth more than $1 million at the time, and gave Jane custody of the boys, Charles recalled.

The news hit the West family hard, particularly Cecile, explained Patricia West Noel. "I liked Janie. I felt sorry for her because I never knew what caused the breakup of that marriage. She raised the children. One time she came in, and we all got together at a restaurant in Charleston. She broke down and cried then. I think it was hard for her to understand, hard for her to take. I never blamed her. When it came time for him to be a father, he was gone all the time. Mother liked Janie a lot. It devastated her when they divorced."

Jane kept the West name, and although she remained embittered by the divorce, she went on to build a successful career for herself in real estate. Many years later, she remarried, to an old boyfriend. West's siblings exchanged numerous letters with Jane after the divorce and wanted to maintain the relationship. "I used to write her," Patricia recalled. "Eventually I quit hearing from her."

"I liked her and admired her," Charles West said. "She put up with a lot."

It was understandable, then, that Jane would wind up with an anger and hurt not unlike his own mother's. West had deceived her, and she would tell others that he was not a good person.

Within two years, on his fortieth birthday in 1978, West would marry Karen Bua, making it official that he had traded his older wife for a younger California girl.

BACK TO THE FUTURE

The Lakers, meanwhile, had done some trading of their own. West's sudden departure in October 1974 proved quite a setback, further complicated by the knee injury of newly acquired free agent Cazzie Russell. The Lakers finished 30–52 and for the first time in fourteen seasons did not make the play-offs.

"I kept thinking, 'It's got to get better,'" Sharman recalled. "But it never did."

Having gone through one season without a superstar, Cooke knew that he didn't want to go through another. The Lakers roster had always featured an exceptional talent. So Newell and Cooke set out to find another one. They didn't have to look too far. In Milwaukee, Kareem Abdul-Jabbar had grown weary of living in a small, cold city and no longer wanted to play for coach Larry Costello. With a year to go on his contract, he informed the team that he wanted to move to New York or Los Angeles.

The choice then fell to the Knicks and Lakers. The Bucks decided they wanted a center and draft choices to replace Kareem. "The Knicks were trying hard to get Kareem too," Newell recalled. "They had a lot of money and no center and no draft choices. We had a center, Elmore Smith, and draft choices."

The Lakers held the second and seventh first-round picks in the 1975 draft, which they used to select David Meyers of UCLA and Junior Bridgeman of Louisville. They packaged those two rookies with Smith and second-year guard Brian Winters for Abdul-Jabbar, a deal that cost the franchise dearly.

Kareem was the NBA's top star, but his brooding image did little to help him win over Milwaukee fans. His last season there had been his first ever as a loser, and many sportswriters read his unemotional response as a lack of interest. Lakers fans, however, mostly remembered Big Lew of UCLA fame. The Dominator. They welcomed him and expected great things.

The troubles, of course, began almost immediately, and the vast majority were not of his making. "We had given up most of our young talent and draft picks to get Kareem," Newell recalled. Kareem arrived to find a mishmash of a roster to greet him. The real complications, however, began on the bench, where the personal tragedies had finally caught up with Sharman.

"I was not a good coach my last two years," he admitted.

Kareem won the rebounding title with a 16.9 average and scored 27.7 points per game, good enough to bring him his fourth league MVP award. But the 1975–76 Lakers could not win on the road and finished 40–42, out of the play-offs for the second consecutive season. Sharman's coaching days were over.

"My contract ran out," Sharman recalled, "and Mr. Cooke didn't renew it. He said, 'Bill, blah, blah, blah, I'd like for you to be the general manager.' So I knew he realized that I wasn't doing the job I did when my voice was good."

Newell had pushed for the hiring of Indiana University's Bobby Knight as the new coach. But with Newell retiring, that option fell through. Sharman moved up, and Cooke set out in hot pursuit of Jerry Tarkanian, coach of the University of Nevada, Las Vegas, as the Lakers' next coach. Cooke recalled that he ultimately decided to pass on Tarkanian. But Tarkanian remembered it very differently. He said that he was offered the job and accepted it, only to change his mind. At the time, the UNLV coach was also just beginning a lengthy court battle with the NCAA. "I was afraid that if I took the Lakers job, the case would be dropped, and my name would never be cleared," Tarkanian recalled. "I backed out at the last minute. The press conference had already been scheduled. So they went ahead and called Jerry West."

Left in need of money by his divorce, West badly needed a job, and he wanted to coach the Lakers. But he was too proud to campaign for it and too proud to kiss Cooke's ring to get it. For public relations reasons, the owner needed to reconcile with West, but he too hesitated.

"He didn't want Jerry West right away," Sharman recalled. "He mentioned different people. He was looking very strongly at Jerry Tarkanian. I was general manager then, and I thought Jerry West would do a good job, so I was pushing Jerry West. Jerry was kind of apprehensive. He didn't sound real eager. But at that time, he wasn't involved in anything else. And he wanted to get back into basketball."

Finally Cooke agreed on West, only to find that West wouldn't return his calls. Actually, West dreamed of coaching the Lakers but still couldn't bring himself to talk to Cooke. Adjusting to retirement had been a nightmare for West, who had indulged himself in golf, travel, and what the writers called his "penchant for stewardesses during the days of bachelorhood."

"I found out it wasn't a very good way to live," he once said. "I won't go into detail, but that period played hell with my marriage."

The summer of 1976 dragged on like a bad dream. The divorce settlement had all but eliminated West's personal wealth. He wasn't in the same situation as his father had been in 1948 after the strike backfired in his face, but the desperation and the lack of direction had a similar reek to it. The big difference for West was that his community still loved him. The LA Bicentennial Committee buried a time capsule on July fourth that was designated for opening in July 2076. It contained a Pet Rock, a Cher dress, and West's Lakers jersey. It wasn't exactly immortality, but considering his circumstances, it was something.

Finally, desperate to get in touch with West one morning later that same month, Cooke ordered Chick Hearn to find him. The broadcaster tracked him down at a local golf course and instructed the pro to have West phone between rounds. Still West refused to budge. When Cooke ordered Hearn to try yet again, he angrily resigned as the voice of the Lakers, only to take the job back moments later when Cooke phoned to patch things up.

West eventually relented and talked with Cooke late that July. "I am so happy we have reestablished communication," Cooke told reporters afterward. "My fondness for Jerry is well known, and the meeting today simply increases that fondness." But the agreement for West to coach the team didn't come until August after Cooke reportedly agreed to bring in more talent. Sportswriter Mitch Chortkoff said that West's hiring, announced August 19 in a Forum press conference, was part of a settlement of his suit against the team. Cooke, however, denied it, saying it was merely a "coincidence" that the suit was settled at the same time West was hired. West has long refused to discuss the suit in interviews.

"I needed something to do with my life besides play golf," he said of his decision to coach.

"West is back in the Forum," announced John Hall in the *LA Times*. "The sun is in its heaven."

Chamberlain, though, was immediately miffed by the announcement. "Jerry's lost more games than I've lost—lost more championships than I've lost—but he's never been called a loser [by the press]," Chamberlain said. "And I can't say the same about myself. I'd like to know, how did Jerry West get to be a candidate, considering he's suing the Lakers and he's never really coached before?"

Others felt he would make a fine coach—if he could keep his temper in check. Fred Schaus pointed out that even as a high school player, West had displayed a great eye for talent, an ability that had grown at every level he played the game. "Jerry is a great student of the game," Butch van Breda Kolff agreed. "He really knew the people he played against, their idiosyncrasies. But Jerry is going to have to understand there are only so many Jerry Wests around. That might be a little problem he'll have."

West himself allowed as much. "I might not have the right temperament to handle men," he admitted.

To help with that issue, he promptly hired two assistants, Stan Albeck for offense and Jack McCloskey for defense, when most NBA teams only had one. "I wanted to coach the Lakers one day," West explained a few months later. "I mean, I love the Lakers. I always felt that loyalty was a tremendously important part in the life of an athlete. But I had this lawsuit going against Cooke, and I figured that would do it for me as coach of the Lakers. Then Cooke asked me if I wanted to coach the team. It was a tremendous adjustment. I guess I'd seen one Lakers game in two years. I called all of the players and told them I would be honest with them and that we were going to have fun. I went out and hired Stan and Jack because I hated organizational work and I needed a crutch to help me through that part. I'm still nervous. Sometimes I don't know what to say to players after a game. I'm still learning."

It would soon become apparent, however, that the coach was the best guard on the roster. Every time the team would go into overtime, Albeck would turn to West and say, "Suit up, Jerry. Just five minutes. Then you can retire again."

If only the solution were that easy, but the problems were larger than the team itself. The California drug culture was in full bloom in

1976. Since Lou Mohs first ran the team in the sixties, Lakers management had employed off-duty LA police detectives to identify hookers hanging around the team's locker room. As drugs became more prevalent later in the decade, team officials had asked their security consultants to keep track of that too. At first the concern was only marijuana. Then, as the seventies progressed, freebasing cocaine, or playing "baseball," became the Hollywood party rage.

"You worried like hell," Newell recalled. "Marijuana and drugs always seemed to break out at parties. The players were celebrities, so they were always invited. And they were anxious to meet the people they saw in the movies. A lot of Hollywood power people liked to showcase the athletes."

"There was a lot of coke going on," recalled sportswriter Doug Krikorian. "Everyone did coke in those days. Late seventies, early eighties, it was everywhere. Anyone that's ever done cocaine, and I have, it makes one feel . . . If you've done it, you know how it makes one feel. Anyone who says he doesn't like it is a liar. It was everywhere in those days. It was everywhere. Everyone tried it. Anyone who tells me they didn't try it is a liar. There are some people, I guess, that didn't try it. But it was a problem on some Lakers teams. The late seventies. I won't name names. They were heavily involved."

It was an issue from the start on West's first Lakers team. He already had trouble with players' commitment to the game before drug usage became an issue.

"I remember hearing stories on the road about one player going to another player's room and giving him an envelope full of drugs," recalled Joe McDonnell, a longtime LA sports radio personality who covered West's first team. "It was just commonplace in those days. I had a member of the team in 1976–77, which was the best record in the league that year. They were 53–29 under Jerry West. This member of the team told me that ninety percent of the guys were doing some kind of drug. Ninety percent."

"We really didn't test the players for drugs because cocaine was not something that was feared that much back then," Newell explained.

Having admitted to experimenting with cocaine and heroin in college, Abdul-Jabbar said that he had little interest in the coke crowd that sought him out, although there were Lakers who did. After all, it could be had at every stop on the road. Hotels around the league were transformed into party palaces that drew regular crowds eager to greet the players as the teams came and went.

"The marijuana smell, if you stayed one place in Oakland, it would keep you awake it was so pungent," Newell recalled. "The place was wall-to-wall hookers. And the lounge was a nonstop party."

"I think we were in an awkward era for the league itself," West said. "It was floundering, and we didn't have any direction."

With the league front office unprepared or unwilling to take on the drug issue, the Lakers protected their interests the best they could.

"We had two detectives that worked the Hollywood beat in terms of drugs and gambling," Newell explained. "We were mainly looking if a player kept the wrong company. Then we'd try to intervene."

Pro basketball survived in an atmosphere of decline in 1976. The ABA was on its last legs, and the NBA lagged behind the NFL and pro baseball in popularity; it was widely viewed as a second-rate sport. It was often portrayed as a black game struggling to find support in white America. To make matters worse, the league's television contract was measly, which suggested limited potential. These conditions weren't as bad as they appeared, but in so many ways, perception was what mattered.

Although these larger issues affected West, he wasted little time with them at the outset of his coaching career. His main focus was the Lakers' shortage of talent. The ABA folded operations after the 1976 play-offs, and NBA teams were greedily gobbling up the rosters of its defunct teams. The New York Nets would survive to join the NBA, along with three other ABA franchises, but they were willing to peddle their star player, Julius Erving, to any team with the cash. The Philadelphia 76ers stepped up and offered a $6 million package, half to Erving, half to the Nets, for Dr. J's rights.

West knew that acquiring Erving would be the one step that could set the Lakers on the right path for the coming decade. Erving playing alongside Kareem? It was one of those rare great opportunities, and it was sitting right there. But Cooke wanted nothing to do with it, despite the assurances he had given in getting West to take the job.

"Obviously, we weren't going to do anything to spend a little bit of money to make us better," West recalled. "We could have gotten Julius Erving. That's the only time I ever got involved. I told Mr.

Cooke, 'You should take this guy. He's very exciting. Plus he's a terrific player.' He told me it wasn't my money; it was his money. So be
it. I never talked to him about those things anymore. The only time I
knew about personnel changes, I'd show up at practice; we'd have a
different face there. Cooke would tell me how great the guy was, and
we'd have picked him up off of waivers. We picked up a lot of people
that were retreads. It was like an open-door policy. We had a lot of
guys running in and out of there. It wasn't a very comforting thing.
When you're letting people who don't know a damn thing about basketball make your decisions, you're going to have a problem eventually."

When he met West to offer him the Lakers coaching job in July,
Cooke had sported a broken arm, which he had sustained just days
earlier trying to stop Jeannie, his wife of forty-two years, from driving
away from their vacation home in the Sierra Nevadas. Jeannie,
though, finally made a clean getaway from the marriage she had tried
to escape for the previous decade. Weary of life with Cooke and his
endless schedule of sporting events, she'd attempted suicide four
times. "I can't measure up to your competitive nature," she explained
in one note.

Bereft, Cooke would eventually pack up his life and move to Las
Vegas, becoming an absentee owner and ruling the Lakers with daily
long-distance phone calls. He had yet to leave in the fall of 1976, but
he had already begun the process of checking out mentally.

Even so, he disagreed strongly with West's take on how the Lakers
lost Erving. "Jerry was excusing himself for the dreadful job he did as
coach," he said. "That is sheer balderdash. My record speaks for itself.
My God, we acquired the giants of basketball: Wilt Chamberlain, Kareem Abdul-Jabbar. There is no truth whatsoever to it."

Sharman, though, acknowledged the circumstances. "When I was
general manager, he said, 'Bill, I don't want you to talk to the coaches
about players. Any time you talk to a coach, they want the best players in the league, and it kind of gets out of hand.' So he left it up to the
general managers pretty much. Mr. Cooke was a real competitor, too.
He loved to win, but he was also a financial genius. When it came to
making money, saving money, negotiating contracts, he might have
been the best ever. He wanted to have a profit, but he also wanted to
win."

Three months after taking over as coach, West figured that the

Lakers were spending $1.4 million on their payroll, while the Philadelphia 76ers were spending twice that. "Shit," he said, "we've got the bodies of a YMCA pickup team . . . The only thing going for us is that we have fun, and we have Kareem. Cooke promised me some help. He promised. Then these players come up, and he doesn't move."

The circumstances seeded West's disillusionment even before he had coached his first game. He did have Abdul-Jabbar, however, and one of West's first moves as coach was to set up a meeting with the center. You don't know me, and I don't know you, West told him. But you need to know what I believe in. I don't know much about offense, because I never had to have plays run for me. West said he thought he could help the team in building a defensive mentality.

"I was one always to believe in chain of command," Abdul-Jabbar recalled. "I agreed with Jerry. Who's going to doubt one of the best players of all time?"

Soon opponents noticed a new life in Kareem and the team. "With Jerry, there was something in the atmosphere that became infectious," he recalled. "Everybody wanted to feel about the team the way Jerry did. He was never arrogant. He had great intuition. He wanted to see what each of us could do. When you get that kind of atmosphere going, it does something to bring you near the top of your skills. Maybe something like that happened with me."

Unfortunately, despite their great hopes, West's teams remained undermanned, and it was Abdul-Jabbar who would bear the blame for their shortcomings. The 1976–77 team started slowly, winning 4 and losing 6, but they found some chemistry on an early eastern trip and ran off a 28–10 streak from there. By March, they were challenging for the best record in the league, which they achieved in a win over Denver. But that same night, power forward Kermit Washington was lost for the season to a knee injury. Then guard Lucius Allen went next. The Lakers still finished with the best record in the league, 53–29, but they had lost what help Abdul-Jabbar had.

"In 1977 we could have won the world championship had we not had Kermit Washington and Lucius Allen get hurt in the last month of the season," Abdul-Jabbar recalled. "Prior to their getting hurt, we had beaten Portland every time. After they got hurt, we never beat Portland again. We had a chance to win the world championship, and it got away."

Lost with the opportunity was the special atmosphere West had created. Four times in eleven play-off games, Kareem scored better than 40 points. But Bill Walton and the Trailblazers swept Los Angeles in the second round, leading to media criticism that Kareem had been outplayed. "I'm a target," the center responded. "Always have been. Too big to miss."

Over the next two seasons, this criticism of Kareem would gain momentum, leaving West furious at two reporters, Ted Green of the *LA Times* and Rich Levin of the *Herald Examiner.*

"We had two writers that were killing him in the newspaper that should have been fired," West recalled. "It was unfounded bias. People expected more than what he was doing. It was never good enough."

Yet West himself contributed to this atmosphere, at one point calling Kareem a dog after a bad game, then losing his temper when the quote made the morning papers.

"He never could understand why his players couldn't go at it with the same ardor and passion that he did," recalled Jack Ramsay from his days coaching against West. "You could see that. I remember before a game one time—he always came over to say hello and shake hands—I said, 'How are things going?' He said, 'I've got that big stiff. I don't know what I'm going to do with him.' I'm thinking, 'Who's he talking about?' Then I realized he's talking about Kareem, you know."

"I should never have coached," West said, looking back. "My personal life was in turmoil. It just wasn't a good time for me. That spilled over into it and made me do and say things I should never have said."

Still, West would look back with a measure of satisfaction after that first year, despite the loss to Portland and despite his disappointment over Cooke's refusal to acquire Erving.

"In some respects, of all the things I've been involved in, that was the most fun year I've ever had in basketball," he told *Sports Illustrated,* adding that he even could handle what had become Cooke's constant meddling. "Mr. Cooke was good to me, other than him wanting to be my assistant coach."

For all its trauma, the 1976–77 season closed with Kareem being named the league MVP for a fifth time. "Those teams in the late 1970s would have been lucky to win twenty games without him," West said of his center. "Yet we were always in the play-offs. We just didn't have enough pieces."

It was hard to watch his inexperienced, outmanned team and not think of how easy it would have been to acquire Julius Erving. But West simply suffered in silence. "I know Jerry was miserable," said Stu Lantz, who played on West's Lakers teams. "He was such a perfectionist, he has always taken losses very difficult. Losses were harder on Jerry than winning was good for him. Winning was great, but losing was that much worse for Jerry. It was always very, very difficult for him."

Even with the patchwork roster, hopes increased for the 1977–78 season. Kermit Washington had returned from his knee injury as a player who could again help Abdul-Jabbar in the frontcourt. Yet all of that promise would be lost in a strange turn of violent events. The trouble started just hours into the campaign when Kareem exploded in anger at Milwaukee rookie Kent Benson for shooting a forearm into his solar plexus. Abdul-Jabbar knocked him unconscious with a punch. The blow broke Kareem's hand, forcing him to miss twenty games, and left Washington to man the boards alone. Such brouhahas were standard fare in the NBA of the 1970s, and Washington was one of the regular participants. The league issued fines on occasion but generally responded as if it considered these flare-ups part of the business. (Kareem was fined $5,000 by new commissioner Larry O'Brien but received no suspension.) A few games after Kareem punched out Benson, Washington took on the Buffalo Braves in a wild melee. "Kermit was hit from behind and beside in Buffalo, which left him gun-shy," Stu Lantz recalled.

The tragedy that these circumstances set up came in a December game in the Forum. Kevin Kunnert of the Houston Rockets was headed upcourt when Washington grabbed his shorts to hold him back. Kunnert turned and threw a couple of punches. When both players squared off, their teammates rushed in to help. Kareem, who had returned to action, grabbed Kunnert and swung him around away from Washington to break up the fight.

At the same time, Houston's Rudy Tomjanovich ran up to help his teammate. Washington abruptly whirled and struck Tomjanovich.

"I was sitting at the scorer's table a few feet away," said Lakers statistician John Radcliffe. "The blow sounded like a melon striking concrete."

Tomjanovich's face collapsed, releasing a shower of blood.

"It was the most physical blow I've ever seen anybody throw or receive," Newell said. "When Washington saw this uniform coming at him, from then on it was a blur. He responded almost instinctively."

Videotape of the gruesome incident was replayed regularly on television, creating further furor. His face shattered, Tomjanovich missed the rest of the season while undergoing a series of reconstructive operations. A former all-star, he resumed his career the next season, yet he never achieved his previous level of play. Washington was fined and suspended without pay for sixty days, bringing an additional $50,000 in salary losses. Shortly after the incident, the Lakers traded Washington and Don Chaney to the Boston Celtics for Charlie Scott. Tomjanovich later filed a civil suit against the Lakers and won. The incident and its aftermath cast a decided pall over the Lakers.

"All of a sudden, we were the negative people," said former Laker Lou Hudson.

With Washington gone, the Lakers had only small forwards Don Ford and Jamaal Wilkes to play the power position, and subsequently lost to the Seattle Supersonics in the 1978 play-offs.

"You know how far we went with them," said Abdul-Jabbar. "It was unbelievable how all of that turned around. We couldn't rebuild it."

From the great calamity of West's second season as coach, the Lakers headed into 1978–79 with some promising developments in personnel. With former Bulls GM Jerry Krause as a scout, the team had begun upgrading its roster through the draft. Among the three first-round picks he found for the Lakers that year was a quick young guard out of Duquesne named Norm Nixon. In short time, he would become "Mr. Big" to the Lakers and a favorite target of West, the coach.

"That's the year they had three number one picks: Norm, Kenny Carr, and Brad Davis," said LA sports radio personality Joe McDonnell. "In Norm, they got one of the quicker point guards in the league to match up with the guys of that time who were really fast, like Johnny Davis and Maurice Cheeks. Norm and Jerry West just didn't like each other. Norm always felt that West was using him as his whipping boy."

Point guard is a challenging position in the NBA, and traditionally it has proved nearly impossible for rookies to play well at the point. Nixon faced that challenge with a perfectionist guiding him. "He obviously was a hard-working coach, but certain mistakes out on the floor just rubbed him the wrong way, especially if they were mistakes made by a backcourt player," Stu Lantz explained. "Sometimes great backcourt players or great centers or forwards are hardest on their positions. For guards to make certain mistakes, I always looked upon it like, 'Jerry would never had made that mistake, so he doesn't understand why someone else does.' I always thought he was too much of a perfectionist to be a coach."

Guard Ron Carter was a rookie that season with the Lakers and found West a troubled man. "He exacerbated the problem by being a poor communicator," Carter explained. "It wasn't that he didn't have the skills; he couldn't articulate what he was seeing and feeling in a nonattacking, nonaggressive way. Jerry would just blow up and go on a diatribe. At the end of it, he hadn't said anything other than 'I'm mad as hell.' It would be like, 'Coach, are we gonna run something? Now that you've cursed us out for the entire time-out.' When he would do that, you could look at the body posture of the players and see this was not right. It was no good. Kareem was the first one. He would always be at the end of the bench, as far away from Jerry as he could be, with his head down. You didn't know if he was listening or not. I'm sure that helped to infuriate Jerry. Because guys weren't giving the eye contact and the 'Yes, we're in this together.' That wasn't happening. My first game—my very first game—we're at the Spectrum in Philadelphia, and Jerry punches a blackboard, he's so damn mad. The first game. I think he broke his pinkie finger. It was over some simple thing. We had made four or five transitions up the floor, and we didn't get Kareem the ball. . . . We got into halftime down a point, and Jerry West is so mad he punches the blackboard and breaks his finger. I'm not sure if he breaks it, but he ends up putting it in ice. He's ranting and raving."

"He didn't try to put the handcuffs on players," Stu Lantz remembered. "But a lot of the players then did not have the mental capacity to make quick decisions or to be intuitively decisive in their decision making, and that would drive Jerry crazy. Especially a flashy player like a John Neumann. There were nights at halftime where Jerry would be totally upset because Johnny had tried a wraparound pass that went up in the stands."

"Our guards never could seem to get the job done to his satisfaction," Abdul-Jabbar said. "But you wouldn't hear a lot about it. Jerry usually was not vocal at all, especially if you were doing a good job.

He would just say supportive things. He wouldn't get into any critiques."

"I'm surprised Jerry had any hair, because Johnny Neuman used to make him pull his hair out," Lantz said. "A lot of his game was similar to Pete Maravich's. A lot of flair, and Jerry West as a player never really dribbled behind his back, between his legs. Always a fundamental player. When Johnny would do one of those fancy plays, honestly, Jerry would see red."

"I used to go sit by Jerry," Lou Hudson recalled. "That way, I knew I would get more playing time. He'd get upset at what was going on and put whoever was next to him back in the game. Whenever I came out of the game, I was always preparing to go back in. Jerry put himself under a lot of stress because he was always expecting the team to win all the time."

No one disliked these circumstances more than West himself. Each day became an invitation to nausea. "I did not like myself," he said. "I was absolutely miserable." Portland coach Jack Ramsay watched the drama play out from the other bench. "I had great admiration for Jerry as a player," Ramsay explained. "I know his team was prepared. I liked Jerry as a person. I know he worked hard as a coach. It's very hard for a great player to then coach. The only player that comes to my mind is Lenny Wilkens. Lenny was a Hall of Fame player and became an outstanding coach. Most of your great coaches are not guys who were great players. They're guys who worked hard at their own game and learned it, learned how to teach it. Examined it carefully. Guys who had to figure it out how to get a shot. Conversely, your great players—Jerry West, Bob Cousy, Willis Reed, Bill Russell—they did not have the success they had as players when they turned to coaching. Jerry didn't have a complete team, either. He was plugging in guys to fill holes."

It wasn't just West, however. The entire franchise was adrift. Caught in his nasty divorce, Cooke had packed up, moved to Las Vegas, and tried to micromanage the team from afar. For urgent matters, Bill Sharman would jump a flight to Vegas to confer with Cooke in person.

"It was difficult having an absentee owner," Sharman recalled. "He wanted to be active in the club. He wanted to know what was going on and make decisions like he always did. So you'd have to fly over there and have meetings or talk on the phone. I'd call him after every home game and give him a rundown on who did what, the box scores and everything."

The Lakers owner became even more of a tyrant after the separation. For years, the rule around Forum offices had been that if the phone on your desk rang three times, you were fired. And when you answered, you had better know the starting times for all major Forum events. If you didn't, that would get you a pink slip too. The tales of Cooke's insensitivity grew with each passing season. Supposedly, there was an occasion when he stood on the Kings' hockey ice, holding his dog Coco and talking to a Forum employee. I need your coat, Cooke told the employee, who quickly surrendered it only to watch him wrap the dog. Cooke has denied these and many other stories of his brash style, but along with the fabulous Forum, the Kings, and the Lakers, they remain part of his legacy in Los Angeles.

Forum employees saw the first indication that this reign was coming to an end in 1979, when Jeannie Cooke finally collected the payback for her decades of misery. Judge Joseph Wapner, who would go on to television fame on the syndicated *The People's Court,* hit Cooke with a $41 million divorce settlement. At the time, the *Guinness Book of World Records* decreed it the largest in history. To pay up, Cooke would have to sell his Forum sports empire, and when it happened, that too would go down as another record deal. "It didn't take me by surprise that Mr. Cooke wanted to sell the team," Sharman said. "I had heard rumors for four or five years that he might sell. He was involved in so many businesses. You always heard stories about Mr. Cooke buying and selling."

No one could have been more pleased by this news than Jerry West. It wasn't exactly clear who would be running the team, but things had to get better. "It was time for a change," West recalled. "It was a positive divorce, that's what it was."

Among their many differences, there was one final subject upon which Cooke and West agreed. "It was a terrible mistake on my part to make him coach," the owner said. "Like other great athletes, Jerry West couldn't understand why the players he coached couldn't duplicate his feats."

Not everyone felt that way, not by a long shot. Jerry Buss, the new owner of the Lakers, got down on bended knee in 1979 and begged West to remain with the team as coach. But the legend had a pretty new wife and a new baby boy on the way. In the throes of coaching

through a heartsick season, West could ▮
and go days without speaking to her. It was▮
to explain later, but he knew that was no way▮
a wife. He was not destined to win championshi▮
too. And if he continued to coach, he would be dest▮
ery and loneliness. Everywhere he turned, people were▮
coach, to give it another try for one more year to see if t▮
improve. But West knew. He had made the full effort and e▮
everything he had in the process. Now it was over. It was time t▮
the dream's embrace.

"Those winter nights as a kid," he said then, "playing until your
fingers cracked and bled. Dreaming. Winning the game with a last-
second shot, being somebody you could look up to. All those things
came true for me, everything happened except one thing, and that's
winning a championship (over the Celtics). And I thought I had the
ability to do something like that. I thought I was gifted with greater
skills. I thought I was responsible. I've often wondered what my life
would have been like if we'd won."

He was speaking mostly about beating the Celtics, of course. And
now that Russell had taken all the prizes and gone, nothing else really
mattered all that much. At least that was how it seemed at the time. In
those dreary final days on the bench, he had no way of knowing that
sweet redemption lay just ahead, waiting where he least expected it.

T • 361

till slip into one of h
nothing personal, he w
to live, no way to keep
os. He believed that
ned only for mis-
asking him to
ings didn't
pended
slip

was so passionate about what I

—Jerry West

THE AFTER LIFE

JERRY WEST WAS JUST TOO DAMNED LONG OFF THE TEES. THAT'S why pro golfers always hated being paired with him in the pro-am events that peppered his off-season schedule. No pro liked to have an amateur outdrive him, even if the amateur was Mr. Clutch. As it was, his local golfing buddies at the club didn't care much for the experience either. West had a knack for leaving them lighter in the pocket. "Never mind the PGA earnings list," the *LA Times* quipped. "Word is that West is California's leading money winner."

West apparently was destined for a fabulous moment in golf, and it came dead smack in the wake of his midlife crisis. In late June 1978, just days after his fortieth birthday and his marriage to Karen Bua, as his coaching career was wending toward its frustrating conclusion, West shot a 28 on the back nine at Bel-Air Country Club. At the time, the best-played round of golf in professional history was a 27, carded first in 1955 by Mike Souchak and again twenty years later by Andy North.

West laid down his sublime round on six birdies and three pars. "Excitement only begins to describe what I was feeling that day,"

West told *LA Times* writer Ted Green. "For a while, the hole looked as big as a washtub. I was so excited I could hardly play after that."

Sensing he had a chance to shoot 60 for the round, he charged into the front nine and promptly gave back some strokes, shot a 37 and finished at 65, still tying his personal best and leaving him with just a splash of Southern California links immortality.

He loved football and baseball, but golf was the sport, other than basketball, that he fantasized about. He even admitted to spending time in front of the TV watching pro events and thinking, "I could do that." The game soon corrected that false assumption. He did whip Jack Nicklaus in a couple of friendly rounds, but he knew that he could never do the same in a professional event. "Too much pressure," he concluded. Surprisingly, the game showed him that while he could handle pressure on the basketball court, the fairways were another story. He was set to qualify for the U. S. Amateur in 1976 when he goofed up and hit somebody else's ball, a gaffe that cost him two penalty strokes. He finished and missed the cut by just those two strokes. He said the experience taught him new lessons about controlling his emotions, just one of the reasons he loved the game. It wasn't boring, that was for sure, not with pin positions and wind and all the other variables you didn't encounter on a gym floor. "In basketball, if you shoot the ball perfectly, it always goes in," he observed. Not so with golf.

It was also the game of choice of his oldest son David, who that same year won the second of two straight city golf championships for Palisades High and then accepted a scholarship to play at Arizona State University. David had been a good basketball player coming up, but he knew not to go there. "It would be awfully hard to follow in Dad's footsteps," he told an interviewer. "There would be too much pressure on me because of Dad's reputation. I expect too much of myself. I guess I got that from my dad."

Just being the son of a celebrity in Los Angeles was tough enough in the untamed seventies. Chick Hearn lost his only son to a drug overdose, and West's second son, Michael, got caught up in his own troubles. The local papers reported that Michael West was charged with burglary and receiving stolen goods, one of several public notices that documented West's struggles to deal with his middle son's personal issues. Afterward, West would sometimes talk of his relationship with basketball in terms of addiction. It had been his drug. He may not have had an easy answer for his son's problems, but he understood them.

West would sometimes address these personal difficulties with *Times* writer Scott Ostler. "He would tell me intimate details about his family, about his problems he was having with one of his sons," Ostler recalled. "I was flattered. It seemed he just needed to talk with someone about that stuff."

In time, West would offer Ostler a window into what was going on with the Lakers and with his own life. They had gotten to be friends in West's last season as Lakers coach. Ostler was assigned to cover the team on one of its eastern road trips. "I grew up with this guy as my hero," Ostler said. "As sportswriters, we want to be objective, but in this case I was starstruck. *This is fuckin' Jerry West talkin' to me.* He was cordial and helpful. In some ways he tried to help me be part of the group." The Lakers still traveled commercially in those days, and they comprised a tight clique with the players, coaches, and staff, and the small contingency of media covering the team, all inhabiting a rare, nomadic life together. That West would even attempt to include him made an instant impression on Ostler.

The Lakers had a long plane flight into the cold Northeast, he remembered. "Lou Hudson had on this almost ankle-length fur coat. It must have cost a trillion dollars. I didn't even bring a jacket. We're set to take the bus from the airport to our hotel. It was pretty cold. West gets on the bus, and as he's walking down the aisle he stops by me. He said, 'Can I ask you a question? You don't wear a jacket? Are you fuckin' crazy?'"

The trip was the beginning of a friendship, one that would allow Ostler to share many off-the-record conversations with West. West told the writer things, then noticed that those things remained confidential. A trust formed.

"He was a funny, charming guy to hang out with," Ostler explained. "He had a lot of funny stories. He knew how to dish a little dirt. I also got the impression he was very tightly wound.

"He took his coaching very seriously," Ostler said. "There'd be sort of two press conferences after every game. There'd be the one where he'd come out right away and say, 'We sort of played a good game, but we didn't do this and that.' But if you ran into him an hour later or so, after he'd thought about it, you'd get his off-the-record stuff. *'Fuckin' Kareem. Jesus fuckin' Christ! What the hell . . . '* You'd get the real stuff."

West would get uptight during games, but away from the floor, he seemed surprisingly comfortable in his own skin, able to entertain with dozens of great inside stories from the game. But Ostler didn't have to spend too much time with West to understand that he wanted away from it all.

"In my days as a Laker, I hated attention," West explained.

For the better part of two decades, he had played the basketball hero, not just in Los Angeles but in all places where people cared even remotely about the sport. Even in his three lost seasons as a coach, he had managed to inspire hope at a time when optimism ran scarce around the Lakers organization. But when he was finally done with competing, he was unwavering in his decision to step away.

His time in the spotlight had taught him everything he needed to know about greatness. "It is a burden," West said.

It was then, knowing that he wanted no more of the burden and realizing that golf was not going to be the rest of his life, that he settled back into the idea of becoming a basketball executive. The mission would be fairly simple: to guarantee the sound running of the franchise he loved, to provide the stability for the organization that he never saw as a player. And so the next year, at age forty-one, he hustled away from coaching as quickly as possible. Ostensibly he began as a personnel consultant, although he soon assumed the title of player personnel director for Jerry Buss's new team. What it really meant was that he got to spend long hours watching the next generation of players in the game he loved and knew so well. And he got to spend that time with people he really respected, people like Pete Newell. For those who know a game and truly understand it, the scouting life is a paradise. In that regard, he revolutionized the position of executive in the sport. West dug in and did the nitty-gritty work, loved doing it, and he would continue to do this his entire executive life. Whereas other GMs tended to stay in their offices, West remained in the field, intensely studying the game, longtime scout Hal Wissel explained. "He was always out there working."

The work itself became the reward for all the time he had put into basketball. It meant that as an aging man, he still had a legitimate means of engaging his obsession, something that a lot of players from the era, especially black players, weren't offered the opportunity to do. West knew he was fortunate to be able to do it.

Yet it was different for him. For the former players and coaches lucky enough to get an NBA personnel job, scouting talent was mostly a low-key pursuit. But for West, there was no such thing. First, his great passion for the game still burned. It was so different channeling that passion into scouting and evaluating, rather than playing or coaching. But the passion itself remained his credential. He may have hated attention, but he found it virtually every place he turned.

"Scouts travel in packs," Pete Newell explained. "For the most part, they have an anonymous life. But when Jerry would go to an arena to scout games, it seemed like there were always twenty kids around him. I've never seen him walk by an autograph yet. I don't know how many times I and other scouts have gone to arenas with Jerry and had to stand there and wait while he signed autographs. We all marveled at him, at his patience."

His only real annoyance with the autographs was that they sometimes kept him from devouring the game. He longed to get lost in it. To others, it appeared that it was easy for him to be really good at evaluating players, but that's only because they didn't know the hours he put into it.

"I don't know if I've run across anybody that's a better judge of talent than Jerry," said Stu Lantz, the Lakers' longtime broadcaster. "That's a rarity. There are a lot of people who claim to be judges of talent. They'll draft a guy or trade for a guy, and it never pans out. But if Jerry says a guy can play, then I'll take that to the bank."

Such ability translated into yet another level of respect. It wasn't just the autograph seekers who coveted his presence. Scouts, coaches, personnel figures from around the NBA—even the league's executives themselves—conferred tremendous cachet on West. The most obvious evidence of this came each summer at the NBA's predraft camp where team officials and coaches could evaluate the college and amateur players hoping to be picked by the league. West would settle in to watch drills and games, and a number of other scouts and coaches would soon gather around him, drawn like moths to a flame, trying to see what he saw, trying to learn which players he liked. In short time, his opinion came to be considered the best inside information.

Mostly, West continued absorbing the game and, as a result, was able to change with it—and, more important, to play a role in shaping those changes. This learning process began immediately upon his taking on the role in 1979. He found an instant challenge as a personnel man with the Lakers, as the team had the first overall pick of the 1979 draft. The choice had been narrowed to Michigan State University sophomore Earvin "Magic" Johnson, a six-foot-nine forward with the versatility of a guard, and Sidney Moncrief, another spectacular guard and tremendous defensive presence out of the University of Arkansas. West could easily see that Moncrief was destined to be an outstanding pro guard. Johnson, on the other hand, was something of an odd duck, although he had just led his college team to the NCAA championship over Larry Bird's Indiana State University Sycamores. Johnson handled the ball in extraordinary but unorthodox fashion, but he was far from polished. Moncrief was a much safer pick, West argued in playing devil's advocate to the rest of the Lakers' management staff, all of whom, like new owner Jerry Buss, were leaning toward Johnson. Sharman saw Magic's ability and nudged the organization in that direction.

"I thought he would be a very good player," West said of Johnson. "I had no idea he would get to the level that he did. No idea."

The experience reminded West of just how much heart can factor into greatness. "See, you don't know what's inside of people," he explained, looking back. "Physically, you can see what they can do on the court. The things you could see, you loved. But you wondered where he was gonna play in the NBA, how he would be able to do it. Through hard work, he just willed himself to take his game to another level. I don't think anyone knew he had that kind of greatness in him. The athletic ability is the easiest thing to see, but it does not constitute what a great basketball player is."

The Lakers got their Magic in the draft, and the new team owner continued his campaign to get West to rethink his decision to stop coaching. Buss, a bright and persuasive man who had made his millions in real estate, was used to getting what he wanted, but not on this issue. West wanted no part of the bench.

Even so, Buss had a decided agenda. He wanted to turn Lakers games into Showtime, a blend of athletic spectacle and sex. The sex would be provided by the new Laker girls, who would dance and shake their assets for the fans. Buss himself had a fantasy life that rivaled that of Hugh Hefner's. The owner exuded informality with his blue jeans and open-collared shirts. He fancied himself a playboy and took great delight in dating beautiful young women. "He liked the girls," said former Laker Ron Carter, who later worked for Buss in real estate. "The girls were always around. They were always very young. That took some doing . . . That kind of stuff. A crazy, crazy life. It was Showtime. Anywhere that we went, we were the party."

That quickly came to include the owner's skybox at Laker games in the Forum. The owner's box became the ultimate place to entertain his real estate clients and new best friends among Hollywood's elite.

"That was really fun up there," recalled longtime Lakers writer Doug Krikorian. "He'd bring young girls. I was single at the time. It was unbelievable, having dinner with Jerry beforehand at the Forum with all his celebrities, and then going up there to his box."

Buss dated scores of the young women, kept photo albums of each of his dates, and even had something of a street team to acquire them. When such dates led to a conquest, he wasn't above boasting about it, even to the media representatives covering the team. Some critics charged that Buss presented a textbook case of arrested development, but there was no arguing with the results. The owner was absolutely dedicated to building great teams that won championships, and on that basis, he and West connected in a very big way. It stood to reason, then, that if Buss wanted to create the ultimate show, he had wanted Mr. Clutch to play a visible part of it.

"He asked me in his office to coach," West said. "That's something I didn't want to do. It wasn't the right thing to do. We'd had a better player than [Magic] in Abdul-Jabbar. Earvin Johnson was a young guy who was gonna be a great player. He was also gonna give the team direction, which it needed greatly. He was also gonna rebound. Those were the two areas we needed most. He was a young player starting his career. You knew you were gonna have two great players, but I didn't want to coach. Period."

That resolve didn't weaken even after the Lakers' Showtime era opened with Johnson and Abdul-Jabbar playing brilliantly. With Magic's electrifying play, the Lakers' fast break took off. Overnight the Forum morphed into ground zero for a reenergized Los Angeles. And the big payoff came right away that first season, with Johnson and Abdul-Jabbar leading Los Angeles to the 1980 championship over Julius Erving and the Philadelphia 76ers.

The only hang-ups came with a series of coaching difficulties. First,

new coach Jack McKinney suffered a serious head injury in a bicycle
wreck even before Showtime officially started. McKinney was replaced by Paul Westhead, his assistant, who coached the team to the
1980 title. But Westhead ran into a player revolt as the 1981–82 season
was getting underway and was abruptly fired. Buss again wanted West
to coach and called an awkward press conference where the owner
announced that West would serve as co-coach with thirty-six-year-old
assistant Pat Riley, only to have West clarify on the spot that he would
help Riley get started a bit, but there was no way he was coaching the
Lakers. Instead West served as an assistant to Pat Riley for two weeks,
until Bill Bertka was hired.

After some initial unsteadiness, Riley found his footing and directed Johnson, Abdul-Jabbar, and company to yet another championship in the spring of 1982. Once denied the title at every turn, West
was now involved with a Lakers organization that seemed primed to
win a run of them. Fittingly, Sharman assumed the presidency of the
Lakers in the 1982 off-season, and West became the team's new general manager. Although West would run the club, Sharman remained
a presence for decades. Each year, he would prepare a report on the
team and its personnel that would be read only by Buss.

West's immediate challenge in 1982 was yet another first overall
pick in the draft and another difficult choice. Should he take Dominique Wilkins, an obvious superstar forward from the University of
Georgia, or James Worthy, who had just helped the University of
North Carolina to the NCAA championship?

"One of the most painful things in my career was to take James
Worthy," West said in looking back at his efforts to build the Lakers.
He said he could see Wilkins's immense talent and knew that with his
ability, he could electrify Forum crowds. Yet Wilkins was a dominant
talent who would need the ball in his hands. The Lakers were already
struggling with Johnson and guard Norm Nixon both wanting the ball
on offense. Worthy possessed great speed and would be a strong fin-
isher on fast-breaks run by Johnson. Already close with Wilkins, West
contacted the Georgia star and explained his decision. Wilkins had
been thrilled at the idea of playing in Los Angeles and was deeply disappointed, but he explained later that he respected West and understood the reasons for the decision.

"I felt Worthy would be a better fit for us," West said. "He
wouldn't have to dominate the ball."

It didn't help that Worthy looked terrible in his debut for the Lakers, just as it didn't help that the Lakers were swept by the Philadelphia 76ers in the 1983 championship series, West's first postseason as general manager.

It was obvious that there was too much conflict between Johnson and Nixon, who was immensely popular among Lakers players and fans. What made it more difficult was that West as a coach had been particularly tough on Nixon as a young guard. There was the perception that the two men did not like each other. West decided to trade Nixon to the San Diego Clippers for rookie Byron Scott. It proved to be a bitter moment.

"We made that trade because Byron was better for Magic Johnson," West said. "He needed the ball in his hands just about all the time."

The trade left West with no doubt that Norm Nixon hated him. "His wife hated me," West said of Nixon's famous bride, actress Debbie Allen. "It was a hard trade. I'd go to bed at night asking myself, 'Did I do the right thing?' I'm a tough son of a bitch, but I'm also sensitive."

Those questions intensified when the Lakers soared along during the 1984 season toward a collision course with Larry Bird and the Boston Celtics in the championship series. The Lakers were clearly the better team, but a series of mental errors and ball-handling miscues cost them the title in seven games. Afterward, West's Celtics demons were not only alive and well, they were grinning at him derisively, sneering at him in his dreams, as they were for many of his old Lakers teammates.

"It would take an act of God to dispel the Celtics curse," West said.

First he would have to fight to keep the team together. After the embarrassment of the 1984 championship series, Buss was furious and determined to trade James Worthy. Only a GM of West's stature could have stood up to the owner and persuaded him to set aside his anger. "His relationship with Jerry Buss was pretty good," Scott Ostler said, "but it really hit a bump with the Worthy stuff. Jerry Buss really wanted to trade him."

West was adamant that trading Worthy would in effect break up a team that was set to win championships. It was a difficult stand to take. West had been in charge of the team for two years, and it had suffered two embarrassing losses in the championship series. It all seemed a huge riff on the old questions. Was West truly cursed?

It took an almost maniacal effort by Riley to drive the Lakers to the 1985 championship over the Celtics in six games. A huge part of the fierceness was supplied by the team's sixth man, Michael Cooper, who had grown up in Pasadena under tough circumstances. As a kid, Cooper had hit free throws to win a scholarship to West's basketball camp. When Cooper came to the Lakers in 1979 as a skinny, high-flying rookie out of the University of New Mexico, he told West about his adolescent delight in attending that camp. Long and bony, with tremendous leaping ability and raw skills, Cooper in some ways reminded West of himself as a rookie. Cooper, too, was a tremendous worker who blossomed into a competitive force playing alongside Johnson. Cooper said his finest moment as a Laker came after that 1985 championship when he was able to go to West and look him in the eye and know that the curse had been broken.

"I didn't have to say a word," Cooper said. "It was a very special moment, to be able to deliver that for him."

"I cared about him and he knew it," West said of Cooper.

Vanquishing Boston didn't just ease the burden of West's past, it fueled his growing aura as the best GM in the game. Before long, the league itself was hesitating to take steps or make decisions without first seeking out his opinions and concerns. Clearly, his status as "the Logo" meant that he had tremendous influence, yet his power came just as much from his tact and judiciousness. Yes, he had a temper that tossed off what the writers called his "F-bombs," but even his anger he was able to channel to great effect. He sensed this power and soon developed into a deft operator who knew how to exercise it with just a phone call. One of the NBA's veteran PR officials once let slip a piece of key information about the Lakers before first advising West of it. Furious when he learned about the slip, West phoned the man and told him the only reason he was receiving a call was because of West's high regard for him. Otherwise, West said, he would have taken the issue directly to the commissioner and had the man's job.

The Celtics reclaimed the title in 1986 as the Lakers stumbled in the play-offs against Houston, but West made a move to acquire forward Mychal Thompson, which pushed them back to the title in '87, another immensely satisfying triumph over the Celtics. Then they followed that up the next year with their fifth title of the decade by outlasting the Detroit Pistons in seven games. The days of West's frustration in losing the title seemed like a dim memory.

Watching from afar while still alienated from his longtime star, Fred Schaus paid him the ultimate compliment. Schaus said that West had become the premier general manager of his time. What Red Auerbach did with the Celtics in the 1960s and 1970s, West had done with the Lakers in the 1980s. "I admired Auerbach in the past, and I admire West now," Schaus said. "Their teams are finishing high in the standings and they're drafting low. That's why it's so hard to remain competitive."

West was every bit as cagey as Auerbach once was, Abdul-Jabbar agreed, but the success didn't seem to make the GM any happier. "Jerry always seems like he's having a terrible time, or something bad is impending," Kareem Abdul-Jabbar observed. "He's always worried."

The Lakers center chuckled and said that West reminded him of the pilots in the film *Catch-22* who are about to fly off into combat. His sense of foreboding always kept his angst spinning.

The talk of greatness and his misery wore on West. I don't want to be Red Auerbach, he replied. I want to be myself. He maintained that his success as a general manager—"If I've had any"—had nothing to do with the competitiveness he showed as a player.

"I have to disagree with him," Schaus said. "Play golf with him, or any game of skill. Cards or anything. He's such a competitor. He wants to be the very best at doing anything." Told of Schaus's comment, West acknowledged that competitiveness did drive him as a GM. "But it's so different," he said. "Being a player, it's a wonderful feeling to win an important ball game, to compete against the best players. Being a general manager is so much more subtle, so much more frustrating. It's a completely different feeling. Every once in a while, when you get something done as a general manager, you really feel good about it. You really do. Finding and drafting players and watching them develop, that's where you get your satisfaction."

By and large, Abdul-Jabbar was correct. West got far more agony than satisfaction from his job. During games, he was a bundle of nervous energy and sometimes wound up out in the Forum parking lot while the outcome was being settled. Or he could be seen standing near section 26, peeking past the ushers at the action, his body twisted with tension.

West still was easily offended if the game wasn't played right.

For the 1989 play-offs, the Lakers again seemed dominant and headed for a third straight title, but Riley drove them too hard in practice before their rematch with Detroit in the championship series. Both Johnson and Scott were sidelined by hamstring injuries early in the series, and the Pistons swept Los Angeles. Abdul-Jabbar retired afterward, and his reward for that was missing out on the contentious 1990 season when the players rebelled against Riley's hard-driving style.

West's dealings with his old teammate had become strained and difficult as well. "He had a terrible relationship with Pat Riley," Ostler remembered. "The Lakers lost a game, and the next day I went to his office. His door was always open to his office. I walked in, and he didn't say hello or anything. He just said, '*Fuckin' Riley.*' They didn't hit it off. He didn't like Riley."

There was the strong perception that Riley's ego had become amazingly distended; that he had come to believe it was he, not the players, responsible for all the Showtime success.

"There are certain coaches that draw attention and want attention," West said when asked about Riley. "And there are others that don't. I think the ones who don't want it, their natures are different. Pat is a little bit more flamboyant in his approach to things. He's out there more than a John Kundla [the unassuming coach of the old Minneapolis Lakers teams that won six pro basketball titles] would be. Red Auerbach, his nature would make him more exposed. It's a personality to some people that puts them in a mode. Coaches succeed because of their teams. They do a wonderful job in the context of things. I've seen coaches get too much credit and too much blame. That's really true. But you can't win without players. That's not a knock at the coach. You take a great coach with no players, and he can't win a game.

"The talent is ultimately what's going to decide your fate."

Still, West said, it was not his decision to fire Riley. "People think I hated Pat Riley or didn't like him. That's not true either," West said. "I've removed two coaches, and both of those were in Memphis. Other people have removed the coaches in Los Angeles. Sometimes it's ugly, and you hate it."

Players and staff members alike have agreed that it was time for Riley to exit. Although they were estranged for years, Riley and West would eventually make their peace, a deal closed when Riley asked

West to be his presenter upon his entry into the Hall of Fame. West had apparently learned the importance of making peace after losing his father abruptly in 1967. West even made amends with Jack Kent Cooke before the sports owner died, Charles West revealed. It apparently took some effort, but the two men had lunch together and set aside their differences.

"Nevertheless, I really didn't like Jack Kent Cooke," West said.

BACK HOME

Cecile West had always found it hard to relax, which only made her later years more difficult. Daughter Hannah once invited her to attend one of her bridge club gatherings in hopes that some broadened interests might help her adjust.

"She did embroidery, she crocheted, she knitted," Hannah explained. "It was my turn to have bridge, and the ladies came, and whoever was dummy would go talk to her. She was sociable and charming and everything. After they all left, she said, 'This is the dumbest thing I ever saw in my life, a bunch of women sitting on their asses all day doing nothing.' I thought she really enjoyed it, so I was kind of taken aback. But my mother was just a hard-working woman. I wish she would have stopped and smelled the roses a little bit."

Caught up in running the Lakers, West had found little time to visit home as his time in California stretched out. He tried to offer support to his mother, but she was too proud and refused much of what West offered, Willie Akers recalled.

By the mid-1980s, her health had worsened. "She had a bad stroke," Barbara West explained, "and that diminished her physical ability on her right side. As is often the case with stroke victims, you will have the early onset of dementia. In her late seventies, she started to lose her memory."

West lost his mother in April just as the 1991 play-offs were set to open. It was a year that would prove difficult for him personally in many ways. In the wake of Riley's departure, he had hired Mike Dunleavy to coach the Lakers, and Johnson again carried them to the championship series against Michael Jordan and the Chicago Bulls. The Lakers won the first game in Chicago, but then Phil Jackson's coaching staff realized that Johnson struggled when guarded by long-armed Scottie Pippen. They put Pippen on Johnson, and the Lakers won four straight games.

That November, as a new season was set to open, Magic Johnson announced to the world that he was HIV-positive, a stunning event that brought revelations about the climate of sexual frivolity around the Lakers. Johnson admitted he had been sleeping with three hundred to five hundred people a year. The team's locker room, and its sauna, had been a place where the star and other players had entertained women, even right after games. Johnson would retire to the sauna after a game, have sex, then put on a robe and return to the locker room for his postgame media interviews. How far had the team gone in condoning such questionable behavior?

"I cared," West said in his interviews for this book. "I did things for those guys. It was ridiculous, some of the things I did for those guys. If the public knew, they'd be outraged. It was a pretty crazy period for us."

The announcement, Johnson's sudden retirement, and then his failed attempts to return from that retirement sent the franchise reeling through years of difficult transition.

Throughout his tenure, West had been possessed by one relentless goal: winning each season's championship. As the pressure mounted on him to find the team's next wave of talent, he suffered from ulcers and sleepless nights in the early 1990s, particularly after games, when he would twist and turn, running back every play in his mind. For a time, a spot had mysteriously appeared on his lung, frightening West and his family. It later went away, but doctors weren't sure what it was. The fear made him appreciate his family more, but it didn't dull his drive.

"I do think this job is wearing," he said at the time. "There's a lot of pressure on you."

The translation, of course, was that he put tremendous pressure on himself, and indirectly on the coaches and players.

"Maybe I'm spoiled," West said. "Maybe the success of this team has spoiled me a little bit. I try to be objective. It makes no sense that I'm not happy. I should be happy. The reason I tend not to be happy is goal setting. You want to stretch yourself. You want to stretch your players and make them try to take that last step, and that's to end their season with a win. If you do that, you're gonna have a fun sum-mer."

In Los Angeles, the basketball tradition, like the entertainment in-dustry itself, was star driven. "Since I came here in 1960," West said at the time, "the Lakers have always had one or two players that have been at the top of the league in talent. In perpetuating this franchise, our next move is, where do we find another one of those guys?"

With Johnson's departure, West embarked on what would prove to be an extended period of maneuvering to pull together another championship chemistry. Admitting that any franchise would be lucky to have one Magic Johnson in a lifetime, he nevertheless became ob-sessed with finding the next great one, "that one unique player who can get through the tough losses and come back and compete the next night. Those players are rare in this league. They'll play hard every night. They'll play in every building. They'll play in every circum-stance. That kind of person is the most difficult to find."

Seeing the athletic talent would be easy, he said. The hard part would be identifying what couldn't be seen. He knew this would be nearly impossible, particularly when he hadn't seen it in Johnson the first time around. Then he had to manipulate the NBA's byzantine personnel structure so that the Lakers could get the rights to that spe-cial player. That had become nearly impossible with the league's salary cap and expansion.

"The problem is, it's like a poker game," he explained. "Any team that has a player play ten years is probably going to be out of chips pretty soon. So you have to try like crazy within the scope of this league to keep your team young and productive. In the past, we've been able to bring in younger players and phase out older players at the end of their careers."

Despite his determination, that replenishing process stalled in the seasons after Johnson's retirement, as the franchise sorted through an array of players and coaches, trying to find a competitive mix.

For five long seasons, the circumstances dragged on, with West tor-turing himself looking for answers. Meanwhile, the Lakers plodded through one unproductive season after another. Always a bundle of nervous energy during games, he grew into a picture of anxiety.

The circumstances pushed him to search harder around the league, looking for a sign that some supremely talented young player would emerge from the amateur ranks or that some impressive veteran from another team would find the contractual freedom to become a Laker. While the situation stretched his patience, West busied himself by acquiring the finest complementary players he could find, so that he would have the pieces in place for adding the prize talent for which he was searching.

THE MIND-BREAKING DEAL

Finally, early in the 1996 off-season, two very special opportunities presented themselves. Both a talented young amateur and the most impressive of veterans were available. But getting them would require a huge gamble, meaning that if he miscalculated, all of his hard work of the last five years would be wasted. It was a risk that would cost tens of millions, but after years of yearning to compete for a championship, both West and Jerry Buss were willing. That the two developments converged so nicely almost made them seem preordained.

Because he was seventeen and there were so many concerns about his suitability for NBA life, Kobe Bryant agreed to perform an unusual number of workouts for teams as the 1996 draft appeared. He jetted from point to point on the NBA map, hoping to show teams just why they should take a chance on someone so young.

In Los Angeles, Bryant found an organization that immediately understood his potential. His workout left West raving. The Lakers scouting staff may have questioned Bryant's willingness to involve teammates, but West watched him move and shoot during the workout, then saw him battle assistant coach and former Lakers defensive star Michael Cooper. There was length, there was strength, there were physical talents, but to go with them was a beautifully polished set of skills, the kind of skills that a seventeen-year-old could possess only after long hours of dedicated work. The skills themselves said much about the issue of work ethic and that hardest-to-read factor: the player's heart.

It was the single best workout West had ever seen. "He has the potential to be an all-star," he excitedly told people within the organization.

Even so, there didn't seem to be much of an immediate opportunity for Kobe to become a Laker. His father, Joe Bryant, who had played pro basketball in America and Europe, had done his research and figured that his son would go somewhere in the top fifteen picks. The Lakers were drafting much lower than that.

First West had to take the huge gamble of trading veteran center Vlade Divac to the Charlotte Hornets for their thirteenth pick in the draft. Then he learned that John Calipari, the coach of the New Jersey Nets, planned to take Bryant with the eighth pick before the Lakers could snare him at thirteen.

"Jerry wanted Kobe, so he basically called up and talked Cal out of drafting Kobe," explained Hal Wissel, who was with the Nets at the time. West encouraged the Bryant family to talk to Calipari and explain that their son really wanted to play for the Lakers. "He knew if we didn't take him at eight, he'd drop to Charlotte, and he could make the deal with Charlotte," Wissel recalled. "Cal was young in the league and, hey, it's Jerry West on the phone."

It was the image of the Logo that carried the day behind the scenes. West used all of his charm in talking Calipari out of taking Bryant for the Nets.

Perhaps most impressive about West's effort is that he made it work all the while structuring a huge deal to sign Shaquille O'Neal as a free agent. At seven foot one, 330 pounds, he presented an intimidating package of strength and athletic ability and seemed certain to net an offer worth tens of millions as a free agent. Some observers were stunned that O'Neal would think of leaving the Orlando Magic and the opportunity to play with gifted young guard Anfernee "Penny" Hardaway. ESPN declared that there was no way O'Neal would be foolish enough to go, because playing in Orlando presented the best opportunity to win championships.

Other observers, though, began to question the Magic's chemistry. There were whispers that Hardaway's immensely successful "Li'l Penny" marketing campaign had created a persona so large that it crimped even O'Neal's style. Another factor was his team's losses in the '95 and '96 play-offs. In Orlando, it was O'Neal—not Hardaway, the coaches, or his teammates—who bore the pressure for those losses, both sweeps. In 1995, the Magic fell 4–0 to Houston in the NBA finals. In 1996, it was the Bulls who took them 4–0 in the Eastern Conference championship series. O'Neal had wept after both of those series.

It helped immensely that West had been a superstar himself. He knew the pressures, the misunderstandings, the problems that players of stature face. It could be argued that no NBA executive went to the effort that West did to protect and nurture young stars. West and his staff saw that they had a shot at signing O'Neal but that it could cost them as much as $100 million, a figure large enough to frighten off most suitors. The situation left West struggling to find room under the salary cap to sign the big center.

"If you have to give up your entire team for a cornerstone player such as Shaquille, you'd consider it," West said.

It soon became clear that he could have a shot at both players, Bryant and O'Neal, if he could trade Divac and his $4 million salary to Charlotte for the rights to Bryant. The only problem with that strategy was that the Lakers would be sunk if they traded their center for Bryant only to later discover that they couldn't swing the final deal for O'Neal. "It really was a gamble," said Jerry Buss. "We could have been left high and dry. We laid it out there and could have lost just as easily. From the time we traded Vlade, we were out on a limb. We were either going to be very sorry or ecstatic."

West figured that he would have to come up with a $95 million offer to get his prize. But ultimately that would prove to be many millions short of what was needed. To create more room under the salary cap over seven seasons, West practically gave away guard Anthony Peeler and reserve forward George Lynch, sending them to the Vancouver Grizzlies.

"The Lakers could have folded," said O'Neal's agent, Leonard Armato. "They may have been on the verge of it a few times. But Jerry West wouldn't do that. He was Mr. Clutch as a player and again in these dealings."

The Orlando offer jumped to $115 million, then a little more. The anxiety climbed to unbearable levels for West and his staff. To push their offer to $123 million, they renounced the rights to seven players, including the retired Magic Johnson. Dumping their roster of players seemed to border on lunacy. If O'Neal stayed in Florida, the Lakers would be forced to bring in a host of low-rated talent to fill the gap.

The Magic could have paid more to sign their own free agent, well above the Lakers' $123 million. But it became apparent that, as O'Neal claimed, money wasn't the key factor. Actually, the Orlando deal was front-loaded with as much as $20 million in cash the first year, but West had persuaded O'Neal to head west. "If this had gone much longer, we were dead," West, who bordered on nervous exhaustion following days of anxious maneuvering to get O'Neal, told reporters after announcing the deal. "To get this prize," he said, "I think is something that when I look back on history and the time that I've spent with this team, this might be the single most important thing we've ever done."

If his efforts had failed, West joked that he might well have jumped out of the window of Leonard Armato's high rise offices.

With the team's tradition came the expectations in the Great Western Forum, where Hollywood stars then paid $700 nightly for courtside seats to be entertained by basketball's best. With O'Neal's contract, those ticket holders knew prices were headed up.

Then Lakers coach Del Harris was understandably ecstatic and characteristically understated. "This will be better," he told reporters. O'Neal was joining a team that West had packed with Bryant, Eddie Jones, Nick Van Exel, and Elden Campbell, all of them young and talented and seemingly poised on the verge of greatness, immediately if not sooner. That certainly was the hope in Los Angeles, where happy endings were concocted daily in the celluloid screening rooms of the film industry. Without a doubt, it was the hour of West's greatest achievement as a general manager.

However, no one knew better than West that translating the talent into wins would prove elusive, and eventually all the talent he had collected would weigh as expectations that could serve to end his historic tenure with the team. Knowing he could pay the ultimate price for such effort might have given someone else reason for pause. Not West. He cared only about the team. For decades, his rather complex competitive nature had driven the franchise, first as a player, then as a frustrated coach and finally as an executive, working, as he explained it, "in my own weird way." He was the club's past, present, and future—the compass that allowed his team to proceed with a purpose across the strange landscape of the NBA.

"The bottom line is, my number one priority in life is to see this franchise prosper," West explained. "That's my life. It goes beyond being paid. It goes to something that's been a great source of pride. I would like people to know that I do care. It's not a self-interest thing. I do care about the winning and the perpetuation of the franchise. That's the one thing I care most about. I don't care about the pelts and the tributes. I like to work in my own weird way, working toward one goal; that's a winning team here."

West's own expectations had brought tremendous pressure for Lakers coaches over the years, but Harris perhaps felt it more than any other. His talent-laden teams showed big gains in games won for two consecutive seasons, but in 1997 and again in 1998, they flopped in the play-offs, so Buss fired him and hired Kurt Rambis in 1999. When the Lakers again stumbled that spring, Buss wanted to change coaches again.

Part of the problem was that West wanted success so badly, Harris confided later. "Jerry was for me, but it never was the coach's team. It was always Jerry's team and what Jerry had put together and so forth. Ultimately, Riley got some success and recognition toward the end. It was slow coming, but inevitable when you win so many games. But I know our players, when I was there, were really more concerned about pleasing Jerry than they were about pleasing me. I always knew when I was there that I was coaching Jerry's team. It wasn't my team, and I knew the players were loyal to him. The proof of that is the night we won our sixtieth game, my last full year there, the headlines the next day were, 'West Might Retire.' And then on the second line, they had a little line that we had won our sixtieth game. To put that in perspective, no team won sixty games in 2001. It's not easy to win sixty games. The players were saying, 'If Jerry leaves, I'll leave. I don't know if I'll stay.' It should have been one of the highlight moments of my life, winning my sixtieth game. Instead it was this other story. It wasn't a team event at all, and the players were saying they weren't sure if they wanted to be on the team."

Harris said he was fired because Buss lost faith in West's plan for success. "Just think where they'd be if Buss hadn't panicked," Harris said. "He alienated Jerry West. He started listening to other people . . . He really didn't listen to Jerry West. There were just so many things that happened. The trust was broken, and Jerry West won't admit it. The trust was broken between him and Jerry Buss."

West's relationship with Buss had been punctuated by disagreements over the years, sometimes followed by West considering attractive offers to take over other franchises. But he could never bring himself to leave. However, the upheaval had left a tenuous situation, made even touchier by West's desire for a pay raise.

After years of making little as a general manager, West had discovered in the late 1990s just how underpaid he was, said Charles West. He wrangled with Buss until he was presented with a substantial contract and pay raise, but the process of that had further alienated him from Buss, although the owner was about to realize huge gains from the team.

"When the Lakers moved to Staples Center [in 1999], I'm not sure Jerry Buss realized how important that was," West revealed. "It was a license to print money. Jerry has been a great operator and a terrific owner. We used to talk almost every day when he was in the office. But then he quit coming to the office."

With Buss no longer around, they were not as close, West said.

All of these events played into the hiring of Phil Jackson in the summer of 1999. "My feeling is that Jerry West was pretty much forced to hire Phil," said Tex Winter, Jackson's longtime assistant. "I don't feel he was ever comfortable with Phil there."

While West obviously had doubts about his future with the team once Jackson joined it, he agreed to hire him for the same reason he did everything as a GM. He would make any move if he thought it improved the team—and that apparently included downsizing himself.

"People think I hate Phil Jackson," West recalled. "I don't hate him. I really didn't know Phil. We are so different in terms of how he interacts with people. I was used to kidding around with people."

West had always had an open door for Lakers employees, but the whole atmosphere changed. He said he was used to "being friendly when you see someone in a hallway." Jackson, though, met him with stony and uncomfortable silence at such moments.

"Phil was just different," West said.

They disagreed over NBA bad boy Dennis Rodman, who had played for Jackson in Chicago. In 1999 Buss had insisted on bringing Rodman to the Lakers, but when Rodman showed up for practice one day drunk, without his shoes, West promptly dismissed him.

"Jerry said that's the last game he'll ever play for the Lakers," confided one Lakers staff member. "Phil wanted to bring him back, but Jerry said the uniforms were purple and gold, and if you're going to wear this uniform, you're going to be proud of it."

West was obviously a tremendous asset to the organization, Winter confided during the 1999–2000 season. But Jackson was quite adept at corporate in-fighting after his experience with the Bulls.

"Phil wanted him out," Winter said in a 2005 interview.

As the Lakers made their way through the 2000 play-offs to claim a surprising championship in Jackson's first year, a rumor began making the rounds that West was planning to leave the team. West had seemingly contemplated retirement, or at least contemplated leaving the organization, virtually every year for a decade, but now, according to the rumor, he had finally come to the end.

Since Jackson had taken over as coach, West had largely kept his distance from the team, and by spring seemed thoroughly detached from the proceedings. He had made appearances at a few play-off games, but for many others he stayed away, trusting one friend or another to keep him abreast of the score with a call to his cell phone.

As he had every summer for years, West began agonizing over his future with the team, only this time he stayed away from the office the entire summer of 2000 and offered virtually little input on the personnel decisions the team would have to make. Word of West's plans reached the press not long after the team celebrated its championship victory with a parade through downtown LA, but no one in the organization would confirm that West planned to retire.

Then, in July, broadcaster Larry Burnett, working as a freelancer for the CBS affiliate in Los Angeles, contacted Jackson at his summer home in Montana and received on-the-record confirmation that indeed West's forty-year tenure with the team was finished. It would be weeks before West himself would make that declaration, after a wry aside about Jackson's sense of timing. West made his announcement in early August in a brief written statement that thanked many but made no mention of Jackson, even though the coach had just directed West's beloved Lakers to a championship.

At the time, news reports out of Los Angeles indicated that West was unhappy that Jackson, after the breakup of his marriage to wife, June, had taken up with Jeanie Buss, the owner's daughter and a marketing executive with the team.

Not long after West's announcement, a new sort of rumor began making the rounds of the league's innermost circles. According to the story, Jackson had "kicked West out" of the Lakers locker room at one point during the postseason as the team was making its run to the NBA title. Although most were reluctant to discuss it publicly, an official with the Bulls said he had heard about the incident, as did Eddie Jones, the former Laker, who talked frequently with many of his former teammates, including Bryant and O'Neal. "How do you like that?" the Bulls official said. "Phil kicked the Logo out of his locker room. How smart is that?"

Jones, a West admirer, had spoken with West privately before the Hall of Famer announced his retirement from the team that August. Inside NBA coaching circles, it was said that West's competitive streak, his obsessiveness about his team, made the Lakers difficult to coach. Jones, an all-star who played four years in Los Angeles before being traded to Charlotte in the middle of the 1999 season, had witnessed the situation firsthand. Jones said he wasn't surprised that Jackson had moved to exclude West from the team.

"I knew it was coming," Jones acknowledged. "As a coach, you gotta have guys' confidence, you gotta have guys who believe in what you're saying. You don't want anybody in their ear saying this and saying that."

Actually, Jackson had asked West out of the locker room rather than "kicked him out." Sources within Jackson's tight inner circle said it happened at the end of a game, when Jackson liked to speak privately with his players for a few moments without interruption. The moment came immediately after a game during the Lakers' play-off series with Portland.

Tex Winter confirmed that, coming into the job, Jackson had concluded he would not be able to coexist with West in Los Angeles. Jackson saw West as too weird, too unpredictable, possessing too much ego—which to some sounded much like Jackson himself. Even one very loyal longtime Lakers staff member acknowledged that West had always been "an active general manager," brilliant in his acquisition of players but sometimes too anxiety ridden and meddlesome to allow the team to settle down and function smoothly.

Winter said Jackson had calculated that West's pride would be hurt by Jackson requesting that he step out of the Lakers' locker room so that the coach could have a word with the team. It was seemingly a subtle thing, yet its implication rang like a hammer through the organization. By doing it, Jackson had sent this message: Jerry West, who had lived and breathed the Lakers for forty years, was not part of the team. The coach, it seemed, had found the perfect way to nudge the sixty-two-year-old icon out of the organization. As coach of the Bulls, Jackson had used a similar technique and called it "setting boundaries." Only a few select people were allowed inside the team circle. In LA, West was no longer one of them.

"Only someone with six rings could have done it," Del Harris, the former Lakers coach, said of Jackson's move. "I don't know if it was so much Phil as it was his status. I don't know that that needed to be done. I always felt Jerry was a plus for us, not only by getting the players there. Yes, the Lakers had always been Jerry's team, but if there were other issues that came up, I could always count on Jerry to good-guy, bad-guy it. It's true that Jerry's involvement was a factor, but I didn't necessarily see it as a negative thing."

Not surprisingly, West didn't show for the press conference announcing his departure. "If you knew Jerry, I think you knew he wouldn't be here," Mitch Kupchak, his successor as Lakers' vice president in charge of basketball operations, told the gathered media.

"Obviously, Jerry West is irreplaceable," Jerry Buss, who also failed to appear, said in a prepared statement. "What he has meant to the Lakers' franchise over the past forty years is immeasurable."

Jackson's dislodging of West from the organization would later prove to have far-reaching implications. The team would win two more championships after West left, but in 2004 O'Neal would be traded after getting into a fuss with Buss over a contract extension.

Breaking up a team that had won three championships was easily one of the most disastrous moves in the Lakers' history. Asked about it, O'Neal confided that after West left the organization, there was no one he could trust, and thus not a basis for him working out his difficulties with the team. O'Neal and Bryant had sometimes faced a major disconnect during their seasons together, but the one thing they agreed upon was their immensely high regard for West. Indeed, West remained a mentor and confidant for Bryant, who celebrated one of the Lakers championships by wearing a number 44 West jersey in the team's championship parade. If West had remained with the Lakers, they might never had broken up their championship combination.

As it was, the circumstances freed West from the Lakers, which meant that he went on the open market as a GM and was able to reap millions in salary from the Memphis Grizzlies, a miserable team that he would build into a play-off contender. One of West's moves in setting the tone for the Grizzlies was to rip a player for smiling in the team photo. As ever, winning was all business with West.

But also as ever, basketball did more for West than provide tension and glory: it shaped his life. It was, after all, Memphis team owner Michael Heisley who financed the West statue outside the basketball arena at West Virginia University. And things had come full circle for the West family in Morgantown when his fifth and youngest son, Jonny, accepted a basketball scholarship to play for the Mountaineers.

Some fans ignorantly think it was West who traded center Pau Gasol from Memphis to Los Angeles in order to help them become a championship contender and win their 2009 title. The truth is that West had long retired from the Grizzlies when the deal was made in 2008. Certainly the people he hired in Memphis wanted to please him, and so in that sense, perhaps the Logo's power and influence were felt once again, although technically he had nothing to do with such a decision. But it's easy to see why fans suspected this, because he had made so many moves for the Lakers, and because he continued to prize his time with the team. "My love for the Lakers was incredible," he said. "It was like being a drug addict, for chrissakes. Your highs are never high enough and your lows are unbearably low. We'd have losses in the play-offs where I'd want to kill myself. Then I'd realize, 'What more could you do?' Winning was never good enough, never good enough."

That, as much as anything, explains his powerful drive to excel, from his first moments lofting a lopsided ball up to the makeshift goal in his muddy backyard in West Virginia. It's what drove him along the path from the depths of disappointment to the heights of the game. "I've lived a very interesting life," he said.

Fans today sometimes wonder where West the player would fit in the modern NBA. That answer was relatively simple for Johnny "Red" Kerr, who spent years playing, coaching, and broadcasting the NBA. "Until Michael and Magic, West and Robertson were the all-time guards in the league," Kerr once observed. "And I don't really put them in the backseat even today because if you're picking teams and somebody else picks Michael and Magic, I'd pick those two guys, West and Robertson. Both good defensive players, good passers, good rebounders, great shooters, the whole package. When West would come down the floor, he'd really put it in second gear. You'd be really trying to keep up with him. All of a sudden, he'd put on the brakes, and he would go up and almost jump a little bit backward. You couldn't keep up with him. He was just *boom,* the perfect shot. A quick hard dribble and up. That's the NBA logo."

ACKNOWLEDGMENTS

I want to thank all of those who granted interviews for this project, especially Charles West and Eddie Barrett, who both talked extensively in multiple sessions, as did Jerry West, who was gracious with his time even though he was engaged in other projects. Of special note are the guiding efforts of agent Matthew Carnicelli and editor Mark Tavani and the entire staff at Random House.

My wife, Karen, and daughter, Jenna, both of whom spent many hours helping me transcribe interview tapes, provided the kind of support that only family can.

Then there are those who agreed to read portions of the manuscript and offered help in shaping it: Diddy Dean, Ric Moore, Jorge Ribeiro. They are the best friends a writer can have.

Critical research efforts were provided by Matt Taylor, Sam Healy, and Delilah Anders.

Thank you all.

INTRODUCTION

Author interviews with Jerry West, Eddie Barrett, Pete Newell, Willie Akers, Charles West, Tex Winter, Gery Woeffel, Fred Schaus, Bill Sharman, and Rod Hundley.

Text sources include *Mr. Clutch* (Prentice Hall, 1969) by Jerry West with Bill Libby; *The Show* (McGraw-Hill, 2005) by Roland Lazenby.

Genealogy sources include West family research and research by the author on Ancestry.com.

Chapter 1 SAGA

Author interviews with Patricia West Noel, Charles West, Hannah West Lilly, and Barbara West.

Text sources include extensive background on the life of American farm women before rural electrification from *The Path to Power* (Alfred A. Knopf, 1982) by Robert Caro. Other background from *Squires and Dames of Old Virginia* (Miller, 1950) by Evelyn Kinder Donaldson; *West Virginia: A History* (University of Kentucky Press, 1994) by Otis K. Rice and Stephen W. Brown; *West Virginia History* (West Virginia University Press, 2003) by John A. Williams; *The West Virginia Mine Wars: An Anthology* (Appalachian Editions, 1998) by David Alan Corbin (editor); *A History of Lewis County, West Virginia* (self-published, 1920) by Edward Conrad Smith; *A History of Harrison County, West Virginia,* (Acme, 1910) by Henry Haymond.

Author researched U.S. Census Bureau records; West Virginia birth, death, marriage records; Accomack County (Va) court records; and West Virginia state archives.

Genealogy sources include West family research and research by the author on Ancestry.com.

Chapter 2 WEST, BY GOD, VIRGINIA

Author interviews with Rene Henry, Barbara West, Hannah West Lilly, Charles West, Patricia West Noel, and James Creasey.

Text sources include *Robert C. Byrd, Child of the Appalachian Coal Fields* (West Virginia University Press, Morgantown, 2005) by Robert C. Byrd; *King Coal* (Macmillan, 1917) by Upton Sinclair; *The Glory and the Dream* (Little, Brown, 1973) by William Manchester; *West Virginia: A History* (University of Kentucky Press, 1994) by Otis K. Rice and Stephen W. Brown; *West Virginia History* (West Virginia University Press, 2003) by John A. Williams; *The West Virginia Mine Wars: An Anthology* (Appalachian Editions, 1998) by David Alan Corbin (editor).

Author researched U.S. Census Bureau records, 1920.

Chapter 3 HEARTBREAK

Author interviews with Joe Chrest, Barbara West, Jerry West, Charles West, Hannah West Lilly, Patricia West Noel, and James Creasey.

Text sources include *Mr. Clutch* (Prentice Hall, 1969) by Jerry West with Bill Libby; *The Show* (McGraw-Hill, 2005) by Roland Lazenby; *The Glory and the Dream* (Little, Brown, 1973) by William Manchester; *The Coldest Winter* (Hyperion, 2007) by David Halberstam.

Other sources include ESPN archives, Jerry West interview.

Chapter 4 THE LOCOMOTIVE

Author interviews with Marty Blake, Jerry West, Joe Chrest, Charles West, K. C. Jones, Barbara West, Patricia West Noel, Hannah West Lilly, Richard Gregg, Eddie Barrett, Fred Schaus, Rene Henry, Hazel Dawson Hawkins, Aileen Holbrook Kelly, Ken Gregory, Willie Akers, J. A. Adande, and Rod Thorn.

Text sources include *Basketball My Way* (Prentice Hall, 1973) by Jerry West with Bill Libby; *Mr. Clutch* (Prentice Hall, 1969) by Jerry West with Bill Libby; *The Show* (McGraw-Hill, 2005) by Roland Lazenby; *The Glory and the Dream* (Little, Brown, 1973) by William Manchester; *The Lakers* (St. Martin's Press, 1993) by Roland Lazenby; *The Golden Game* (Taylor, 1992) by Billy Packer and Roland Lazenby; *The NBA Finals* (Taylor, 1990) by Roland Lazenby.

Newspaper sources for West's high school years include the work of Bob Wills, editor of the *Raleigh Register* (Beckley, W.Va.); Tom Stimmel of the Associated Press, Fred Ferris of the United Press; Bob McKowen of the United Press; George Springer, sports editor of the *Beckley Post-Herald* (W. Va.); Skip Johnson of the *Charleston Gazette;* Bob Baker of the *Charleston Gazette;* Bill Dwyre of the *Los Angeles Times;* Tony Constantine of the *Morgantown Post;* C. J. McQuade of the *Raleigh Register* (Beckley, W.Va.).

Staff reports are from the *Weirton Daily Times* (W.Va.), the *Charleston Sunday Gazette Mail,* the *Morgantown Dominion-News,* the *Raleigh Register* (Beckley, W.Va.), the *Morgantown Post,* and the *Charleston Gazette.*

Other sources include ESPN archives, Jerry West interview.

Chapter 5 THE DISCOVERY

Author interviews with Eddie Barrett, Willie Akers, Charles West, K. C. Jones, Barbara West, Patricia West Noel, Hannah West Lilly, Richard Gregg, Fred Schaus, Rene Henry, Rod Thorn, Dick Kepley, Lee Patrone, Nemo Nearman, Mike Strickler, and Pete Newell.

Text sources include *Basketball My Way* (Prentice Hall, 1973) by Jerry West with Bill Libby; *Clown* (Cowles Book Co., 1970) by Rod Hundley and Bill Libby; *Mr. Clutch* (Prentice Hall, 1969) by Jerry West with Bill Libby; *The Show* (McGraw-Hill, 2005) by Roland Lazenby; *The Glory and the Dream* (Little, Brown, 1973) by William Manchester; *The Lakers* (St. Martin's Press, 1993) by Roland Lazenby; *The Golden Game* (Taylor, 1992) by Billy Packer and Roland Lazenby; *The Official NBA Encyclopedia* (Doubleday, 2000), by Jan Hubbard (editor); *The NBA Finals* (Taylor, 1990) by Roland Lazenby; *The Pistol* (Free Press, 2007) by Mark Kriegel; West Virginia University Basketball Media Guide.

Article and magazine sources: "They Stood Tall" by David Fox, *Minneapolis Star-Tribune,* March 21, 2009; "Smashing Hurrah for the Lakers" by John Underwood, *Sports Illustrated,* February 8, 1965; "A Teddy Bear's Picnic" by Frank De-Ford, *Sports Illustrated,* February 2, 1972; "The Man Behind Show Time" by Scott Ostler, *The National Sports Daily,* February 2, 1990.

Other sources include ESPN Archives, Jerry West interview.

Newspaper sources for West's college years include the work of Bob Wills, editor of the *Raleigh Register* (Beckley, W.Va.); Tom Stimmel of the Associated Press; Fred Ferris of the United Press; Bob McKowen of the United Press; George Springer, sports editor of the *Beckley Post-Herald* (W. Va.); Skip Johnson of the *Charleston Gazette;* Bob Baker of the *Charleston Gazette;* Tony Constantine of the *Morgantown Post;* C. J. McQuade of the *Raleigh Register* (Beckley, W.Va.).

Staff reports are from the *Weirton Daily Times* (W.Va.), the *Charleston Sunday Gazette Mail,* the *Morgantown Dominion-News,* the *Raleigh Register* (Beckley, W.Va.), the *Morgantown Post,* the *Charleston Gazette.*

Other sources include ESPN archives, Jerry West interview.

Chapter 6 THE MOUNTAINEER

Author interviews with Eddie Barrett, Lee Patrone, Jerry West, Willie Akers, Phil Jackson, Charles West, Patricia West Noel, Hannah West Lilly, Lou Adler, Steve Springer, Hal Wissel, Mac McEver, Fred Schaus, Rene Henry, Rod Thorn, John McLendon, Pete Newell, and Jack Ramsay.

Text sources for West's college accomplishments include Mike Douchant's work in *Total Basketball* (Sport Media Publishing, 2003). Other text sources include *Basketball My Way* (Prentice Hall, 1973) by Jerry West with Bill Libby; *Clown* (Cowles Book Co., 1970) by Rod Hundley and Bill Libby; *Mr. Clutch* (Prentice Hall, 1969) by Jerry West with Bill Libby; *The Show* (McGraw-Hill, 2005) by Roland Lazenby; *Mad Game* (Master's Press, 1999) by Roland Lazenby; *Blood on the Horns* (Addax Publishing, 1998) by Roland Lazenby; *A Good Man: The Pete Newell Story* (Frog Ltd., 1999) by Bruce Jenkins; *50 Years of the Final Four* (Taylor, 1987) by Billy Packer and Roland Lazenby; West Virginia University Basketball Media Guide.

Article and magazine sources: "They Stood Tall" by David Fox, *Minneapolis Star-Tribune,* March 21, 2009; "Smashing Hurrah for the Lakers" by John Underwood, *Sports Illustrated,* February 8, 1965; "A Teddy Bear's Picnic" by Frank De-Ford, *Sports Illustrated,* February 2, 1972; "The Man Behind Show Time" by Scott Ostler, *The National Sports Daily,* February 2, 1990.

Other sources include ESPN Archives, Jerry West interview.

Newspaper sources for West's college years include the work of Bob Wills, editor of the *Raleigh Register* (Beckley, W.Va.); Tom Stimmel of the Associated Press; Fred Ferris of the United Press; Bob McKowen of the United Press; George Springer, sports editor of the *Beckley Post-Herald* (W.Va.); Jack Bogaczyk, Skip Johnson, and A. I. Hardman of the *Charleston Gazette;* Bob Baker of the *Charleston Gazette;* Mickey Furfari of the *Morgantown Dominion-News;* Tony

Constantine of the *Morgantown Post;* C. J. McQuade of the *Raleigh Register* (Beckley, W.Va.); Ron Green of the *Charlotte News.*

Staff reports are from the *Weirton Daily Times* (W.Va.), the *Charleston Sunday Gazette Mail,* the *Morgantown Dominion-News,* the *Raleigh Register* (Beckley, W.Va.), the *Morgantown Post,* the *Charleston Gazette.*

Other sources include ESPN archives, Jerry West interview.

Chapter 7 THE HOPEFUL

Author interviews with Eddie Barrett, Lee Patrone, Jerry West, Willie Akers, Charles West, Patricia West Noel, Hannah West Lilly, Mike Strickler, Fred Schaus, Rene Henry, Rod Thorn, John McLenden, Jim Pollard, Pete Newell, and Jack Ramsay.

Text sources for West's college accomplishments include Mike Douchant's work in *Total Basketball* (Sport Media Publishing, 2003). Other text sources include *Basketball My Way* (Prentice Hall, 1973) by Jerry West with Bill Libby; *Clown* (Cowles Book Co., 1970) by Rod Hundley and Bill Libby; *Mr. Clutch* (Prentice Hall, 1969) by Jerry West with Bill Libby; *The Show* (McGraw-Hill, 2005) by Roland Lazenby; *A Good Man: The Pete Newell Story* (Frog Ltd., 1999) by Bruce Jenkins; *50 Years of the Final Four* (Taylor, 1987) by Billy Packer and Roland Lazenby; West Virginia University Basketball Media Guide; *Rome 1960* (Simon & Schuster, 2008) by David Maraniss.

Article and magazine sources: "Smashing Hurrah for the Lakers" by John Underwood, *Sports Illustrated,* February 8, 1965; "A Teddy Bear's Picnic" by Frank DeFord, *Sports Illustrated,* February 2, 1972.

Sources for the Los Angeles Classic included Mal Florence's coverage of the tournament in the *Los Angeles Times,* including "Unbeaten West Virginia Inspired by Jerry's Talents," December 24, 1959.

Sources for the 1960 Olympics include the work of Paul Zimmerman and Mal Florence in the *Los Angeles Times.*

Newspaper sources for West's senior year in college include the work of Bob Wills, editor of the *Raleigh Register* (Beckley, W.Va.); Tom Stimmel of the Associated Press; Fred Ferris of the United Press; Bob McKowen of the United Press; George Springer, sports editor of the *Beckley Post-Herald* (W.Va.); Jack Bogaczyk, Skip Johnson, and A. I. Hardman of the *Charleston Gazette;* Bob Baker of the *Charleston Gazette;* Mickey Furfari of the *Morgantown Dominion-News;* Tony Constantine of the *Morgantown Post;* C. J. McQuade of the *Raleigh Register* (Beckley, W.Va.); Ron Green of the *Charlotte News.*

Staff reports are from the *Weirton Daily Times* (W.Va.), the *Charleston Sunday Gazette Mail,* the *Morgantown Dominion-News,* the *Raleigh Register* (Beckley, W.Va.), the *Morgantown Post,* the *Charleston Gazette.*

Other sources include ESPN archives, Jerry West interview.

Chapter 8 THE LAKER

Author interviews with Jerry West, Charles West, Fred Schaus, Chick Hearn, Bob Cousy, Tommy Heinsohn, Gene Shue, Johnny Most, Bob Ryan, Mitch Chortkoff, Mike Waldner, John "Red" Kerr, Red Auerbach, Kareem Abdul-Jabbar, John Radcliffe, Merv Harris, Barbara West, Rod Hundley, Elgin Baylor, K. C. Jones, and Jack Kent Cooke.

Text sources for West's rookie year in Los Angeles include *A Wife's Guide to Pro Basketball* (Viking, 1970) by Jane West and Michael Rich; *Basketball My Way* (Prentice Hall, 1973) by Jerry West with Bill Libby; *Clown* (Cowles Book Co., 1970) by Rod Hundley and Bill Libby; *Mr. Clutch* (Prentice Hall, 1969) by Jerry West with Bill Libby; *On Court with the Superstars of the NBA* (Viking, 1973) by Merv Harris.

Article and magazine sources: "Smashing Hurrah for the Lakers" by John Underwood, *Sports Illustrated,* February 8, 1965; "A Teddy Bear's Picnic" by Frank DeFord, *Sports Illustrated,* February 2, 1972; "The Man Behind Show Time" by Scott Ostler, *The National Sports Daily,* February 2, 1990.

Newspaper sources for West's pro years include the work of Mel Zikes, Dan Hafner, and Mal Florence, the longtime Lakers beat writers for the *Los Angeles Times,* plus *Times* columnists and writers John Hall, Jim Murray, Art Ryon, Charles Maher, and Paul Zimmerman.

Chapter 9 THE HORROR

Author interviews with Jerry West, Charles West, Fred Schaus, Chick Hearn, Bob Cousy, Tommy Heinsohn, Gene Shue, Johnny Most, Bob Ryan, Mitch Chortkoff, Mike Waldner, John "Red" Kerr, Red Auerbach, John Radcliffe, Merv Harris, Barbara West, Rod Hundley, Elgin Baylor, K. C. Jones, and Jack Kent Cooke.

Text sources for West in Los Angeles, 1962–1965, include *A Wife's Guide to Pro Basketball* (Viking, 1970) by Jane West and Michael Rich; *Basketball My Way*

(Prentice Hall, 1973) by Jerry West with Bill Libby; *Clown* (Cowles Book Co., 1970) by Rod Hundley and Bill Libby; *Mr. Clutch* (Prentice Hall, 1969) by Jerry West with Bill Libby; *Winnin' Time* by Scott Ostler and Steve Springer; *On Court with the Superstars of the NBA* (Viking, 1973) by Merv Harris; *The Show* (McGraw-Hill, 2005) by Roland Lazenby; *Tall Tales* (Simon & Schuster, 1992) by Terry Pluto; *The Glory and the Dream* (Little, Brown, 1973) by William Manchester; *The Lakers* (St. Martin's Press, 1993) by Roland Lazenby; *The Golden Game* (Taylor, 1992) by Billy Packer and Roland Lazenby; *The NBA Finals* (Taylor, 1990) by Roland Lazenby; *The Boston Celtics Greenbook* (Taylor, 1988) by Roland Lazenby; *Second Wind, The Memoirs of an Opinionated Man* (Random House, 1979) by Bill Russell and Taylor Branch.

Article and magazine sources: "Smashing Hurrah for the Lakers" by John Underwood, *Sports Illustrated,* February 8, 1965; "A Teddy Bear's Picnic" by Frank DeFord, *Sports Illustrated,* February 2, 1972; "The Man Behind Show Time" by Scott Ostler, *The National Sports Daily,* February 2, 1990.

Newspaper sources for West in Los Angeles, 1962–1965, include the work of Dan Hafner and Mal Florence, the longtime Lakers beat writers for the *Los Angeles Times,* plus *Times* columnists and writers John Hall, Jim Murray, Mel Zikes, Charles Maher, and Paul Zimmerman.

Chapter 10 MISERY

Author interviews with Marty Blake, Bill Sharman, Jerry West, John Radcliffe, Elgin Baylor, Merv Harris, Fred Schaus, Bill Bertka, Jack Kent Cooke, Mitch Chortkoff, Barbara West, Bailey Howell, Dick Harp, Bob Cousy, Jack Ramsay, Doug Krikorian, Tommy Heinsohn, Sam Jones, and Chick Hearn.

Text sources for West in Los Angeles, 1965–1969, include *A Wife's Guide to Pro Basketball* (Viking, 1970) by Jane West and Michael Rich; *Basketball My Way* (Prentice Hall, 1973) by Jerry West with Bill Libby; *Clown* (Cowles Book Co., 1970) by Rod Hundley and Bill Libby; *Mr. Clutch* (Prentice Hall, 1969) by Jerry West with Bill Libby; *Winnin' Time* (Macmillan, 1986) by Scott Ostler and Steve Springer; *On Court with the Superstars of the NBA* (Viking, 1973) by Merv Harris; *The Show* (McGraw-Hill, 2005) by Roland Lazenby; *Tall Tales* (Simon & Schuster, 1992) by Terry Pluto; *The Glory and the Dream* (Little, Brown, 1973) by William Manchester; *The Lakers* (St. Martin's Press, 1993) by Roland Lazenby; *The Golden Game* (Taylor, 1992) by Billy Packer and Roland Lazenby; *The NBA Finals* (Taylor, 1990) by Roland Lazenby; *The Boston Celtics Greenbook* (Taylor, 1988) by Roland Lazenby; *Second Wind, The Memoirs of an Opinionated Man* (Random House, 1979) by Bill Russell and Taylor Branch.

Article and magazine sources: "Smashing Hurrah for the Lakers" by John Underwood, *Sports Illustrated,* February 8, 1965; "A Teddy Bear's Picnic" by Frank DeFord, *Sports Illustrated,* February 2, 1972; "The Man Behind Show Time" by Scott Ostler, *The National Sports Daily,* February 2, 1990.

Newspaper sources for West in Los Angeles, 1962–1965, include the work of Dan Hafner and Mal Florence, the longtime Lakers beat writers for the *Los Angeles Times,* plus *Times* columnists and writers John Hall, Jim Murray, Mel Zikes, Charles Maher, and Paul Zimmerman; also Merv Harris of the *Los Angeles Herald Examiner.*

Article and magazine sources: "A Teddy Bear's Picnic" by Frank DeFord, *Sports Illustrated,* February 2, 1972.

Newspaper sources for West's pro years include the work of Dan Hafner and Mal Florence, the longtime Lakers beat writers for the *Los Angeles Times,* plus *Times* columnists and writers John Hall, Jim Murray, Mel Zikes, Charles Maher, and Paul Zimmerman; also Merv Harris of the *Los Angeles Herald Examiner.*

Chapter 11 THE LOGO

Author interviews with Jerry Sloan, Jerry West, Bill Walton, Jack McCallum, Mark Heisler, J. A. Adande, Charles West, Mitch Chortkoff, Mike Waldner, Doug Krikorian, Merv Harris, and Walt Frazier.

Text sources for West in Los Angeles, 1969–1971, include *Wilt* (Macmillan Publishing, 1973) by Wilt Chamberlain and David Shaw; *A Wife's Guide to Pro Basketball* (Viking, 1970) by Jane West and Michael Rich; *Basketball My Way* (Prentice Hall, 1973) by Jerry West with Bill Libby; *Clown* (Cowles Book Co., 1970) by Rod Hundley and Bill Libby; *Mr. Clutch* (Prentice Hall, 1969) by Jerry West with Bill Libby; *Winnin' Times* (Macmillan, 1986) by Scott Ostler and Steve Springer; *On Court with the Superstars of the NBA* (Viking, 1973) by Merv Harris; *The Show* (McGraw-Hill, 2005) by Roland Lazenby; *Tall Tales* (Simon & Schuster, 1992) by Terry Pluto; *The Glory and the Dream* (Little, Brown, 1973) by William Manchester; *The Lakers* (St. Martin's Press, 1993) by Roland Lazenby; *The Golden Game* (Taylor, 1992) by Billy Packer and Roland Lazenby; *The NBA Finals* (Taylor, 1990) by Roland Lazenby; *The Boston Celtics Greenbook* (Taylor, 1988) by Roland Lazenby; *Second Wind, The Memoirs of an Opinionated Man* (Random House, 1979) by Bill Russell and Taylor Branch.

Article and magazine sources: "A Teddy Bear's Picnic" by Frank DeFord, *Sports Illustrated,* February 2, 1972.

Newspaper sources for West's pro years include the work of Dan Hafner and Mal Florence, the longtime Lakers beat writers for the *Los Angeles Times,* plus

Times columnists and writers John Hall, Jim Murray, Mel Zikes, Charles Maher, and Paul Zimmerman; also Merv Harris of the *Los Angeles Herald Examiner.*

Chapter 12 THE LAST CHANCE

Author interviews with Bill Walton, Bill Sharman, Mitch Chortkoff, Jerry West, Bill Bertka, Tex Winter, Doug Krikorian, Rod Hundley, Pat Riley, Fred Schaus, Jack Kent Cooke, and Pete Newell.

Text sources for West in Los Angeles, 1971–72, include *Wilt* (Macmillan Publishing, 1973) by Wilt Chamberlain and David Shaw; *The Pivotal Season* (St. Martin's Press, 2005) by Charley Rosen; *A Wife's Guide to Pro Basketball* (Viking, 1970) by Jane West and Michael Rich; *Basketball My Way* (Prentice Hall, 1973) by Jerry West with Bill Libby; *Clown* (Cowles Book Co., 1970) by Rod Hundley and Bill Libby; *Mr. Clutch* (Prentice Hall, 1969) by Jerry West with Bill Libby; *Winnin' Times* (Macmillan, 1986) by Scott Ostler and Steve Springer; *On Court with the Superstars of the NBA* (Viking, 1973) by Merv Harris; *The Show* (McGraw-Hill, 2005) by Roland Lazenby; *Tall Tales* (Simon & Schuster, 1992) by Terry Pluto; *The Glory and the Dream* (Little, Brown, 1973) by William Manchester; *The Lakers* (St. Martin's Press, 1993) by Roland Lazenby; *The Golden Game* (Taylor, 1992) by Billy Packer and Roland Lazenby; *The NBA Finals* (Taylor, 1990) by Roland Lazenby.

Article and magazine sources: "A Professional Pfffffft," by Peter Carry, *Sports Illustrated,* June 5, 1972; "Swish and They're In" by Peter Carry, *Sports Illustrated,* May 15, 1972; "As West Goes—So Goes the West" by Peter Carry, *Sports Illustrated,* May 1, 1972; "Bombs Away Out West" by Peter Carry, *Sports Illustrated,* April 24, 1972; "Another Knockdown Coming Up" by Peter Carry, *Sports Illustrated,* April 10, 1972; "A Teddy Bear's Picnic" by Frank DeFord, *Sports Illustrated,* February 2, 1972; "The Man Behind Show Time" by Scott Ostler, *The National Sports Daily,* February 2, 1990.

Newspaper sources for West's pro years, 1971–1972, include the work of Dan Hafner and Mal Florence, the longtime Lakers beat writers for the *Los Angeles Times,* plus *Times* columnists and writers John Hall, Jim Murray, Mel Zikes, Charles Maher, and Paul Zimmerman; also Merv Harris of the *Los Angeles Herald Examiner.*

Chapter 13 A "WEARING THING"

Author interviews with Gar Heard, Norm Van Lier, Doug Krikorian, Pete Newell, Mike Waldner, Jerry West, Jack Kent Cooke, Chick Hearn, Richard Gregg, Patricia

West Noel, Charles West, Bill Sharman, Jerry Tarkanian, Kareem Abdul-Jabbar, Stu Lantz, Ron Carter, Jack Ramsay, Lou Hudson, and Joe McDonnell.

Text sources for West in Los Angeles, 1972–79, include *Wilt* (Macmillan Publishing, 1973) by Wilt Chamberlain and David Shaw; *The Pivotal Season* (St. Martin's Press, 2005) by Charley Rosen; *A Wife's Guide to Pro Basketball* (Viking, 1970) by Jane West and Michael Rich; *Winnin' Times* (Macmillan, 1986) by Scott Ostler and Steve Springer; *The Show* (McGraw-Hill, 2005) by Roland Lazenby; *Tall Tales* (Simon & Schuster, 1992) by Terry Pluto; *The Lakers* (St. Martin's Press, 1993) by Roland Lazenby; *The Golden Game* (Taylor, 1992) by Billy Packer and Roland Lazenby; *The NBA Finals* (Taylor, 1990) by Roland Lazenby.

Article and magazine sources: "The Not-So-Grand Finales" by Peter Carry, *Sports Illustrated,* May 14, 1973; "In Seven, as in Heaven" by Peter Carry, *Sports Illustrated,* May 7, 1973; "A Teddy Bear's Picnic" by Frank DeFord, *Sports Illustrated,* February 2, 1972; "The Man Behind Show Time" by Scott Ostler, *The National Sports Daily,* February 2, 1990.

Newspaper sources for West's career, 1972–1979, include the work of Ted Green, Scott Ostler, Dan Hafner, and Mal Florence, the longtime Lakers beat writers for the *Los Angeles Times,* plus *Times* columnists and writers John Hall, Jim Murray, Mel Zikes, Charles Maher, and Paul Zimmerman; also Merv Harris and Rich Levin of the *Los Angeles Herald Examiner.*

Chapter 14 THE AFTER LIFE

Author interviews with Ted Green, Jerry West, Scott Ostler, Steve Springer, Pete Newell, Dominique Wilkins, Michael Cooper, Kareem Abdul-Jabbar, Fred Schaus, Hannah West Lilly, Johnny "Red" Kerr, Hal Wissel, Del Harris, and Tex Winter.

Text sources for West's career, 1979–2009, include *Winnin' Times* (Macmillan, 1986) by Scott Ostler and Steve Springer; *The Show* (McGraw-Hill, 2005) by Roland Lazenby; *Tall Tales* (Simon & Schuster, 1992) by Terry Pluto; *The Lakers* (St. Martin's Press, 1993) by Roland Lazenby.

Article and magazine sources: "Mister Clutch, Master Builder" by Richard Hoffer, *Sports Illustrated,* April 23, 1990; "The Man Behind Show Time" by Scott Ostler, *The National Sports Daily,* February 2, 1990.

Newspaper sources for West's career, 1979–2009, include the work of Ted Green, Scott Ostler, Steve Springer, Scott Howard-Cooper, and Tim Kawakami for the *Los Angeles Times,* plus *Times* columnists and writers J. A. Adande, Mark Heisler, John Hall, Jim Murray, Mel Zikes, Charles Maher, and Paul Zimmerman; also Rich Levin of the *Los Angeles Herald Examiner,* Kelly Carter and Kevin Ding of the *Orange County Register,* and Howard Beck of the *Los Angeles Daily News.*

BIBLIOGRAPHY

THE WRITERS

Background sources include the works of other newspaper and magazine writers, including J. A. Adande, Mitch Albom, David Aldridge, Jim Alexander, Elliott Almond, Neil Amdur, Dave Anderson, Howard Beck, Ira Berkow, Steve Bisheff, Greg Boeck, Mike Bresnahan, Cliff Brown, Tim Brown, Ric Bucher, Bryan Burwell, E. Jean Carroll, Kelly Carter, Mitch Chortkoff, Marlene Cimons, Doug Cress, Karen Crouse, Tim Deady, Frank DeFord, Kevin Ding, Larry Donald, Mike Downey, Ron Dungee, David Dupree, Melvin Durslag, David Ferrell, Joe Fitzgerald, Mal Florence, John Freeman, Tom Friend, Bud Furillo, Frank Girardot, Sam Goldaper, Brian Golden, Alan Goldstein, Ted Green, Allen Greenberg, Don Greenberg, Milton Gross, Donald Hall, Merv Harris, Randy Harvey, Mark Heisler, Steve Henson, Randy Hill, Bruce Horovitz, Scott Howard-Cooper, Mary Ann Hudson, Bob Hunter, Michael Hurd, Doug Ives, Bruce Jenkins, Roy S. Johnson, William Oscar Johnson, Tim Kawakami, Dave Kindred, Leonard Koppett, Tony Kornheiser, Doug Krikorian, Rich Levin, Leonard Lewin, Bill Libby, Mike Littwin, Jackie MacMullen, Jack Madden, Allan Malamud, Jack McCallum, Sam McManis, John L. Mitchell, Kevin Modesti, David Leon Moore, Morton Moss, Bruce Newman, Scott Ostler, Sandy Padwe, Chris Palmer, John Papanek, Charles Pierce, Bill Plaschke, Diane Pucin, Pat Putnam, Brad Pye, Jr., Ron Rapoport, Bob Ryan, Steve Springer, Bill Steigerwald, Marc Stein, Larry Stewart, Eric Tracy, Brad Turner, George Vecsey, Peter Vecsey, Michael Ventre, Lesley Visser, Mike Waldner, Peter Warner, Mark Whicker, and Alex Wolff.
A number of excellent books and periodicals provided me with background for this project.

MAGAZINES AND NEWSPAPERS

Extensive use was made of a variety of publications, including *AirCal, Basketball Times, Boston Globe, Boston Herald, BusinessWeek, The Charlotte Observer, Chicago Sun Times, Chicago Tribune, The Detroit Free Press, The Detroit News, ESPN The Magazine, Esquire, Flint Journal, Forbes, GQ, Hartford Courant, Hoop Magazine, Houston Post, L.A. Herald Examiner, Let's Talk!, Lindy's Pro Basketball Annual, Los Angeles Business Journal, Los Angeles Daily News, Los Angeles Lakers Illustrated, Los Angeles Sentinel, Los Angeles Times, The National, New West, New York Daily News, New York Post, The New York Times, The Oakland Press, The Orange County Register, Philadelphia Inquirer, The Roanoke Times & World-News, San Diego Tribune, Sport, The Sporting News, Sports Illustrated, Street & Smith's Pro Basketball Yearbook, USA Today, Vanity Fair,* and *The Washington Post.*

BOOKS

Abdul-Jabbar, Kareem, and Peter Knobler, *Giant Steps,* Bantam, New York, 1983.
Abdul-Jabbar, Kareem, and Mignon McCarthy, *Kareem,* Random House, New York, 1990.
Anderson, Dave, *The Story of Basketball,* William Morrow, New York, 1988.
Barry, Rick, and Jordan E. Cohn, *Rick Barry's Pro Basketball Scouting Report,* Bonus Books, Chicago, 1989.
Bell, Marty, *The Legend of Dr. J,* New American Library, New York, 1981.
Berger, Phil, *Miracle on 34th Street,* Simon & Schuster, New York, 1970.
Caro, Robert, *The Path to Power,* Knopf, New York, 1982.
Caughey, John and Laree (eds.), *Los Angeles. Biography of a City,* University of California Press, 1977.
Chamberlain, Wilt, *A View from Above,* Signet Books, New York, 1992,
Chamberlain, Wilt, and David Shaw, *Wilt,* Macmillan, New York, 1986.
Clary, Jack, *Basketball's Great Dynasties: The Lakers,* Smithmark Publishers, New York, 1992.
Corbin, David Alan (ed.), *The West Virginia Mine Wars: An Anthology,* Appalachian Editions, Charleston, 1998.
Dickey, Glenn, *The History of Professional Basketball Since 1896,* Stein and Day, New York, 1982.
Donaldson, Evelyn Kinder, *Squires and Dames of Old Virginia,* Miller, Los Angeles, 1950.
Douchant, Mike, *Total Basketball,* Sport Media Publishing, 2003.
Frazier, Walt, and Neil Offen, *Walt Frazier,* Times Books, New York, 1988.

Goodrich, Gail, and Rich Levin, *Gail Goodrich's Winning Basketball,* Contemporary, Chicago, 1976.

Green, Lee, *Sportswit,* Fawcett, New York, 1986.

Halberstam, David, *The Breaks of the Game,* Knopf, New York, 1981.

Haymond, Henry, *A History of Harrison County, West Virginia,* Acme, Morgantown, 1910.

Heisler, Mark, and Roland Lazenby, *Giants,* Triumph Books, Chicago, 2003.

Heisler, Mark, *The Lives of Riley,* Macmillan, New York, 1994.

Hession, Joseph, *Lakers,* Foghorn Press, San Francisco, 1994.

Hollander, Zander, (ed.), *Basketball's Greatest Games,* Prentice Hall, Englewood Cliffs, 1971.

Hollander, Zander, *The Modern Basketball Encyclopedia,* Dolphin, Garden City, NY, 1979.

Hollander, Zander, and Alex Sachare (eds.), *The Official NBA Basketball Encyclopedia,* Villard, New York, 1989.

Holtzman, Red, and Harvey Frommer, *Holtzman on Hoops,* Taylor Publishing, Dallas, 1991.

Hundley, Jessica, and Jon Alain Guzik (eds.), *Horny Los Angeles,* Really Great Books, Los Angeles, 2001.

Jenkins, Bruce, *A Good Man: The Pete Newell Story,* Frog Ltd., Berkeley, 1999.

Johnson, Earvin, and Rich Levine, *Magic,* Viking, New York, 1983.

Johnson, Magic, and Roy S. Johnson, *Magic's Touch,* Addison Wesley, Boston, 1989.

Johnson, Earvin, and William Novak, *My Life,* Random House, New York, 1992.

Koppett, Leonard, *Championship NBA,* Dial Press, New York, 1970.

Koppett, Leonard, *24 Seconds to Shoot,* Macmillan, New York, 1980.

Kriegel, Mark, *Pistol,* Free Press, New York, 2007.

Lazenby, Roland, *Blood on the Horns,* Addax Publishing, Lenexa, 1998.

Lazenby, Roland, *The Lakers, A Basketball Journey,* St. Martin's Press, New York, 1993.

Lazenby, Roland, *Mad Game,* Master's Press, Lincolnwood, 1999.

Lazenby, Roland, *The NBA Finals,* Taylor Publishing, Dallas, 1990.

Libby, Bill, *Clown,* Cowles Book Co., New York, 1970.

Manchester, William, *The Glory and the Dream,* Little, Brown, Boston, 1974.

Murray, Jim, *The Jim Murray Collection,* Taylor Publishing, Dallas, 1989.

Nadel, Eric, *The Night Wilt Scored 100,* Taylor Publishing, Dallas, 1990.

Neft, David S., and Richard M. Cohen, *The Sports Encyclopedia, Pro Basketball,* St. Martin's Press, New York, 1992.

Ostler, Steve, and Steve Springer, *Winnin' Time,* Macmillan, New York, 1986.

Packer, Billy, and Roland Lazenby, *College Basketball's 25 Greatest Teams,* The Sporting News, St. Louis, 1989.

Packer, Billy, and Roland Lazenby, *50 Years of the Final Four,* Taylor Publishing, Dallas, 1987.

Padwe, Sandy, *Basketball's Hall of Fame,* Grossett & Dunlap, New York, 1973.

Patterson, Wayne, and Lisa Fisher, *100 Greatest Basketball Players,* Bison Books, Greenwich, CT., 1988.

Peterson, Robert, *Cages to Jump Shots,* Oxford, New York, 1990.

Pluto, Terry, *Tall Tales,* Simon & Schuster, New York, 1992.

Reisner, Marc, *A Dangerous Place,* Pantheon Books, New York 2003.

Rice, Otis K., and Stephen W. Brown, *West Virginia: A History,* University Press of Kentucky, Lexington, KY, 1994.

Riley, Pat, and Byron Laursen, *Showtime,* Warner Books, New York, 1987.

Rosen, Charley, *The Pivotal Season,* St. Martin's Press, New York, 2005.

Russell, Bill, and Taylor Branch, *Second Wind, The Memoirs of an Opinionated Man,* Random House, New York, 1979.

Salzberg, Charles, *From Set Shot to Slam Dunk,* Dutton, New York, 1987.

Smith, Edward Conrad, *A History of Lewis County, West Virginia,* self-published, 1920.

Springer, Steve, *The Los Angeles Times Encyclopedia of the Lakers, Los Angeles Times,* 1998.

Stauth, Cameron, *The Golden Boys,* Pocket Books, New York, 1992.

Vessey, George, *Pro Basketball Champions,* Scholastic, New York, 1970.

West, Jane, and Michael Rich, *A Wife's Guide to Pro Basketball,* Viking, New York, 1970.

West, Jerry, with Bill Libby, *Basketball My Way,* Prentice Hall, Englewood Cliffs, 1973.

West, Jerry, with Bill Libby, *Mr. Clutch,* Grosset & Dunlap, New York, 1969.

Williams, John A., *West Virginia History,* West Virginia University Press, Morgantown, 2003.

Wolff, Alexander, *100 Years of Hoops,* Oxmoor House, Birmingham, 1992.

Wooden, John, and Jack Tobin, *They Call Me Coach,* Word, Waco, TX., 1972.

Hearn, Chick, 97, 146, 148, 194–96,
202, 210–11, 226, 228, 238, 250,
251, 260, 279, 310, 338, 349
loses son to drug overdose, 364
on Russell, 279
uses "Zeke" nickname in
broadcasts, 205
West's popularity and, 283–84
on West's retirement, 343
Heinson, Tommy, 196, 197, 200, 212,
214–17, 221, 223, 233, 239, 240,
243, 311
Heisler, Mark, 285, 287, 328
Heisley, Michael, 386–87
Helms Foundation, 135, 178
Henderson, Cam, 86, 120–21
Henry, Rene, 100–101, 104–5, 121,
125, 126, 207
Herald Examiner, 204, 243, 270, 329,
355
Highcoal, West Virginia, 40
Hoffman, Dustin, 292
Holy Cross University, 154, 155
Holzman, Red, 292, 294
Hoover, Herbert, 50
Hosket, Bill, 294
Houston Rockets, 334, 379
Howell, Bailey, 217, 238, 263, 272,
273
Huddleston, Paddy, 30, 31
Hudson, Lou, 291, 357, 359, 365
Hughes, Jesse, 13, 15
Hughes, Martha, 14
Humphrey, Hubert, 183–84
Hundley, Hot Rod, xx, 145, 206–7,
241, 260, 275
on Baylor, 202, 204
in Charleston summer league, 129
on Cooke, 251
decline in skills and career of,
237–38
on drafting West, 181
Hollywood celebrities and, 226,
237
as Laker, 125–26, 192, 200, 201,
208, 209, 226, 229, 233–35,
237–38

on LaRusso, 229–30
on Schaus, 207
on West, 196, 305
as WVU player, 86, 91, 101, 104,
106, 109, 116–27, 160
Huntington East High School, 103
Hurt, Howard, 93, 95–96, 101

Iba, Hank, 154
Imhoff, Darrall, 164, 168, 169,
185–86, 241, 256, 262, 268
Indiana State University, 368
Indian attacks, 11–15
Inman, Stu, 343

Jackson, Phil, 166
on alpha males, 146–47
as Bulls coach, 375–76
as Knicks player, 337
as Lakers coach, xv, 383–86
West and, xiv, xv, 337, 383–86
Jackson, Scoop, 199
Jacobs, Jay, 130
Jefferson, Thomas, 30
Jerry West Night, 296
Johnson, Earvin "Magic," 148, 199,
368–71, 374–77, 380, 387
Johnson, Hollis, 300–302
Johnson, Skip, 62
Johnston, Neil, 222–23, 265
Jones, Eddie, 381, 384, 385
Jones, K. C., 79, 196, 197, 217, 220,
221, 239, 240, 242, 243, 256, 310
Jones, Mary Harris "Mother," 22–23
Jones, Sam, 196, 197, 217, 231, 233,
239, 240, 243, 263, 272–76, 279
Jordan, Michael, xv, xix, 146–47, 149,
214, 216, 241, 254, 311, 375, 387

Kanawha County Board of
Education, 106
Kanawha Hotel, 205
Kanawha Valley, West Virginia, 14,
20, 26, 27

ABOUT THE AUTHOR

ROLAND LAZENBY has taught journalism at Virginia Tech and Radford University for two decades and is the author of *Mindgames: Phil Jackson's Long Strange Journey* and *The Show: The Inside Story of the Spectacular Los Angeles Lakers, in the Words of Those Who Lived It,* among other books. He is a frequent contributor to sports documentaries, including ESPN's *Sports-Century,* and a regular guest on television and radio programs. Lazenby's work has been cited in numerous publications and websites, including *Sports Illustrated, The Washington Post,* and NBA.com.

ABOUT THE TYPE

This book was set in Times Roman, designed by Stanley Morrison specifically for *The Times* of London. The typeface was introduced in the newspaper in 1932. Times Roman had its greatest success in the United States as a book and commercial typeface, rather than one used in newspapers.